ELDER ADVOCACY

ELDER ADVOCACY

Essential Knowledge and Skills Across Settings

RUTH HUBER

Kent School of Social Work
University of Louisville

H. WAYNE NELSON

Department of Health Sciences
Towson University

F. ELLEN NETTING

School of Social Work
Virginia Commonwealth University

KEVIN W. BORDERS

Kent School of Social Work
University of Louisville

THOMSON
™
BROOKS/COLE

AUSTRALIA • BRAZIL • CANADA • MEXICO • SINGAPORE • SPAIN
UNITED KINGDOM • UNITED STATES

THOMSON

✶ ™

BROOKS/COLE

Elder Advocacy: Essential Knowledge and Skills Across Settings
Ruth Huber, H. Wayne Nelson, F. Ellen Netting, Kevin W. Borders

Acquisitions Editor: *Dan Alpert*
Development Editor: *Tangelique Williams*
Assistant Editor: *Ann Lee Richards*
Editorial Assistant: *Stephanie Rue*
Technology Project Manager: *Julie Aguilar*
Marketing Manager: *Meghan McCullough*
Marketing Assistant: *Teresa Marino*
Marketing Communications Manager: *Shemika Britt*
Project Manager, Editorial Production:
   Christy Krueger
Creative Director: *Rob Hugel*

Art Director: *Vernon Boes*
Print Buyer: *Doreen Suruki*
Permissions Editor: *Roberta Broyer*
Production Service: *Aaron Downey/Matrix Productions Inc.*
Copy Editor: *Kay Mikel*
Illustrator: *Maria Sas/NuGraphic Design*
Cover Designer: *Larry Didona*
Cover Printer: *Thomson West*
Compositor: *ICC Macmillan Inc.*
Printer: *Thomson West*

Thomson Higher Education
10 Davis Drive
Belmont, CA 94002-3098
USA

Printed in the United States of America
1 2 3 4 5 6 7 11 10 09 08 07

For more information about our products,
contact us at:
Thomson Learning Academic Resource Center
1-800-423-0563
For permission to use material from this text or
product, submit a request online at
http://www.thomsonrights.com.
Any additional questions about permissions
can be submitted by e-mail to
thomsonrights@thomson.com.

Library of Congress Control Number: 2006934672

ISBN-13: 978-0-495-00004-4
ISBN-10: 0-495-00004-3

From Ruth Huber

To my Don
(and we all appreciate his patience!)

From Wayne Nelson

To my children
Cameron W. Nelson and Sarah E. Nelson
and to my parents Hugh and Sandy

From Ellen Netting

In memory of Howard N. Hinds,
East Tennessee Long-Term Care Ombudsman

From Kevin Borders

In memory of my grandparents
John and Eunice Borders
and
Charles and Hattie Daugherty
and
to my parents
Merwyn and Linda Borders

BRIEF CONTENTS

CONTENTS

PREFACE

Twenty-five years later, just as the United States is about to experience the most significant demographic phenomenon in its history—the aging of the baby boomers—advocacy for aging policies and programs at the national level seems to have lost its compass. STONE (2004, p. 59)

Robyn Stone's sentiments mirror our own, eloquently reflecting the reason we wrote this book. We know that there are still advocates in the field who care deeply about older people and are incredibly committed. You may be one of those people, and for you we are grateful. But we also know that we live in an increasingly complicated world and that the "compass" originally held by such great leaders as Dr. Arthur Fleming, Claude Pepper, Maggie Kuhn, and a host of others does not seem as certain as in the early days when we witnessed the excitement about an emerging aging network. This raises the question, Where have all the advocates for elders gone?

This book is for practitioners, students, and others who work with elders, which will eventually include virtually all of us. We provide a conceptual framework for understanding when and how to use different advocacy strategies and practical methods for intervening when elders need help in negotiating diverse and complex service delivery systems. *Elder Advocacy* is relevant to clinicians (who work one on one and with families) as well as to macro practitioners who focus their efforts in the organizational, community, and policy arenas. Our basic premise is that gerontological advocacy requires committed, ethically grounded, compassionate, and not infrequently courageous promoters and champions who can systematically and effectively change the hearts and minds of more powerful decision makers in unique and often unpredictable situations that threaten the vested interests of aging persons.

Other textbooks provide general overviews of aging in various settings or focus on the demographics and the knowledge base one needs in an aging society, and still others provide guidance for one-on-one work with elders. *Elder Advocacy* is unique in that our focus is on the *how to* of dealing with complex situations in which elders and their allies, surrogates, and advocates often find themselves. We repeatedly illustrate the interface and inseparability of micro and macro practice. Moreover, we do not shy away from the thornier issues surrounding elder care but present examples of lawfully mandated elder care advocates who sometimes clash with other advocates.

Our overarching goal is to empower both future and practicing advocates by imparting skills that inculcate the self-assurance and capacity to effectively solve client problems in the often highly charged, highly contingent, and interactive elder-service environment. More specifically, our goals are to show helping professionals and others how to (a) conceptualize difficult situations and (b) select strategies and tactics that will facilitate their being more effective advocates for our nation's elderly. *Elder Advocacy* is not about radical social reform, although that certainly may be a long-term goal given the problems that arise. We are talking about daily, ongoing attempts to find the right fit between organizational and community practice to ensure that elders' needs are met.

As educators, caregivers, providers, elders, students, children of elders, and even parents of elders, each of us must assume part of the responsibility. Are we not training, encouraging, inspiring, and motivating our students and colleagues to consider careers in the aging arena? When we think about the thousands of health and social service workers who either work directly with elders or routinely encounter them across a wide variety of settings and services, we are hard pressed to think of even one job or position that would not be strengthened by workers, both paid and volunteer, honing their advocacy skills.

We are aware that educators in a number of disciplines, including nursing, medicine and the allied health professions, public health, psychology, and social work, are adding content on aging to their curricula. We also know that many laypeople from all walks of life are thrust into positions of needing to advocate for themselves or for aging family members even as they, too, are aging. The demographic shift will affect everyone, and we must all possess considerable knowledge and skills to be effective advocates. Dr. Stone is right: just when we most need strong leadership in advocating for elders, we must look hard and long at why those leaders are not on center stage and at what we, personally, can do about it. We believe we can all do something about it, even if our efforts are focused inwardly. Each of us can become a skilled advocate for elders.

Organization of This Book

Elder Advocacy is divided into three parts, each with three chapters, and is full of how-to models, lists, boxes, figures, tables, stories, discussion questions and exercises, and recommendations for additional reading. We have drawn heavily from our own experiences and have shared with one another what we had learned in our respective work with elders. Each chapter begins with a story from which we launch the chapter's main topic, and some chapters contain additional stories to illustrate points along the way.

Part I is all about understanding contexts—the elder's physical, economic, health-related, personal relationship, financial, and familial contexts. Here we lay the groundwork and explain the theoretical underpinnings on which we build the rest of the book. Chapter 1 is about complex delivery systems, specifically focusing on social and health care delivery systems, each of which seems almost impenetrable at times yet must be

negotiated. We question our own assumptions and describe four types of aging services: prevention, treatment, protection and support, and resource brokerage/linkage services. In Chapter 2 we introduce different theoretical perspectives and close with four guiding contextual principles to aid in understanding contexts and settings—themes that are woven throughout the book. In Chapter 3 we delve into the complex web of roles and relationships that surround elderly people and their advocates to bring some clarity to that melee. Types of advocates include self-advocates, third party citizen advocates, provider and legal advocates, hybrid advocates and their organizations, and advocates who are internal or external to the targets of their advocacy work.

Part II focuses on gathering and analyzing information. In Chapter 4 we work through the critical task of carefully assessing the problem by discussing a series of questions: *Why* assess? *What* to assess? *Who* should be assessed? *When* to assess? and *Who* should conduct the assessment? Four major assessment tasks are also explained. Chapter 5 is about investigating and analyzing situations. Investigations are comprised of interviews and collecting and analyzing the resulting data. Topics include the three rules of evidence, the competing values of autonomy and beneficence, and informed consent. Chapter 6 describes planning interventions and introduces the situational conflict model and its four main conflict resolution strategies: building alliances, consultation, persuading and forcing, and problem solving.

Part III focuses on practicing advocacy, applying what you've learned to the practice of advocacy and touching on how to evaluate advocacy outcomes. Chapter 7 adds tactics to the strategies of the situational conflict model to advocate for an individual, and closes with the role of mediation in elder advocacy, including activist mediation, hard and soft negotiations, and negotiated consent. Chapter 8 continues this discussion and applies it to macro-level interventions, providing a menu of five different approaches: policy, program, project, personnel, and practice. These are user-friendly approaches that make intuitive sense. Chapter 9 provides a brief introduction to evaluating advocacy outcomes. Using a simple codebook format, we illustrate how you can construct a database to facilitate data collection that will enable you to evaluate the outcomes of your advocacy practice.

This book is intended for advocacy work in the United States, and the premises and strategies posed and recommended here cannot be used internationally without careful consideration of local cultures and the context of the situations encountered there. Indeed, in other countries some of the ways U.S. citizens can safely advocate for individual rights, for example, would be dangerous to the advocates and to the individuals for whom they would advocate, as well as their causes. We urge you to be cognizant of the context in which you are working.

A companion website for this book is maintained by Thomson Brooks/Cole: www.thomsonedu.com/social_work/huber. At the end of each chapter of the website, readers will find the exercises, additional readings, glossary items, crossword puzzles, and flashcards.

Finally, we are very interested in readers' comments and especially your suggestions for improving any future editions. Please send them to ruth.huber@louisville.edu.

Acknowledgments

We thank those who helped us bring this manuscript to completion. Three patient souls proofread and provided salient feedback. Margaret Moore, Ruth Huber's 86-year-old aunt not only found errors but also corrected grammar and provided countless other kinds of help and information. Cindy Conley proofread from a doctoral student's perspective and provided different and insightful views and suggestions. She spent countless hours searching for obscure information to complete citations. Another doctoral student, Theresa Hayden, also found sources seemingly on a moment's notice.

The librarians at the University of Louisville dug deep and wide to find fugitive and otherwise elusive literature and proper citations.

A large *thank-you* goes out to these dedicated professionals: Anna Marie Johnson, Director of the Ekstrom Library, and members of her staff: Barbara Whitener, Felix Garza, Margo Smith, and Mildred Franks; and Michel Atlas in the Health Sciences Library. Ongoing appreciation goes to the small and dedicated group in Distance Learning Library Services led by Sharon Edge, and to Melissa Crain and Jason Friedman. More than anyone, perhaps, we owe much to the patience of our spouses and other family members.

We are fortunate to have positions in three universities, all of which recognize the importance of including aging in social work and health sciences programs. To our deans, Terry Singer, Frank Baskind, and Charlotte Exner, who have all been instrumental in advocating for aging to be part of the social work curriculum, we thank you for the support you continue to provide.

We also wish to thank the following reviewers for their insightful suggestions: Priscilla Allen, Louisiana State University; Amanda Barusch, University of Utah; Alice Chomesky, New Mexico State University; Connie Corley, California State University, Los Angeles; William Daily Jr., California State University, Fresno; Molly Davis, George Mason University; Kathy Elpers, University of Southern Indiana; Susan Eve, University of North Texas; Daphne Joslin, William Patterson University; Rosalie Kane, University of Minnesota; Waldo C. Klein, University of Connecticut; and Howard Palley, University of Maryland, Baltimore.

Finally, our appreciation goes to the professionals at Thomson Brooks/Cole who took our work and turned it into this book. Many people were behind the scenes making it all happen and we are thankful for them, as well as those who held our hands and answered endless questions: Dan Alpert, Christy Krueger, and Ann Richards at Thomson Brooks/Cole; Aaron Downey at Matrix Productions; our copyeditor, Kay Mikel; and Maria Sas at NuGraphic Design. Without these experts, we just had ideas.

For 16 years we have worked together as a research team. We have published numerous conceptual and empirically based articles in refereed journals and have given multiple presentations together at professional conferences. A prevailing theme in our work has been how volunteers and paid staff work together in elder advocacy programs. As a team, we dreamed of writing a book that would bring together what we have learned over the years. *Elder Advocacy* is that book, and it is a product of more than 75 years of our combined work, practice, advocacy, teaching, and research experiences with and about elders. Some of us are more theoretically oriented than others, but in this book we were all committed to providing the skills and knowledge you will need to successfully advocate for the elders you serve. We wish you well.

Ruth Huber is professor of social work and director of the doctoral program at the Kent School of Social Work at the University of Louisville in Louisville, Kentucky. She has expertise in the National Long-Term Care Ombudsman Program, hospice, and advanced directives.

H. Wayne Nelson is associate professor in the Department of Health Sciences at Towson University in Baltimore, Maryland. He served for 16 years as deputy director of the Oregon State Long-Term Care Ombudsman Program where he trained and supervised numerous volunteers.

F. Ellen Netting is professor of social work at Virginia Commonwealth University in Richmond, Virginia. She practiced within the aging network in East Tennessee where she gained expertise in working with elders in diverse community-based settings. Drs. Huber, Nelson, and Netting are Fellows within the Gerontological Society of America (GSA).

Kevin Borders is an assistant professor research faculty member at the Kent School of Social Work at the University of Louisville, Louisville, Kentucky, where he directs various grant projects and continues his research on institutional abuse and aging.

UNDERSTANDING CONTEXTS

CHAPTER ONE

Approaching Complex Delivery Systems

*Everyone does advocacy—it's just that some are advocating
for the status quo.* EZELL (2001)

BOX 1.1

JEANINE: Kidnapping or a Daughter's Right?

Jeanine was an 85-year-old woman who contentedly lived in an adult foster care home in the small coastal community where she had lived her whole life. Jeanine was estranged from her daughter, Trudy, who suffered from a long history of drug addiction and a borderline personality diagnosis. Until 4 years ago, Trudy had been her mother's caregiver, but now she was, at best, inattentive—except when it came to spending Jeanine's money.

Jeanine wanted nothing more to do with her daughter. She often refused to take Trudy's frequent calls, which always involved a plea to Jeanine to return to Trudy's care. Jeanine repeatedly told her caregiver and her Medicaid case manager that she never wanted to live with her daughter again—and was not even sure she wanted to see her. One day, Jeanine received a letter from Trudy informing her that Trudy was coming up for a visit—just for a few minutes and a cup of coffee. Jeanine immediately told her provider not to let Trudy in under any circumstances.

Several days later Trudy showed up demanding to see her mother. The caregiver relayed Jeanine's wishes, but Trudy became alternatively belligerent and hysterical. Jeanine, hiding in her room, overheard the mounting drama. Trudy shouted past the hapless caregiver and pleaded with her mother to come out for a few minutes: "I want to see you for just a moment, I promise, nothing more. I have news," she pleaded. "Can't we just go out for a cup of coffee? I'll go home then, right away, I promise, I have really good news." Jeanine gave in, just to keep the scene from escalating further. Putting on a brave face, she told her caregiver that they would go down the street to the Seaside Cafe for some lunch. Trudy apologized for her display and reassured the caregiver that everything would be fine. However, Jeanine failed to come home in a few minutes, or a few hours.

Fearing the worst, the caregiver called the police and accused Trudy of kidnapping her mother. The police asked if there had been any formal charges filed against Trudy concerning her mother. "Not to my knowledge," she admitted. "But Jeanine was very persistent in not wanting to go home with her daughter. Besides," she said, "she's left all of her things here." But the police would do nothing. The next day the caregiver explained the situation to Jeanine's Medicaid case manager, who also called the police, who still refused to act. Finally, the case manager called the state's long-term care ombudsman* for assistance.

---

*While we support gender-neutral language, the leaders of the National Long-Term Care Ombudsman Program have decided to retain the name as it originated in Sweden and we acquiesce to their preference of terms.

The deputy state ombudsman called the police sergeant who was familiar with the case. The ombudsman asked why the police were not searching for Jeanine: "Why isn't this a kidnapping?"

"Because all we have here is a daughter picking up her elderly mother and taking her home," he responded. "I think an adult child has the right to do that with a very old parent, don't you? I mean if I were 85-years-old and lived 150 miles from my son, and he picked me up to bring me home, I wouldn't call that a kidnapping, would you?"

"Yes, if it was against my will," retorted the ombudsman. "And at what age do you assume that your son gets control over you?"

"Well, I guess most people would say that someone in their 80s who requires care should be taken care of by their kids. The roles sort of reverse now, don't they?"

The ombudsman had heard this logic many times and could not contain himself. "Well, I guess you know very little about elder law." Not a wise thing to tell a police officer. Things got decidedly hotter.

"I don't need to know about elder law," said the sergeant. "What I do know is that we don't even know that Jeanine was taken against her will, now do we?"

"However, we do know that she had repeatedly told her caregiver and her case manager that she did not want to live with her daughter. We do know that her daughter promised to bring her right back, but did not. Moreover, we do know Jeanine has not called any of her contacts here, and that she has not picked up any of her belongings. If Jeanine were a 7-year-old child, I bet you'd do something," pressed the ombudsman.

"Of course we would," huffed the cop. "But that's totally different. Most kids are snatched by someone they know . . ."

"Often a noncustodial parent," the ombudsmen finished for him. "It happens all the time."

"The charge of kidnapping is ridiculous," growled the cop.

"Why?" asked the ombudsman. "If she had been taken against her will by her daughter, why wouldn't that be kidnapping?"

After a short pause the sergeant began to calm down and listen. The ombudsman, too, became conciliatory. "I'm not really serious about pushing the charge of kidnapping," explained the ombudsman. "What I am concerned about is that a woman, who is mentally quite sound, is missing under circumstances that suggest that she was deceived or forcefully taken against her will."

The sergeant became increasingly helpful. A statewide search was initiated, and in less than a week Jeanine was found, at her daughter's home, where she was being held against her will. She returned to her caregiver and community, secured a restraining order against her daughter, but refused to press further charges.

At some point in life, virtually everyone advocates for elders. They may be family members advocating for their relatives, or, as in Jeanine's case, caregivers advocating for elders to *protect them* from family members. They may be colleagues, clients, friends, neighbors, or even strangers. If you live long enough, you will need to know how to advocate for yourself as an elder member of a society that is not always sensitive to your needs. Some advocates will assume the roles of both formal and informal caregivers. Many will advocate as private citizens, acting individually as consumer self-advocates or as members of organized social reform groups. Direct practitioners with titles such as social worker, nurse, physician, occupational therapist, vocational therapist, chaplain, or home health aide will find themselves in advocacy roles. Many of these practitioners will work with or through the aging system's more formally prescribed advocates including long-term care ombudsmen, hospital patient representatives, discharge planners, case managers, and adult protective service workers, to name a few.

Helping professionals, government regulators, public servants, paid employees, administrators, and managers at all levels of public and private sector (both nonprofit and for profit) organizations will be faced with choices that involve advocating against situations that seem unfair, unjust, inhumane, or even life threatening. Not a few will engage in the stringent juridical forms of adversarial case and class advocacy as elder-law attorneys or as their growing numbers of highly trained and specialized legal assistants. Indeed, it sometimes seems that the nation's virtually boundless humanitarian instinct to help will assure no shortage of those willing to don the advocacy mantle.

This move toward advocacy raises some paradoxical questions. If so many people think of themselves as advocates, won't they be stepping on one another's toes when they disagree about what needs to change, not to mention the appropriate course of action? Might they be at odds with one another, often latently, blatantly, and even aggressively? Is it conceivable that helping professionals who sincerely believe that they provide good care could be challenged by others who are convinced that their older clients are not receiving the services they need? If you consider yourself an elder advocate, you probably answered "Yes" to all of these questions.

☹ DEFINING ADVOCACY IN CONTEXT

The term *advocate* has been adopted by almost everyone, which clouds its meaning and leads to "multiple interpretations and lack of clarity" regarding its values, goals, methods, means, function, and role (Mallik, 1997, p. 130). It is important, therefore, to tackle this fundamental confusion. Consider the following questions:

1. For whom do you need to advocate? An individual? Or a group of people? And what is your relationship with these elders?
2. Who is going to advocate? The older persons themselves? You? Another practitioner? A lawyer? And what types of advocacy organizations might be involved?
3. To whom/what are your advocacy efforts targeted? Are you trying to get a person, group, organization, or system to do something different?
4. Why are you advocating? Is it to convince others to support or protest a policy, rule, or practice? What do you want out of this effort?
5. How will advocacy be conducted? What strategies and tactics are needed to make the change?

Throughout the book we return to these questions because they frame any advocacy effort.

Reflecting on these questions will be more enlightening if you first identify your own assumptions and values regarding the older population and the concept of advocacy. Our intent is to lead you away from accepting advocacy as a simple generic construct and toward an awareness of at least five types of elder advocates. We will explain how they are distinguished by competing values and drives that shape their respective orientations toward the older person's status, role, and needs. But first, it is important to define the concept—what is advocacy?

Our Definition of Advocacy

There are many ways to label, categorize, and describe advocacy, but the term *advocacy* itself derives from the ancient Latin verb *advocare*, "to call out." This reflects the idea that advocacy is fundamentally an act of communication. Whether with aggressive panache or in psychological subtlety, advocates *call out* about simple problems, urgent wrongs, injuries, and injustices. They draw attention to any problems needing resolution.

For the purposes of this book, we define **elder advocacy** as vigilant efforts by, with, or on behalf of older persons to influence decision makers in structures of imbalanced power and to promote justice in providing for, assisting with, or allowing needs to be met. *Vigilant efforts* implies a constant monitoring and attention devoted to the situation because it is too easy for people to fall through the cracks, particularly if they are highly vulnerable. *By, with, or on behalf of older persons* means that every effort will be made to empower older persons themselves to do what needs to be

TABLE 1.1 The Elements of Elder Advocacy

Element	Advocacy Requirements
Vigilant efforts	Constant monitoring Attention devoted to the situation Recognition of high vulnerability
By, with, and on behalf of older people	Empower older people to advocate for themselves Work together when needed In extreme cases of vulnerability, work on behalf of another
Influencing decision makers in structures of imbalanced power	Know who decision makers are Target persons who can make choices Assess power imbalances
Promoting justice in providing for, assisting with, or allowing needs to be met	Recognize power differentials Know the law Build a case to convince a reasonable person

done, but sometimes it takes people working together to get things done. At other times, when persons are particularly vulnerable or live in cultures different from their advocates' cultures, advocates may work on behalf of others. Different cultures value different roles for elderly people. In the United States, for example, self-advocacy and independence are positive attributes, but in other cultures elders' families are respected more if they assume full responsibility for their aging family members.

To influence decision makers in structures of imbalanced power indicates that persons who can make choices about who gets care, who qualifies for services, how services are delivered, and what rights will be honored have power. Power imbalances are sometimes overwhelming just because consumers do not understand how the organization works or know what rights they have. Being ill, for example, can be disempowering because individuals do not have the energy to figure out how to negotiate within the system for their own care. *To promote justice in providing for, assisting with, or allowing needs to be met* reflects an absence of balance or equity in individual, group, organizational, and societal relationships. Services or accommodations that are either lawfully mandated or are what a reasonable person would expect to be delivered are not forthcoming. Table 1.1 summarizes these elements of advocacy.

Scholars have dissected the various traits of advocacy in terms of the advocate's motives, goals, methods, focus, strategic orientation, and core values, as well as the advocate's fundamental relationship to the client. Butler and Webster (2003) comprehensively reviewed definitions for advocacy and introduced a basic vocabulary surrounding advocacy. A broad summary of these concepts portrays advocacy as being (a) an effort to change individual or group positions, system's processes, or policies that are perceived to be (b) flawed, dangerous, unresponsive, unfair, or insensitive. This change can be corrective, complementary, supplemental, or entirely punitive. The common goals of advocacy are to (c) improve conditions, avoid harm, meet needs, protect rights, defend general interests, or, more broadly, to rectify injustices affecting the interests of (d) oneself, other individuals, or groups or classes of elders with specific characteristics (Cohen, 2004) who share little in common other than being generally above a certain age and being in some sense vulnerable and influentially disadvantaged.

Our Assumptions

In this section we reveal some of the assumptions about elder advocacy that caused us to write this book. You do not have to agree with our assumptions—we just want to be transparent about some

TABLE 1.2 Our Assumptions Questioned

Assumption Questions	Short Answers
1. What does the elder want?	Ask them. Elders' wants and needs are paramount over those of family members and advocates. If they have sufficient cognition, just ask them.
2. Why aren't systems more systematic?	Systems (a) must always be flexible and adaptable to work at all, and (b) people with different (often conflicting) assumptions run them.
3. When do providers need to call in outside help?	Providers need to call in outside help when (a) they are too busy or overwhelmed or when (b) their positions could be in jeopardy if they advocate against their employers or their policies.
4. Is conflict inevitable?	Yes. Well, usually. Advocates must work for win-win outcomes whenever possible, but they also need to be creative in their efforts.

of our biases. We pose four questions for your consideration.

1. What does the elder want?
2. Why aren't systems more systematic?
3. When do providers need to call in outside help?
4. Is conflict inevitable?

By raising these questions, you have probably guessed that we (a) caution you about forgetting to hear the voices/wishes/desires/needs of the older persons for whom you are advocating, (b) are skeptical about the systematic nature of systems, (c) believe that there are indeed times in which outside help is needed, and (d) are convinced that conflict is virtually inevitable. Table 1.2 provides four questions that challenge our assumptions, along with candid short answers.

1. What Does the Elder Want?

We offer this example. In years past, nursing home workers were concerned about the serious injuries sustained by elders who fell out of their wheelchairs. Some simply leaned too far forward and fell, and others fell while getting out of their chairs, so workers began tying elders into their chairs to prevent injuries. The intent was to protect elders from harm. In doing so, however, workers crossed the line into violating individuals' autonomy. We

are not sufficiently naive to believe that the sole reason for restraining older people was always the desire to protect them from harm—sometimes it was to restrain those who were combative (or noncompliant, perhaps not understanding where they were and why they were taken from their homes) or those who wandered off, sometimes into other residents' rooms or even away from the nursing home (troublesome residents). Thus, what began as protection crossed the line into taking away individuals' freedom of movement, which further exacerbated their quality of life. In this example, because being tied down would frustrate *them*, advocates assumed that it would frustrate most everyone, but we do not know that. Being tied down could have made some residents feel more secure. Their personal histories and cultures may have generated strong feelings or experiences of being restrained, both positively and negatively.

In another example, when nursing home reform was on the lips of hundreds of advocates and providers were trying to be responsive, there was a general assumption that nursing homes should look and feel more like homes than institutions. One idea was that workers need not wear uniforms because regular street dress would make residents feel more at home, and for some it did. Others, however, were confused because they could not tell a registered nurse (RN) from a nurse's aide and preferred that staff go back to wearing uniforms.

A third example comes from the early days of the development of the congregate meals program under Title III of the Older Americans Act (OAA). (A link to this act is on the companion website.) A great deal of effort went into distinguishing between elders who were homebound and really needed a home-delivered meal and older persons who were able to get out each day and go to congregate meal sites. The push to get people out of their homes and socializing with others was seen as almost as important as the nutrition provided by having a balanced meal every day. Advocates who strongly believed in the activity theory of aging—that older people need to replace lost roles and continue being active as long as possible—assumed that it was important for everyone who could get out to go to a congregate meal site should do so, rather than receive a meal at home in isolation. These assumptions undergirded the program, perhaps dismissing the legitimate desire of some older persons to eat in the privacy of their own homes.

In a fourth example, a daughter moved her mother from a two-bedroom apartment in a high-rise for seniors to a studio apartment in the assisted living unit of a continuing care retirement community (CCRC). The daughter assumed that she should consult her mother about every piece of furniture and all the contents within her apartment because they would have to dispose of at least two thirds of the mother's belongings. Running back and forth between the larger apartment to the assisted living unit across the street, the daughter asked her mother about every item, trying desperately to include her mother in every decision (and there were many). Finally, the mother gently said to her daughter, "You are wearing me out. I just want you to decide. I trust you to make these decisions." The daughter had assumed that her mother wanted to be included in every decision, no matter how small, but this was her assumption, not her mother's.

And as a fifth example, McCann (2003) wrote a poignant account of nursing home residents with Alzheimer's dementia. (A link to the Alzheimer's Association is on the companion website.) Before or in the early stages of Alzheimer's disease, holocaust survivors generally managed to lead fairly normal lives by not thinking about the horrors of the past. The progression of the dementia, however, took away their ability to block out those memories. One of McCann's examples was how upset residents became when staff lined up their wheelchairs for showers. The staff did not realize that *showers*, to these elderly Jewish residents, meant being gassed to death! Advocates realized that the much younger employees of the nursing home had no idea why residents were terrified of showers and men in uniforms with authoritative voices, and they arranged for comprehensive training for staff (McCann, 2003). This was a good experience for advocates because no one lost, everyone won: staff understood residents' behaviors and learned to avoid circumstances that upset residents who, in turn, became less frightened and combative.

In all five examples across three different types of settings (the nursing home, the congregate meal site, and the CCRC), assumptions were being made. One of the assumptions we bring to this book is that whenever possible it is critically important to ask older persons what *they* want and recognize when their assumptions vary from those of well-meaning advocates. The point is *not* that we should not make assumptions, but that we must recognize them and check to see whether they are getting in the way of that which is best for the person you are trying to help.

There will always be assumptions among providers, within organizations, and even in whole communities. Cultural assumptions that disempower may be hidden in provider practices and even reinforced in organizational, regulatory, state, and/or federal policies. In other words, people can be following their best practice standards to the letter, yet still be doing things that diminish the quality of elders' lives.

2. Why Aren't Systems More Systematic?

We frequently use the term *system* in this book, and you hear it a lot in practice. By definition, a system sounds like something that comes together in a cohesive manner. Some entities that

BOX 1.2

A Simple System Gone Awry

Accompanied by her 85-year-old Aunt Margaret, one of the authors was trying to buy an over-the-counter medication that was also popular with local crack producers. Management had implemented a simple system to deal with the problem: tags were hung with the names and pictures of medications, consumers were to take a tag to the pharmacy counter, and the person there would get the medication from under the counter. I took a tag to the counter and stood in line to pay for it. After a 10-minute wait the clerk said, "Oh, we don't have that in stock, just hang the tag back where it was." And I said, "Why hang it back up if you don't have any in stock?" And she replied, "That's our system. If you don't want to hang it back up, I will." Clearly the clerk knew the system but had no concern for unintended consequences—elderly people waiting in line unnecessarily.

we call systems, however, are actually an array of unconnected health care providers, each a complex organization in itself, each with its own expertise and self-interests. Each may be competing with the others for business and third party reimbursements (i.e., private insurance, Medicare, and Medicaid). (Links to Medicare and Medicaid are on the companion website.)

Some systems work fairly well. Others simply do not work very well, and some appear to be anything but systematic. Although there are usually logical reasons for what happens in a particular setting, unintended consequences can be oppressive and even discriminatory against elders. Interorganizational relationships may be ragged and require extra vigilance, and people can get lost between the cracks. Therefore, it behooves the advocate to watch for these unintended consequences and not to be surprised when they happen. Box 1.2 describes a very simple, well-intentioned system gone awry.

No matter the setting, you will encounter people with good intentions (e.g., providers, family members, and volunteers) whose well-meaning actions are not in the best interests of elders. You may even encounter persons whose intentions are simply *not* good. When consequences are unintended, when indifference occurs, or when intentional harm is done, elders are at risk of neglect, exploitation, and abuse.

3. When Do Providers Need to Call in Outside Help?

One of our assumptions is that most entities in these somewhat nonsystems provide very good care for their patients. The work is demanding, the pace fast, and complex problems seem never ending. Nevertheless, one of the strongest incentives for providers to do their jobs is that they feel like they are making a difference in their patients' lives. We believe that most providers and their representatives are trying to do decent, competent work. We also recognize that individuals and whole groups of people can buy into decisions and methods that seem logical at the time but that disempower and even wrong the very persons whom they are trying to serve.

For example, physically or chemically restraining nursing home residents became known as tools for patient management, which finally came to be seen as a form of kidnapping—restraining people against their will. Imagine a newly hired nurse's aide working in a long-term care facility that had restrained elders since the home opened in 1950, but the aide hated doing it, partly because *he* wouldn't want to be tied to a wheelchair and partly because he had to physically fight the residents to get it done every day. He knew that he would lose his job if he tried to tell the nurses and administrators that they shouldn't be doing this. He was an advocate at heart whose hands were tied by his need to keep his job, but he could get support from elsewhere in the aging community.

Led by the National Citizens Coalition for Nursing Home Reform (NCCNHR), advocates combined forces to lobby against physical and chemical restraints, and they were successful. Since passage of the Federal Nursing Home Reform Act as part of the Omnibus Budget Reconciliation Act of 1987 (commonly referred to as OBRA 87), the use of antipsychotic drugs has declined between 28% and 36% and physical restraints have declined approximately 40% (Turnham, n.d.). (Links to the coalition and to these acts are on the companion website.)

We recognize that clinicians are busy, thus they may see additional advocacy work as requiring more vigilance than they have time to invest. You may become such a clinician. If geriatric and elder service workers are too busy or overwhelmed by their primary duties to advocate against injustices or inequities, they can contact local advocates and work with them to resolve problems. If you are a helping professional employed in a system where advocacy is needed, you may not be able to take the same actions (risks) as external advocates. There may even be risks in calling them in. Sometimes you will have to make hard choices, using your best judgment.

4. Is Conflict Inevitable?

Yes. If you are going to advocate for anything, some degree of conflict is inevitable. In fact, conflict is invited by adopting widespread solutions and interventions. Conflict can also occur on a smaller scale, such as between two care planners. For example, if one resident's care plan includes "must have more privacy" and his roommate's plan calls for "more human interaction," there will be conflict. Conflict at all possible levels of intervention is inevitable. No matter how collaborative you are, there will be resistance. This resistance may come from unlikely sources because of political and personal relationships. Conflict is part of daily life, and in some families it is simply the communication style. Advocates should not be put off, therefore, if the elder for whom they are advocating appears to be a bit hostile or even adversarial—cultural contexts vary and often surprise advocates.

The overwhelming consensus is that advocacy begins with a polite appeal, through education, or by forming alliances and working collaboratively. But beyond this, "the task of the advocate is to be argumentative, inquisitive, indignant or apologetic as the occasion demands, and always persuasive" (Pannick, 1992, and cited in Bateman, 2000, p. 27). Advocacy entails gentle and sometimes not so gentle confrontation because much of what disempowers older persons can be hidden in provider practices, values, and competing priorities. Disempowerment can be reinforced in organizational, regulatory, state, and federal policies. Confronting practices, values, priorities, and even policies can breed controversy and opposition. Conversely, consider that there may even be times when the conflict is between you and the person or persons for whom you are advocating. We provide more about how to handle and use conflict in later chapters.

Based on their unique knowledge and experiences, most people hold assumptions about other people, events, services, and organizations, and we encourage you to consider the assumptions you hold about aging, about health and human service delivery systems, and about yourself as an advocate for elders. These assumptions emanate from our own cultures. The trick is to identify your assumptions, then look behind and underneath them to see whether they are helpful or harmful. Your analysis of whether your assumptions are helpful or harmful will probably depend on the specific situation you are confronting.

Defining "Elder"

No matter what terms are used, we realize that someone will be offended, so we apologize in advance. In past years, the word *senior* was used to describe persons over a certain age. *Elderly* was and still is often heard, but it has been replaced by *elderly persons* or *elders* because "elderly" is an adjective rather than a noun, and no one wants to simply be a description! In the literature, *older persons* is often used as well as the term *the aging*. We see aging as a process that everyone is engaged

BOX 1.3

Who Are We, Anyway?

Advocates for elders? Elder advocates? Yes. Just as we interchangeably use at least two terms to describe the focus of this book, *elders* and *older persons*, so do we use at least two labels for people who advocate for elderly people: *elder advocates* and *advocates for elders*. Today's elderly population is fortunate to have a small but dedicated army of supporters who advocate for elder persons' myriad needs on a daily basis. Many are young, which brings us back to the topic at hand in this section—just what is *old?* (The first author has the answer: "My age plus 20.")

in from birth onward, so *the aging* refers to everyone. Therefore, in the interest of offending as few people as possible, we will use the terms *older person* and *elder* interchangeably throughout this book. Box 1.3 touches on this same conundrum pertaining to elder advocates.

The target population for elder advocacy includes a heterogeneous range of individuals who are grouped as having reached the chronological age of 60 or 65. This is consistent with important legal definitions of aging such as the Older Americans Act's authorization to Area Agencies on Aging (AAAs) to serve persons from the age of 60 years, the Social Security System's normal retirement age (67), or Medicare's eligibility trigger age of 65. (Links to these agencies are on the companion website.) The widely recognized problems with these time-dependent definitions of old age is their poor compatibility with biological, psychological, functional, and social definitions of aging that better reflect the tremendous interindividual variability that exists among older adults.

For example, almost everyone knows at least one 50-year-old who is more physically, financially, and mentally fragile than individuals who are decades older. More physically challenged younger persons who are transitioning between middle age and being young-old may really need the services of an advocate who knows the aging network. Even though they may barely qualify for membership in the American Association of Retired Persons (AARP [age 50]), they may well need help in navigating the plethora of complex systems that may be less psychologically geared

up for chronologically younger but no less needy individuals. (A link to the association is on the companion website.)

Still, logic predicts that the so-called **young-old** (ages 65 to 74) may be more active and independent than the frail **old-old** (ages 75 to 85), who are in turn more empowered than the very fragile **oldest-of-the-old** (over age 85) who are unquestionably in greatest need of third party empowerment and advocacy (Hooyman & Kiyak, 1999). Logic predicts that as an advocate you will be needed more by the oldest-of-the-old, especially if they have a number of conditions that limit functioning.

Still, in operationalizing the term *elder*, we should avoid being too restrictive. For example, if we rigidly stick to an age of, say, 65 and older, then advocates wishing to address the issue of age-related job discrimination will have difficulties because the Age Discrimination Employment Act of 1967 (ADEA) identifies people over 40 as needing protection from an ageist culture. (A link to the act is on the companion website.) Also, our experience indicates that clearly designated elder-care advocates, like the Older American's Act ombudsmen, routinely tackle problems lodged by or on behalf of younger persons, including infants, who are housed in the nation's long-stay facilities. Thus, even though ombudsmen invariably self-identify as elder-care advocates, they do not limit their services based on any age criteria.

We take a similar approach here. Although older persons for whom and with whom you may advocate will normally be individuals over age 60, we expect that the need for advocacy will increase in direct proportion not only to persons' advanced chronological ages but also in proportion to sociodemographic characteristics that predispose older persons to increased vulnerabilities. Such vulnerabilities might include poor physical health, mental illness, poverty, inadequate education, lack of social support, dysfunctional family structure, or being a member of a minority group or of a different culture.

☾ FUTURE NEEDS

In assessing the future need for advocacy, consider (a) that the cohort of persons over 65 is growing at more than two and a half times the rate of the general population and (b) that there are now twice as many people over age 65 as there were in 1960 (Freidland & Summer, 1999). Moreover, this factor will double again in just another 25 years when the United States will embrace 70 million citizens over age 65. By 2050 at least 31% of these citizens will be members of minority groups who experience disproportionate need, as will the fastest growing age group, the very vulnerable oldest-of-the-old (age 85+), whose numbers will swell from nearly 4 million, to 8 million, to nearly 21 million by 2040 (Freidland & Summer, 1999).

Conventional wisdom suggests that the growth of these last two groups in particular will present many dilemmas that pit national resources against America's impulse for social justice. Some argue that the pressure on Social Security, Medicare, Medicaid, and other aging support systems will severely burden the relatively few younger taxpayers who will be called upon to support the spiking elder service need. This situation may be compounded by the fact that health care costs generally grow at nearly double the inflation rate. Gloom prophets forecast particularly grim scenarios for certain segments of the aging service arena. For example, challenges to providing long-term care include a surging demand by the very old at the same time that the female caregiving population declines—both in real numbers and in apparent willingness to serve in the typically poorly compensated, demanding job of being a certified nursing assistant (CNA) or a personal attendant (Van Kleuned & Wilner, 2000).

Clearly, the U.S. population is shifting from the traditional population pyramid (more younger people at the base and fewer older people at the top), toward a vertical rectangle. This shift may even become an *inverted* pyramid due to older people living longer (at the top) and fewer children at the base. Elders represent nearly half of hospital days and patients in critical care, two-thirds of home care services, and over 80% of nursing home residents. One anticipated effect is that fewer young people will be financially supporting more elderly people. Another view is that higher elder health care and human service costs will be offset by diminished costs for education and other youth-related social expenditures, and by improved medical procedures, technological advances, better care management, improved prevention, and enhanced knowledge and clinical practice skills in how to acclimate aging individuals to their social living environments. Even though the economic effect is a wild card, any positive change in market forces could easily help offset any increased costs for age-related services.

Without a reliable crystal ball, we simply cannot predict the future, be it rosy or catastrophic. Thus we cannot reliably forecast the future need for elder advocacy. It is clearly safe, however, to say that this need will grow.

Just as elders are heterogeneous, so are the situations in which they find themselves. It is not as simple as saying that an older person lives at home or resides in an assisted living setting because elders move in and out of different settings according to changing needs. We now turn to these diverse settings in which advocacy may take place.

☾ ELDER ADVOCACY SETTINGS AND SERVICES

Elder services are offered in an array of health and human service settings, making it particularly hard for the uninitiated observer to fathom—even veteran advocates pause to scratch their heads in bemusement from time to time. Perhaps the main reason for this complexity is that elders must navigate not one system but myriad somewhat disconnected services and agencies to get their needs met. There is rarely one-stop shopping. Table 1.3 provides an

TABLE 1.3 The Labyrinth of Services

Prevention

Home- and community-based education services

Case management services

Outreach services

Wellness clinics

Health screenings

Exercise programs

Home-delivered meal services

Flu immunizations

Depression screenings

Suicide awareness and prevention programs

Elder abuse/neglect prevention services

Stress management

Smoking cessation

Preventive tests such as Pap, bone resorption, and mammograms

Treatment

Outpatient mental and physical health

Inpatient mental and physical health

Acute hospitalization

Ambulatory care services

Urgent care clinics

Physician visits

Health maintenance

Skilled nursing care

Protection and Support

Adult protective services

Long-term care ombudsman services

Family caregiver services

Senior companion and friendly visiting services

Homemaker services

Volunteer shopping services

Services for grandparents parenting grandchildren

Legal aid services:
- living wills
- health proxies
- benefits
- involuntary transfers
- probate
- consumer fraud
- financial exploitation
- housing
- medical malpractice

Brokerage and Linkages

Information and referral services

Telephone hotlines

Case management services

---

overview of possible services offered by diverse organizations. It may be helpful to think about how one elderly woman entered this labyrinth.

Margaret Enters the System

The nature of the doctor-patient relationship often results in doctors retiring just as their patients of 40 years enter their 60s and 70s, which, in turn, results in patients being referred to new, young, and very busy physicians, perhaps in practice groups of 10 or 20 physicians. This is what happened to Margaret, an 85-year-old woman who is preparing for the first visit to her new physician. First, she must complete a comprehensive life history and send it ahead or take it with her when she goes for her first visit, which may be difficult if she has not kept good medical records. When she arrives at the doctor's office, she must sign in, wait, then provide proof of insurance or demonstrate how she is going to pay her medical bills. She must also sign four or five forms written in small print legalese and put them in the receptionist's waiting hand. Then she waits until she is called by the next stranger.

Stranger 2 takes her medical history again, including information about all of Margaret's medications including each medication's start date, purpose, dosage, and frequency. This person or another then weighs her and takes her temperature, blood pressure, and heart rate and tells her to completely undress and put on the ubiquitous paper gown and "hop up on this table," which she cannot do. She struggles, however, and crawls up on the high steel (and cold) table and waits. She must have a complete physical because the new doctor does not know her, so Stranger 3, the new doctor, comes in, perhaps with a medical student in tow, and these two or three strangers then poke and squeeze various parts of her body and insert cold steel utensils or fingers into her private orifices. Oh yes, it is 60° in the exam room, and they yell at her, assuming that she is hard of hearing, which she isn't.

Next, let's assume that this doctor knows to go out and give her a chance to get dressed before sitting down to talk to her about what's next. She is given new prescriptions for high blood pressure and cholesterol and referred for testing for the cause of slight tremors, lower back pain, and a chronic upset stomach. She has two more stops before she leaves. First, she waits to meet with Stranger 4, who schedules appointments with specialists in those areas (neurologist, nephrologist, and gastroenterologist). Each of these specialists will first meet with her (repeating the whole new patient regimen) and then refer her for their respective tests (again repeating the new patient regimen). Appointments with new doctors made, she finally waits again to check out (pay her bill) and make her next appointment with this doctor.

Recall that this is just a brief snapshot of Margaret *entering* the health care system—never mind that she must continue to negotiate her way through this maze of caregivers over time. You get the picture. It's little wonder that Margaret soon said, "no more new doctors."

Aging Services: Four Types

Understanding the complexities of the service delivery system is aided by breaking the process down into discretely manageable units of analysis. Ward (1979, as cited in Beaver, 1983) provided a much-used classification scheme of geriatric services that embraces a broad range of local, public nonprofit, proprietary, and faith-based providers. This approach classifies services into four basic areas: (a) prevention, (b) treatment, (c) adult protection and support, and (d) resource brokerage/linkage services.

Prevention Services

Prevention services include home- and community-based educational, case management, and other outreach efforts that promote elder wellness and early intervention strategies. These services are designed to increase elders' likelihood of successfully aging in place. The Older Americans Act funds a wide range of these services through local AAAs and their associated senior centers. Services typically include a variety of health screenings, exercise programs, home meal delivery, congregate meals, influenza immunization initiatives, depression assessment and suicide awareness and prevention programs, elder abuse and self-neglect prevention services, and stress management, smoking cessation, and other programs intended to reduce the incidence of stroke among older persons. Medicare also covers a variety of prevention assessments including Pap tests, bone resorption assessments, and breast exams.

Treatment

Treatment services include a wide range of public and private institutional and community-based health and allied social services designed for elders. Providers include inpatient and outpatient mental and physical health units, acute care hospitals and ambulatory care units, urgent care clinics, solo and group general medical practices, and a range of geriatric specialist practices. Treatment services also include the long-term care continuum, which consists of institutional and community-based residential settings that combine treatment and health maintenance functions with services intended to promote residents' socioemotional well being (Pratt, 2004). At the end of this continuum is the nursing home, which provides medical and skilled nursing services and assistance with activities of daily living (ADLs include feeding, grooming, bathing, toileting, and transferring, for example, from wheelchairs to beds) to convalescing elders (and others) who are unable to live at home but do not require hospitalization. Most of the work done in nursing homes is custodial and is performed by paraprofessional nurse's aides. Subacute care is an intermediate type of medical institution between a nursing home and a hospital. It provides more intense, but shorter duration care than a nursing home but is lower tech, longer stay, and less expensive than a hospital. Home health care is also part of this continuum.

The Department of Veterans Affairs (DVA) runs inpatient and outpatient facilities spanning the continuum of care, but it is increasingly shifting its resources to long-term care as America's veterans age. (A link to the department is on the companion website.) The DVA is a leader in developing hospital-based, multidisciplinary geriatric research, education, and clinical centers (GRECCs), which disseminate best practice information to providers throughout the health care system.

In addition to the nursing home, a growing list of noninstitutional, community-based residential alternatives provide older residents with ADL assistance but not with nursing care. These settings include residential care and assisted living facilities (that typically house from 5 to 100 or more residents), adult foster or boarding care homes (with 5 or fewer residents in a single-family homelike dwelling), and adult day care facilities where family caregivers can drop off a loved one for fewer than 24 hours of respite care. Palliative care units and hospice programs provide comfort care for dying individuals.

Community-based treatment services also include case management, preinstitutional assessment and placement services, and a range of visiting practitioner programs and specialized services such as outpatient substance abuse treatment, grief management counseling, and individual and family therapy.

Protection and Support Services

These services are geared to defend the older individuals' health and rights and to make their experiences in the community safe and secure. These services are provided by a variety of private and public, sectarian and nonsectarian agencies and programs, including the AAAs, local law enforcement agencies, the long-term care ombudsman program, state and county health departments, and many others. Services include adult protective service programs that work with police and ombudsman programs to investigate, document, and refer cases of elder abuse, neglect, or financial exploitation to the appropriate authorities for intervention and corrective legal action. In this connection, most communities provide a range of family caregiver assistance activities that are designed to reduce caregiver stress and lessen the incidence of elder neglect and abuse. Senior companion, friendly visitor, homemaker, and volunteer shopper assistant programs are targeted to protect at-risk older, socially isolated and homebound people who may not be able to fend for themselves, and more and more programs are being designed to help older individuals who are parenting their grandchildren.

The Area Agency on Aging maintains a legal assistance developer who organizes legal aid advice and counsel, either directly or by referral, for low-income elders. Advocacy services are wide ranging and include (a) help with living wills and other health proxy issues, (b) diverse government benefit problems ranging from Medicaid to disability law problems, (c) nursing home involuntary transfers (moves to different rooms, roommates, wings, buildings, and levels of care) and (d) other long-term care issues, (e) probate, (f) consumer fraud and financial exploitation troubles, (g) subsidized housing issues, and (h) medical malpractice, as well as nearly every other kind of routine (and not so routine) legal problem encountered by older people.

Resource Brokerage/Linkage Services

These services are largely coordinated by the AAAs and include services that are designed to connect older people with any of the staggering array of services previously listed. Much of this is done through information hotlines, phone banks, and confidential referral services that identify specific service options for individuals with special needs. Culturally competent linkage services assess diverse values and needs, striving to reduce language barriers between users and providers and to provide direct assistance to clients in filling out applications and circumventing other barriers to access.

Layers of Complexities

Beyond the dizzying array of these often fragmented service options, the older individual's access and use is complicated by many other factors, including (a) availability and access to specialized geriatric and elder-oriented services, (b) the individual's level of social support, and perhaps most important, (c) the elder's health insurance and other financial resources.

The availability of health and mental health services is not usually a barrier for elders living in urban areas, but it can be troublesome for rural elders. Consider how an older individual's transportation problems might pose a greater challenge in a rural community without public transportation where distances between service providers might be considerably greater. For example, the continuum of care is truncated in rural areas. Alternatives to institutional care are fewer because it is not economically feasible to develop these options privately, and public policy regarding the Medicaid waiver program that supports these noninstitutional alternatives targets cities.

We are aware of a federally funded, university sponsored interdisciplinary health screening program designed to set up free clinics in rural and underserved areas. This program sends teams of faculty and students from social work, nursing, medicine, and dentistry into rural areas to conduct screening and make referrals during summer semesters. Local Area Health Education Centers (AHECs) do the advance work of finding sites and advertising the coming 4- or 5-day free clinic. (A link to these centers is on the companion website.) This is good for rural communities and an excellent learning opportunity for faculty and students, but some team members are concerned that they may be making hollow referrals if (a) the needed services are not available, (b) elders cannot reach them due to transportation barriers, or (c) elders cannot afford them. These team members are laying the groundwork, however, to advocate for resources to actually provide more

of the services needed. Currently, only minimal services are being provided, which may include dental checkups, weight, temperature, blood pressure and heart rate tests by medical faculty and students, and social workers who gather case histories and assess for destructive activities in patients' homes. Writing the grants to put such services in place is a prime example of advocacy.

Elders may be more motivated to keep health-related appointments and follow up on referrals if they are surrounded by positive social support from family, friends, or even professionals who can take the time for follow-up phone calls or send reminder postcards—all forms of advocacy for elders to access the services they need. Absent this support, or worse, the elder's social network may not facilitate health care use, and advocacy is much more difficult.

Health insurance and financial resources may be the most intractable layer of complexity. The first question from most health care providers is about money—how are you going to pay? Do you have insurance? Are you on Medicare? Medicaid? Do you have prescription drug coverage? The answers often drive access to the services provided, including medications and referrals for testing and specialists.

☾ SUMMARY

We exposed our assumptions about elder advocacy: (a) it is important to carefully listen to what elders want and need, (b) systems are not always very systematic, (c) most providers try to provide good care, and (d) conflict is inevitable. We introduced terms associated with older people and acknowledged that age is purely a chronological classifications scheme. There are vital people of all ages and others who have multiple needs regardless of age. Elder advocacy settings and services were discussed, using the example of Margaret who enters a physician's practice and finds the routine very dehumanizing. Four types of aging services were identified: prevention, treatment, protection and support, and resource brokerage/linkage services. These services are not mutually exclusive; in fact, there are layers of complexity in their delivery across and within diverse settings.

We framed advocacy in the context of four sets of questions focused on for whom one advocates, who advocates, to whom the effort is directed, the reasons behind advocating, and how advocacy will be conducted. The remainder of the book is directed toward the reasons for advocating and the guidelines for how you can advocate for elders. We defined advocacy as vigilant efforts by, with, or on behalf of older persons to influence decision makers in structures of imbalanced power and to promote justice in providing for, assisting with, or allowing needs to be met. We examined five types of advocates, recognizing that they will often overlap. It is important to consider the difference between being an internal or external advocate as well as how to identify decision makers who have the power to change situations.

DISCUSSION QUESTIONS AND EXERCISES

1. Everyone advocates for their needs to be met. In some situations, you will need to draw on others to assist in the advocacy process. What situation can you identify in which you needed help to get your needs met? What makes this situation different from those times you were able to advocate without assistance?

2. In this chapter we revealed our assumptions about elders' wants, systems, providers, and conflict. How do these assumptions differ from yours? What assumptions do you have about the eldercare delivery system? How do your assumptions influence the way in which you will approach elder advocacy?

3. The example of Margaret entering the system through the physician's office is but one step in what may be an extended journey with the health care system. Reread this example and think about what you would do if you were Margaret's relative or friend. How might you advocate with and for her? Now assume that you are the physician or someone who works in this medical practice. How might you advocate for change in the care of elder clients?

4. We proposed a definition of elder advocacy. What is your definition of elder advocacy? How does it differ from the one we have proposed and why?

5. Being an internal advocate has its strengths and limitations, as does being an external advocate. Can you think of times in which an internal advocate may actually become an external advocate and vice versa as elders move in and out of various settings? How do the dynamics change as you move from the position of being within a particular setting to advocating for your client who has gone into another setting?

6. At times you may be the decision maker targeted by a persuasive advocate who truly believes that something needs to change. Given your current position or what you are training to do, can you think of situations in which you might actually be the targeted decision maker rather than the advocate? Similarly, can you envision yourself simultaneously being the decision maker and the advocate? Discuss what that might be like.

7. Reread the case at the beginning of the chapter. If you had been the adult foster care provider in Jeanine's story, what would you have done differently? What advocacy roles are being played out in this situation and by whom? How does the definition of advocacy used in this chapter fit with what happened in this case?

ADDITIONAL READINGS

Baldridge, D. (2004, Spring). Double jeopardy: Advocating for Indian elders. *Generations, 28*(1), 75–78.

Binstock, R. H. (2004, Spring). Advocacy in an era of neoconservatism: Responses of national aging organizations. *Generations, 28*(1), 49–54.

Blancato, R. B. (2004, Spring). Advocacy and aging policy: The prognosis. *Generations, 28*(1), 65–69.

Callahan, J. J. (2004, Spring). The world of interest-group advocacy: An "Insider's" view. *Generations 28*(1), 36–40.

Fisher, R., Ury, W., & Patton, B. (1991). *Getting to yes: Negotiating agreement without giving in.* New York: Penguin Books.

Freeman, I. C. (2004, Spring). Advocacy in aging policy: Working the bills on Capitol Hill(s). *Generations, 28*(1), 41–47.

Haynes, K. S., & Mickelson, J. S. (2000). *Affecting change* (4th ed.). Needham, MA: Allyn & Bacon.

Hornbostel, R. (2004, Spring). The power of local advocacy: Funding for senior services in Ohio. *Generations, 28*(1), 79–81.

Hudson, R. B. (2004, Spring). Advocacy and policy success in aging. *Generations, 28*(1), 17–24.

Kane, R. A. (2004, Spring). The circumscribed sometimes-advocacy of the case manager and the care provider. *Generations, 28*(1), 70–74.

Kapp, M. B. (2004, Spring). Advocacy in an aging society: The varied roles of attorneys. *Generations, 28*(1), 31–35.

Kelly, M. A. (2004, Spring). Developing an advocacy coalition with varied interests and agendas: A Pennsylvanian experience. *Generations, 28*(1), 83–85.

Lens, V. (2004, July). Principled negotiation: A new tool for case advocacy. *Social Work, 49*(3), 506–513.

Lowenberg, F., & Dolgoff, R. (1988). *Ethical decisions for social work practice* (3rd ed.). Itasca, IL: F. E. Peacock.

McConnell, S. (2004, Spring). Advocacy in organizations: The elements of success. *Generations, 28*(1), 25–30.

National Association of Social Workers. (1999). *The code of ethics.* Washington, DC: Author.

Reish, M. (1986). From cause to case and back again: The re-emergence of advocacy in social work. *The Urban and Social Exchange Review,* 20–24.

Rother, K. (2004, Spring). Why haven't we been more successful advocates for elders? *Generations, 28*(1), 55–58.

Rubin, J. S. (1994). Models of conflict management. *Journal of Social Issues, 30,* 34–45.

Stone, R. (2004, Spring). Where have all the advocates gone? *Generations, 28*(1), 59–64.

Zimny, G. H., & Grossberg, G. T. (1998). *Guardianship of the elderly: Psychiatric and judicial aspects.* New York: Springer.

CHAPTER TWO

Theoretical Frameworks for Understanding Context and Settings

The whole is greater than the sum of its parts. BOTAN (1988, p. 114)

 BOX 2.1

PATRICE

Patrice, an African American woman, lived in her neighborhood for over 75 years. A participant in the Foster Grandparent Program, she was proud to call herself a charter member of the program. Even with limited income, she had been able to live in her family home her entire life. She had been the caregiver for both her parents before they died, and she had never married. Her dogs were the joy of her life. She was characterized by her outgoing personality and ready smile.

Patrice was still driving and anxious to maintain her independence. However, she was having more and more trouble seeing to drive and was absolutely sure that she should not drive at night. When she went to have her glasses changed, she learned that she had macular degeneration and that it was dangerous for her to drive. As she left the ophthalmologist's office, she was very preoccupied, trying to sort through what she could do without a car. The city bus did run within a couple of blocks of her house, and she still knew a few neighbors who had cars.

As she left the parking lot and pulled out on the street, Patrice was hit by a passing car. She never saw the car coming, and the next thing she remembers is waking up in a sterile white hospital room. She was confused and her head kept spinning. She asked where she was, but nothing seemed to compute. The persons who swirled around her seemed to be mumbling and talking over her, not to her. Over the course of 3 days, she learned that she had several broken bones and that she would be moving to a rehabilitation facility by week's end. She felt as if she had lost all track of time, and all she could think about was whether anyone was feeding her dogs. When she asked the nurse if Jack and Ralph were okay, the nurse would say things like, "There, there, don't worry about anyone else."

The nurse told the social worker that from all they could tell this was a single woman who lived alone but that she kept asking about two men. The social worker visited Patrice, only to find her sobbing uncontrollably. She was unable to get anything out of her other than she might as well be dead as being in the condition she was in. Patrice had given up any hope of being able to communicate with any of the hospital staff, and when she was transferred to rehab, she appeared to have given up. The rehab team assessed her as severely depressed and referred her to the nursing home where she could "rest" since she did not appear motivated enough to benefit from the rehabilitation process. When a neighbor stopped by to see her, just 10 days after her accident, he did not recognize the vital woman he had known. The nursing home nurse told him that the only thing she had talked about was Jack and Ralph and asked if he might be either of them. "No," he replied, "They are her dogs! I've been feeding Jack and Ralph while she's been laid up."

The cultures of the complex systems in which Patrice found herself apparently were not open to hearing what Patrice had to say. In addition, her caregivers were not adept at active listening; their interactions were one-way communications. With no one to advocate for her, Patrice very quickly became a victim of at least two helping systems, the hospital and the nursing home. Although we do not know *the rest of the story*, if the neighbor who cared for Jack and Ralph could also intervene on Patrice's behalf, she should be able to recoup some of her losses. If he could get representatives from the rehab center, the nursing home, and her colleagues in the Foster Grandparent Program to work together, he will have proven Botan's (1988) theory that the *whole* (the collective of these players and the results of their collaborating to help Patrice) is greater than the sum of its parts: each of these entities acting—or not—individually without including the rest of Patrice's social system. Thus the layperson in the picture may accomplish that which the professionals missed in this situation.

Botan's statement and the resulting notion of synergy resound throughout this book. In the first chapter we focused on the complex delivery system in which elder advocacy occurs. In this chapter we turn to theoretical perspectives that may help in understanding these diverse contexts and settings.

There are volumes about theories that inform practice, so we have been selective, offering some guidance in other theoretical perspectives beyond what we can provide here. We briefly highlight three theoretical streams of thought: (a) complex social systems theory, (b) organizational culture theory, and (c) theories of interaction, including power, social exchange, and conflict. These perspectives are particularly helpful in setting the stage for the remainder of the book.

☽ THREE THEORETICAL PERSPECTIVES

Complex systems theory is useful in understanding how the aging network is made up of many subsystems of other systems nested within one another. Systems thinking respects the possibility that things do not always happen in a linear manner—that "the whole is greater than the sum of its parts" (Botan, 1988, p. 144). This is often referred to as synergy, the idea that the aging network is not merely a group of agencies all lined up on a menu for elders to access as needed (this would be a sum of its parts). Instead, in a well-functioning aging network, agencies work together to build a supportive network, or a system, for an elder. Thus the aging network is something greater than a list of agencies. It is built on the premise, or ideology, that society bears some responsibility for its elders.

On a larger scale, systemic thinking reveals how effective macro-level public policy advocacy can have critical consequences for other, more local levels within larger systems. Conversely, it provides clues to how individual case and administrative level advocacy can, in turn, influence and even reshape the larger social environment.

Complex systems may contain a host of formal and informal structures, including groups, organizations, and communities. Therefore, we have chosen a second theoretical school of thought that we have found particularly helpful in understanding the organizational cultures of the settings in which elder advocacy occurs, or that elder advocacy efforts are intended to alter in some way. **Organizational culture theory** focuses introspectively at the self-maintaining attitudes, values, habits, rituals, and goals that comprise a given agency's procedural, social, and psychological belief system. Knowing an organization's culture

TABLE 2.1 Overview of Three Theoretical Perspectives

Theory	Perspective
Complex Systems Theory	A basic tenet of this theory is the acknowledgment that systems do not work with any linearity. Even looking at lists of aging service agencies does not convey that they work together; rather, they are simply lists of parts, not unlike a list of car parts. Botan's (1988) mantra that "the whole is greater than the sum of its parts" (p. 114) is exactly true of cars. Compared with cars, however, the aging network is closer to being a misnomer than a truism. Ever optimistic, however, those who provide services to elders continue to strive to make it truly a network in which the parts work more closely together so that the collective result of aging services is greater than your list of providers.
Organizational Culture Theory	This theory can be physically seen in organizations that strive to maintain the status quo. Change is anathema to organizations that look introspectively at their values, habits, and goals and determine that they are good, and that outsiders who suggest change are threats to their stability—clearly a tougher challenge for advocates who deign to target them for change.
Theories of Interaction	These theories address power in various dynamic forms, (for example, social exchange and conflict theories). Tensions can be high as agencies vie for funding, recognition, staff, volunteers, and high-profile supporters. These competitive dynamics can, however, increase public awareness and critical thinking about aging issues.

provides crucial insights into the habits of mind, thought, and action that can enhance or stifle consumer priorities as well as advocacy efforts.

A third theoretical perspective is offered to assist in understanding the human behaviors that occur within complex systems, as well as within and between organizational cultures. **Theories of interaction**, including power, social exchange, and conflict theories, convey the pervasive tension and the inevitable conflicts that occur between people in the aging service arena where scarce resources, lean staffing, and burgeoning service needs can create many frustrations. These tensions and dynamics can thwart client needs, driving home how people with power in specific arenas can control those with less or no power, thus setting in place the need for advocacy.

Looking at the disparities between these three perspectives, it is little wonder that they have not emerged as an open and collegial system with a common mission. Collectively, these three theoretical perspectives (complex systems, organizational culture, and interaction theories) enable advocates to more clearly assess the larger context in which older persons find themselves. Simultaneously, they can advance critical thinking about the assumptions and norms within each specific service setting. These perspectives may be helpful in identifying and understanding the causes behind circumstances that may seem paradoxical or even unethical. We provide this theoretical backdrop to frame situationally effective solutions to potential problems (Table 2.1). Understanding these theories is one thing, but being able to use what you know for productive action is yet another. The purpose of this chapter is to ground the remaining chapters in theory so that you will have a conceptual guide to carry you through the rest of the book.

Complex Systems Theory

Students in the helping professions have long been taught about systems theory, but there are multiple types of systems theory. Whereas general systems theory is helpful when it comes to negotiating health and human service delivery systems, complex systems theory is particularly useful in helping advocates understand why

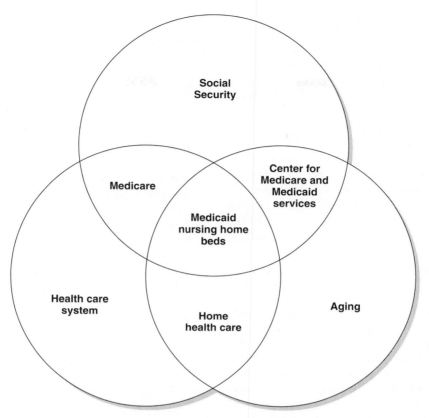

FIGURE 2.1 Venn Diagram Showing Intersections Between the Aging Network and the Health Care and Social Security Systems

service delivery is not always logical, linear, nor effective in meeting older persons' needs.

Put briefly, the aging service network is comprised of interdependent and reciprocally influential subunits that include individuals, groups, associations, organizations, communities, and larger social systems (such as the health care system and the national aging network) that are all aspects of the societal suprasystem. For example, an adult day program may be under the auspices of an aging services organization, which in turn is situated in a community that receives monies from the state. The program is a system that can be analyzed, but it cannot be fully understood without recognizing the nuances of the larger aging services organization (and it's organizational culture), community context, and state and

federal politics concerning the distribution of funds (Figure 2.1).

These systems interact in exceedingly complex and nonlinear ways that are made all the more difficult to comprehend because of constant and often rapid change. Case managers will tell willing listeners that everything can change very quickly. Elders who live independently and can perform all activities of daily living by themselves can fall and break a hip in a matter of minutes. "A fall is often a seminal event for an older person. . . . Many older people describe a fall as a dreaded event that could precipitate a cascade of problems that will rob them of their independence" (Tennstedt, 2002, p. 5). Yet minutes earlier these same persons were receiving only light housekeeping services and driving their own automobiles. The trajectory of what occurs next is nonlinear and depends on the ups and downs of what happens in a series of hospital, rehabilitation, and follow-up care scenarios. The process is fraught with unpredictable dynamics, probably brought on by the convergence of what insurance the person has, the attitudes toward older persons and level of stress felt by discharge planners, the motivational level and social supports of the patient, and a host of other factors that arise in the process. The care plan, so carefully conceived the day before, can become obsolete instantly, and a new assessment process then begins. Each person's story is written somewhat differently as the person encounters different systems and subsystems.

Our goal here is to shed light on the fundamental tension between change and stability in social systems (Anderson, Carter, & Lowe, 1999). This is crucial because change is a constant, often unpredictable consequence of advocacy. Consider, for example, at a practice level, what gerontologists have known for years: no matter how complete a geriatric multidimensional assessment is, it is still based on only a snapshot in time. The minute it is completed, everything can change. Yet case managers often have to proceed as if what is known about needs through the assessment process can be translated into a well-designed care plan with measurable objectives.

System theorists have studied change from a variety of perspectives. Perhaps the most important approach to examining system change comes from analyzing the differences between highly mechanistic or biological views that tend to see systems as operating like machines or biological organisms, always striving to maintain some sense of order and stability, and sharply contrasting views in which constant change and varying degrees of conflict are the focus. We think it is helpful to understand that different people view systems differently, some believing that they are like machines and organisms that will seek to maintain their structures and sense of order, whereas others will see that systems are in constant change with a new order always emerging. It is our experience that different systems hold different assumptions and that no two systems are identical.

Mechanical and Biological Views of Systems

Mechanical systems perspectives are based on machine metaphors. It is assumed that everything will run smoothly, that the system is closed, stable, orderly, and predictable—just like a well-oiled machine (Burns & Stalker, 1961). Conflict is seen as symptomatic of a problem and should be reduced so that uncertainty and change are kept to a minimum. The goal of a mechanical system is to return to the best state of equilibrium (sometimes called homeostasis or the steady state).

Persons who view the service delivery system from a mechanical systems perspective want everything to work in a consistent way. If an older person has an acute health care episode, the medical goal is to get that person well and back to the previous state of functioning by curing the diseased part—fixing the machine, as it were. In short, assumptions of mechanical systems are that things should remain the same and that change should be kept to the minimum. Problems are seen as something to be diminished with the least possible change. This view may work in acute care episodes, but it fails miserably in chronic care situations. Mechanistic systems are said to be morphostatic, which means "structure maintaining" (Anderson et al., 1999, p. 26). As long as everyone does their jobs, everything should go well. The mechanistic perspective is also used to explain certain types of human behavior. Box 2.2 illustrates this mechanistic perspective in action.

Organizations with Mechanistic and Biological Views

It is not only individuals who have mechanistic views of how systems should work. Some organizations are designed from a mechanistic perspective. Most notable among these are the numerous government and medical bureaucracies that comprise much of the aging services network.

Mechanistic and biological analogies emphasize getting back to the way things were, but people who work in the field of aging know that this rarely happens. Certainly this might be the hoped-for goal of a person like John, but even in his compliance and attempt to maintain a steady

BOX 2.2

John, the Engineer

John was a 92-year-old mechanical engineer who had Parkinson's disease and was becoming increasingly frail. He was perplexed that his limbs did not always respond to what he wanted them to do. He also needed a heart valve replacement. He asked his daughter repeatedly, "Why can't they fix this?" From an engineering perspective, he had watched his diet, taken his medication, been totally compliant with all physicians' instructions, and done his part in every conceivable way. He thought of his body as a machine—predictable, manageable, definable, and programmable—and he figured that if one of his parts needed replacing, then it should be replaced. Advocating for him involved recognizing that he had no intention of acknowledging his own mortality and no understanding that his condition was a result of almost imponderably complex changes, many taking place below the clinical horizon, that were not diagnosable. Client-centered advocacy required his daughter to recognize that her father wanted as much done as possible to keep him going, even when others might have given up. He also expected the health care system to function with the same set of assumptions and to have the skills to perform machine maintenance in a way that would keep him going indefinitely.

His primary physician, on the other hand, had a different set of assumptions. He did not want to "put John through" excessive neurological testing for his Parkinson's and was convinced that he would not survive any heart surgery. A wise psychogeriatrician advised the daughter differently: "Everyone has given up hope on him, and hope is what's keeping him alive. If he wants to go through the tests, it is his choice, and you should push to have them. His view is that his body is a machine and that he has done everything he was asked to do. He needs to see the system as working in machinelike fashion to do everything *it* is supposed to do." The daughter was pushing the physician to line up tests literally as her father died quietly in his sleep, not because she believed it would repair his body but because of her father's set of mechanistic assumptions about what he had expected would work, and what he demanded, and, consequently, what he deserved to have respected.

state, his physical body did not cooperate and he died. Similarly, those working in acute care systems are often trying to get individuals back to their former states of being, but even these caregivers must admit that accommodations (sometimes *major* accommodations) have to be made in the process. Nothing remains exactly the same.

Biological views of systems are much more animated and alive than mechanistic views. Viewing societies, communities, organizations, and groups as biological organisms is part of common parlance. When people refer to "heads of state" or "arms of government," there is a general understanding of what this means. When medical people refer to case managers as their "eyes and ears" in the community, they are using biological analogies.

Like persons who view systems as machines, there is the hope that biological systems will work in a routine manner, that each part has a function, and that all the parts will work together as a whole. Such systems have to perform various functions to survive. Talcott Parsons's (1960) structural-functionalism introduced four states that systems need to achieve to survive: adaptation, goal attainment, integration, and pattern maintenance. If there is conflict or stress, one assumption in a biological system is that the members should be working together to return to a state of harmony through consensus and cooperation among the necessary subsystems.

Professionals in health care systems are very familiar with biological systems, thus it is only a little stretch to apply this analogy to a long-term care facility or a retirement community. Because biological systems are open to environmental forces, unlike machine analogies, it is assumed that these systems must recognize the importance of the larger environment.

Both mechanistic and biological analogies in general systems theory have been heavily criticized. For example, Hudson (2000) wrote, "The common assumption that organisms seek equilibrium ignores findings from chaos theory that show that many complex adaptive systems rarely established equilibrium, and that they never exactly repeat themselves" (p. 218). Hudson argued that homeostasis is a false assumption because it fails to consider the importance of feedback loops. Positive feedback actually amplifies deviation from the way things are, allowing the system to understand growth and change. Negative feedback demonstrates just how much change has occurred, serving as a type of thermostat.

Certainly advocates may sometimes think in terms of consensus building, maintaining the status quo, and returning to a state of harmony, but most of the time advocacy involves some degree of conflict. An example is the Long-Term Care Ombudsman Program, a nationally mandated advocacy program designed to provide a voice for consumers receiving long-term care services in various settings. One of the biggest challenges faced by the paid staff and volunteers is knowing when a collaborative approach needs to be taken and when it is necessary to directly engage in conflict of an adversarial nature. Collaboration is sometimes needed when the goals include returning to a former state of equilibrium, yet there are many other times when changes must occur for people to have what they need to deal with changing situations in which it is impossible (and not even desirable) to go back to business as usual.

Open and Dynamic Views of Complex Systems

Martin and O'Connor (1989) reflected on three analogies that view systems as highly open, dynamic, and changing: morphogenic, factional,

and catastrophic. These analogies are particularly helpful in beginning to understand complex systems theory because they are based on assumptions that recognize the inevitability of change and conflict.

Morphogenic means structure changing. This analogy is very different from mechanical or biological views of systems in which there is a desire to maintain current structures at all costs. Morphogenesis recognizes that systems are not only constantly changing but that people will face conflict. It is through change that new ways of doing things emerge, and fundamental change is not out of the question. In these types of systems, people generally cooperate with one another in the change process.

Factional analogies view systems as special interest groups, all with their own agendas and cultures, divided into factions and bent on conflict. Note that there is much more tension in this approach than in a morphogenic approach. "A factional analogy employs concepts such as conflict, domination, disorder, competition, and co-optation in place of consensus-oriented terms such as cooperation, integration, and consensus" (Martin & O'Connor, 1989, p. 57).

And last, a **catastrophic** analogy is a system in constant flux. Everything is random or in motion. Events contradict one another rather than forming a pattern. To gain any sense of stability, the system has to collapse and be reborn, and only then is it no longer catastrophic. We suspect that some exhausted advocates reading this book may at times see the aging service delivery system in this way, needing a complete overhaul and rebirth.

In recent years helping professionals have looked to chaos theory, "characterized by periodic, nonlinear, dynamic, and transitional elements" (Hudson, 2000, p. 219), as part of complex systems theory. It is not our intent to try to explain chaos theory here, other than to remind you that traditional views of systems have tended to be highly mechanistic, seeking to hold things constant. The idea is that an input will logically lead to an outcome, when in actuality older persons' lives and the organizations with which they interact are much more complicated than that. It is important to recognize that things are constantly changing and that even nonlinear dynamics can be somewhat deterministic even though they differ from linear assumptions (Warren, Franklin, & Streeter, 1998).

Organizational Culture Theory

Having identified how perspectives on order, change, and conflict can differ in understanding complex systems, we now focus on theories that probe the assumptions held by organizations that interact in elder delivery systems. An advocate is typically tethered to an organization or group of some sort, and it is likely that that organization or group will be more compatible with some other organizations and groups and less compatible with others. It is incumbent upon advocates to know the strengths and constraints of the cultural base from which they operate and to understand that other systems will have different sets of deeply held assumptions about elder care.

Organizational culture theory emerged in reaction to the entrenched structuralist perspective that has dominated our own discussion to this point. Organization culturists recognized that subtle characteristics of organizations were being missed or forgotten. These theorists are interested in understanding how organizational cultures form and change and how culture affects leadership and relationships in establishing organizational directions. As a result, organizations began to be understood in more symbolic ways (Martin & Frost, 1996).

This school of thought brings another set of assumptions to theory. First, organizational culturists believe that how participants *interpret* what is happening is more important than what is *actually* happening. Perceptions, then, become reality. Second, ambiguity and uncertainty are prevalent in most organizations and may override rational problem solving and decision making. Third, symbols and metaphors are used to reduce uncertainty and to gain a sense of control (Shafritz & Ott, 2001).

Schein (1992) defined organizational culture as "a pattern of shared basic assumptions that the group learned as it solved its problems of external adaptation and internal integration, that has worked well enough to be considered valid and,

therefore, to be taught to new members as the correct way to perceive, think, and feel in relation to those problems" (p. 12). Once these shared ways of thinking have been integrated into the organization's culture, they become a matter of course. People conform to these norms without giving them a second thought. Schein listed factors required for internal integration of an organization's culture, including (a) the development of a common language and conceptual categories, (b) group boundaries, (c) power and status dimensions, (d) norms concerning relationships, (e) rewards and punishments, and (f) ways to explain uncontrollable events. These factors also remind us of the cultures of families. Chapter 4, on assessment, includes a section on cultural competency and proficiency, but advocates must *always* be aware of cultural differences, be they in families or in larger systems. Schein explained that cultural assumptions provide a filter for how one views the world and that if one is stripped of that filter, anxiety and overload will be experienced.

Cultural solutions offer routine answers to what would normally be complex problems, and these answers are not always valid, merely embedded in a culture that may need to change. The major reason organizational members resist cultural change is because it challenges deeply held assumptions that stabilize their world—it questions the status quo. As a result, members of a dysfunctional culture might choose to retain prevailing assumptions rather than risk having their cultural roots challenged. Identification with artifacts (for example, organizational processes, architecture, language, and organizational stories), values, and assumptions allow the group to develop, and group development results in culture (Schein, 1992). These are also clues to an outsider about how to get to know an organization's culture, how to work with it, how to communicate in its language, or how to recognize what needs changing.

Some organizational culturists face the challenge of conflict head on, believing that a good organizational study cannot ignore the complexities of deep-rooted conflict, inconsistencies, and differences in interpretation among cultural members. Given their predisposition to focus on

BOX 2.3

Fran and Maria in the ICU

Maria, a 75-year-old woman with no living kin, was admitted to a large teaching hospital with a life-threatening illness. Fran, a case manager in a small, rural, informal Area Agency on Aging, had worked with Maria for several years in packaging in-home services for her so that she could remain in her own small-town home. Fran visited Maria in the intensive care unit at this prestigious big city hospital and was immediately intimidated by its reputation. The plaques on the wall, the donors' list in the entryway, the officious manner in which staff dealt with her, and the marbled corridors all contributed to her discomfort. Yet as a case manager, she recognized that despite the hospital's daunting reputation, there were aspects of Maria's care that were disturbing and needed attention. Everything about the organizational culture of this huge facility screamed competence, authority, certitude, control, and absolute dominance. Yet elements of Maria's quality of care were lacking—things weren't happening that

should, and other things were being done that shouldn't have been done.

When Fran gently approached Maria's nurse, she was told that she could not have any information due to the privacy act. When Fran countered that she was not seeking information but that she knew Maria well and could provide information to the staff that might be helpful, she was met with a cold, condescending stare.

Undaunted, Fran executed a simple plan. She went directly to Maria's primary care physician who had privileges at this hospital and asked this physician to intervene so that Maria had the best possible care. The physician had the real and symbolic authority to be listened to within the hospital's culture. He had functioned within this culture for years, whereas Fran was not a part of the culture, nor did she know the nuances of the culture in order to navigate the system alone. Fran, the advocate, had to solicit an empowering alliance with yet another advocate who would not be unsettled by the hospital's cultural norms.

conflict and inconsistencies, they draw heavily from conflict theory (Martin & Frost, 1996). The clash of cultures can be seen in the example of Fran and Maria in Box 2.3.

As an advocate, Fran realized that she could not approach this situation in a collaborative mode, that she was not recognized as a legitimate—let alone professional—source of information in this culture; there would be no willing reciprocity here! Yet Fran also had an obligation to help Maria, who was extremely ill. Fran recognized a moral duty to convey whatever she could to the persons responsible for her care. In this situation, the organizational culture served as a cocoon, isolating and protecting the system from the intrusion of outsiders. If Fran had quit at that point, she would have been unable to break through the cultural wall—and the culture would have fulfilled what Stein (1994) warns about, the hospital

caregivers would not know "precisely what they need to know" to get Maria well (p. 71).

We could just as easily have offered a scenario in which the organization's culture was highly receptive to internal or external advocacy, or one in which the physician was a woman of color. Regardless, to devise optimal change strategies, effective advocacy requires accurate assessment of these governing cultural variables.

THEORIES OF INTERACTION: POWER, EXCHANGE, AND CONFLICT

Power Theory

Those who study the many classifications and categories of power agree that the best general summary of its effect is the influence that a person, group, or system has to cause or affect some change, action, or circumstance in another person, group, system, or thing. Although *power* can have negative connotations (Giordano & Rich, 2001), we use it here because of its common use in systems, communication, conflict, organizational, and sociological theories and because we believe that power can be a positive force when used appropriately.

The study of power points to the need for aging service advocates who can acquire and use power to influence system decision makers. After all, advocacy is really all about the acquisition and use of power at every system level.

For example, at the macro level, debate swirls around whether older Americans, as a group, wield significant political power (Hooyman & Kiyak, 1999). Proponents of the subculture of aging theory, for example, say "Yes" and argue that older Americans comprise a powerful force that will fend off threats to their ever mounting health care and other service needs (Dychtwald, 1999). Others, however, worry that older Americans do not, in fact, comprise a cohesive subculture with common goals and a shared vision that would empower them to advance common interests. One perspective sees elders as empowered to advance common interests such as the protection of Medicare and other entitlement programs, whereas others are not so sure. Either way, both internal and external advocates are needed to ensure that promises to elders are honored.

This is no less true at the community level. For example, Hardina (2002) explained that community organizations must have power to acquire goods and resources and the authority to make decisions. She listed three implications of power dependency theory for community practice: (a) powerful external funding sources may limit efforts to push for social change, (b) persons who are dependent on free services may be reluctant to advocate for themselves for fear of losing those services, and (c) social change is fraught with political realities such as powerful persons who are elected to office or who receive political favors or jobs, and are, therefore, often obligated to vote, act, and advocate in certain ways.

Power is also central to understanding organizational level advocacy and politics because organizations are essentially "political systems" that interactively maneuver to gain and use power to achieve goals (Luthans, 1981, p. 405). In service organizations, power is lodged in legitimate roles, usually in the organization's higher income-producing departments that compete with each other for resources, and is increasingly concentrated in higher managerial levels. Power is also held by informal cliques and internal factions, resides in professional roles, and is held by health care and service employees generally. For instance, nurse's aides have tremendous power over elder persons on a daily basis (Nelson, 2000). Power can be dispersed quite differently in grassroots organizations in which members generate and influence the oversight of collective values. Although the study of power in organizations is highly complex, one thing is constant—politics and conflict will ensue when you advocate for change, either internally or externally (Luthans, 1981). Of course, knowing where the power lies is also paramount in advocating within smaller systems, such as families, and is key to understanding each family's culture.

Social Exchange Theory

The expression of power at the individual level is examined in the widely used theory of social exchange. Here, the central principle is reciprocity. When two parties have equal power, equity or reciprocity is in effect. In the aging service arena, however, many power relationships are unequal (nonreciprocal), such as one between a frail, elderly parent and an adult child who is neglecting the parent, or among older residents and staff.

Nelson (2000) reviewed a number of studies conducted in nursing homes that focused on reciprocity and nonreciprocity. The favorable effects of reciprocity, such as trust, communication, and decision making, may result in better care, adjustment, attention, autonomy, and a host of other benefits. Conversely, when nonreciprocity occurs, there can be conflict and feelings of alienation. Even relatively powerful (within their systems) nursing home administrators may choose

BOX 2.4

Lester and Dorothy in the Hospital

Lester was a vital 85-year-old man who was the primary caregiver of his wife, Dorothy. She was in and out of the hospital with various chronic conditions, on oxygen 24 hours a day, and the center of his world. He spoiled her by bringing her whatever foods she wanted, chicken tenders being a favorite. On his last trip to take her to the hospital for a bladder infection and back pain, he drove back to their apartment, parked the car, and went for a walk. Coming down the incline to the apartment, he fell off the curb, breaking his left arm, left hip, and hitting his head. The apartment manager called an ambulance and sent him to the emergency room of the same hospital to which his wife had been admitted just hours earlier. The office manager agreed to look after the cat (Mikie), which was now alone in the apartment. The following day Lester had surgery to pin his hip.

Lester and his wife had only a modest retirement income and had lived a minimalist lifestyle. This made them invisible to powerful people in the community. They were essentially the have-nots in the local power structure. They had spent most of their time in the apartment, with Lester making forays into the community to pick up groceries and mail, and they were fairly self-sufficient as long as Dorothy's oxygen was delivered every few days. Their only relatives were a sister-in-law who was in her early 80s and a niece who lived out of town. Lester was an eccentric person, a loner, who often ranted and raved about politics.

No one in the hospital liked Lester. He had no advocate, and his fate rested in the hands of a discharge planner to whom he was not endeared. He was a difficult patient, trying to pull out tubes and angry over his condition. The potential for conflict was high, and access to decision-making authority was limited, Once discharged to a rehabilitation or nursing facility, he would literally be out of sight and out of mind, placing him at risk of even more total domination. The discharge planner decided to discharge Lester to the first locally available

to leave their positions when they have feelings of nonreciprocity in decision making, autonomy, and expected awards from their boss or corporate structure (Singh & Schwab, 1998).

Another way of viewing reciprocity is by seeing it as a condition in which two parties are equally dependent on each other, which makes their power equal. Inequality exists when one person is dependent on another. This inverse relation of power and dependence results in nonreciprocity. For example, the assisted living administrator's power over the resident equals the resident's dependence on the assisted living administrator. Here, the power disparity is nearly absolute: the resident is totally dependent on the assisted living facility for virtually everything. The resident cannot harm the administrator, so the administrator is, theoretically, free to dominate or ignore the resident. To be a good advocate, the administrator must literally give power to the resident when the latter holds a legitimate opposition. If not, the resident will need an external advocate to rebalance power so that a condition of reciprocity (fairness) might exist, making the chance of collaboration more likely and meaningful. If push comes to shove, advocates have a fair chance at pressuring administrators if they continue to resist.

The thoughtful use of power can be seen as a form of executional autonomy, which is the ability to control one's fate. Nelson (2000, p. 41) extended earlier work by Blau (1964) to identify six autonomy/fate control dynamics that influence social exchange: (a) options, (b) physical capacity, (c) mental capacity, (d) strategies and resources (material and instrumental behaviors), nursing home bed, even though Lester wanted to return home.

Lester protested mightily and requested that if he really had to go to a nursing home for a while, that it be the one near his home. However, there wouldn't be a bed available there for a week or so. The discharge planner's mind was made up, and Lester needed to go now. Lester's pleas fell on deaf ears. He became angry and raised his voice. This was met with an exasperated tirade about his unruly ungrateful behavior and a stern warning to calm down or he would be sedated. Lester was powerless. Sure, he could shout and yell, but this was counterproductive. He didn't have the inducements or leverage through threat of harm to intimidate a staff that was closed to reasoning—and he wasn't very good at reasoning himself. In short, he had no money, no status, no pull, no lawyer, and hence, no rights, but he did have his niece.

Lester called her to explain what the hospital was planning to do and how the discharge planner had threatened to sedate him if he didn't calm down. The niece called the discharge planner to politely request that Dorothy and Lester be released to the facility near where they lived. But the discharge planner brusquely advised the niece that Lester was problematic and that the staff had other people to care for and didn't have time for Lester's antics.

"What do you mean antics? I don't think raising your voice when you're being denied your rights is an antic, and I think that threatening someone with sedation who is clearly not harmful to himself or others is a problem. Now, can we settle this amicably, or do I need to talk to your boss or take legal action? It's your call," the niece said with intensity.

The discharge planner, weighing the weakness of her position against the possible harm from resisting further, changed her tone. "Well, I think there's been a misunderstanding here, I'll call the facility near Lester's home and make arrangements for the next possible bed. They owe me one, don't worry."

(e) coercive power, and (f) expectancy (the perceived probability of achieving a goal). Nelson contended that diminished capacity in any of these six dynamics would reduce one's autonomous ability to exercise power. Box 2.4 provides an example of power politics in action.

Applying the six autonomy/fate control dynamics to Lester and Dorothy's situation, we can create the following analysis. Lester's *options* and *physical capacity* were changed overnight. His wife's *options* suffered a tremendous blow as well because Lester was her primary caregiver and she could not go home without him. Facing a long stint in rehabilitation, exacerbated by having broken his arm and his hip, Lester's *expectancy* toward future goals was less than had he simply broken one extremity. Stress reduced *mental capacity* for both, each worrying about the fate of the other; the possibility of using *coercive power* was subsequently diminished by their increased dependence. Discharge planners assumed control over their lives.

This illustration is a reminder that when anyone is hospitalized it is almost impossible for that person to maintain any sense of autonomy and control. If persons are sick enough to be in the hospital, it is likely that they are not physically able to maintain autonomy and to participate in decision making without someone to assist in this process. In this case, Dorothy and Lester became wards of a system that sought to get them discharged to another facility as quickly as possible given the powerful nature of financial reimbursement. In sum, Lester's fate (executional power) was severely compromised by fate itself. He and his wife desperately needed an advocate. Theoretically, the discharge planner could have served in that role, but she was frustrated by Lester's noncompliant and abrasive behavior. The niece intervened as an external advocate.

This story could have been quite different with different cultural dynamics. Suppose, for instance, that Lester had been a man of high standing in the community, perhaps on the hospital's board of directors. Then he would not have had to rant and rave to get his housing wishes honored—his personal physician would have seen to them personally and immediately. Or suppose that Lester was a very large, very dark man of color whose very presence was threatening, and the young Caucasian discharge planner was afraid to *not* honor his wishes—never mind that he would never harm anyone. The point is that culture always matters, regardless of whether the topic is how theories play out, power, or autonomy, among others.

Social Conflict Theory

Social conflict theory also sheds light on clashing waves of influence that constitute power dynamics within systems. Classic conflict theory asserts that there are two fundamental dynamics at play in any given system: conflict and domination (Collins, 1994). This means, for example, that elders or their allies are striving to maintain threatened benefits or to increase them through conflict, or, if they are not engaged in conflict, they are being controlled or dominated by provider system decision makers. One should not view this control as being necessarily oppressive or exploitative. In fact, in service bureaucracies it is more likely to manifest as some procedural rule or resource constraint designed to control the distribution of limited resources. Agencies can save money when a case manager denies service to an impoverished older woman because her income barely exceeds the state's needs test, when an occupational therapist discontinues needed treatment because the Medicare reimbursement cap is met, or when an older man is sent to a nursing home against his wishes due to the unavailability of community certified beds. The conundrum, however, is that if those same

agencies are not efficient, they will cease to exist and the problem switches from *limited* services to *no* services.

Other provider controls are entirely beneficent and are designed to promote client well-being by requiring client compliance to some treatment or social intervention. At other times, however, provider controls may be self-serving, such as when nursing home patients are illegally physically or chemically restrained for convenience sake. At any rate, all elder service organizations control or dominate their clients through rules, regulations, policies, procedures, schedules, patterns of staffing, and myriad other managerial control processes. These are designed to maximize efficient resource allocation by restricting nonconforming client behaviors that would undermine the service organization's legitimate efficiency goals. Again, conflict theory indicates that elderly clients must either submit to these restraints or try to resist or change them.

These conditions create *haves* and *have-nots*, the latter group being especially marginalized for various reasons such as race, gender, age, disability, intelligence, knowledge, religion, or sexual orientation. The goal of empowerment is to draw on strengths of the have-nots and increase their access to decision-making authority (Hardina, 2002).

Not surprisingly, classic conflict theory tends to characterize the provider system's dominance as unfair and illegitimate, recommending tactics and solutions that are respectively more adversarial and reformist in nature (Litwin, 1982). However, remember that conflict has both collaborative and adversarial functions. It is likely to be collaborative if both parties respect each other and share basic assumptions about the system's goals (better service and care, for example), or it can be adversarial if involved parties see the goals as false and they lack respect for each other's positions. In other words, in the big picture view, if the advocate sees the target person, group, organization, or institution as working on illegitimate goals, and the targeted decision makers are focused on preserving their system (morphostasis), then adversarial conflict is likely, and may even be necessary to cause change.

Implications of Theoretical Perspectives

We have briefly touched on three sets of theoretical perspectives: complex systems theory, organizational culture theory, and theories of interaction about power, exchange, and conflict. For a deeper elaboration of these perspectives, we recommend Clegg, Hardy, and Nord (1996) and Shafritz and Ott (2001). In reviewing these perspectives, four guiding principles have emerged that may help in navigating advocacy seas, be they calm or choppy: (a) service-driven systems are complex and unpredictable, (b) each unit within these systems has its own unique organizational culture, (c) sources of power and conflict need to be identified, and (d) sharp, analytic skills are needed to determine the appropriate point on the collaboration-to-adversarial-conflict continuum for your intervention.

Four Guiding Principles

1. Health and Human Service Systems Move in Both Linear and Nonlinear Ways

Health and human service systems are complex because their patterns do not always conform to cause and effect conceptualizations. Systems theory provides a number of concepts that are helpful to the practitioner who is trying to understand how an organization or community works (or doesn't). For example, John, the 92-year-old engineer introduced earlier in this chapter, expected the health care delivery system to be a mechanical, organized, predictable structure. However, a mechanistic view was unrealistic in a system that serves human beings who are anything but mechanistic. As long as mechanical or biological metaphors are used in trying to understand complex systems, conflict may be denied or not pursued depending on the pressure applied, and practitioners as well as consumers may make unrealistic assumptions about human service delivery.

This has huge implications for advocates who must trigger exactly what mechanistic bureaucracies resist most: change. And they must do this by communicating, by exerting energy into a machine that doesn't want to change, at least not

much, nor fast, and certainly not under pressure. But precisely because mechanistic bureaucracies are relatively closed systems, change often has to be induced from the outside, sometimes forcefully. After all, machines don't repair themselves; it takes a mechanic. Whether this repair is accomplished by cutting red tape, bucking rules, altering policies, streamlining procedures, or fixing a thousand other systemic glitches, the advocate-as-mechanic will often have to fix things by altering the bureaucratic mind-set, which can only be done through communication. Fortunately, other systems may be more open and easier to move.

2. Every Unit Within a Service Delivery System Has Its Own Organizational Culture

The analogies identified in systems theory (mechanistic, biological, morphogenic, factional, and catastrophic) imply very different cultural assumptions about, and attitudes toward, conflict and change. Recognizing the culture of one's own base of operations is one thing, but being able to assess the culture of another organization or group of organizations is equally important, particularly if an advocate wants to be able to intervene to help an older person or persons negotiate the system. For example, recall the example of Fran and Maria. Fran, a case manager from a small AAA, was somewhat intimidated by the large city hospital in which Maria found herself. The culture of the small AAA was very different in almost every way from the large bureaucracy Fran encountered in the hospital. Yet Fran had to negotiate this culture to help Maria who was captive in the intensive care unit. Fran understood the power dynamics within this new system in which she found herself, and she gained power by aligning herself with a physician who could influence Maria's care.

Both external and internal advocates will have an easier time communicating with persons in more receptive and open cultures. Consequently, conflict is more likely to be collaborative in nature, including fair negotiation and bargaining, which are, in essence, open and equitable exchanges of energy through communication. Even though some organizations may be easier to access and influence than highly mechanistic bureaucracies, their structure-maintaining goal (morphostasis) is pitted against their willingness to change their structure and function. Consider how small grassroots organizations, unfettered by rigid, formalized rules and processes may have different cultures than large systems, but never underestimate the importance of understanding their cultures, which may present very different dynamics but will be no less difficult to change.

3. Human Service Systems Do Not Always Return to a Previous Equilibrium

We highlighted theories of power, exchange, and conflict because it is in the interactions that occur between people, within various cultures, embedded in layers of systems, that millions of daily advocacy efforts occur. These interactions within health and human service systems may be collaborative, but they are inherently conflictual. As change occurs, conflict may be accelerated. Human service systems do not necessarily work toward returning to a previous steady state or equilibrium, even though there may be people who want this to happen and systems may be essentially self-preserving. This means that advocates, practitioners, and consumers will be living with ongoing change, and in some cases, change may be volatile. Conflict is inevitable, and how it is handled will depend on the power and value dynamics between the interacting parties. In factional and catastrophic systems, conflict is ongoing as different interests compete. Organizational cultures are often the arenas in which power dynamics are played out in the service delivery system. It is important to recognize that some cultures will tolerate conflict more than others.

4. Advocates Must Be Able to Analyze Complex Systems and Face Change and Conflict Directly

Advocates must be able to analyze complex systems, face change and conflict in a direct manner, and assess the culture in which they are engaged

with or on behalf of older persons. Advocates must become multicultural to navigate the various settings in which older persons find themselves. When a particular setting is unknown or the advocate cannot break into the culture, forming alliances with others is critically important. One of the biggest challenges faced by advocates is balancing when a collaborative approach needs to be taken and when it is necessary to engage in adversarial conflict.

Aging service organizations fall along a continuum of mechanistic to catastrophic, and most blend different cultural elements, sometimes paradoxically. Advocates will face multiple, complex systems in which multiple and diverse cultures exist, and the human dynamics and interactions that transpire run the gamut from status quo enhancing to highly conflictual.

As advocates, you will have your own unique views of how all this comes together. The four principles we have discussed are summarized in Table 2.2. Our intent is to raise the possibilities and to set a framework for the remainder of the book in which we focus more and more on the actual practice of elder advocacy. There is no one right way to approach organizations targeted for change, whether you are advocating for an individual or another organization. Making the right choices hinges on your analytic observations and critical thinking skills.

☾ SUMMARY

In this chapter we highlighted three theoretical perspectives: complex systems theory, organizational culture theory, and interactional theories of power, exchange, and conflict. Different types of systems analogies were provided, including comparisons to machines and biological organisms that are typically oriented around the status quo. The morphogenic, factional, and catastrophic analogies, in contrast, are based on expected change and range from moderate to very high conflict.

We introduced organizational culture theory, the focus of which is on the artifacts, values (norms), and underlying assumptions that people within a system begin to believe in so strongly

TABLE 2.2 Four Guiding Advocacy Principles

Principle	Description
1. Health and human service systems are complex and move in both linear and nonlinear ways.	Complex systems do not exhibit cause and effect interactions and do not fix themselves. Even though John, our 92-year-old engineer, wanted doctors to repair his body, human beings are not as easily fixed as cars. Advocates must be the mechanics, and communication is the tool of first choice to try and effect change in highly mechanistic organizations such as the health care system.
2. Each service delivery system has its own organizational culture.	You, as the advocate, must be able to conduct deep homework to understand a target organization's culture before you intervene. Regardless of whether the target organization is mechanistic, biological, morphogenic, factional, catastrophic, or a hybrid of several, large or small, you must understand it to be effective. That which you learn each time will add to your skills for the next time, similar to Fran understanding the power dynamics of the big city hospital. She then built a small alliance to add the power of a physician so that she could successfully penetrate the very closed medical system.
3. Human service systems do not always return to a previous steady state or equilibrium.	The nature of systems is self-preserving, and they can become volatile and conflictual when change is forced upon them. Conflict is inevitable and affects a system's suprasystem. Nothing happens in isolation, and changes may resemble the effects of the proverbial pebble thrown into the ocean—the ripples are infinite.
4. Advocates must be able to analyze complex systems and face conflict directly.	You must know how to assess individuals' and organizations' cultures and work with or within them, using them to advance your clients' goals rather than allowing them to defeat your purposes. You must know when a collaborative approach that has worked is no longer working and, thus, when to change to an adversarial approach.

that they become core tenets of the organization's identity. The tie to systems theory is important here, as systems theory typically examines organizations in their environment. Some systems want to close out a turbulent environment, and others embrace the stimulation of environmental change. Culturally, however, organizations may embrace assumptions about the larger environment and their place in it that make them more or less susceptible to change.

We then focused on theories of power, exchange, and conflict that examined the interactions among various stakeholders in systems.

Health and human service delivery systems vary structurally and functionally and employ multiple personnel to serve increasingly diverse elder populations. It is inevitable that there will be chances for collaboration across some systems and less chance among others when cultural values clash. It is necessary for any person who seeks to influence change (in small or large ways) to understand context (in both large systems and organizational levels) and the dynamics within those contexts. In Chapter 3 we examine and clarify the advocacy and decision-making roles.

DISCUSSION QUESTIONS AND EXERCISES

1. Consider an organization with which you have an affiliation. Think about the embeddedness of that system in answering the following questions. Of what community or community systems is this organization a part? How many other types of organizations like this one exist in this community? What are the relationships among similar organizations: cooperative, collaborative, competitive, or conflictual?

2. In the case of John, the 92-year-old engineer, what do you think about his expectations of the system? As an advocate, would you have pushed his physician to provide a series of tests even when John's death was imminent? Why or why not?

3. Think about the health and human service delivery system within a community with which you are familiar. How does this system address the needs of elders in the community? What changes would you like to see in these systems, and why?

4. Identify at least two organizations with which you are familiar. Compare their organizational cultures. How are their artifacts, values, and underlying assumptions similar or different, and why?

5. In the example of Maria and Fran, how would you assess the hospital's culture? What clues would tell you about the culture and how might you use those clues to assist Maria? How might the two cultures (the small, informal AAA and the large city hospital) in which Fran was involved have influenced her actions, and why? What might a large health care system do to be more culturally friendly to elders?

6. What are your attitudes about power, exchange, and conflict? How do these attitudes influence your ability to be an elder advocate? Are there certain settings in which you would rather work or volunteer, and if so, how are power, exchange, and conflict viewed in these settings?

7. Are there certain elder-care settings that you consider ideal? What are their characteristics, and how might what you can learn from these settings be embedded in the cultures of other elder-care settings?

8. In the case of Lester and Dorothy, how would you have handled this situation had you been the discharge planner? The niece? Why was conflict inevitable?

ADDITIONAL READINGS

Burrell, G., & Morgan, G. (1979). *Sociological paradigms and organisational analysis.* London: Heineman.

Cameron, K. S., & Quinn, R. E. (1999). *Diagnosing and changing organizational culture: Based on the competing values framework.* Reading, MA: Addison-Wesley.

Martin, J. (2002). *Organizational culture: Mapping the terrain.* Thousand Oaks, CA: Sage.

Morgan, G. (1997). *Images of organization* (2nd ed.). Thousand Oaks, CA: Sage.

Netting, F. E., Kettner, P. M., & McMurtry, S. L. (2004). *Social work macro practice.* Boston: Allyn & Bacon.

Reed, M., & Hughes, M. (1992). *Rethinking organization: New directions in organizational theory and analysis.* Newbury Park, CA: Sage.

Schultz, M. (1995). *On studying organizational cultures: Diagnosis and understanding.* New York: Walter de Gruyter.

Weick, K. E. (1995). *Sensemaking in organizations.* Thousand Oaks, CA: Sage.

Clarifying Advocacy Roles and Relationships

Role tension between the professional's curative function and patient advocacy . . . breeds strife, tension, and stress. BIRD (1994)

BOX 3.1

CLARA

Clara is a 96-year-old widowed patient who is recovering from two broken ankles that she suffered in a fall. She also has unstable congestive heart failure, diabetes mellitus, glaucoma, and acute lymphocyte leukemia. The latter will probably kill her within 6 months.

Clara has two daughters, Anna and Suzanne. Clara has appointed Suzanne, her eldest daughter, as health care power of attorney in fact to make medical decisions for her in the event that she should become incapable of making them for herself (de facto incompetent). Despite anxiety about her condition and secondary depression, Clara is rational and oriented to her environment.

Clara had a private apartment in an assisted living facility close to Suzanne and her grandchildren. After surgery, Clara was transferred from the hospital for rehabilitation at Mounthaven Nursing Home. Clara was told that she would need to spend about a month in this facility before being returning to her apartment where she would eventually receive hospice care.

After several painful sessions, Clara refused physical therapy. She only wanted to stay in bed to reminisce, watch TV, or ruminate over her failing health and current circumstance. She really only cared about her daughters' visits, and during those times she pleaded to be taken home.

Although it was a hard choice, Suzanne thought it would be best for Clara to stay in the facility. Anna, however, wanted her mother to be wherever she would be happiest in her final days. The physician and the social worker recognized that Clara had the right to refuse therapy but nevertheless believed it would be best for Clara to stay at Mounthaven Nursing Home.

Anna met with the facility social worker to try to arrange for Clara's return home. The social worker, backed with the physician's recommendations, argued that, at the very least, Clara should not leave until the therapist had gotten Clara to a point where she could function at home. Anna countered with "time is so short and mother's happiness depends upon going home." Anna promised to hire a personal aide and argued that with her and her sister's help, along with hospice, Clara would be fine at home. The social worker reminded Anna that her sister had the legal authority to make medical decisions for Clara, whose judgment was certainly influenced if not clouded by depression and anxiety. However, the social worker recognized the importance of Clara's socioemotional well-being and suggested a formal care planning meeting that would bring all partners together to problem solve.

It appears that Clara has at least four advocates (the good news): her two daughters, her doctor, and the facility social worker. But the not-so-good news is that they do not agree on what is best for Clara. We have defined advocacy as vigilant efforts by, with, or on behalf of older persons to influence decision makers in structures of imbalanced power and to promote justice in providing for, assisting with, or allowing needs to be met. Sure enough, in Clara's situation there is an imbalance of power, and you must not underestimate the implications of that imbalance.

In this chapter we focus on the roles of all of the players in advocacy efforts as well as the complex relationships inherent in advocacy work. Sosin and Caulum (1983) identified three principal agents involved in advocacy efforts: (a) the person in need, (b) the advocate, and (c) the person with the power to change the situation. Ideally, all three would be the same person. In most situations they are different persons, sometimes with very different perspectives.

First, according to our definition, vigilant efforts may be performed by older persons themselves, with older persons, or on behalf of older persons. Thus our advocacy efforts focus on older people in need of something to happen—or not. Accurately assessing the needs of older persons is so important that Chapter 4 is fully devoted to how to assess needs.

Second, advocates are the persons who engage in these vigilant efforts designed to influence change. Advocates may play multiple roles and may, in fact, be older persons themselves. This chapter is all about the plethora of roles in which advocates work.

And third, persons with the power to change situations are located in various settings as well. They may include a caregiver in the community who is insensitive to an elder's needs or a relative who is neglectful or abusive. Persons with the power to change situations may be representatives of structures that, for whatever reason, reflect an imbalance of power and thus in some way create a barrier to meeting an individual's or group's needs. These barriers are not always evident, and they may or may not be formalized. They could be the result of attitudes or assumptions that are part of a professional or organizational culture, held so deeply that their oppressive nature is neither intended nor recognized. On the other hand, they may be intentionally created to serve collective needs but not be intended to harm individuals. Understanding how to identify, target, communicate with, and influence persons who have the power to make change is an important advocacy skill.

Whatever the need for change, older people, advocates, and persons in controlling, powerful, or decision-making positions engage in an interactive process. As discussed earlier, the conflict between parties is not always obvious. Advocacy begins when there is conflict between two nonequal principals: the less powerful client and those who control more resources. This conflict may be either latent or blatant. If latent, those with power may not even be aware that their actions (or their organizational norms) are blocking consumers' wants or needs. Regardless, this initial two party relationship reflects a fundamental difference in power and status that makes it difficult for older persons to achieve their goals without the help of an allied third party. The mere presence of this third person (this may be you, the advocate) may create sufficient parity in the power dynamic to motivate those with the power either to change things or at least to be more likely to listen, negotiate, or comply (Copp, 1993; Donohue & Kolt, 1992; Hocker & Wilmot, 1991; Nelson, 2000). To help you decide what kind of advocacy most appeals to you or fits your personality, we next look at the roles of different kinds of advocates.

☺ TYPES OF ADVOCATES

At the bedrock level, there are two kinds of advocates: the self-interested and the other-oriented. The self-interested advocate pursues personal goals, and the other-oriented advocate pursues the goals of others. However, to truly understand elder advocacy, we must move beyond this basic dichotomy to distinguish other useful categories, which are based on the following characteristics:

1. The advocate's relationship to the client (self- or other-oriented)
2. Level of role formality (informal versus legally formal)

3. Organizational placement (internal versus external)
4. Degree of conflict (a simple dyad between two people or multiple players)

The result is a general classification system that suggests at least four basic types of advocates:

1. Self-advocate (individual or collective efforts)
2. Third party citizen advocate (friend, family member, neighbor, volunteer)
3. Provider advocate (professional or paraprofessional who works with elders on a daily basis and performs multiple roles)
4. Legal advocate (designated by position or mandate)

As with any classification scheme, this one is intended to facilitate understanding, not to establish rigid prototypes. In fact, later in the chapter we discuss hybrid models that combine features of these four types (Bateman, 2000).

Self-Advocates

By far the most common type of advocate is the individual self-advocate who feels certain wants and needs and is motivated and able to strive for them. Individual self-advocacy is an everyday, informal activity. It occurs when you act to assert influence over your external environment to meet a blocked need. However, self-advocacy sometimes requires a collective effort. Self-advocacy can be an isolated, individual activity or a collective venture. We briefly look at both types.

Individual Self-Advocacy

You do self-advocacy all the time, and you will continue to do it into your old age, as long as you are physically and mentally able. It will occur when you (a) educate others about your needs, (b) persuade others to grant you access to services, (c) work with your caregiver to improve service, or (d) question your physician about options and demand meaningful answers. It will manifest when you seek more choice and control by promoting nontraditional therapies or lifestyle changes or by joining a senior center advisory board to influence future activities. It also occurs when you contribute to a political campaign to advance your general self-interest or the interests of others.

Collective Self-Advocacy

By definition, the efforts of the individual self-advocate are not typically channeled though an organized group. Once you decide to work on a political campaign, for example, you are no longer an individual self-advocate; you have joined an organization to work purposely with others.

Sometimes self-advocates work cooperatively (Bateman, 2000). The salient difference between individual and collective self-advocacy is that in the latter individuals join with others in cooperative efforts (often under the leadership of paid coordinating staff) to promote shared interests. Collective self-advocacy takes the form of more than a thousand nongovernmental, nonprofit, grassroots, and voluntary aging interest groups (Binstock & Day, 1996) that exert pressure on external entities that are the focus of their change efforts.

Self-advocates may have joined an organization because they need help in getting their own needs met or to help close friends or family members avoid a plight that also affects the advocate in some personal way. Commonly, the self-advocate is providing the friend or family member with some form of physical, financial, or emotional support. For example, the self-advocate may be a caregiver who joins the Alzheimer's Association to advocate for more research into the causes of the disease and for more viable long-term care options for its victims and caregivers. (A link to the association is on the companion website.)

There are many collective self-advocacy efforts, but they differ widely in their size, scope, and specific goals. For instance, The United Seniors Association is a million-plus member organization that mobilizes older activists who are concerned about Social Security, Medicare, and other financial matters that affect their lives. The National Council on Aging (NCOA, n.d.), composed of nearly 4,000 aging programs ranging from senior centers to retirement communities, advocates for improved Medicare and Medicaid reimbursement rates for home health care and other community services and to expand the Older Americans Act programs generally, especially nutrition and

BOX 3.2

Self-Advocates

Individual Self-Advocates . . .	Collective Self-Advocates . . .
Advocate everyday, informal activity	Cooperate with others in collective effort
Advocate usually for themselves	Have needs that are also the needs of others in the collective
Educate and persuade others to grant access to services	Are tied to a group, association, or organization
Typically are not channeled through an organized group	Can be local or large scale
	Can be focused on broader scale change

caregiver support. The Older Women's League (OWL) pursues similar goals but bases its advocacy for pension and Social Security reform, among other issues, on a model that looks to gender discrimination as a primary motivation to improve the welfare of older women. Members of the National Association of Retired Federal Employees work primarily (but not only) to safeguard their own economic futures and to ward off general threats by raising money for Alzheimer's research, for example, or to push for Medicaid reform and access to prescription drugs. (Links to all of these organizations are on the companion website.)

The name most recognized of all collective self-advocacy organizations that focus on aging is the American Association of Retired Persons (AARP). (A link to the association is on the companion website.) One of the largest nonprofit associations in the world, AARP's goal is to "improve every aspect of living for older people" (Dychtwald, 1999, p. 24); hence, it purportedly represents the vested interests of all elders. By the mid-1990s, AARP's role in killing the Balanced Budget Amendment recast it as a recognized champion of "grassroots activism that can put an instant stranglehold on its opponents' efforts" (p. 27). Some would say that the AARP is ideologically diffuse and that its focus on business and organization building detracts from its advocacy goals (Reisch, 1986). Others might counter that the bonds among AARP's older members translate into broadly similar interests and political points of view that can be advanced through partisan political advocacy (Thompson, 1993). Box 3.2 summarizes the characteristics of self-advocates.

Collective self-advocacy efforts also take the form of health-related advocacy organizations such as the National Parkinson's Disease Foundation, the National Ataxia Foundation, the Coalition of Institutionalized Aged and Disabled, the National Organization of Rare Disorders, the National Diabetes Association, or the Y-Me Breast Cancer Association. (Links to these organizations are on the companion website.) These associations typically raise money for publicity, promotion, publications, and, at least in the larger organizations, for the paid professional advocate/lobbyist whose job it is to "win a competitive advantage" for the collective membership in the public policy arena (Gibelman & Kraft, 1996, p. 43). Of course, smaller collective advocacy organizations often rely on a single executive director or on volunteers (or both) to do this work. But they can be just as effective locally as long as they are capable and committed.

Examples of the smallest type of collective advocacy groups include the thousands of family and resident councils that exist in many of the nation's nursing homes. Here, the respective family members and the residents themselves band together to voice concerns and recommend changes. Although resident councils tend to be facility focused, family councils also raise concerns about the entire long-term care system and provide a forum for residents' loved ones to be heard (O'Boyle, 1999).

BOX 3.3

Third Party Citizen Advocates

- Are seen as altruistic because they do not share the need of the persons for whom they are advocating
- Can be paid or unpaid

- Focus on protection or empowerment of persons who cannot advocate for themselves
- May engage in outreach to vulnerable persons or groups

Third Party Citizen Advocates

A citizen advocate is distinguished by altruistic involvement on the behalf of dissimilar others. Bateman (2000) characterized what he called "third party citizen advocacy" as a joint venture "between a person with a disability and an able-bodied person" (p. 24). To this we add that the citizen advocate does not share the client's medical or service need, nor do citizen advocates gain any direct benefit by their advocacy. On the face of it, then, citizen advocates' motives are altruistic because they are third parties, not directly affected by the situation at hand.

The notion that citizen advocates are motivated by altruism finds support in at least one study (Nelson, Hooker, Dehart, Edwards, & Lanning, 2004). However, third party citizen advocates may have motives other than altruism because people often act out of a variety of personal needs and drives that are not always clear. For example, these volunteers may be seeking new skills or honing existing ones or looking for social contacts, status, or to replace roles lost to retirement (Nelson, Pratt, Carpenter & Walter, 1995; Nelson et al., 2004). Others may be trying to protect their own futures by reforming systems that may be important to them down the road (Nelson et al., 1995), and pay may be a motive for citizen advocates who are employed by nongovernmental grassroots organizations.

Third party citizen advocates are at least professedly devoted to protecting or empowering those who cannot effectively defend or fend for themselves. This casts them in the roles of proxy spokespersons, allies, or conflict **surrogates** who are willing to engage in a wide range of persuasive efforts, both mild and strong, that are intended to aid or empower vulnerable others (Nelson, 2000) either on their behalf or under their direction.

Individual citizen advocates can be found in all sorts of advocacy organizations, serving as board members, assisting in fund-raising activities, and performing direct client advocacy or legislative advocacy. Examples include the trained older volunteers serving in the Medicare Patrols of the Administration on Aging who uncover and investigate Medicare and Medicaid abuse and educate other older individuals on how to be better-informed consumers (Box 3.3). The pioneering volunteers of the old Nursing Home Long-Term Care Committee of the United Hospital Fund of New York were third party citizen advocates. They cruised New York nursing homes compiling reports and sending them to hospitals and other placement agencies to advocate for better standards (Agress, 1985). The Little Brothers Friends of the Elderly (LBFRE) sends its paid and volunteer staff out into the community to locate resources for socially isolated elders. They prod local agencies to refocus energy on serving older people by providing direct outreach to homebound elders as well as health assessments and help with legal aid, housekeeping services, food stamps, and utilities. (Links to all of these organizations are on the companion website.)

Provider Advocates

Provider advocates are undoubtedly the most inclusive, but arguably the least "pure" type of advocate because they do not always primarily self-identify as advocates. Advocacy is just one aspect of their professional identity, and thus this type of advocate can be referred to as an "intrarole advocate" (Bateman, 2000).

Provider advocates can be any elder-service worker who sees something not working for an older person and speaks out or takes action. It could be a social worker, physician, nurse, or any other allied health professional; or a case manager, health facility aide, hospice worker, administrator, direct caregiver, or even a vendor or any other ancillary support person. The act of advocacy might be fairly straightforward, such as when a nurse's aide reminds fellow workers that a patient has the right to refuse a meal and receive a decent substitute, or when a social worker asks a colleague to stop talking about older patients in their presence as if they weren't there. Advocacy of this type may even consist of a nursing home administrator defending a resident's choice to leave the facility for home against the nursing staff's clinical judgment. Such acts are invariably well intended but might also be morally ambiguous such as when a physician exaggerates an impoverished patient's symptoms or diagnosis to assure that a patient is authorized to receive care by a Health Maintenance Organization (HMO)—a practice that appears to be widespread (Alspach, 1998).

Nursing home administrators must apply their skills to efficiently run a facility to meet the collective health needs of all residents, and by the laws of distributive justice, they cannot maximize the wishes of one resident over the conflicting, but stipulated rights and needs of others. Consider how the physician's primary duty to diagnose and cure patient maladies contradicts the need to respect the patient's right to noncompliance. Consider also the evidence from a study of 113 hospital patient representatives. When polled about their client orientation, fully one third reported that their managers would expect them to uphold hospital interests over patient interests (Charters, 1993). These examples illustrate the central defining characteristic of provider advocates—inherent role conflicts between their professional/occupational roles and their advocacy roles.

Intrarole conflict occurs in most professions. For example, social workers' advocacy efforts are sometimes incompatible with their other social work roles, creating role conflict, and the social worker must decide which role will prevail (Beaver, 1983). This provider conflict is reflected in both the social work and nursing literature (Gibelman & Kraft, 1996; Mallik, 1997). In geriatric nursing, the appropriateness of advocacy is hotly debated, partly because advocacy is a relatively recent addition to their discipline, although codes of nursing ethics clearly push advocacy. They require nurses to respect client autonomy and rights and to vigorously defend patients, especially the most vulnerable (including elders) not only from ill health but from powerful, high-status medical authorities and the unyielding efficiency structures for which they work (Copp, 1993). Role tension between the nurse's curative function and patient advocacy is clearly reflected in the literature where it often becomes quite paternalistic (Bird, 1994).

Role conflict is directly mirrored in provider advocates' professional societies and trade associations, which, despite their advocacy goals, are essentially provider organizations. These include the American Nurses Association, the National Association of Social Workers, the American Medical Association (AMA), the American Health Care Association (for nursing home leaders), the Association of Rehabilitation Nurses, the American College of Health Care Administrators, the National Hospice and Palliative Care Organization, the American Occupational Therapy Association, and a host of others. (Links to these organizations are on the companion website.) The professional society's duty is to protect and promote the profession, to assure best standards of practice, to control access to the profession, to safeguard the profession's economic livelihood, to advance professional knowledge—and, in sum, to assure the profession's hegemony as a purveyor of certain types of services (Sullivan, 2000). Trade associations are designed to advocate for benefits for the self-interests of their members.

This self-interested advocacy is just as natural as your own self-advocacy or that of an older person's for that matter. Moreover, provider group goals incur clear benefits to consumers through improved professional competence. However, it is also true that provider group client advocacy tends to assume the same secondary status in the public policy arena as it does among these groups' constituents in the interpersonal sphere. Moreover, Lee and Estes (1994) reminded us that provider interest groups have had a much greater

BOX 3.4

Provider or Intrarole Advocates

- Constitute the most inclusive but least pure type
- Have advocacy as just one aspect of their identities
- Are professionals who have other responsibilities and thus may experience role conflict (e.g., social workers and nurses)

impact on health policies and practices because they have more at stake, and that 90% of advocacy efforts are funded by providers (Dunning, cited in Cohen, 1994), leading one to question, is this bad? No, at least not necessarily. As we have indicated, self-advocacy often benefits the client, but not always. Besides, to varying degrees these provider groups have taken powerful public stands on a variety of issues that are vitally important to their elder clients, and they will undoubtedly continue to do so in the future.

The important point is that the dominance of provider advocacy organizations at the public policy level mirrors the same imbalance of power that exists between the provider advocate's professional role and the client at the interpersonal level. You will find that provider advocates show up as often in our book as decision makers or persons in control of the situation as they do as third party advocates (Box 3.4).

Legal Advocates

Legal advocates are part of a group of paid professional agents whose duties are prescribed by law or administrative rule. Core agents of legal advocacy are elder-law attorneys, but in the elder-service arena legal assistants, who may be nurses or social workers, perform activities (often investigative in nature) that are ancillary to an attorney's usual litigation or arbitration efforts. The legal advocate's central purpose is to forcefully defend the rights and welfare of older clients. Much, if not all, of this work is adversarial and uncompromising—at least theoretically.

Experts on legal advocacy (Krauskopf, Brown, Tokarz, & Bogutz, 1993) stressed how much vulnerable older persons rely on attorneys to assure

them of due process as they navigate through the highly complex, superregulated service delivery systems, even as the elders depend on those very systems. Certainly, elder-law attorneys engage in many routine activities including estate, disability, trust, and chronic care planning. However, they also aggressively pursue civil and criminal remedies for gross medical negligence and malpractice, age discrimination, consumer fraud, financial exploitation, physical abuse, and many other care and general welfare problems. They safeguard client rights and welfare interests in guardianship and conservatorship hearings, execute a variety of health proxy documents, assure that advanced directives are followed, and help older people with other mental capacity issues. They protect older clients' access to rental housing, food stamps, Social Security, Medicare, and Veterans and other benefits (Krauskopf et al., 1993).

The highest stake legal advocacy involves life and death decisions, such as a client's right to life support or, conversely, to a natural death. In one state, it could mean advocating for a person's right to a physician's aid in dying. Although Oregon is the only state that has codified such a right, the Vermont chapter of Compassion and Choices has been involved in legislative efforts for an Oregon-style law for the last few years, and Washington state is considering similar legislative efforts (Marsha Temple, personal communication, October 27, 2006). In the future clients may travel to other countries for aid in dying. For example, a new end-of-life choice law came into effect at the end of 2006 in Israel. According to Chris Coker (personal communication, October 30, 2006), board member of the World Federation of Right to Die Societies, "It is a passive and limited law, only allowing mentally competent, terminally ill or injured adults to decline life-extending treatments; it specifically does not allow for euthanasia, active deeds to hasten death, or any 'double effect' actions. Nevertheless, it is a new law in yet another country that provides a legal anchor for the concept that the right to die with dignity is part of the right to live with dignity." (Links to these organizations are on the companion website.)

Elder-care attorneys can join several professional societies including the American Bar Association (ABA), which sponsors a Senior Lawyers Division. The ABA also publishes the *Bifocal* (Bar Association's Focus on Aging and the Law), which shares "how-to" information dealing with all manner of specialized elder rights subjects. The National Academy of Elder Law Attorneys (NAELA) promotes the interests of aging individuals by improving the advocacy skills of elder lawyers. In 1993 NAELA founded the National Elder Law Foundation, which was recognized in 1995 by the ABA as the certification authority for a specialty in elder law. (Links to these associations are on the companion website.)

Other legal roles that carry an explicit advocacy component include court appointed guardians/conservators who act as health proxies, providing for the general and financial welfare of older principals (called wards) under their custody. **Guardians** constitute a subcategory of involuntary surrogate advocates (Zimny & Grossberg, 1998) because they are judicially imposed upon older persons (or anyone else, for that matter) who have been legally deemed mentally incapable (de facto incompetent) or are otherwise unable to provide for their own care. Guardians/conservators who assume the ward's full rights (*sui juris*) are **plenary guardians;** as such, the ward assumes a status that is very similar to that of an unemancipated child. However, courts can limit guardians' authority in specific ways. Regardless, both plenary and limited guardians are supervised by the courts, and they must regularly report to the court.

Although we classify guardians/conservators as client advocates, which is consistent with the legal intent of the role, the great power that these custodians wield over highly vulnerable individuals has led to incidents of abuse and exploitation. This is an ongoing concern, and some patients' rights advocates view guardianships as too often representing a final act of disempowerment that should be avoided in all but the rarest cases.

Public guardians represent another form of the involuntary surrogate type of legal advocate. These officials are appointed in some jurisdictions to protect the legal and financial rights of individuals who are unable to manage their own affairs, usually due to mental incapacity. A different type of legal advocate are the so-called **attorneys-in-fact** (which does not mean lawyers) who are health proxy advocates with legally binding powers to make decisions on behalf of older individuals on the basis of personal trust, by executing a durable health care power of attorney. They are voluntary surrogates (Zimny & Grossberg, 1998) because their authority derives from the client (called principal), not from a court. Typically, the attorney-in-fact's decision-making power is not activated until the appointing authorities (the older individuals) are no longer able to make decisions for themselves.

Other advocates include the **guardian *ad litem,*** or court visitors, who advocate for the rights and best interests of older persons in guardianship proceedings. They base their advocacy work on investigations of the older persons' circumstances and make recommendations to the court as to whether guardians are needed.

A distinct subtype of legal advocates includes a whole range of government officials whose roles entail some specific legal duty to protect older clients. Personnel from regulatory enforcement agencies such as Centers for Medicare and Medicaid Services (CMS) or the various state health departments who inspect nursing homes, for example, clearly perform some very legalistic forms of advocacy to control social problems even though advocacy is not central to their roles. Still, regulatory leaders are frequently involved in initiatives to promote residents' interests, individually and collectively, by improving enforcement through corrective actions by working on quality improvement task forces or testifying before state legislatures on the need for protective regulation.

BOX 3.5

Legal Advocates

- Are typically paid professional agents whose duties are prescribed by law or administrative rule
- Defend in a forceful manner and can be highly adversarial

- Stress due process and legal mandates
- Include attorneys, legal assistants, guardians, conservators, and government officials

---

Consider, also, how regulatory involvement invariably entails adversarial and trial-like due processes, such as hearings designed to fundamentally defend client/consumer interests. Bateman (2000) pointed out that government advocates often utilize the same tactics as lawyers although they are less technical. This is illustrated by one of the author's recollections as Deputy State Ombudsman. An attorney on staff joked about how she had technically left the practice of law, which she did not enjoy, only to end up as an ombudsman who spent even more time practicing (de facto) law. This suggests the importance of the law as leverage for nonregulatory, formally designated governmental elder-care advocates (Nelson, 2000). These governmental legal advocates fundamentally differ from attorneys in that they are not directly paid by the client, which is no small distinction.

At the federal level, the premier elder advocacy agency, legally mandated through the Older Americans Act (OAA), is the Administration on Aging (AoA) located in the U.S. Department of Health and Human Services. This agency administers the OAA, which funds State Units on Aging (SUAs) to promote policies and programs designed to improve older persons' dignity, health, independence, safety, and socioemotional well-being. The OAA specifically mandates advocacy services for vulnerable elders by requiring SUAs to work with the local Area Agencies on Aging (AAAs, often called the "Triple As") to support the Long-Term Care Ombudsman Program and to promote other services that prevent elder abuse and exploitation, thus enhancing the

provision of elder legal services. (Links to these organizations are on the companion website.)

AAAs frequently don the advocacy mantle when their clients fail to receive needed information or require access to available services. Other legally mandated government advocates include the various states' Adult Protective Services (APS) workers, who work with local law enforcement agencies to prevent both community and institutional abuse and who investigate and intervene when abuse happens (Box 3.5).

Hybrid Advocates and Their Organizations

If you feel somewhat confused trying to sort out what advocacy role you play or will play, rest assured that these roles are not mutually exclusive. In addition, no matter the type or target of your advocacy work, culture must always be taken into consideration. There is some overlap in all types of advocates, and in certain cases hybrid models emerge. A prime example is the Long-Term Care Ombudsman Program. State offices of the ombudsman program are authorized under Title VII of the Older American Act, further empowered by the National Nursing Home Reform Act of 1987 (often called OBRA 87, as this act and others fell within an Omnibus Budget Reconciliation Act) and procedurally guided by state enabling laws and administrative codes. (Links to these acts are on the companion website.) Ombudsmen rely heavily on legalistic methods, such as using stringent nursing home regulations to leverage their resident defense claims and system reform goals. As such, ombudsmen

BOX 3.6

Hybrid Advocates and Their Organizations

Hybrid Advocates . . .

Are procedurally *guided by state* enabling laws, statutes, and administrative codes

Are *fully informed* on policies and practice standards

Use *all types of advocacy*

Encourage *member participation* (for example, by people affected by target problem)

. . . And Work in Organizations Like These.

National Citizens Coalition for Nursing Home Reform (NCCNHR, commonly pronounced Nickner)

The National Association of Retired Federal Employees

The Coalition of Institutionalized Aged and Disabled

Long-Term Care Ombudsmen

The Older Women's League

The National Council on the Aging

The Alzheimer's Association

American Association of Retired Persons (AARP)

The National Parkinson's Disease Foundation

The National Ataxia Foundation

The National Organization of Rare Disorders

The National Diabetes Association

Y-Me Breast Cancer Association

meet the criteria of being legal advocates. On the other hand, such advocates overwhelmingly rely on mobilized grassroots citizen volunteers, who, by law, must have no vested interest in the long-term care system (Nelson, Netting, Huber, & Borders, 2001b), so the program is also a touchstone for third party citizen advocacy.

Analysis of the membership dynamics of many other elder-oriented pressure groups reveal hybrid elements. Various advocacy organizations encourage member participation of consumers who are negatively affected directly by a given problem and who are simultaneously the subjects of the agency's rescue efforts. The National Citizens Coalition on Nursing Home Reform (NCCNHR), for example, encourages long-term care residents and their families to join NCCNHR as members. (A link to the coalition is on the companion website.) This reflects NCCNHR's collective self-advocacy orientation. On the other hand, most NCCNHR members hold staff positions in local not-for-profit citizen advocacy groups, paid and unpaid, including a very prominent showing of both state and local, past and present, long-term care ombudsman program leaders. This reflects NCCNHR's third party citizen advocacy

function, which is supplemented by academicians, elder-law attorneys, and other public and private sector leaders. Consequently, NCCNHR is a hybrid type of advocacy organization that effectively combines a mix of advocacy types who cooperate to influence the external focus of their change efforts. This broaches yet another subject: how advocates' tactics and effectiveness are powerfully influenced by whether they are external to or members of the organizational system that is targeted for change (i.e., long-term care facilities). These are summarized in Box 3.6.

Internal Versus External Advocates

Advocates who stand outside the organization or larger system needing change can be more zealous in their advocacy as they are not fettered by employment concerns or a need to maintain good relations with coworkers (Rubin, 1994). However, this doesn't necessarily mean that they are more effective. Third parties, including ombudsmen, regulators, attorneys, and even relatives of clients, can spark dysfunctional conflict by their forcefulness and uncompromising zeal. They sometimes make bad things worse by promoting personal agendas, infusing bias against the target

BOX 3.7

Internal Versus External Advocates

Internal Advocates . . .	External Advocates . . .
Work from within their own organizations or agencies	Can be more zealous with their jobs not on the line
Usually have firsthand knowledge	May be more objective
Know the players	
Know the politics and may hold some authority for changes	
Are usually more invested	
HOWEVER,	HOWEVER,
May be placing their jobs on the line	May not be as invested
May be under pressure to maintain the status quo	May not understand all of the internal dynamics
May alienate colleagues	
May damage relationships with colleagues with whom they work every day	

organization or decision makers (Rubin, 1994), or by not understanding the culture of targeted people and organizations.

Conversely, internal advocates (who are likely to be of the legal type) face numerous structural pressures that can restrain their client-centered advocacy work. Their employment status, for example, can result in pressure to *keep a lid on things* and to protect organizational or professional interests, to say nothing of their own jobs. Still, the internal advocate often has the connections, system savvy, and authority to get things done for clients.

Both internal and external advocates have a place, and both face special challenges unique to their respective roles. Each type faces very different dynamics when they target the persons who have the power to change situations (Box 3.7).

LEVELS OF ADVOCACY

There is a well-established literature on levels of advocacy. Focusing on advocacy levels brings the question back to whether one is advocating for individuals or much larger groups of older people. Whether you become a self-advocate, a citizen advocate, a provider advocate, or a legal

advocate, depending on the level of intervention needed, you may be engaged in case or class advocacy. Chances are that you may be engaged in both simultaneously, advocating for individuals in need but also joining efforts with others to advocate for changes that will affect large numbers of older persons over the long run.

Case Advocacy

Ezell (2001) reviewed the types of advocacy found in the literature. "Citizen, clinical, self, and direct service advocacy are similar in their focus on individual cases and are distinguished by who does the advocacy, a citizen, a practitioner, or a client" (p. 28). He considers all of these types as case advocacy because the focus is on individuals.

Schneider and Lester (2001) defined the purpose of advocacy as protecting individuals' rights, services, and other benefits to which they are entitled. They defined clients broadly, as individuals alone or in families or groups, and even as communities and organizations. This is an important distinction. There is a tendency to think of a person as an individual case, and it is easy to forget that a family unit, a small group, a specific organization, or even a community

BOX 3.8
Levels of Advocacy

Case Advocacy . . .	Class or Cause Advocacy . . .
Focuses mainly on individual clients but can include families, communities, and small organizations	Focuses on laws, policies, regulations, practices, and even political agendas that affect large populations

with established boundaries can be a client. Thus we see **case advocacy** as situations in which an identified, individual case (whether it is a person or a larger unit) is the subject of change efforts.

Case advocacy includes situations in which advocates plead for some desired change that will result in direct benefits to themselves or to a client. Examples include a case where an ambulatory, mentally capable nursing home resident asks to take a stroll but is denied by the charge nurse, who worries not only about the resident's safety but also about the facility's liability should an accident occur. The facility social worker hears of this and tactfully reminds the nurse of residents' rights to go for walks and helps the nurse understand how liability risks can be minimized by documenting the resident's sound mental capacity and informed assumption of risk. The nurse changes her stance, and this single incident, or case, is closed. Another example would be when a nurse challenges a physician who is strong-arming compliance against a patient's repeated, if somewhat timid, objections.

Class Advocacy

A class implies more than one client, and that is exactly the meaning that we intend by this term. **Class advocacy** means to champion the needs or rights of groups of people, groups of organizations, and even multiple communities with the same problems or in similar situations (Ezell, 2001). Class advocacy has a broader scope than case advocacy and focuses on bringing about change in policies and practices for those who are disabled, victims of domestic violence and other crimes, welfare recipients, and elderly newcomers to the United States (Schneider & Lester, 2001). Other terms used for this concept are *systems advocacy* and *policy advocacy* (Ezell, 2001; Box 3.8).

Class advocacy can occur at the group, organizational, community, or broader policy levels in what are often called macro arenas. For example, administrative advocacy (Schneider & Lester, 2001) occurs at the organizational or local community level, where the internal or external advocate pushes for change in policies, processes, or protocols by implanting new ideas, recommending new practices, and changing attitudes. Examples include the AAA director who motivates her staff to more aggressively assess depression in elderly males who are at increased risk for suicide, or nursing home administrators who change their organizational cultures to make them more sensitive to patients' rights (Giordano & Rich, 2001). Others include rural, faith-based outreach program leaders who build alliances with local businesses, public service providers, and citizens to develop an elderly and disabled persons transportation service for the community.

Class advocacy can also involve political change at the highest social level as pushed, prodded, and pursued by broad-based, threat-oriented, citizen-based coalitions who desire to, for example, increase outputs for Medicare, Social Security, or other national programs. Class advocacy could include the mobilization of social reform groups, such as the collective self-advocacy organizations referred to earlier. These threat-sensitive organizations martial resources to effect change at the national level and could include efforts to influence policy makers to increase Medicare coverage for home health care or intermediate nursing home care, for example, or exert pressure on legislators to increase funding for research on a particular condition that affects older people. Table 3.1 brings these various types of advocates together for a more comprehensive overview.

TABLE 3.1 Types of Advocacy and Typical Characteristics

Self-Advocates

Individual Self-Advocates . . .	Collective Self-Advocates . . .
Advocate everyday, informal activity	Cooperate with others in collective effort
Advocate usually for themselves	Have needs that are also the needs of others in the collective
Educate and persuade others to grant access to services	
	Are tied to a group, association, or organization
Typically are not channeled through an organized group	Can be local or large scale
	Can be focused on broader scale change

Third Party Citizen Advocates . . .

Are seen as altruistic because they do not share the need as the persons for whom they are advocating

Can be paid or unpaid

Focus on protection or empowerment of persons who cannot advocate for themselves

May engage in outreach to vulnerable persons/groups

Provider or Intrarole Advocates . . .

Constitute the most inclusive but least pure type

Have advocacy as just one aspect of their identities

Are professionals who have other responsibilities in addition to advocacy and may experience role conflict (social workers and nurses)

Legal Advocates . . .

Are typically paid professional agents whose duties are prescribed by law or administrative rule

Defend in a forceful manner and can be highly adversarial

Stress due process and legal mandates

Include attorneys, legal assistants, guardians, conservators, and government officials

Hybrid Advocates . . .

Are procedurally guided by state enabling laws, statutes, and administrative codes

Are fully informed on policies and practice standards

Use all types of advocacy

Encourage member participation by people affected by target problem

Internal Versus External Advocates

Internal Advocates . . .	External Advocates . . .
Work from within their own organizations or agencies	Can be more zealous with their jobs not on the line
Usually have firsthand knowledge	May be more objective
Know the players	
Know the politics and may hold some authority for changes	
Are usually more invested	
HOWEVER,	HOWEVER,
May be placing their jobs on the line	May not be as invested
May be under pressure to maintain status quo	May not understand all of the internal dynamics

(Continued)

TABLE 3.1 *Continued*

May alienate colleagues

May damage relationships with colleagues with whom they work every day

Levels of Advocacy

Case Advocacy . . .	Class or Cause Advocacy . . .
Focuses mainly on individual clients but can include individual people, families, communities, and small organizations	Focuses on laws, policies, regulations, practices, and even political agendas that affect large populations

Targeting Decision Makers

No matter the role played or the level of interaction, advocates ask questions such as these: Who has the authority and the power to change this situation? Is it an individual or a group? Is this informal power such as in the case of caregivers and family members, or is this person in a position of power or authority? Is the person or persons to be targeted a decision maker or a series of decision makers in a formal agency or institutional setting? Do I understand the cultural dynamics?

Sometimes people are eager and active allies in solving client problems. Just because they have the power to control the situation does not mean they want to control it or are overtly trying to keep older persons from having their needs met. Many providers easily respond to the advocate's simple request for help or to the suggestion that a problem exists. Certainly, persons in control are not always resistant, and in fact, many of you will be the very decision makers advocates will target for change. Decision makers and change agents can even be the same persons.

Informal Decision Makers

Informal decision makers do not hold roles of authority within established organizations or groups. Their power derives from their roles in relation to older persons—relationships in which they have the ability to influence the quality of care and the quality of life of those persons. Examples are informal caregivers, friends, family members, neighbors, and a host of other persons with whom the older person might have a relationship.

We consider these persons decision makers because they have the ability to make choices and to take action, no matter how little impact they have on older people. For example, a daughter who sees her mother as a hypochondriac may discourage her from seeking medical care when she really needs it. Her experience is that her mother has "cried wolf once too often," but in this situation her mother may have a legitimate need. Since the daughter provides transportation for her mother and is her primary caregiver, her inattention in responding to the mother's symptoms could endanger her mother. The advocate in a situation like this might be a close personal friend of the family who recognizes that the daughter is not intending to neglect her mother's care but who can persuade the daughter to get her mother to a physician.

Advocates target informal decision makers all the time, yet they don't always conceptualize the process as one of advocacy. For example, a volunteer in an interfaith, friendly visiting program discovers that the elder she is visiting lives in a filthy apartment with a number of animals that are frequently left unattended and in poor health. When the volunteer asks the older woman if she may help her clean up the apartment and possibly locate homes for at least some of her pets, she is met with a blank stare. Not only does the older woman not see any need for this kind of help, but also she is confused as to why the volunteer would even suggest it. In this situation, the decision maker and the older person for whom the volunteer is advocating are one and the same. Feeling that the situation is a threat to the older person's health, the volunteer begins trying to persuade her to at least consider the possibility of a change.

Formal Decision Makers

Formal decision makers are persons who have the power and authority to promote, influence, control, or maintain group, professional, or organizational norms that sometimes (even in highly functional prosocial systems) block the legitimate interests of less powerful people. They are *formal* because they have positions within established agencies and institutions.

Potential service barriers that are influenced by the decision maker may include market demands, political climate, economic policies, public and private law and rules, and plans, procedures, values, and norms. At the community and organizational levels, decision makers have even greater control over organizational policies and procedures, the use of technology, professional habits and rituals, communication patterns, modes of dispute management, and leadership practices, among other factors that influence an operating system's ability to meet elder clients' needs. At the individual level, decision makers may have the greatest degree of control over their own communication and management style, professional and personal goals, ethics, and values that may block valid concerns.

Decision makers can be found everywhere—from the micro, individual level to the macro, sociopolitical level—but the decision maker's personal authority to change a system diminishes as the problem moves from micro to macro concerns. Consider, for example, that individual decision makers have the most power to change their own stances or values, but they have generally somewhat less influence over groups or organizational norms. Put simply, then, the advocate will generally find it easier to induce change through decision makers at, successively, the individual, group, or organizational levels, followed by the community or slightly higher social institutional levels. Most difficult to change is the highest level of national policy where advocates must influence large groups of decision makers, many of whom will disagree among themselves as to what needs to change. Regardless of the advocate's level of influence, effective advocates must identify and work with, through, or even against genuine decision makers if they want to effectively influence the power that is working against the interests of elders.

☾ SUMMARY

After opening this chapter with Clara's story, we identified the three principal agents in elder advocacy: older persons, advocates, and persons with the power to effect changes (or defeat them). Next we introduced four different types of advocates, acknowledging that they are not mutually exclusive.

Self-advocates may work alone, attempting to persuade others that their needs should be met. Self-advocates often find that others are advocating for the same or similar causes and that joining in collective advocacy efforts will assist in addressing their needs.

Citizen advocates are persons who do not have the condition or problem for which they are advocating, but for whatever reason they are working to make things better for older people who do face these conditions/problems. Although they may not stand to gain directly, there are benefits gained in the process that make their efforts worth pursuing.

Provider advocates are employed by formal organizations, and they perform multiple roles in their daily practices. Advocacy may be one of many roles they play as they go about the work of elder care. Providers are often professionals and paraprofessionals who are guided by codes of ethics that provide direction in terms of when advocacy is warranted. Because they function in provider roles, they are sometimes targeted for change by advocates outside the system.

Legal advocates are mandated through some formal process to perform advocacy roles. They may provide legal counsel, guardianship, power of attorney, and legal assistance.

All types of advocates engage in both case and class advocacy. Although self- and citizen advocates by definition tend to function outside of established, formal systems, provider and legal advocates often perform within established structures. However, this does not mean that the latter do not perform external advocacy roles when they confront injustices in systems other than their own.

We concluded with a view of decision makers and the roles they play. Distinguishing between informal and formal decision makers is critically important because power can be highly informal and just as formidable as authority within formal systems. As we move to subsequent chapters, we will reexamine relationships between advocates and decision makers and how to develop strategies to address elders' needs in collaborative as well as contentious situations.

DISCUSSION QUESTIONS AND EXERCISES

1. Being an internal advocate has its strengths and limitations, as does being an external advocate. Can you think of times in which an internal advocate may actually become an external advocate and vice versa as elders move in and out of various settings? How do the dynamics change as you move from the position of being within a particular setting to advocating for your client who has gone into another setting?

2. Case and class advocacy are not always mutually exclusive. Can you think of situations in which it is hard to determine if one is doing case or class advocacy? Is it possible to be doing both at the same time? Explain your response.

3. At times you may be the decision maker targeted by a persuasive advocate who truly believes that something needs to change. Given your current position or what you are training to do, can you think of situations in which you might actually be the targeted decision maker rather than the advocate? Similarly, can you envision yourself simultaneously being the decision maker and the advocate? Discuss what that might be like.

4. Reread the opening story about Clara and her two daughters, Anna and Suzanne, and address the following questions:
   • What are the roles of all of the players?
   • Who are the advocates?
   • What are the legitimate and illegitimate sources of influence (power) in this case?
   • Who are the critical decision makers—the targets?
   • What prima facie values are at play in this case?
   • Is there a legally correct course of action here?

5. Read the following case and answer these questions:
   • Who is the person in need in this case? What do you know about her strengths and challenges?
   • Who are the advocates in this case? What types of advocates are they?
   • Who has the power to change this situation? How does this power shift and change as Hazel travels from setting to setting?
   • What are the points of conflict in this situation? Who is in conflict?
   • There are multiple roles played in this case: Hazel, friends, family members, and professionals in various settings. How do these roles and relationships offer strengths and challenges in this situation?
   • If you were the niece, what would you do at this point?
   • What is your assessment of this situation?

Hazel, a widow of 25 years, lives alone in a continuing care retirement community (CCRC). Hazel is 85 and has lived in this same location for 20 years. She has no children but has several nieces and nephews and two sisters who are both in their 80s but who live far away. She is on the sixth floor of a high-rise apartment building in a convenient location. Within a mile of the building is a mall where Hazel and her friends go to walk in the mornings; it has services such as banks and restaurants and a number of health care facilities. Although the area is very convenient, it has also become quite congested over the years. Walking to these various places is not safe, and sidewalks do not line all the roadways. Until last autumn Hazel drove about town, but due to the progression of macular degeneration she gave up her car. This was a hard decision, but she knew that this would eventually happen. More recently she often rides to stores and services with friends who live in the same building.

One day a grandniece, who lives about 30 miles away in another town, had gone to pick up groceries for Hazel. When the grandniece rang the buzzer, Hazel stood up from her chair and slumped to the floor, breaking her hip. When Hazel didn't respond, the grandniece got a neighbor to let her in. She found Hazel on the floor in pain. An ambulance was called, and Hazel was admitted to the hospital. Fortunately, she did not require a hip replacement, but she did undergo surgery and the hip was pinned. After 4 days in the hospital, she was discharged to the rehabilitation hospital.

As soon as Hazel entered the rehabilitation hospital, another niece, who lives about 300 miles away, called to check on her because this niece has her health care power of attorney. The case manager was very anxious to have all the appropriate documentation on file, which included the health care power of attorney, insurance information, and Hazel's living will. The niece called the case manager and inquired about Hazel, who had just been admitted.

The case manager told the niece that in situations like this when persons are 85 and fall and break their hip, they usually recommend assisted living. The niece was somewhat taken aback that the case manager would suggest that Hazel consider assisted living since she was currently living in an independent living unit. The niece was also angry that anyone would simply assess an older person on the basis of age without having done a complete assessment of the situation. The case manager explained that the aunt would be case conferenced the next Tuesday and that the rehab team would do a complete assessment before making a recommendation.

Hazel is not happy about being in the rehab hospital, but she is determined to make progress and to show that she can maximize her physical therapy. On the third day in the rehab hospital, it is rainy and cold outside (the winter weather seems to be lingering into late March this year). The physical therapist comes in and announces that Hazel and several other patients will be going to the mall to demonstrate that they can begin to move into the outside world. Hazel is a genteel person and likes to comply with professional requests, but she asks not to go. It is cold outside, and she is only a week postsurgery. She has no coat or hat with her because she did not bring them from home. However, the physical therapist insists. Hazel reluctantly complies, wrapping a towel around her head and a blanket around her body to keep warm. She is lifted in a wheelchair into the van and transported to the mall.

When the niece calls that evening, Hazel is exhausted. She says, "I was mortified that someone I knew would see me. You know we walk in the mall. I just knew they would see how I look and the whole building would know that I have gone down hill." The niece decides she has to drive down to visit her aunt that weekend as soon as she can get away because she wants to confront the physical therapist who had the audacity to place her aunt in such an embarrassing and dehumanizing position.

When the rehab team meets late that week, they note that Hazel complained about going to the mall, indicating that she was resisting her therapy. They decide that they would recommend another week in the rehab hospital and then a discharge to assisted living. They also view her as somewhat noncompliant and send the facility's psychologist in to ask why Hazel was resisting treatment (going to the mall).

The case manager goes to Hazel's room and tells her that a psychologist will be visiting and that the team's recommendation is that she go to assisted living. Hazel is frightened because she knows that going to assisted living is exactly what the owners of the apartment building want to happen. She is in a CCRC, and she has one of the original life care contracts that they have quit selling. She had never owned a home and had worked all her life to support herself and a disabled husband. She had moved back to her hometown after her husband had died. She had always been very frugal and had managed to save a nest egg of $30,000. Twenty-five years ago she had bought into the CCRC by paying the $25,000 nonrefundable entry fee. She was one of the charter residents in the building, and the owners very much want to resell the apartments because the going rate in today's market is around $200,000. If they could get Hazel into a small assisted living unit, it would free up her two-bedroom apartment for someone else to buy. Hazel is very aware that she is vulnerable to being transferred to assisted living against her will.

Hazel is afraid. She knows that the rehab team is composed of five professionals, and if her apartment building manager learns of their recommendation, it would be just what the manager needs to transfer her out of her home of 20 years. Just a week and a half away from having lived independently, she now faces the prospects of losing her home. Not only that, but she faces the overwhelming sadness that she would be moving away from an older man who lives in the same building and with whom she is in love.

When the niece learns of the rehab team's recommendation, she is very concerned. The niece manages to advocate for Hazel. Because the case manager in the rehab hospital does not know the staff in the CCRC, the rehab team's recommendation is never shared. Hazel is discharged from the rehab hospital to the personal care unit of the CCRC where she has a 30-day grace period. If she can get back to her apartment before the 30 days are up, she has the right to go back to her independent apartment. This becomes her goal. Her 80-year-old sister from New Mexico flies in 2 weeks later, and Hazel goes back to her apartment with her sister there. Hazel is elated to be home.

Temporary home health services are put in place by the niece. The physical therapist is amazed at Hazel's progress. She is definitely motivated to get well, and her male friend arrives every afternoon to play a game of dominoes with her. He always lifts her spirits.

Suddenly, one week into her return home, Hazel gets very ill. She is so dizzy she can't get up and she has a severe headache. Her sister (who is still staying with her) calls the nurse in the nursing unit at the retirement home. Hazel is rushed to the hospital, where they do some tests and send her home. A list of medications reveals that no one medication or no medication interaction would have caused such a rapid rise in blood pressure. She had not eaten anything unusual that day, nor had she come off any medication recently. She said that she felt depressed and had no stamina but couldn't think of anything else to tell the emergency room physicians.

The next day she feels much better. She has a *good* day. Two days later she has a headache and her blood pressure spikes dangerously high (238/98). The nurse comes but says that Hazel needs to go to the emergency room. An EKG and CAT scan reveal no problem. With a new medication (Procardia), she is able to go home.

Hazel's sister is in a quandary. In 4 days she has a return flight to New Mexico. She wants to support and advocate for Hazel's desire to remain at home, but she is beginning to wonder if she can really make it on her own. She confidentially talks with the niece about the possibility of Hazel moving to assisted living, wondering out loud whether the rehab team had been right. Hazel keeps saying, "I'm not ready to give up yet," and the niece says that if she is aware of the risk that she should be allowed to stay in her independent living unit.

Source: Adapted from Netting, F. E. (1998). Interdisciplinary practice and the geriatric care manager. *Geriatric Case Management Journal,* *8*(1), 20–24.

ADDITIONAL READINGS

Baldridge, D. (2004, Spring). Double jeopardy: Advocating for Indian elders. *Generations, 28*(1), 75–78.

Blancato, R. B. (2004, Spring). Advocacy and aging policy: The prognosis. *Generations, 28*(1), 65–69.

Callahan, J. J. (2004, Spring). The world of interest-group advocacy: An "insider's" view. *Generations, 28*(1), 36–40.

Fisher, R., Ury, W., & Patton, B. (1991). *Getting to yes: Negotiating agreement without giving in.* New York: Penguin Books.

Freeman, I. C. (2004, Spring). Advocacy in aging policy: Working the bills on Capitol Hill(s). *Generations, 28*(1), 41–47.

Freeman, I. C. (2000). Uneasy allies: Nursing home regulators and consumer advocates. *Journal of Aging & Social Policy, 11*(2/3), 127–135.

Haynes, K. S., & Mickelson, J. S. (2000). *Affecting change* (4th ed.). Needham, MA: Allyn & Bacon.

Hornbostel, R. (2004, Spring). The power of local advocacy: Funding for senior services in Ohio. *Generations, 28*(1), 79–81.

Hudson, R. B. (2004, Spring). Advocacy and policy success in aging. *Generations, 28*(1), 17–24.

Kane, R. A. (2004, Spring). The circumscribed sometimes-advocacy of the case manager and the care provider. *Generations, 28*(1), 70–74.

Kapp, M. B. (2004, Spring). Advocacy in an aging society: The varied roles of attorneys. *Generations, 28*(1), 31–35.

Kelly, M. A. (2004, Spring). Developing an advocacy coalition with varied interests and agendas: A Pennsylvanian experience. *Generations, 28*(1), 83–85.

Lowenberg, F., & Dolgoff, R. (1988). *Ethical decisions for social work practice* (3rd ed.). Itasca, IL: F. E. Peacock.

Lens, V. (2004, July). Principled negotiation: A new tool for case advocacy. *Social Work, 49*(3), 506–513.

McConnell, S. (2004, Spring). Advocacy in organizations: The elements of success. *Generations, 28*(1), 25–30.

McNutt, J. G. (2002). New horizons in social work advocacy. *Electronic Journal of Social Work, 1*(1), 1–13.

Moxley, D. P., & Hyduk, C. A. (2003). The logic of personal advocacy with older adults and its implications for program management in community-based gerontology. *Administration in Social Work, 27*(4), 5–23.

Rother, K. (2004, Spring). Why haven't we been more successful advocates for elders? *Generations, 28*(1), 55–58.

Stone, R. (2004, Spring). Where have all the advocates gone? *Generations, 28*(1), 59–64.

GATHERING INFORMATION

Assessing Elders' Needs in Context

Try to become *the client.*   RADER (1992)

BOX 4.1

ALICE

An advocate for elders received a beautifully written letter from Alice who was in a nursing home in a locked Alzheimer's unit. Alice was mad and bitter that her daughter had tricked her into moving into the locked unit. Her daughter had asked her if she wanted to take a ride. When Alice said "Yes," her daughter drove her to the nursing home and had her admitted. Alice is 67 years old, and all she wanted was to go home. It was a highly effective plea.

Alice and her husband had built their home 45 years ago, sharing it together until he died a few years ago. It was a place she never wanted to leave, and she described her home in loving detail. The letter revealed a very logical plea to be released to the familiarity of her home.

The advocate took the letter to his supervisor who was truly struck by its power. The advocate was outraged by Alice's plight and was determined to help her. With the supervisor's permission, the advocate immediately left to go to the facility to begin his assessment and investigation.

He first visited Alice and corroborated the story. He reported that Alice spoke of her home in deep detail and remembered that dark day that her daughter stole her life away by forcing her into Sparkdown Manor. The advocate was convinced that a heinous wrong had been perpetrated on Alice. When he reported what he had found, staff members were excited about having a powerful case that perfectly highlighted their worst fears of elder exploitation. They could relate to Alice's plight and wanted to be successful in addressing it.

The advocate informed the facility that Alice's rights had been violated, that she had the right to go home, and that she was inappropriately housed in a locked Alzheimer's unit. The facility countered with a strong argument that the advocate was terribly mistaken, that the woman did, in fact, suffer from dementia, that she was legally incompetent, and that the daughter had guardianship over her mother. Given this strong opposition, the advocate did not know what to do. He asked his supervisor to intervene.

The supervisor could not believe that her staff advocate could be so wrong about this situation. They had talked at length about Alice's situation and were convinced that her claim was valid. But the facility was making a strong and unambiguous counterargument. The supervisor bought a little time by saying that she would personally investigate the case further, and if she and her staff advocate were wrong, the agency would certainly change its position. She left the office to talk with the facility staff and to spend some time with Alice.

At the facility the supervisor was introduced to Alice, and she greeted her pleasantly. Alice ushered her to a table, and they began a nice chat. She seemed alert and oriented and answered many questions about her home; in fact, she waxed quite eloquently on her home, her favorite subject. They talked for some time, and Alice had the staff bring coffee (which the supervisor would not drink, as it would appear that she was accepting something from the facility). It was a pleasant and seemingly normal conversation. She understood what Alice was saying, and Alice's reasoning seemed fine: she was pleasant, animated, and friendly.

Now that they had developed rapport, the supervisor thought that it was time to start seriously trying to figure out Alice's mental status, but there would be no formal mental status testing—it would be informal. She asked Alice if she would show her around, and being an elegant and graceful hostess, Alice obliged. She asked who this staff person was, and who that staff person was. Alice's answers began to sound unrealistic, but not extraordinarily so: "Oh, they're just the help, they do what we tell them to."

As they passed a window, Alice explained how she could never take a walk and that she would love to go outside, but that this wasn't allowed.

The supervisor complimented her on the facility—saying that it was an exceptionally nice home. The supervisor then asked Alice to show her the shower. When they had passed it three times—it was clearly labeled—but Alice kept looking for it, the supervisor began to see problems.

Later they found Alice's room, and she invited the supervisor to sit on her bed. She was sitting there and Alice was telling her about her lovely lost home when Alice's roommate wandered in. Alice became very angry: "That woman is always lost, and she always comes in here. Get her out, I don't know who she is."

More questions raised more concerns. The supervisor asked Alice if she was pleased with the service there, and Alice replied that it wasn't as good as she got at home from her cat. When the supervisor asked Alice how long she had had her cat, she said, "Oh, I would never have a cat, I'm allergic to cats!" More questions led to more bizarre answers. The supervisor soon came to the sad conclusion that Alice had fluctuating mental capacity. She seemed to have apparently broad windows of lucidity when she presented well, but upon deeper probing she showed severe memory deficits and disturbed cognitive processing.

The supervisor realized that her staff advocate had conducted a faulty assessment, had been blinded by emotion, and had not taken the time to do a thorough informal assessment. A further review of the written evidence showed that the court visitor had documented that Alice was unaware of her own safety needs. Moreover, the daughter was Alice's legal guardian, but it was a limited guardianship that precluded the daughter from moving her mother out of her house. In fact, the court was to have been informed if the daughter felt that a move was unavoidable, and she did not do that.

Alice had sufficient financial resources for in-home care, so the advocates had the leverage to get her back in her house, even though they had to admit that they were remiss in their initial assessment. This left them in somewhat of a quandary—they could assist Alice in doing what she desperately wanted to do on a technicality, but they were beginning to recognize that she would probably not be able to function solely on her own.

☽ MULTIDIMENSIONAL ASSESSMENT

Multidimensional assessment is no stranger to gerontological practice, and some assessments are a great deal more complicated than others, as in Clara's case in Chapter 3 and Alice's case here. Nevertheless, a thorough assessment is a core component of effective advocacy. Regardless of your role, some type of assessment of elders' needs must occur. Such appraisals typically include clients' functional abilities, finances, physical and mental health, social relationships, environment, spirituality, and perhaps other aspects of their lives. Assessments must also include the elder's personal cultural history, past and present, and if a move to another setting is under discussion, the culture of that facility and the differences between the client's and the facility's cultures. This requires culturally competent assessors, addressed later in this chapter.

In many programs assessment is a standardized process in which agreed-upon (even mandated) tools are used (e.g. Diwan, Shugarman, & Fries, 2004). In others, the assessment process may be less standardized or even highly informal. Nevertheless, one thing is certain: assessment is critical to anything you plan to do with and for older people because whatever action you take must be based on some method of assessing the needs from the older person's perspective. This bears special emphasis for advocates, who are sometimes so results oriented that they give short shrift to assessing the intricacies of clients' needs. Even when advocates recognize the importance of assessment, they may not have time to evaluate client needs in the context of the larger environment, and they must sometimes move ahead with only fragments of the whole mosaic.

Conducting systematic assessments of older persons' needs is indispensable to effective advocacy. Gerontological advocates must know how to select and use assessment tools and be adept at assessing the broader contexts in which elders live. Our primary focus here is on assessing elders' immediate needs, including their settings or environments.

This person-in-environment approach requires assessing the system in which practitioners and elders are located—the interface between multiple provider systems and elders' immediate organizational environments. We say *immediate* because their settings/locations may change rapidly. For example, an older person may enter the hospital, be transferred to a step-down unit, and be discharged to a rehab hospital within a few days. Assessing these various settings requires case management skills and the ability to reassess quickly as situations change, contextualizing given incidents, problems, and cultures, and understanding what life is like for the elder in such rapidly changing environments. Incidents that call for advocacy do not happen in isolation or in a vacuum. To be an effective advocate, practitioners must understand all of the overt and covert factors as well as the dynamics and nuances among them.

This chapter focuses on the assessment process to ensure that advocacy efforts are appropriate for the presenting situation. We begin with the five questions posed by Kane and Kane (2000) as an assessment guide: why, what, when, whom to assess, and who should conduct the assessment? We then discuss the vulnerability of elders, even when they are in the care of providers. This is followed by examples across settings and the importance of being a culturally competent advocate.

We continue with a discussion of six general issues that must be viewed in context when considering elders' quality of care and the quality of their lives. Finally, we discuss four tasks that the advocate must consider in the assessment phase; each includes a case illustration and questions to be considered if you are an advocate in that scenario.

Multiple examples in this chapter demonstrate how difficult it can be to identify the problems in a complex situation. The threads that can be pulled through the examples presented are (a) that elder vulnerability within systems is not always easy to understand and (b) that the uniqueness of individuals (e.g., their preferences, values, cultures, and experiences) must never be lost in the process. The older person's situation and uniqueness form the context within which you have to assess the problem or issues at hand, and most situations are multiproblematic. The initial problem may be a medical condition that becomes a crisis, yet the problem the advocate encounters concerns the way in which providers of every type can, or cannot, resolve it. Providers (the individuals providing care for elderly persons in various settings) in any given situation may not know how to alleviate a problem, may be hindered by the philosophies, policies, and attitudes of their employers, or may not understand the importance of cultural considerations. We begin our walk through Kane and Kane's (2000) assessment guide by examining the five *Ws* of assessment.

☾ THE FIVE WS OF ASSESSMENT

Years ago assessment tools began to appear in the gerontological literature. Scales that could be used to assess such things as functional ability or perceived health were soon joined by multidimensional tools that looked at all aspects or domains of an older person's life. In the early 1980s, Robert and Rosalie Kane designed an assessment tool for nursing home residents, identifying the various tools that were available. The process of locating these tools was not easy, and many were inaccessible. Organizing the tools they had located turned into a book titled *Assessing the Elderly* (Kane & Kane, 1981). In 2000, Kane and Kane edited a sequel called *Assessing Older Persons* in which the following assessment content areas are examined: functional ability, physical well-being and health, cognition, emotions, social functioning, quality of life, values and preferences, satisfaction, spirituality, caregiving, and physical environments. In selecting assessment tools or techniques, they asked the following questions: Why assess? What to assess? When to assess? Whom to assess? and Who should conduct the assessment? We examine each of these questions in turn.

Why Assess?

Why assess depends on the purpose of the assessment. Eligibility for services or requirements of a funding source may require certain types of assessment. Assessment may be needed to screen for or diagnose a problem and determine a treatment or placement plan for an older person. Assessment can be used to evaluate an intervention that is intended to make a difference in a person's life (e.g., better functioning, improved health, or comfort; Kane, 2000). Regardless of the context, assessment of the older client's need is an essential prerequisite to developing an action plan. It may also be the key to compel decision makers to pay attention to the issue and help resolve it. Advocates cannot

resolve client problems without identifying the gap between "what is and what ought to be"—the pivotal goal of assessment (Windsor, Baranowski, Clark, & Cutter, 1994, p. 63).

What to Assess?

What to assess emerges from having a clear understanding of what needs to be measured or examined. Does the client need assistance with activities of daily living (ADLs)? Can the client recognize her safety needs, handle her finances, and manage her shopping and personal hygiene? Is the client socially isolated or suffering undue grief, stress, sexual dysfunction, malnourishment, or memory loss? Does the client have different cultural values that give meaning to the situation that may inform the need for a culturally sensitive action plan? These questions bespeak a need for a strong conceptual understanding of clients' problems and their underlying causes and origins. In other words, if you want to know how older persons are able to function in their apartments, functional assessment tools that measure ADLs and instrumental activities of daily living (IADLs) such as writing checks, shopping, and scheduling appointments are appropriate. If you want to know how a partner is feeling about being cast in a caregiving role, a tool targeted to caregiving is appropriate. If your client faces medical threats, geriatrically trained medical professionals have a whole range of special diagnostic techniques appropriate for older people that lay advocates might urge practitioners to consider, especially in light of mounting concerns that diagnostic techniques for the general adult population may not be appropriate for the oldest-of-the-old (Larson & Shadlen, 1999).

Choosing the right tool or technique to best measure what you want to assess is not always easy because the name of an assessment instrument does not always indicate what it actually measures. Furthermore, just because you have an assessment tool that is used in your place of employment does not mean that it will fit all situations. Perhaps for eligibility purposes a specific tool needs to be used, but additional tools might be helpful if the instrument does not tell you what you need to know for you to fully understand what is happening.

Whom to Assess?

Whom to assess may be affected by several factors. It is critically important to get as much information directly from the older person as possible. In some instances the older person may not be able to respond (perhaps temporarily) and the advocate must seek information from caregivers and friends or must directly observe the client's circumstances or behaviors. In other instances, being in contact with others may assist in confirming information or gaining alternative perspectives (Kane, 2000).

There may be a tendency to rely on the explanations of others for what very sick and frail older persons may need. As an advocate, however, it is important to start with the older persons themselves if at all possible. Certainly you do not want to wear your client out by administering an excessively long assessment tool or by asking a battery of questions to someone with reduced stamina. In those circumstances, it may be important to gather needed data over several shorter visits rather than trying to do everything at once. In other words, even if it is more time consuming and difficult to assess older persons themselves, if they are capable and willing to give you the information you need, they are your best source.

When to Assess?

When to assess is often dictated by what happens. If community-based older persons are getting along quite well, there may be little need for assessment beyond physicians' diagnoses. If the client is very concrete about getting help for a specific need, the advocate's assessment might also be fairly straightforward and may not go much beyond an attentive intake interview or a casual observation. However, if a person has a precipitating event, such as an accident, or if a family member requests help for a loved one with functional, socioemotional, or financial problems, a more thorough assessment is usually needed. Depending on the situation, when to assess literally depends on what has happened, how much follow-up is needed (reassessment), and the nature of the situation (Kane, 2000).

Who Should Assess?

Who should conduct the assessment also depends on the situation. If an older driver is concerned about his vision or reaction time, the person administering the driving exam is performing an assessment. If a case manager is working with an older couple in the community and following their progress with in-home services, the case manager will assess and reassess their situation on a regular basis. If a long-term care ombudsman enters a nursing home to investigate a complaint, the ombudsman will assess the situation. Professionals, paraprofessionals, and volunteers are constantly assessing situations, using formal tools and asking questions about the identified situation. Many advocates will not have the technical knowledge or credentials required to perform certain clinical or psychological assessments and will need to ask for help from appropriate experts. Indeed, much of the advocacy undertaken by one of the authors was conducted in highly technical medical settings where he had neither the medical knowledge nor credentials to perform formal diagnostic tests. If he had questions, he would, with his client's permission, typically turn to the organization's staff to test or verify his observations concerning the client's needs. This usually worked, but if he doubted the staff's veracity or encountered resistance, he merely turned to external experts he had cultivated as colleagues for help. The fact is, any advocate, whether employed to do so or not, whether professional or family member, whether friend or self, has to assess the situation in some way, regardless of whether the advocate uses formal tools designed for that purpose. The main points of the five *W* questions are summarized in Table 4.1. In the next two sections we ask you to think deeply about the vulnerability of older people and the importance of being a culturally competent advocate.

Elders' Vulnerability

Examine the pros and cons of intervening at all, and select different strategies for different situations to avoid tactics that sabotage the elder's care. It is particularly important in gerontological advocacy that you recognize situations in which

TABLE 4.1 The Five Ws of Assessment

Why does the assessment need to be made?

- Eligibility for services
- Funding requirements
- To screen for a diagnosis or treatment plan
- Periodic reassessment to set a baseline or compare with previous assessment
- To evaluate the treatment plan
- To identify the gap between "what is and what ought to be"

What should be assessed; what needs to be measured or examined?

- To screen for a diagnosis or treatment plan
- Depends on the why and intervention goals
- May be ADLs and IADLs, physical or mental health functioning
- May be psychosocial or environmental
- Myriad instruments are available (see Chapter 9)
- Check on the validity of standardized instruments

Whom do you assess, or to whom do you go for information?

- If at all possible, go first and most often to the elders themselves
- Question those named as being related to any problems, be they family, friends, or professionals
- You may need to consult with collegial professionals such as attorneys, social workers, nurses, or physicians
- Question the older person's landlord and neighbors if appropriate

When do you assess, or how urgent is the situation?

- The degree of urgency will inform your decision about when
- Availability of the older person and other parties will help you assess the when question
- The functional abilities of the older person will also inform you of when to assess

Who should conduct the assessments?

- Isolate the problem using the first four Ws; for example, to determine whether the elder is capable of driving, consult the local drivers licensing authority and, when needed, an optometrist or audiologist
- Case managers
- If cognition or reasoning problems are at issue, mental health professionals should assess
- If ADLs or IADLs are involved, physicians, nurses, and physical and occupational therapists may assess abilities

older people may be in an extremely vulnerable position if an advocate alienates a provider or caregiver. The legendary first canon for physicians is to *first do no harm,* and advocates would be smart to pause early on and think about this. Have you ever inadvertently harmed someone when your intention was to help? This sad phenomenon is sometimes referred to as unintended consequences—something you really want to avoid, which is why it is so important to start where your clients are and not do anything without their permission. If clients perceive that your well-intended efforts will jeopardize them or their loved ones in any way, your hands may be tied.

Suppose you lodge a complaint that the night shift nurses' aides in the hospital are not leaving water for your client. Perhaps it will not happen again, but aides have very frustrating jobs and have been known to occasionally lose their patience (as have most of us). In fact, it is within the realm of possibility that if the aide is called in and scolded by his supervisor, the next night he might pour cold water on your client saying, "You want water, here's water!" That client may hesitate to allow you to advocate for her again. Every tactic must be carefully considered, with as much input from the elder as is feasible. Helping the client often threatens the interests of someone else, or worse, makes the elder vulnerable to retaliation.

Consider, for instance, what might happen within a continuing care retirement community if you recommend that your client's financial resources be liquidated to pay for a private room in the adjacent assisted living facility that is much more expensive than the client's current apartment. This may incur the resistance of the client's family who might resent the diminution of their inheritance or oppose the move because it is symbolic that their relative is becoming increasingly frail. Older people might also be reluctant to tap into funds saved over many years—money that was set aside for a rainy day or to guard against the fear of running out of money. You may need to gently change their minds if they truly need assisted living care.

Financial issues loom large for elders, especially if they remember the Great Depression (1929–1939). Very few families escaped this disaster unscathed, and many children and young people of that time grew up determined to never, never be without money and be as vulnerable as their families had been. Many scrimped, sacrificed, and saved for a rainy day so they would have the money needed to sustain them if another disaster ever struck (and many would not trust those funds to banks for many years thereafter, if ever).

Accept the premise that elders who were 5 years old during those years (which would include elders currently 72 and older) could well remember the dire effects of America's financial catastrophe on their families, families around them, and even the nation. One author's elderly aunt (86) recalls that her father was in his mid-50s during that period, lost his job at the Chamber of Commerce, and could not find another job—even

younger men could not find jobs of any kind. In this family's situation, her father had the money to pay off the mortgage on their house *but would not do so*. The banker was stunned and said, "But you'll ruin your credit if you just let your house go!" He replied, "I don't care about my credit; what would you have me do, sit here in a debt-free house with good credit, but no job, and let my wife and daughter starve?" He moved his family to a farm they had purchased in recent years, turned the Graham Paige into a farm truck, and they grew their own food.

Hospice social workers sometimes have to convince elders that "this *is* the rainy day for which you have saved. Your wife needs 24/7 care." Tapping into this rainy day fund for which they had scrimped and sacrificed for 20 to 50 years is extremely frightening. Those funds have been their safety net, and as long as they remain intact, elders feel that they will not lose everything as had their families.

The dilemma of moving to a higher (and more costly) level of care is complicated. Consider also how labor intensive elder-care settings are, and you can see why they are resistant to providing more costly interventions that eat up precious staff time. Facility managers face many obligations that can make meeting your client's individual needs seem onerous, unrealistic, or impossible. Providers have valid obligations to other residents and to other business realities including liability, as well as to residents' family members (Nelson, 2000).

On the other hand, if your client really needs assisted living and is trying to make it in an independent living unit with the help of in-home services, this may be a safety hazard if not enough in-home services are in place. Furthermore, the actual cost of providing sufficient in-home services to allow elders to live in their own apartments may exceed what it would cost to move to assisted living because the in-home services are provided by outside agencies. At least in assisted living in-house staff are available around the clock for your client. But there are opposing interests at play here: your client needs a higher level of care, but it will be more costly for the provider and may stretch the facility's budget to the

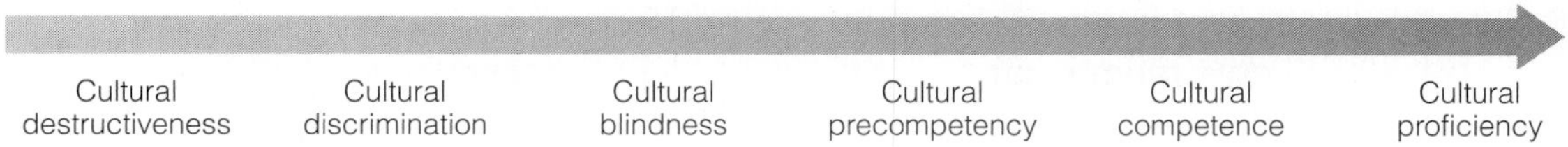

Cultural destructiveness	Cultural discrimination	Cultural blindness	Cultural precompetency	Cultural competence	Cultural proficiency

FIGURE 4.1 Six Stages of Cultural Proficiency
Source: Cross, 1988.

point of being a *dis*service to the other 100-plus residents.

Respecting diverse individual needs within group settings can be challenging. Social agencies are no less immune to pursuing efficiency goals that sometimes block their beneficiaries' interests. Consider, for example, how the rule of distributive justice would compel some service providers to allocate limited resources equitably among all beneficiaries, even though this actually cheats some clients who "need a greater share of these resources than others" (Loewenberg & Dolgoff, 1988, p. 46). In other cases, the client's valid choice may be at odds with your own personal value system, such that you may even be the one tempted to block the client's goals (Lowenberg & Dolgoff, 1988). This creates what Bisno (1988) called an interpsychic conflict of interest between your duties as an advocate to support the client's valid choice and your own personal interests.

There is so much to sort out. You are always reassessing, reanalyzing, and altering your plan depending on what happens in each situation. You must assess whether the target is a person whose views need to change or a setting where practices are harming residents and whose policies promote or permit harmful practices. You must assess your leverage and the likelihood of support or resistance, what resources to mobilize, and whether your involvement is effective. All the assessing, investigating, and analyzing are for naught unless the plan is effectively implemented.

Does the situation call for a collegial or an adversarial approach? Gentleness or pressure? Will allies be needed? Should the intervention occur on several levels simultaneously or in succession? Effective advocates must analyze all of these factors and anticipate their targets' concerns, counterarguments, and needs to present

cogent cases that minimize the decision maker's perception of harm (and hence, resistance) and maximize the expected benefit to clients and even to the decision makers, if appropriate (Ziegelmueller & Kay, 1997). You must also advance cases in ways that minimize harm to you personally and limit anger, the chance of revenge, and other unproductive forms of conflict, and if at all possible, even build bridges to future cooperation. In the next section we discuss the basic elements of being a culturally competent assessor and advocate.

☾ CULTURAL COMPETENCY

Professional **cultural competence** was defined by Kohli (2003) as the ability to work successfully with people from various cultural backgrounds, including race, culture, gender, sexual orientation, physical or mental abilities, age, and national origin. She distinguished between cultural competence and cultural chauvinism: the notion that only like people can be effective practitioners (for example, that only recovering alcoholics can work effectively with clients battling alcoholism). Kohli developed a continuum of competency from Cross's (1988) six stages: cultural destructiveness, discrimination, blindness, precompetency, competence, and proficiency (Figure 4.1). Kohli (2003) also proposed a CARE framework for developing cultural competence (Constructionism, Appreciation, Realities, and Education; Figure 4.2). Testing the CARE model resulted in the development of the *Cross-Cultural Awareness Inventory* with three subscales: knowledge (5 items), attitudes and beliefs (6 items), and skills (10 items). Box 4.2 provides another way to think about dynamic cultural differences—as an advocacy dance—as you contextually go from one client to the next in different contexts.

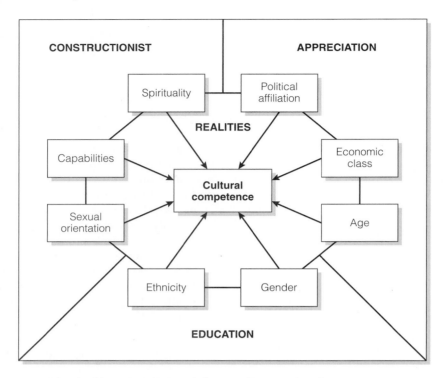

FIGURE 4.2 The *CARE* Framework for Developing Cultural Competence
Source: Kohli, 2003.

Developing Cultural Competence

The United States is experiencing accelerated diversity among culturally plural aging populations. From 1995 to 2025 the White population is expected to increase by 21.6%, the African American population by 16.5%, and the Hispanic population by 44.3% (Campbell, 1996). All advocates must have some understanding of elders in a wide range of cultural groups.

Persons in diverse cultural groups may have very different beliefs, values, mores, habits, rules, and worldviews than those who might wish to advocate on their behalf. Culture encompasses not only values but geographic and racial differences, which might differ within states, within organizations and agencies, within disciplines, within religious denominations, within communities, within families, and across generations. Men and women experience culture differently as do different ethnic groups. Advocates who practice from different theoretical and political perspectives see culture differently, and the disciplines in which they have been trained have very different cultures and perspectives as well.

The Administration on Aging (AoA) defined cultural competence as "a set of cultural behaviors and attitudes integrated into the practice methods of a system, agency, or its professionals, that enables them to work effectively in cross cultural situations" (AoA, 2001, p. 9). (A link to this organization is on the companion website.) Practicing in a culturally competent manner requires that you understand the importance of culture and have knowledge of different cultures. Promoting cultural competency is part of an emerging body of literature that stresses the importance of such practice and suggests how to practice in this manner. The goal of cultural competence is to understand the culture of the people for whom you are advocating and to implement this understanding by advocating for culturally sensitive policies and service delivery.

BOX 4.2

Another Advocacy Dance

Think about an older person as the center of attention, sitting in a comfortable chair at one end of a room. Refreshments are served, and in front of her is an array of her family members and representatives from various agencies in her community's aging network. The dancers include advocates and decision makers, and everyone is respectful of the client and of one another. She is orchestrating the meeting, and based on what she is telling them, they are brainstorming about the best opportunities to get her wants and needs met. She leads, then someone else leads, and she follows until it's her turn to lead again.

In another culture an elderly man is quite ill, and the Shaman or Medicine Man leads the community in rituals for healing. Family members and friends sit in attendance to sing, tell stories, share laughter, and rest quietly and peacefully with the sick man who is out of harmony with his world.

In both examples the elders are surrounded by people who have their best interests at heart, and both, according to their own cultures, have advocacy dancers to assist them. That it does not always happen in this halcyon manner should not prevent you from holding these images as goals for your advocacy work.

Cultural competency has two main dimensions: surface structures and deep structures. **Surface structures** include materials that integrate the obvious characteristics of your advocacy population (AoA, 2001). For example, in a long-term care facility that has a large Hispanic population, information about residents' rights should be translated into Spanish so residents do not have to rely on someone to translate. **Deep structures** include general racial and ethnic population characteristics and the factors that may influence specific behaviors (AoA, 2001). For example, it is important to know (speaking very generally) that African American families have exceptionally strong family helping networks that can be accessed to assist African Americans for whom you are advocating. However, it is equally important to recognize that these strong networks have been used, for many years in some communities, as excuses not to provide services to this population group because they have such strong networks and those networks will care for their own.

There are important cultural differences concerning aging itself. Cross-cultural gerontologists have long recognized Western culture's tendency to devalue older people who are seen as literally worthless because their productive days are

behind them (Helman, 2001). However, culturally competent advocates can expect that some cultural groups will hold elders in much deeper respect. Cultural differences in how to handle pain or incapacity or illness also vary considerably. For example, some cultures do not view dementia with the horror it is typically accorded in Western cultures that value youth and high cognition. In fact, in many non-Western societies, such as China, a certain amount of youthfulness in the very old is seen as a condition to simply be accepted and not as something abnormal or negative that requires an intervention (Helman, 2001).

In view of the many differences between America's growing number of cultural groups, advocating for greater access and opportunity will continue to be a necessity in all forms. This applies across the spectrum of assessment strategies from building empowering alliances and coalitions within the groups themselves to classic individual third party interventions at the case and highest political class or cause levels of advocacy. The needs span all areas of access and opportunity.

Consider, for example, the many health disparities that exist between African Americans and other cultural groups. The former experience greater indigence, leading to reduced health access, which translates into higher rates of hypertension, diabetes, heart attacks, strokes, prostate cancer, and many other problems, including lower rates of early detection and cure for almost all disease groups. In fact, it is a stark reality that people of color "have higher morbidity and mortality rates of almost every disease or illness, and these differentials have not diminished over time" (Syme & Berkman, 1997, p. 30).

The double jeopardy hypothesis predicts that old age may well exacerbate these culturally based inequalities when members of minority groups must deal with being both a member of a minority group *and* being old (McPherson, 1983). For example, one six-state study found that African American men in long-term care facilities were not only more likely to suffer abuse and gross neglect but were much more likely to experience unresponsive staff members than either African American women or Caucasian men or women (Huber, Borders, Netting, & Nelson, 2001). Furthermore, despite the fact that a disproportionately higher percentage of complaints were reported for African American men and women than Caucasians, advocates (who were overwhelmingly White) fully resolved a lower percentage of problems for men and women of color: 40% for African American men, 44% for African American women, 50% for Caucasian men, and 56% for Caucasian women (Huber et al., 2001).

To be sure, it is possible that the cultural lens through which minority individuals viewed the complaint resolution/satisfaction outcome was influenced by their subjective perceptions of the advocacy initiative itself or its outcome. Although speculative, cultural differences may sometimes cloud or otherwise affect communication between minority clients and their Caucasian advocates. Evidence suggests that African Americans may be more distrustful of outsiders generally and more skeptical of government-based advocates involving formal reporting (Huber et al., 2001). This distrust may even extend to caregivers who attempt to undertake internal advocacy roles.

This drives home the need for advocates to be acutely aware of their own cultural attitudes and practices, including any biases toward the client's cultural group that might influence their interactions with clients. Advocates must actively work to understand and respect their clients' subjective perceptions of the problems and desired outcomes. For example, science-oriented advocates from the dominant White culture should expect and respect the greater spiritual orientation toward healing among African Americans and, in some parts of the country, the tendency for poorer African Americans to hold heartfelt beliefs in home remedies that have been handed down through the generations. Respect for such folk practices will improve understanding and cement trust in the advocate–client relationship.

Likewise, African American advocates may experience a heightened sense of within-group solidarity and may lean toward a collectivist perspective that is inconsistent with the highly individualistic orientation of Anglo-Americans. In other words, if you are an African American advocate, you may tend to see yourself as an advocate for all African American clients in a particular facility (or collective of African Americans) rather than for one client with one problem. That said, however, it is (sadly) possible that there may be a culture of discrimination against minorities throughout a facility's staff. All advocates must be vigilant for wrongs of all kinds, and failure to understand this can result in a host of new problems.

When you advocate for people, you are speaking for them. Become adequately informed so that you can do so with credibility. To explore this collectivist tendency among people of color (not just African Americans but Asians, Hispanics, and others as well), we asked a South Korean colleague about her perspective on the culture of South Korea. We present her guidance here to demonstrate a minimal level of understanding that advocates need to have before attempting to advocate for someone of a different culture.

Our South Korean colleague said that societal rights in her country prevail over those of individuals and can be seen in a hierarchy of importance from nation to family to individual. South Korean society privileges authority over liberty, the group over the individual, and duties over rights. These are examples of deep structures that can help in understanding what kind of advocacy Korean individuals might accept and what barriers to service they might encounter. To begin with, she found it curious to hear one of us refer to *South* Korea instead of simply Korea, which, in turn, the author found curious. However, she then spoke more specifically of South Korean culture.

South Koreans' honored values are harmony, cooperation, order, and respect for the existing hierarchy. Their culture in general may be described as a part of East Asian culture, centered on Chinese Confucian tradition and characterized by *extraordinary homogeneity.* Due to the family-centered Confucian social ethics, in addition to the traditional cultural legacy of folkloristic Shamanism that stresses emotion and affections in interpersonal relations, South Koreans place great value on family and family-related matters in their lives. Our colleague refers to this kind of attitude and social behavior as "familism-directed culture" (Suk-hee Kim, personal communication, August 21, 2004).

This brief foray into Korean culture is meant to point out that it is critical to learn about the culture of your clients. This is true regardless of the culture in which you are functioning, be that Buddhism, feminism, conservative politics, Alcoholic Anonymous, or a thousand or so others. You cannot ever see their lives and problems exactly as they do, but at a minimum you must make the effort to learn some basics about how they think and the history behind their thinking. Thanks to the world of information available on the Internet, this is not difficult. When you do so, you have also made a strong statement to your clients that you took the initiative to learn enough about them to be a better informed advocate for their needs and thus more effective.

Effective advocates work hard to see through the eyes of the client. To do this is to practice advocacy through "cultural synthesis" as opposed to advocacy through "cultural invasion" (Freire, as cited in Green & Kreuter, 2005, p. 38), in which the advocate acts based on an uncritical evaluation of the advocate's own value system, without due assessment of the culturally different client's worldview. Conversely, the advocate who employs the cultural synthesis model enters the advocacy situation to learn first and to work with the client or the client's friends and family to solve the problem in a way most consistent with the client's worldview. Here, "cultural synthesis does not deny difference between the two views; indeed it is based on these differences. It does deny the invasion of the one by the other, but affirms the undeniable support each gives to the other" (p. 39).

Culturally sensitive interventions cannot occur outside of the social context of the situation (Huber, Borders, Netting, & Kautz, 2000). Huber and her colleagues pointed out that advocacy without understanding the cultural milieu of the client can result in misinterpreting needs and goals and, therefore, possibly harming clients rather than helping them. The same is true for interventions throughout all helping professions.

Culturally sensitive advocates can identify out-group cultural values by following these steps adapted from O'Donnell's (2002) recommendations to "build supportive cultural environments" (p. 205). Ask clients or involved associates (through interpreters if necessary) the following questions:

1. How do their values, beliefs, and goals relate to the current problem?
2. What would be an acceptable solution to this apparent problem?
3. What are their values and beliefs regarding this solution?
4. How might you help them achieve their desired solution?
5. Who else in the community might support their efforts to obtain a solution?

Having discussed elders' vulnerability and the advocates' cultural competence, we turn to six general issues that effective advocates keep in mind when conducting assessments.

☯ SIX GENERAL ISSUES CONSIDERED IN ASSESSMENTS

Kane (2000) identified six general issues involved in assessing older persons. First, *establish communication*—overcome any visual, auditory, or cognitive barriers at the onset. Be sensitive to speech and hearing difficulties, but do not speak loudly assuming that they have hearing problems. Family members or caregivers will sometimes answer for older persons when it is not necessary—they can usually respond for themselves. Further, having another person in the room may restrict how honestly older persons feel they can respond. If possible, find a private space and limit both the audience and any interruptions, reduce background noise and other distractions, and generally do anything you can to make the client comfortable. Communicate genuine interest and validate the client's message. Above all, mirror the client's communication style and vocabulary. Use vocabulary familiar to the client, but do not talk down to the client. Do whatever you can to see the problem from the client's point of view; try to *become* the client (Rader, 1992) or imagine walking a mile in the client's shoes. Be patient. Do not pressure the client. Do not ask leading questions, and allow elders ample time to respond to open-ended questions. Pay close attention to subtle nonverbal affective and behavioral cues that may convey critical information.

Second, *remember that it takes more time to assess an older person* given a variety of factors, such as slower response time or even an isolated elder's opportunity to talk about other things to an attentive listener (that may be you). Consider the advantages of asking open-ended questions even though this may take longer. It may be time well invested because open-ended questions tend to put people at ease by letting them control the flow of the conversation while affirming the importance of what they have to say. This does not always work, however, and sometimes advocates have to ask pithy and pointed queries to draw out confused or indecisive clients (Rader, 1992). You may need to talk more slowly or enunciate more clearly than you normally do. Adjust to elders' tempos, and ask periodically if they need to take breaks.

Third, although it is generally best to *minimize the number of assessment interviews*, this is not always possible with older clients whose frailty may invite fast fatigue. You may have to break a multidimensional geriatric assessment into several sittings. Batteries of tests that have to be administered in a certain order can also contribute to fatigue. If you return for a second interview, ask if they prefer a different time or place and begin with a summary of your first session.

Fourth, *be sensitive to elders becoming embarrassed by some questions.* Try not to have other people in the room when you are interviewing elders. Embarrassment may result if the assessment requires older persons to perform certain tasks that they can no longer do as well, or if they have to admit having problems of a sensitive nature, such as incontinence or memory loss. Determine (perhaps with your colleagues) whether you can adopt the attitude that nothing on your forms is worth embarrassing older people or causing them anguish. Even advocates may be embarrassed to ask questions about such things as physical problems or financial status.

Fifth, *recognize that assessments are often used by various stakeholders and within different contexts to do opposite things.* Know why the assessment is being conducted, and know the agendas of all interested parties. For example, an eligibility assessment may be used to screen people out; scoring well on health might actually be used to deny service. The same assessment might be used to determine level of need in another problem, opening the door to receiving a service that is needed in order to remain at home. Depending on context, answers to certain assessment questions may result in very different interventions.

Sixth, *consider time and costs of various assessment tools.* Assessments can be costly; carefully consider the cost of copyrighted instruments that must be administered by professionals. Carefully determining what is important to assess thus becomes a matter of efficiency and cost containment, as well as a necessary step in advocating for elders (Kane, 2000). Consider the notion that older people may not like or agree to responding to a battery of forms. If volunteers are conducting the assessments, do not presume that their time is of less value, and never assume that the elder's time is not just as valuable and important as that of professionals. Table 4.2 provides a summary of these six ideas.

TABLE 4.2 Six Issues That Must Be Considered When Assessing Older People

Establish communication

- Take the time before meeting with older people to identify a quiet, private place to minimize interruptions.
- Learn of any cognitive, auditory, or visual barriers before you arrive by networking with relevant professionals such as audiologists and translators.
- Arrange seating so that you are on the same eye level.
- Look older people (as with everyone else) in the eye.
- Talk to elders using words that are familiar to them, but take care not to talk down to them.
- Pay very close attention not only to what they tell you but to their nonverbal communication as well.
- Try to *become* them or see events through their senses.
- Include open-ended questions, and allow ample time for elders to respond.
- Communicate genuine interest and validate their messages.
- Be sensitive to their speech and hearing abilities, but do not begin by speaking loudly and assuming that they have hearing problems.

Avoid overly long sessions

- Interviews with older people may take longer due to their attention span and interests.
- You may need to talk more slowly or enunciate more clearly than you normally do.
- Know that your schedule is not as important as connecting with the elders and adjusting to their tempo and schedules.
- Tell those whom you are interviewing how long it may take, when you are going to move to a different topic, and ask periodically if they need breaks.

Plan for more than one interview session

- Interviews with older people may take longer, and you may need to break them up into shorter visits.
- If you go back for a second interview, begin with a summary of your first session.
- Ask if they prefer a different place or time.

Avoid embarrassment

- Be sensitive to elders being embarrassed about some of your questions, especially about personal care, abilities, and disabilities.
- Try not to have other people in the room when you are interviewing elders.
- Be sensitive to elders' physical needs such as a drink of water and perhaps the need for frequent breaks for personal care.
- Determine (perhaps with your colleagues) whether you can adopt the attitude that nothing on your forms is worth embarrassing older people or causing them anguish.

Consider the context and use of the assessment

- Consider elders' responses in relation to the setting and their circumstances (one reason for privacy).
- Know why the assessment is being conducted.
- Know the agendas of all interested parties.
- The most important thing to do is listen, listen, listen.

Weigh efficiency and cost containment

- Carefully consider the cost of copyrighted instruments.
- Be aware that older people may not like or agree to responding to a battery of forms.
- Carefully consider the time and other costs, regardless of whether you or other professionals or lay volunteers are investing the time.
- If volunteers are conducting the assessments, do not presume that their time is of less value.
- Never assume that the elder's time is not just as valuable and important as that of professionals.

☾ Quality of Care and Quality of Life

Other considerations in the assessment process are quality of care and quality of life. **Quality of care** describes how those responsible for caring for older persons (providers) are doing their jobs. Are older persons being taken care of in a quality manner? **Quality of life** is how older persons perceive their individual situations. Conceivably, one's quality of care could be high but quality of life might be seen as low, given the barriers and challenges of illnesses and aging. If the quality of care is high, however, the quality of life may be better than if care is not being well provided. Kane (2003) provided a view of why quality of life is so difficult to figure out, especially in nursing home settings. It is difficult to operationalize concepts, and quality issues require hearing the voices of older persons and knowing how they perceive the quality of their lives. Another person cannot assess someone else's quality of life for them; it requires knowing what the older person is feeling, thinking, and perceiving. Again, *become* them (Rader, 1992).

Several books examine the pros and cons of geriatric assessment, and we hope you will become familiar with the many options available. Kane and Kane (2000) provide an excellent overview of geriatric assessment. Depending on your own experience, you may be familiar with various geriatric assessment tools. Our intent is to provide guidance in how to assess a situation from the standpoint of an advocate, regardless of whether you are employed by the organization where the older person lives, by another organization in the community, or are a volunteer, friend, or family member. Whatever role you play, the questions we pose and the tasks in the following section will help you assess the needs of elderly people.

☾ Four Tasks of an Assessment Framework

Four assessment tasks are explained in this section: (a) define roles and relationships, (b) determine what is known about the older person, (c) consider the setting and the environmental context, and (d) prepare to constantly reassess and reframe. We now walk you through these tasks in assessing the needs of elderly persons. Each task is explained, then illustrated by a case example. For the most part, these cases come from our collective experiences with older people. Together these four tasks comprise a framework for the assessment process.

Task 1. Define Roles and Relationships

It may seem pretty straightforward to define your relationship to the older person or persons with or for whom you are advocating. If you are a social worker in a senior citizens' center, for example, and you are working with older people who participate in the center's activities, you are a *paid employee* advocating for a consumer of service. If you are a social worker, nurse, or physician treating older patients, you are a *professional service provider.* But relationships are not always easy to define. What if you are a social worker or a physician but have an older relative who needs an advocate? Are you functioning as a professional or as a relative, and what are the differences? Are you an external or an internal advocate? Is your role shifting in the process? Does it matter?

Ferrel

Ferrel is an artist who spent his life freelancing with various studios in the city, working odd hours. Even in his late 70s his hand-drawn illustrations were steady and beautifully designed, but with the advent of computer graphics, graphic design was transformed from time-consuming (costly) hand work to technology-produced work that takes far less time. Ferrel had never considered the possibility that he would not be able to work until he died, and therefore he had no retirement savings or pension plan. In addition, he made some early decisions that would affect his old age.

He was a prisoner of war in World War II, and he had joined the Vietnam War protest movement in the 1960s. He had decided not to pay taxes to a government that would support such a war and had filed no tax returns. He owned no property, held no licenses, had no bank accounts, paid no Social Security, received and paid everything in cash, lived in a single room occupancy hotel, and received health care from the Veterans Administration (VA) hospital, and only when it was desperately needed. For all practical purposes, he did not exist on paper except for his discharge papers from the Army Air Force.

When hand illustration was no longer a viable alternative, Ferrel had no income from any source. He was destitute. His older brother who lived in another state sent him enough money to pay room and board, but this was a drain on the older brother's monthly retirement income. Ferrel had no spouse (he was twice divorced) and no children. His brother's only daughter, a social worker, was concerned about her father trying to support Ferrel, and she knew that Ferrel should be eligible for a VA pension. She was particularly concerned about the strain, both financially and emotionally, that this situation was putting on her father. Thus, her father was her primary concern. She also wanted to seek professional help for Ferrel, but he did not want anyone to know about his situation because he was fearful that the IRS might "come after me after all these years."

The niece suggested to Ferrel that he go to the VA and apply for benefits. He replied, "do you want to put your old uncle in the pokey?" She replied, "If I thought the VA and the IRS had information systems that could talk to one another, I would respond to your question. And even if by some stroke of fate their information systems could interface, at least you would have a roof over your head. Believe me, if you end up in jail, I'll find an advocate in Chicago who will get an 80-year-old POW out of jail." This was not exactly what she would have said to her uncle had he been a client, but this relationship was defined as a niece-uncle relationship. Eventually Ferrel applied for benefits and found that indeed he did qualify for a VA pension. It wasn't a great deal of money, but it would cover rent for a one-room apartment and enough food for the month.

The niece persisted in her attempts to assist, asking Ferrel's permission to contact the local Area Agency on Aging and their case management system. It cost $200 for the case manager to conduct a geriatric assessment, and the niece agreed to pay the cost. Based on the assessment and knowledge of eligibility considerations, the case manager found that Ferrel would qualify for a number of programs including food stamps and senior housing. Ferrel felt that the pension was enough to survive on, and he did not want to use the services for which he qualified. His health care was covered by the VA, and he made periodic treks to the hospital.

Questions to Consider Regarding Ferrel

Ferrel's story raises a number of definitional concerns. It was important for the niece to clarify with Ferrel that she was actually advocating for her father, who was supporting Ferrel, and that her father was her primary concern. She had to persuade Ferrel to physically go to the VA benefits office because he had to present in person. She would not take no for an answer—a stand a niece could take but a professional could not. Once he qualified for the pension and would no longer be a drain on her father's resources, she focused on Ferrel's needs. She advocated for his needs by consulting a case manager who could become a professional advocate for Ferrel, informing him of services for which he would qualify. The case manager was paid by the niece, but her client was Ferrel. Although the niece could have done a geriatric assessment because she had done many in her social work role, she realized that she could not be effective as both a social worker and a niece, and that she needed to be the niece. The case manager, on the other hand, was working strictly in a professional role, as were the health care professionals at the VA hospital who addressed Ferrel's physical needs.

In this situation a niece, an older man, and a case manager interacted. These roles seemed fairly straightforward in the beginning, but the niece was a professional social worker. Perhaps she could have conducted an assessment and not paid another person to do the same thing. Yet, if she wanted to remain in her role as niece, it made sense to clearly define that boundary and hire a professional to conduct the assessment. Being both a family member and a professional can become confusing to everyone when emotions are involved.

In many situations, defining your relationship may seem fairly simple—you are a practitioner who is advocating for a client. But what happens when that older client moves from your senior center to the hospital? Suddenly, you are an outside (external) professional visiting your client in someone else's system. If you want to advocate for your client, you will need to talk with persons who have credibility in the hospital system, perhaps contacting the discharge planner or the social worker. In consideration of privacy issues, they may not feel comfortable even talking with you, plus you are outside your base of operation.

Consider this scenario. You are a nurse in the hospital and have worked with this patient for 2 weeks to get her ready to leave the hospital. You know what medications she is on, what her routine has been, how far she has come, and a host of other things. Your patient is then taken by ambulance to a rehabilitation facility where everyone has to start from scratch to assess their new patient. Even more important, what happens if no one is following this person through the maze of services involved in her recuperation? Is there a family member, friend, or case manager who has the whole picture? Are older people able to advocate for themselves when they have been moved from place to place and are just trying to regain their strength? In other words, roles and relationships will be continually shifting and changing. In defining relationships, consider these questions:

1. What is your role and relationship with this older person now? Are you internal or external in the current setting?
2. How has your role changed or shifted, and do you anticipate having to redefine your role and relationship? If so, what does this redefinition mean for you?
3. Who is playing a significant role in this situation or set of situations? Who has credibility to help you advocate for or with the older person? Are family members or significant others involved?
4. Does anyone have the role of following this person across the continuum of care, and if so, who is that person? Is it your role to do so?

Task 2. Determine What Is Known About the Older Person

We have pointed out that multiple assessment tools focus on all domains of an older person's life. In addition, site-specific assessment tools are required in various settings, and these become part of the permanent record. For example, the law requires that the Minimum Data Set (MDS) assessment be conducted for all residents (no matter how long the stay) in any nursing home in the United States (Mor et al., 2003; Nursing Home Compare, 2002).

When older persons move from one setting to another, chances are they will be asked a multitude of questions in the screening, assessment, and reassessment processes in each location. When the two settings have similar requirements, many of the questions will be redundant. This information can be shared among internal advocates within each system, but the Health Insurance Portability and Accountability Act (HIPAA) restricts the information that can be made available to advocates outside the immediate system. An external advocate may have to have a health care or durable power of attorney to gain access to these assessment data.

Mabel and Roy

Mabel had chronic obstructive pulmonary disease (COPD) and had been on oxygen for several years. She had a number of complaints and ailments that had accumulated over the years. Her best days were ones in which she did not have to take a bath and could watch the cable station with reruns of all the westerns. *Bonanza* and *Gunsmoke* were favorites. Roy, on the other hand, was in reasonably good health. He was Mabel's caregiver, literally making the difference in whether she could remain in their independent living apartment.

Roy had a bad fall and had his hip pinned just as Mabel was undergoing tests at the same hospital. Both were discharged to a nursing home in which they were assigned to the same room. Having no children or living siblings, they depended on several older friends to visit them and to bring them mail from their apartment. Mabel had trouble sleeping, and Roy was not adjusting well to a nursing home environment. He was loud and used language that offended the staff, language he used in their apartment that Mabel had learned to ignore. She was somewhat embarrassed by his antics and suggested they give him a sedative at night so they both could sleep.

Mabel had a couple of really bad days in which she was in a lot of pain and was sent back to the hospital where she subsequently died. Roy was left alone in the nursing home. Mabel had been his durable power of attorney and he was hers, so he was left without anyone in that role. Thinking that they were helping him deal with Mabel's death, staff continued giving him the sedative at night.

When Roy had entered the hospital, he had been taking one prescription drug for acid reflux (heartburn) and an over-the-counter ointment for dry skin. By the time he had gone through the hospital and spent a month in the nursing home, Roy was taking 11 prescription drugs. Mabel had not been able to monitor his medication, and nursing home staff had inherited a number of drugs that were prescribed post-surgery. In addition, Roy had accumulated the sedative and another controlled substance in the course of his rehabilitation, which was not going well. He was just too sleepy and tired to make much progress in rehab, and staff attributed much of his lethargy to his extreme grief over Mabel's death. He remarked to a friend that "I'm surprised that I am so calm over Mabel's death," indicating that he was in somewhat of a drug-induced fog that kept him from fully feeling the impact of losing her.

When another friend visited, she recognized immediately that Roy was not even close to being himself. She asked if she could see a list of his medications, and the certified nursing assistant (CNA) shared the list with her. Although the CNA should never have allowed her to see the list, the friend recognized at least four controlled substances that could have severe interactions in older patients. She began to think about how to advocate for Roy and exactly who to approach at the home or physician's office, yet she recognized that she didn't have a legal leg to stand on. As the friend was pondering her options, Roy took a

sudden turn for the worse: the drugs diminished his oxygen supply, and he died that night.

Mabel and Roy's situation reveals how complicated things can become and how quickly conditions can change. One month prior to Roy's death, he was driving his car, buying groceries, and taking Mabel out to lunch when she felt like it. He provided care for her on a daily basis, helping her with her ADLs and IADLs. Once Roy fell, a series of problems followed: Mabel could not go home without a caregiver, Roy accumulated numerous drugs while in the hospital, and Roy's durable power of attorney (Mabel) died. In a very short period of time, Roy was transformed from an active elder in good health to a person who nodded off while sitting in his chair. Staff began to ask his friends, "When did his dementia start?" and soon he was labeled as demented. His identify as a self-sufficient person living in the community disappeared, and within a month he was dead.

Questions to Consider Regarding Mabel and Roy

Assessments of Mabel and Roy were conducted in the hospital setting. Being in a medical setting, these assessments were appropriately focused on their ability to function and on their physical health, given the nature of that environment and the physical challenges they both faced. Released to the rehab unit of a nursing home, both were assessed using the MDS, and an important focus was on their ability to perform ADLs and IADLs. Mabel's suggestion that Roy could use a sedative added to the number of drugs that he had already accumulated, yet she was recommending this as his durable power of attorney and his wife. She thought this would make sleeping easier for both of them. Once she was dead, staff continued the sedative, and no one was there to question the number of medications he was taking. The physician was not on the premises, and the staff assumed Roy was a demented old man, having never seen him as the vital person he was just one month prior. Friends assumed Roy was grieving and therefore unresponsive, except for the one friend who recognized that he might be overmedicated. As an advocate, she stood little chance of making a difference because she had no power within the system or legal recourse as would a power of attorney, blood relation, or guardian.

In deciding on an assessment plan, consider these questions:

1. What assessments have been conducted, and who has access to these data?
2. What do the assessment data tell you?
3. What additional data need to be collected (e.g., medications) so that you can have a more complete snapshot of the situation?
4. What do these additional data indicate about what needs to change? How do they help you in defining and prioritizing any problems?
5. Whose vigilance brought the problems or incident to light?
6. Does the elder have a health care power of attorney, durable power of attorney, and advanced directive in place?

Task 3. Consider the Setting and the Environmental Context

Advocacy-related concerns arise in multiple settings and often traverse multiple locations. It behooves the advocate to know as much as possible about the setting in which the older person is located. It is particularly important to know the rights you have within this setting and whether they are informally assumed or documented in writing. If you are employed by the group, agency, or institution providing services to the elder, you probably have more credibility within the system than if you come from another setting. Sometimes, however, working in the setting is problematic. You may be too close to the situation to be objective, or you may feel disempowered within your work environment. Knowing whom you can trust to offer alternative perspectives on the situation you are assessing, either within or external to your immediate work location, is helpful.

In Chapter 1 we briefly examined the continuum of care and the many possible settings in which older persons may be located. Possibilities include a full complement of environments from living alone in a single family dwelling to being totally institutionalized in a long-term care

setting. Just because one setting is relevant today, does not mean that others may not be more suitable tomorrow as older persons move through an array of services (hopefully on a continuum of care), being admitted and discharged from facility to facility during chronic or acute care episodes, or as one enters multiple settings as an outpatient or transitory visitor.

Environment or setting can be viewed along four domains—"the physical, social, psychological, and cultural—each composed of characteristics that individually or collectively affect the physical, social, and cognitive functioning of the older person" (Cutler, 2000, p. 360). Whereas the **physical environment** includes everything from stairs to toileting facilities, the **social environment** focuses on the interactions among people in that setting and the degree of privacy or crowdedness. The **psychological environment** includes how the person is affected by the setting. For example, how are the interactions of people or the memories attached to this setting perceived? The **cultural environment** is attuned to values, norms, symbols, and traditions that may or may not be familiar to the older person. Tools are available to assess the fit of older adults within the environmental setting in which they are currently located (Cutler, 2000). You may want to access such tools in order to gain a perspective on the fit of person-in-environment.

In Chapter 2 we presented a brief overview of social systems, referring to different levels of conflict that can arise. Now is the time to assess whether the situation is static or dynamic and how much tension and conflict is present. If the older person must contend with the cultures of multiple settings or groups, understanding the connections across groups and organizations is relevant. Madeline's story, which follows, reflects just how complicated it can be to assess a set of issues across diverse settings. It also points out the importance of carefully assessing context.

Madeline's Story

Madeline is 90, and she has lived in the city her entire life. In fact, she still lives in the home where her extended family (all of whom are now deceased) have resided for more than 100 years. Her large brick house is in disarray, with loose cement breaking through cracks in the outer wall. Paint around the doorways and porch has weathered, and only small patches of color remain.

Madeline served as a missionary for more than 40 years and hoards every useable item she finds. There are few pathways left inside the crumbling walls of her home, which is lined with cardboard boxes filled with every conceivable item one could imagine. She is often seen pushing a grocery cart of items collected from the various city dumpsters within walking distance of her neighborhood. Her backyard, once a place where seasonal plants were groomed, contains a large tent filled with plastic crates of clothing, shoes, children's toys, puzzles, and wicker baskets. She is very clear in saying that nothing should be wasted, as she had witnessed extreme poverty in her missionary work and is appalled at what is thrown away in the United States.

Her junk-filled house is situated among others that are selling for $350,000, and city inspectors have condemned her home. Adult Protective Services workers have conducted multiple assessments and have removed Madeline from her home, placing her in an assisted living facility for lower income elders. Ironically, the assisted living facility is just a few blocks from her home.

A local newspaper reporter learned of Madeline's plight and published a human interest story on the front page of the Sunday paper. She revealed that Madeline had served as a foreign missionary, retiring to her family birthplace when her mother became chronically ill. After her mother died, now more than 25 years ago, Madeline began collecting everything she could find and recycling every item that could be given to needy persons in the community. The reporter described Madeline as a bright intelligent woman with strong, steel gray eyes and a good sense of humor. She walked much faster than most people her age and credited never having driven a car as "keeping me in shape." She was kind to her neighbors, even though she was very aware that they called the authorities about her living conditions and complained that rodents are infesting the property.

The newspaper reporter picked Madeline up at the assisted living facility, and they walked through the yard of her home. As they strolled among piles of what the neighbors have called "garbage," Madeline explained that she realizes they just do not understand but that she has "seen street children in South America who would be thrilled to have even a handful of the items" she stores under the tent in her backyard. Madeline spoke to the reporter in both English and Spanish, facile with her bilingual command of language. She felt her rights had been violated by the city officials who evicted her from her home and remarked that "I don't think it is fair for the public to be subsidizing my care in assisted living, and frankly I don't need assisted living. I devoted my life to God's work, not to the government. I do not even agree with the current administration. I just want to be left alone to find people who can use what I have. God has given me so much."

Questions to Consider Regarding Madeline

Madeline's situation is played out in two basic settings: the neighborhood where people live independently and an assisted living facility where she temporarily resides. A number of groups and organizations are involved in sorting out the dilemmas that have arisen: Madeline's neighbors, city government, Adult Protective Services, and even the staff of the local newspaper and the reading public. Conceivably, once brought to local attention, the religious community will have a perspective on Madeline's plight as well.

Defining and redefining roles and relationships (Task 1) is closely tied to assessing settings and context because multiple stakeholders are inherent in any context. In Madeline's situation, the newspaper reporter with a journalism background is an advocate because she brings Madeline's plight to the attention of the larger community—possibly advocating for her autonomy. Certainly the Adult Protective Services workers are advocating for Madeline to be in a safe, clean location (assisted living), a beneficent stance. They are not necessarily advocating for what Madeline wants for herself: autonomy. Left alone, she would continue to live in her family home and collect as many discarded items as she could find, with the intent of recycling them to people in need.

City building codes, public health laws, neighborhood ordinances, and a host of other legal considerations interfered with Madeline continuing to live as she has chosen. The context in which she lives is a neighborhood in which property values, sanitation concerns, and neighbors' attitudes carry considerable weight. One could even argue that advocates for a healthy neighborhood would have to intervene in Madeline's life for the sake of the greater good versus her own personal desire to continue to hoard.

Context cannot be ignored, and the advocate (no matter the situation) must consider the bigger picture that transcends the specific needs of one person. It is often difficult to balance what is known about the larger context. The following questions are particularly helpful in recognizing the feasibility of individual need in the context of an environment or setting.

1. What is known about the larger environment and the specific setting in which you and the older person find yourselves?
2. What tools are available to help you assess the environment and setting physically? Socially? Psychologically? Culturally?
3. If multiple settings are involved, what is known about the relationships between them?
4. What is the legal or policy context in which you are trying to advocate?

Task 4. Prepare to Constantly Reassess and Reframe

We hope we have demonstrated just how complicated a process assessment really is. First you have to figure out what needs to be assessed and for what purpose; then you need to know what data already exist and what additional data you need to gather. Knowing what data are needed does not solve the challenge of locating ways (tools and methods) of actually conducting the assessment. For many practitioners, that tool is you—a human instrument who can see, hear, and perceive—making judgments on what these data mean. Standardized tools may help, but they provide only a snapshot in time. It is up to you to interpret what the tools reveal and to watch for changes, sometimes subtle and sometimes not so subtle, that reveal new information to be considered in assessing the situation. This process of constantly reassessing and reframing means that the problem or problems originally identified will shift and change.

Changing Conditions

In **Ferrel**'s case, the environment shifted and hand illustrations were no longer in demand. Had technology not changed so radically, he might have been able to support himself by continuing to freelance in the Chicago area. Instead, he was destitute. The setting in which he found himself changed, and rather than being a successful freelance artist he became an old man without any financial resources.

Mabel and Roy lived independently in a rental apartment, and as long as Roy was able to care for Mabel, their quality of life was reasonably high. But one acute episode, Roy's fall and subsequent hospitalization, cast them both in the role of nursing home residents. With the introduction of new medications, Roy was seen as a demented old man—but by whose assessment?

Madeline ended up in an assisted living facility. In one day she went from living at home collecting every useable material for those who had less than she to being labeled a hoarder and having her house condemned. Depending on who was assessing her situation, she was either a strong former missionary with a charitable zeal or an eccentric old woman living in unsanitary, unsafe conditions.

Questions to Consider Regarding Changing Situations

Each situation presented in this chapter, as well as those that you will encounter, can be viewed from multiple perspectives. Assessments will differ depending on who is assessing the situation and the purpose of that assessment. Therefore, in addition to the questions we have already posed, we add a few more that may assist in the continual assessment and reassessment process:

1. How do you define the problem or challenge you are facing? How has your definition shifted in the assessment process?
2. Who are the primary stakeholders? What relationships are strong? Are some relationships damaged?
3. How vulnerable is the elder? Is the older person as involved as possible? Do you need a proxy?
4. What resources are available?
5. What patterns are emerging? Is this an individual situation, or does it affect a group of elders?

Answering these and other questions will assist you in developing an advocacy plan in the next chapter. Note that the last question focuses on whether the situation you have assessed affects one person or many others. This has implications for where you will intervene—on the interpersonal, group, organizational, or community level.

☾ Summary

We began this chapter with an example of a well-intended but faulty assessment and introduced the importance of evaluating clients' needs in the context of the larger environment. The gerontological advocate must know how to assess informally but also must know how to select and use formal assessment tools. The advocate should focus on understanding the person-in-environment, knowing that settings may be changing even as the assessment process continues.

The five assessment Ws were presented. *Why assess* depends on the purpose of the assessment and whether you are simply screening to determine eligibility for services or presenting problems or whether there is a need to conduct a multidimensional assessment. *What to assess* depends on having a clear understanding of what needs to be measured and evaluated. *Whom to assess* is always the older person in need first, but if that person is not able to communicate his or her needs, a proxy may be used. *When to assess* may be dictated by what is happening and whether this is an urgent situation. *Who should assess* depends on the situation as well. There are many contingencies to consider in the assessment process.

Elders are vulnerable in a number of arenas, and it is important to be a culturally competent advocate. We described Cross's six stage continuum of becoming a culturally competent advocate and Kohli's CARE framework. We examined Kane's six general issues to consider when advocating for elders: establishing communication, taking appropriate time, minimizing the assessment time if possible (although this may be very difficult with frail elders), reducing potential embarrassment, knowing what stakeholders will have access to the data collected, and cost containment.

We defined quality of life and quality of care and elaborated on a framework with four tasks: (a) define roles and relationships, (b) determine what is known about the older person, (c) consider the setting and the environmental context, and (d) prepare to constantly reassess and reframe. These four tasks are accompanied by a series of questions that the advocate can use as a guide in the assessment process. The full advocacy assessment framework appears in Table 4.3.

The key to an on-target assessment is investigating the incident at both the client and larger systems levels. Assessment must include information directly from the older person involved, when possible, both formal and informal factors in systems, knowledge of available resources and where the power lies, cultural factors, appropriate assessment tools, and well-honed investigative skills. In Chapter 5 we turn to the importance of investigation.

TABLE 4.3 Advocacy Assessment Framework

Task 1. Define Roles and Relationships

1. What is your role and relationship with this older person now? Are you an internal or external advocate in the current setting?

2. How has your role changed or shifted, and do you anticipate having to redefine your role and relationship? If so, what does this redefinition mean for you?

3. Who are the persons who play significant roles in this situation or set of situations? Who has credibility to help you advocate for or with the older person? Are family members or significant others involved?

4. Does anyone have the role of following this person across the continuum of care, and if so, who is that person? Is it your role to do so?

Task 2. Determine What Is Known About the Older Person

1. What assessments have been conducted, and who has access to these data?

2. What do assessment data indicate about the older person's conditions and needs?

3. What additional data need to be collected (e.g., medications) so that you can have a more complete snapshot of the situation?

4. What do these additional data indicate about what needs to change? How do they help you in defining and prioritizing any problems?

5. Whose vigilance brought the problems or incident to light?

6. Does the elder have a health care power of attorney, durable power of attorney, and advanced directive in place?

Task 3. Consider the Setting and the Environmental Context

1. What is known about the larger environment and the specific settings in which you and the older person find yourselves?

2. What tools are available to help you assess the environment and setting physically, socially, psychologically, and culturally?

3. If multiple settings are involved, what is known about the relationships between them?

4. What is the legal or policy context in which you are trying to advocate?

Task 4. Prepare to Constantly Reassess and Reframe

1. How do you define the problem or challenge you are facing? How has your definition shifted in the assessment process?

2. Who are the primary stakeholders? What relationships are strong? Are some relationships damaged?

3. How vulnerable is the elder? Is the older person as involved as possible? Do you need a proxy?

4. What resources are available?

5. What patterns are emerging? Is this an individual situation, or does it affect a group of elders?

DISCUSSION QUESTIONS AND EXERCISES

1. At the beginning of this chapter you were introduced to Alice, an older person who had been admitted to a locked Alzheimer's unit against her will. Read this case again and answer the questions in the assessment framework from the perspective of the staff advocate in Alice's case. Do you need to add other questions to your assessment to fully understand the situation?

2. Consider the 5 Ws presented in this chapter in light of a situation that you have encountered in your own experience. Using that situation as an example, ask the question posed by each W, and describe how you would respond.

3. How might you overcome communication challenges such as visual and auditory barriers so that you can effectively conduct an assessment?

4. Discuss the trade-offs in efficiency you might make when it takes an excessive amount of time to accurately assess a situation. What other environmental demands might compel you to speed up the assessment process and at what costs to the older person?

5. What factors would you consider in deciding the number of interviews you might need to conduct your assessment?

6. What strategies might you use to reduce embarrassment in the assessment process? Think about what embarrasses you, and discuss what types of questions you might be hesitant to ask. How would you determine if it was your own hesitancy, the older person's embarrassment, or both that are influencing the assessment process?

7. Consider the various uses of even the same assessment process. For example, an eligibility assessment may be used to screen people out if they are in good health or it may open the door for a person to remain at home. What are the potential ethical dilemmas that might arise in situations where assessments are used for multiple purposes?

8. How might you be more culturally sensitive in the assessment process? What principles might you use to assure sensitivity?

9. Discuss the differences in the concepts quality of care and quality of life. Can you think of a situation in which quality of care actually reduces quality of life? Can you think of a situation in which quality of life is high but quality of care is low? How do you see these two concepts interacting, and why is it important to distinguish one from the other?

10. Reread Ferrel's case and answer the questions under Task 1 (define roles and relationships) from the niece's perspective.

11. Reread Mabel and Roy's case and answer the questions under Task 2 (determine what is known about the older person) from their friend's perspective. Answer the same questions from the perspective of a staff person at the nursing home. Do your responses differ depending on the role you play? Why or why not?

12. Reread Madeline's case and answer the questions under Task 3 (consider the setting and the environmental context) from the local newspaper reporter's perspective. Now ask the same questions from the perspective of the Adult Protective Services worker who placed Madeline in assisted living. Are your responses different? Why or why not?

ADDITIONAL READINGS

Allen, R. S., Burgio, L. D., Roth, D. L., Ragsdale, R., Gerstle, J., Bourgeois, M. S., et al. (2003, December). Revised Memory and Behavior Problems Checklist—Nursing Home: Instrument development and measurement of burden among certified nursing assistants. *Psychology & Aging, 18*(4), 886–895.

Binder, E. F., Miller, J. P., & Ball, L. J. (2001, October). Development of a test of physical performance for the nursing home setting. *The Gerontologist, 41*(5), 671–679.

Feinberg, L. F. (2003–2004). The state of the art of caregiver assessment. *Generations, 28*(4), 24–32.

Iverson, G. L., Hopp, G. A., DeWolfe, K., & Solomons, K. (2002, May). Measuring change in psychiatric symptoms using the Neuropsychiatric Inventory: Nursing Home Version. *International Journal of Geriatric Psychiatry, 17*(5), 438–443.

Lange, R. T., Hopp, G. A., & Kang, N. (2004, May). Psychometric properties and factor structure of the Neuropsychiatric Inventory: Nursing Home Version in an elderly neuropsychiatric population. *International Journal of Geriatric Psychiatry, 19*(5), 440–448.

National Citizens Coalition for Nursing Home Reform. (1988). *The rights of nursing home residents.* Washington, DC: Service Employee's International Union (partly funded by the Health Care Financing Administration, contract No. 87-0392, HSQB-87-0013).

Rantz, M. J., Mehr, D. R., Petroski, G. F., Madsen, R. W., Popejoy, L. L., Hicks, L. L., et al. (2000). Initial field testing of an instrument to measure observable indicators of nursing home care quality. *Journal of Nursing Care Quality, 14*(3), 1–12.

Rubenstein, L. Z. (1990). Assessment instruments. In W. B Abrams, R. Berkow, & A. J. Fletcher (Eds.), *The Merck manual of geriatrics* (pp. 1189–1200). Rahway, NJ: Merck Sharp & Dohme Research Laboratories.

Ryden, M. B., Gross, C. R., Savik, K., Snyder, M., Oh, H. L., Jang, Y. P., et al. (2000). Development of a measure of resident satisfaction with the nursing home. *Research in Nursing & Health, 23*(3), 237–245.

Sloane, P. D., Mitchell, C. M., Weisman, G., Zimmerman, S., Long Foley, K. M., Lynn, M., et al. (2002, March). Therapeutic Environment Screening Survey for Nursing Homes (TESS-NH): An observational instrument for assessing the physical environment of institutional settings for persons with dementia. *Journals of Gerontology: Series B: Psychological Sciences and Social Sciences, 57B*(2), S69–S78.

Valk, M., Post, M. W., Cools, M., Cools, H. J., & Schrijvers, G. A. J. P. (2001, May). Measuring disability in nursing home residents: Validity and reliability of a newly developed instrument. *Journals of Gerontology: Series B: Psychological Sciences and Social Sciences, 56B*(3), P187–P191.

CHAPTER FIVE

Investigating and Analyzing Situations

. . . the primary emphasis for advocates is empirical evidence. LENS (2005, p. 233)

BOX 5.1

MOLLY

Molly was recently admitted to Hillside Haven Convalescent Center. She is a nonambulatory patient with late stage dementia, and is totally dependent in almost all of her activities of daily living. Her daughter, Zoe, is dedicated to her care and has stood beside her through some pretty bad experiences in prior hospital and assisted living settings (bed sores, poor grooming, and weight loss). These experiences had been very frustrating to Zoe, and as a result, she had begun to see herself as a reform-oriented patient advocate. In fact, Zoe had developed the perspective that many professional caregivers are frauds and really do not care. "So often," she explained to a friend, "you'll see that they just rush through their routines so they can punch their time cards and go home and forget this place. Yeah, there are some good ones, but they are few and far between." Her expectations for her mother's care were high—the staff felt that they were very unrealistic.

Zoe spent well over 4 hours a day in the facility. When Zoe wasn't with her mother, her daughter, Meg, was often there. Both helped care for Molly. They assisted in Molly's feeding, bathing, and grooming. They believed Molly would suffer if they didn't pitch in. They also involved themselves with the care and welfare of

the other residents, assuming a watchdog role. Ever vigilant, they were quick to jump on errant aides for any and every perceived mistake. Their litany of complaints ranged from concerns about aides with poor communication skills to breaches of infection control. And woe betide any aide with a surly attitude!

Zoe and Meg were highly knowledgeable about nursing home regulations because they had taken the training to become volunteer ombudsmen. However, when they found out that they couldn't be assigned to Hillside Convalescent, they were upset. "I'd like to help in other facilities," Zoe explained to her training coordinator, "but I really want to be assigned to Hillside—I could do a lot of good there if I only had some real power. Besides that, I *know* the place!" The coordinator explained to Zoe that assignment to a facility where her mom lived would be an insurmountable conflict of interest. Zoe left the program a bit disgusted, but at least, she thought, she had learned a great deal. Plus, she had copies of the voluminous nursing home regulations, and her understanding of these regulations would prove to be a formidable source of power.

(continued)

BOX 5.1 *(continued)*

As a rule, the aides cringed whenever Zoe walked into the facility. Meg was more passive, playing more of a silent observer/reporter role. She seldom confronted anybody directly, but she filed regular status reports with her very controlling mom. Meg was quiet, not outgoing at all, and seldom talked to the staff. Zoe was much more outgoing, quite charming when she wasn't angry. When mad, however, she really spun out of control. Her emotions were easily inflamed, and she was highly confrontational—shooting rapid fire from the hip, often making accusations, sometimes backed with facts, sometimes not, and interspersed with questions designed to throw her opponents on the horns of a dilemma. She was a poor listener, used a blaming style, and literally screamed and cried as the arguments heated up.

Although most of the staff saw the terrible twosome as meddlesome, unrealistic, and unfair, Zoe had made close friends with two aides. She lavished attention on Sherry, a highly conscientious and hard working aide, and Mel, a less competent, but affable young man. Zoe had these two over for dinner on several occasions and had even helped them with some personal troubles at home. Sherry and Mel funneled all sorts of insider information to Zoe either directly or through Meg. Consequently, Zoe was acutely aware of many subsurface problems and issues such as who was getting fired and who was on warning.

Zoe tended to blame the Director of Nursing (DoN), Ann, a 52-year-old experienced nurse, for the general state of things at Hillside. Ann was pretty prickly herself—a strong woman who could easily become defensive. She had written Zoe off as a petty person who enjoyed intimidating her staff. She would have none of this. She looked for opportunities to put Zoe in her place. Before long, the angry encounters between Zoe and Ann became legendary. They were so common and ugly that Hillside's administrator, Bob, was finally forced to take action.

Bob is a young administrator (age 30), and this was just his second facility. He is an affable peacemaker, a good communicator who could calm Zoe down a bit and get her to see reason. Bob didn't like to confront, but he recognized that the relationship between Ann and Zoe was irreparable. He had tried to stay out of the feud between the two strong women, but a recent incident at Hillside forced his hand.

Two weeks ago, Meg had been visiting her grandmother and had heard some commotion in the hall. She wandered down the hall to see what was going on but was intercepted by Ann, who told Meg to go back to her grandmother's room and mind her own business. Meg immediately became suspicious and called her mother on the cell phone. "Mom, you'd better get over here, something is going on." In less than an hour Zoe was in the facility. When the coast was clear, she started to do some digging. In short order, she learned from Sherry that a resident named Joe had just died. He had choked to death when an inexperienced aide had served him waffles and sausage instead of his required soft diet. The aide hadn't recognized his special needs and had just left the tray underneath his nose . . . and he soon stopped breathing.

Hearing this, Zoe immediately called the ombudsman program and Adult Protective Services. They undertook an investigation and found the facility negligent. This incident resulted in some heavy fines and some very bad press in the local newspaper.

Ann quickly put two and two together and, through her own investigation, determined that Zoe had called in the authorities. This enraged Ann, and she confronted Bob with an ultimatum: "It's either her or me. She's grinding down my staff, and she's really laying in wait for all of us—including you! This would never have gotten into the papers if it weren't for her and her little spy daughter!" Bob agreed, and together they devised a plan. On the grounds that Zoe was severely disruptive, she would henceforth be barred from all common areas in the facility, or from talking to the staff, except in the case of an emergency. Her time in the facility would be limited to no more than 4 hours in the evening, and she would have to be out of the facility no later than 10 p.m. Her presence was also restricted to the A-wing hallway and her mother's room. If she had any concerns, she would not approach or correct the staff directly but would contact Bob. Bob would share his personal phone number with Zoe.

When Bob presented this plan to Zoe, she went ballistic. "I know who's behind this. You're being led around by your nose by that Ann. She's a bad woman, and she's going to ruin your career. You know better than this!" Bob tried to calm her down. He explained that she was unduly stressing his direct care staff and that this was beginning to negatively affect patient care. But Zoe was not in a listening mood. She launched into blistering language and near hysteria and stormed out of the facility.

Zoe called Ron, the local volunteer ombudsman, and explained the situation. The next day Ron met with Bob. "I think your plan is too restrictive," he advised Bob. "You may have a case to limit Zoe's interaction with your aides, but you cannot bar her from the facility after 10 p.m. nor can you restrict her visitation time to 4 hours each night. This would be a violation of her mother's rights." Bob countered that Molly was incapable of making decisions and thus had no real rights, and that as the administrator he was responsible for the well-being of his staff.

Despite Ron's best efforts, he made no headway with Bob. Things only got worse when Bob invited Ann into the discussion. Ann was characteristically blunt: "Zoe needs therapy—her guilt about her mother's condition makes her irrational. Her harsh treatment of my frontline staff is negatively affecting patient care. She is highly disruptive—end of story." Ron continued to insist that their planned visitation restrictions were without legal justification, but it was clear they had reached an impasse.

Ron reported his failure to Zoe, who exploded. She began attacking Bob and the ombudsman program. "What kind of government program uses volunteers to take on the nursing home industry?" She was scathing: "My mother's rights are being violated. Moreover, this whole cockamamie plan is nothing more than an unlawful retaliation for my reporting Joe's death." This last allegation struck Ron as credible. He called his paid supervisor, Jim, and asked for assistance.

Jim agreed that the nursing home's restrictions were too extreme and that the whole thing seemed retaliatory. He made an appointment to see Bob. After agreeing to meet with Jim, Bob called Ann, who advised Bob to call in a corporate attorney. When Jim showed up to meet with Bob, the administrator's office was full. Sitting next to Bob were Ann and Candice, an attorney from Hillside's corporate office. Jim laid out his case—but to deaf ears. Bob sat in silence. Candice proved to be intractable, and she doggedly attacked Zoe, citing Bob's duty to protect his staff and arguing that Zoe's morale crushing intrusions were seriously disrupting patient care. This meeting ended in another impasse.

Meanwhile, Zoe was digging up more dirt on the facility through Sherry and Mel. She had easily convinced these two that the facility was totally in the wrong and that Ann and her incompetent boss needed to be brought down. All she needed was their help in revealing the *truth* about Hillside. They were only too eager

(continued)

BOX 5.1 *(continued)*

to comply as neither cared for Ann, who they saw as the real power in the facility. In less than a week they had funneled pages of problems to Zoe: bed sores, medication errors, unexplained injuries (apparently due to falls) that had not been reported to Adult Protective Services as required, as well as inappropriate use of restraints and many other issues. Sherry had recruited several other aides to the cause.

Zoe shared this information with Jim, who felt that he had been unfairly ambushed by the facility. Jim called the state ombudsman, Joan, and explained the situation regarding the alleged retaliation against Zoe; he also shared the new allegations of poor care and patient harm. Joan pulled together her top investigators, issued several subpoenas, and ordered her task force to descend on the hapless facility.

And descend they did. They quickly substantiated numerous complaints ranging from cold coffee to negligent physical abuse and determined that the facility's actions regarding Zoe were retaliatory and otherwise unlawful. Joan called Bob for an appointment to discuss her findings. At this meeting, once again Candice (Hillside's corporate attorney) put on a spirited defense. Believing that the best defense is a good offense, Candice even attacked the ombudsman

program on numerous procedural grounds (one of the investigators was not wearing a name tag, another failed to announce her presence upon entering the facility, and the ombudsman had not apprised the facility of the focus of their investigation). This encounter quickly degenerated. Joan tried to maintain a focus on the issues of retaliation and poor care but couldn't deflect Candice's guard dog attacks. Another impasse occurred.

When Joan left the room, she called Zoe to ask if she would be willing to talk to the press. Zoe agreed. Joan then called her old friend Bill Tweed, a newspaper reporter. She reminded Bill of the recent wrongful death and offered him a long list of fresh problems. Bill talked to Zoe, Meg, Sherry, and Mel. In a week, he published a story about a "once good facility that had gone bad—very bad." This story triggered the memory of readers who had also experienced problems at Hillside, and the paper was flooded with allegations and letters of outrage.

Hillside's corporate headquarters put together a team to lobby the legislature about the abusive powers of a reckless and irresponsible ombudsman program but fired Bob and Ann anyway. The ombudsman program survived a legislative attempt to weaken its authority.

In Molly's rather lengthy case, it is striking how Molly becomes a nonperson. Technically, it is her case, but we know almost nothing about her. She is assessed as being nonambulatory, in late stage dementia, and totally dependent on others for assistance with her activities of daily living. Given that information, it appears that no one in this situation is really turning to her for information about her needs. It is also striking that as the process evolves it is not necessarily Molly's care that is in question. Zoe, her daughter, has become the self-appointed watchdog for

whatever happens to anyone in the facility. The dynamics that occur in the process get more and more complicated as each new person enters the scenario (14 in Molly's case), adding to the complexity of the situation. This example, based on an actual situation, demonstrates just how important it is to have investigative and analytical skills. Depending on who is analyzing this situation, it is very likely that the situation will be differently interpreted. And depending on the role being played, each person will have a very different perspective.

☾ Where to Start?

In Chapter 4, we focused on assessing elders' needs, emphasizing how important it is to assess people in their own environments and in the context of their cultures. Whether the assessment process is relatively informal or formal, advocates may discover situations that require attention. However, unless someone labels these situations as "problems," they are simply *conditions*—they exist. Sometimes the older person tells you in no uncertain terms that there is a problem. Other persons may agree or disagree, depending on the situation. At other times, you do not need anyone to tell you that something needs to be done, given its glaring nature. At still other times, it is hard to tell whether this is a problematic situation until more information is collected.

In this chapter we focus on how to move beyond assessment and begin investigating and analyzing the situation to determine appropriate action, if any. Situations that call for corrective action or new services and support may arise due to myriad circumstances, both simple and complex. An ongoing investigative process is required to analyze the situation in context. It is important to investigate and analyze systematically so that you have enough information to proceed. Recognize that both human and system failures may contribute to the situation you encounter. Therefore, just as in Molly's case, it may be difficult to determine who to turn to first to ask the questions that need to be asked.

Several classic questions may spring to mind when you think about where to start in the investigation and analysis process:

1. *Who* did *what* to whom?
2. *Who did not do* what they were supposed to do?
3. *Where* and *when* did they do (or not do) it?

If this sounds like another form of assessment, you are right, it is.

It may be helpful to think of yourself as an advocate sitting across the desk from a decision maker who has the authority to fix, or at least respond to, your client's problem. You have completed the needs assessment and presented your request (plea/demand) for something to be done for your client, for your relative, or for your friend (Chapter 4). But now you must try to understand the context in which the client's identified problem is occurring. A decision maker who has a position within that context can help you make sense of the context and give you guidance about how to analyze and investigate the situation. Without this understanding and an eye for cultural dynamics, it is impossible to devise an appropriate plan of action (the subject of Chapter 6) that will allow you to navigate within the system to advocate for the needed change.

The assessment process and the investigation and analysis process are intertwined. Sometimes you will gain information on the context before you even have access to the client. At other times, as in Molly's case, the needs assessment may be heavily dependent on participant observation and proxy information (for example, from Zoe and Meg). Trying to be systematic is important, but you also have to use your best judgment in these very intense emotional situations. Keeping in mind that assessment is ongoing, new data may emerge during the investigative process that may change the course of your investigation.

There are seven critical tasks in investigating and analyzing situations: (a) know the three rules of best evidence, (b) interview the persons involved, (c) draw information from all available resources, (d) recognize negligence, (e) carefully examine potential rights and ethics issues, (f) develop working hypotheses, and (g) verify the problem (or not). These tasks do not always occur in this order, and each situation is unique. This framework is designed to help you know where you might start. This is not a formula; it is only a guide. Portia's story provides one view of this kind of analysis.

☾ Portia's Broken Leg

Portia is an older woman who is in the hospital with a broken leg. The break may have occurred due to multiple contributing factors that may

FIGURE 5.1 Factors Swirling Around Client Going Home

remain hidden until they are investigated. Figure 5.1 illustrates the factors that might contribute to analyzing Portia's case. The figure looks pretty overwhelming, but it shows why investigation and analysis are needed. Obviously, Portia has a broken leg, and that is a problem. But how did this happen? Some of the possible factors that might bear on her predicament (as well as point to solutions) will literally be swirling in your mind as you approach Portia. The initial emergency room (ER) assessment of her broken leg may, indirectly, reveal needs beyond the physical. Perhaps the ER assessors detected some mental confusion or became suspicious of self-neglect, caregiver neglect, or even violence. If so, it is no longer enough to assess only the physical injury. You must assess the sequence of events that led to the injury to establish whether they were preventable and, if so, to identify what might prevent a reoccurrence. A social worker, a patient representative, a protective service worker, or an advocate by any other name must pursue the initial leads by analyzing what really happened to Portia.

Broken legs rarely just happen as isolated incidents. (You're sitting in class and suddenly your leg is broken? Probably not.) This is what advocates know and do best: you know that nothing happens in isolation, and you automatically wonder and begin to figure out the multiple problems that need to be prioritized in the analysis process. Did something that should have happened fail to happen? Did a home health nurse fail to show up on time? Did a case manager consistently develop service plans that did not truly meet the client's needs? Did a nursing assistant leave Portia's walker across the room, out of Portia's reach, as she did her cleaning? Perhaps Portia's husband (her sole support and chauffeur) died recently, and Portia fell because she walked to church on a very wet and slippery Sunday morning. Perhaps it was the result of an unpreventable accident. Did Portia fall because her leg broke, or did her fall break the leg? No matter how much action the different parties intersecting Portia's life take, no matter how much effort goes into the service planning or how much attention is dedicated to Portia's care, if Portia's needs are not being met, the action is simply wasted effort.

Before you can correct any causal errors or oversights, you must solve the mystery of who, why, how, when, and where by collecting and analyzing the evidence. In some cases, this process entails nothing more than a casual observation of some action, process, system, or structure. A few brief comments from a single complainant may solve some cases. In other cases, you will need to gather and analyze evidence from multiple strings that are difficult to untangle. Analyzing a situation and collecting evidence to support the analysis requires a sound and systematic investigation. Begin with the first of seven investigative tasks: the three rules of best evidence.

☺ TASK 1. CONSIDER THE THREE RULES OF BEST EVIDENCE

Collecting quality evidence depends on your commitment, skill, investigative powers, and access to authority, all of which vary widely among different kinds of advocates. Some legal advocates, including regulators and Adult Protective Services workers, for example, have relatively broad access to people, records, places, and authority, including the ability to impose sanctions for willful resistance or noncompliance.

Other advocates may have more limited powers and no formal authority. However, even if you do not have direct access to medical records,

nothing prevents you from reviewing these records in the company of older clients who have the legal right to read their own records in any health care setting or grant access to others via written permission. Coleman (1985) advised that nonlegal advocates who have no access authority can still investigate problems by allying with advocates who do. You must not transgress the limits of your investigative powers, whatever they may be, so know your authority and its limits.

Because your analysis is only as good as the evidence that supports it, you need to pay attention to the timeliness of data collection. If the older person is at risk, then finding facts demands immediate attention. Even if the case is not urgent, you still need to act quickly because recollections inevitably diminish and change over time. This leads us to the three rules of best evidence.

The **first rule of best evidence** *stipulates that the farther away the investigation is from the time of the incident, the less reliable the investigation.* You must act as quickly as possible.

The **second rule of best evidence** *stipulates that the farther a person is from witnessing what is (or is not) happening, the less you can rely on that person's information to guide you.* If you directly observe the problem yourself, this is the very best evidence as it is hard to argue with an eyewitness. However, many advocates will have to begin a notch down on the best evidence list. If they do not see the problems themselves, they must find and interview credible eyewitnesses to get their perspectives.

The **third rule of best evidence** *warns that evidence is worthless if it cannot be reliably retrieved once it is collected.* Consequently, savvy advocates will carefully write down observations. They will document the names, roles, status, and anything noteworthy about what people tell them. It is helpful to include interviewees' emotional states, physical statuses, apparent psychosocial functioning and attitudes as well as any possible motives that might shade what they tell you. Be careful to note specific observed behaviors, such as slow speech, saying they do not want to talk to you, or cupping their ear to hear. Avoid interpreting behaviors by inferring in your notes that the client was mentally incapable, which may not be the

BOX 5.2

Three Rules of Best Evidence

1. The farther away the investigation is from the time of the incident, the less reliable the investigation.
2. The farther a person is from witnessing what is (or is not) happening, the less you can rely on that person's information to guide you.
3. Evidence is worthless if it cannot be reliably retrieved once it is collected.

case (Sullivan & Rader, 1995). Notes must accurately reflect the person's recollections, including specific quotations about key events. Although tape recorders might intimidate some older clients, if you gain their permission, recorders often prove useful, especially when language difficulties are present.

The third rule also stipulates that you should keep your notes, especially in situations with legal implications. It is wise to make copies in case the originals are subpoenaed. Moreover, many eldercare problems tend to reoccur in troubled systems, and we have found it useful on more than a few occasions to dredge up tattered investigative notes as evidence of the chronic nature of certain deep-rooted problems. These three rules are summarized in Box 5.2.

Good documentation is equally important at both the individual and system advocacy levels. Systems advocates must prove the existence of trends and troubles at the higher administrative, community, and policy levels. Therefore, gathering data for systems advocacy is done on a much larger scale. Successful systems advocacy requires documentation of the numbers of individual problems that batch into clusters of related incidents that demonstrate the existence of broader social needs that can only be resolved through larger scale solutions, such as through the political process. The following example illustrates this.

The director of a small community aging service agency notices her staff complaining about a recent, sharp increase in the inappropriate admissions of mentally ill patients into nursing homes, which are ill prepared to meet these patients' special needs. The agency director asks her staff to document these incidents. After collecting the data indicators for her community, she shares her concern and documentation with other aging service directors at a statewide conference. These attendees share her concerns about this problem in their communities as well and agree that the problem has recently spiked in concert with two trends: (a) the declining availability of beds in more appropriate community-based settings coupled with (b) an increase in empty nursing home beds. Together, these program directors contacted the press, citing the available data that suggest the extent of the problem. As a result, a series of investigative reports pushes the issue into the open. This public concern piques the interest of state lawmakers who pass a bill requiring nursing homes to provide inpatient mental health services. (Lang, n.d.)

This story illustrates how the collection of individual cases can combine to shape successively larger systems, beginning with one individual. These problems are then grouped at the facility, then county, and finally state levels, consistent with the system's theoretical perspective that "the whole [problem] is made up of the sum of its parts" (Anderson et al., 1999, p. 4). If the problem is sufficiently extensive, the aggregated multistate data could reveal the existence of a nationwide problem. These data could be used to convince macro policy makers to make a change. This shows the importance of data, not only to identify and analyze individual problems

TABLE 5.1 Five Questions Linked to the Three Rules of Best Evidence

Three Rules of Best Evidence	Ask Yourself These Questions
1. The farther away the investigation is from the time of the incident, the less reliable the investigation.	1. What is my role, and how much authority and access to information do I have? 2. How quickly can I act?
2. The further a person is from witnessing what is (or is not) happening, the less you can rely on that person's information to guide you.	3. Am I an eyewitness, or do I need others to tell me what happened (or didn't)?
3. Evidence is worthless if it cannot be reliably retrieved once it is collected.	4. What notes do I need to keep to fully document the situation? 5. Is this a situation similar to others I have encountered or heard my peers discuss?

but also to influence macro-level decision makers in the event that these problems affect large numbers of people. In short, organizations and movements that desire to change systems must become the go to places for information (Frank, as cited in Hunt, 2002).

In considering the rules of best evidence, ask yourself these five questions:

1. What is my role, and how much authority and access to information do I have?
2. How quickly can I act?
3. Am I an eyewitness, or do I need others to tell me about what happened (or didn't)?
4. What notes do I need to keep to fully document the situation?
5. Is this a situation similar to others I have encountered or heard my peers discuss?

Table 5.1 links these questions to the three rules of best evidence.

☾ Task 2. Start by Interviewing the People Involved

Once you have considered the rules of evidence and how you need to proceed, it almost goes without saying that you begin with the individual who is most affected by the problem, or who called you or made the first contact—it's a judgment call every time. Some of you may have experience working with older people, but others may not be accustomed to investigating situations with elders. Here are some suggestions for facilitating interviews that fall into four general areas: timing, trust, interviewing skills, and closing interviews.

Preparing to Interview—Time, Setting, and Set-Up

If at all possible, interview the witness/complainant face to face. To do this, you need to set the right amount of time for the interview. Never underestimate the time needed for the interview. Do not rush older interviewees, who generally require a little more time (Cavanaugh & Blanchard-Fields, 2003). Lengthy interviews tend to exhaust older clients, so it is generally best to break up potentially long sessions into several shorter ones.

Avoid scheduling interviews during busy times that may result in interruptions. Pick a place and time that are convenient for the elder. Make sure you have a well-lighted area so the client can read your features, but avoid glare (Rader, 1995a). Ask clients what settings and circumstances they prefer. Identify and compensate (insofar as is practicable) for any communication problems that may hamper your client's comprehension, thought processes, or responses.

Rader (1995b) offers these suggestions for entering the personal space of older people: cultivate a calm approach, approach from the front rather than the side, speak while making eye contact, and position yourself in a lower or equal position.

When talking with older people, face them at eye level, sitting close enough so they can read your facial expressions. This might be no closer than about 24 inches, which is near the range of intimate personal space in most normal social settings, but pay attention for any signs that this proximity is making them uncomfortable. Make sure that no bright lights are shining over your shoulder as the glare may hamper the elder's vision. Pay close attention to your body language, especially when interviewing stroke victims or people with early stage dementia as they are sensitive to nonverbal cues (Rader, 1995a). And always honor cultural differences.

Whom Should You Interview?

Following the first rule of best evidence, begin your investigation by interviewing the person who brought the situation to your attention. This may or may not be the elder for whom you are advocating. The logic for this is threefold:

1. The complainant (whether the victim or a proxy who is reporting on behalf of an elder) typically provides the nature, setting, scope, severity, and priority of the situation.
2. If the complainant is also the victim/client, you must be sure that the complainant is given the opportunity to either direct or influence the problem-solving process. This is essential to staying client centered.
3. If the complaint involves any level of risk to the complainant/victim, the investigator must determine the complainant's mental capacity to make an informed choice of accepting or rejecting your assistance.

Back to the first rule of evidence. If the complainant is someone filing a grievance on behalf of an older client, then ideally the second party you interview after the complainant should be the older person. If the elder does not want you to pursue the case and is mentally capable, you must back off—unless there is evidence of abuse or gross neglect.

If there is evidence of abuse and you are a mandatory reporter (by your state's statutes), you must report the situation to Adult Protective Services regardless of the client's wishes. On the other hand, if the elder is mentally incapable of making an informed choice, and risk is present, then you must pursue the case on the basis of best interest. If there is evidence of abuse or gross neglect but you are not a mandatory reporter by your state's laws, do you still report it on moral grounds? That question, writ large, goes to the heart of a dilemma for later consideration.

In cases involving human error, neglect, abuse, or fraud, it is often a good idea to interview the alleged source of the problem following the initial complainant or victim interviews. This individual is sometimes referred to as the **alleged perpetrator** or AP. A secondary goal of interviewing APs early is to lock in their stories before they have time to manufacture an alibi or a plausible, but false, defense (which is quite likely once they become aware that an investigation is taking place).

If you are an external advocate, your mere appearance in a new setting will often be somewhat of an intervention. For example, you may be closely watched and notice taken of whom you are visiting. This is especially true if the complainant has already raised the issue internally or if the episode is already known in-house. Consequently, if you go into a public or communal setting such as a senior center or a retirement home to interview witnesses, you may want to be discrete by casually visiting a number of uninvolved people before interviewing your key witnesses. It is difficult enough to maintain some sense of confidentiality in any group situation without being obvious about why you are there. These tips are summarized in Box 5.3.

BOX 5.3

Tips on Time, Setting, and Set-Up for Interviews

1. The first person to interview is the victim or proxy if the victim cannot be interviewed.
2. Determine the mental capacity of the person to be interviewed.
3. Stay client centered; let the older person direct the process.
4. Advise clients that you will hold what they tell you in confidence to the extent permitted by law but that you must report danger to self or others.
5. If there is evidence of abuse or gross neglect and you are a mandatory reporter, you must report it to Adult Protective Services (APS) regardless of clients' wishes.
6. If there is such evidence and you are *not* a mandatory reporter, do you report it anyway on moral grounds?
7. Position yourself in front of your client, face to face, at eye level, no closer than 24 inches.
8. Plan on adequate time; don't rush older people.
9. Avoid the busiest time of their day.
10. Use a well-lighted area, and ensure that no bright lights behind you shine in the older person's eyes.
11. Adjust for any communication barriers such as language, culture, or speech impediments.
12. Read the body language, and be sure that your body language sends an open and calm message.
13. If you are an external advocate, consider casually visiting a few other people in the facility before the victim to protect your client from any problems that your presence may cause.
14. If you are interviewing an alleged perpetrator, do so right after the victim interview to get these stories locked in.

Reducing Tension and Building Trust with Interviewees

Basic communication techniques bear some amplification here. First and foremost, when interviewing older persons, be patient and do what you can to make them feel relaxed and at ease. Be pleasant and conversational—this is not an interrogation. Effective interviewers know how to read and react to their interviewees. There is a delicate balance between being overly solicitous and being perceived as condescending. Evidence suggests that older clients recognize and resent such condescension (Ryan, Hamilton, & See, 1994). It is also inappropriate to reassure distressed older people by offering false hope, promising a quick fix, or promising anything that you may not be able to deliver.

Because older residents are often worried about confidentiality, address this issue up front, and always ask if it is all right to take notes. Remember, just because your intentions are good does not mean elder clients will trust you or be confident in your abilities. It often takes time to develop trust, especially if you are an outsider. It may be even more difficult to engage trust if you are an employee of the agency or facility involved in the problem.

Candidly explain your role and your goal of collecting data to analyze the situation. If you see signs of apprehension in elderly clients, ask about the source of their discomfort and determine whether they are worried about someone finding out about the interview or the situation. If so, reassure them by promising to studiously guard their confidentiality, explaining that you

BOX 5.4

Romanian Foster Care Providers

One of the authors recalls how his government status and authority proved problematic on more than one occasion. He recalls how a large community of Romanian adult foster care providers sometimes referred to his agency as being *Securitate* (like the secret police). This puzzled him until he recalled how these providers had recently fled a totalitarian police state. To change their suspicious and hostile behaviors required that he understand why they behaved as they did. At first his own ethnocentricity got in the way, and he relied on his official authority and even threats to compel access. Later he used a softer, more educational approach to request compliance, with much better results. Thinking contextually and being sensitive to cultural experiences was critical to working effectively with this population.

will not divulge their names nor release information that might allow someone to guess their identities without their permission. Be careful, however, not to make such promises unless you are sure you can honor them. Despite your best efforts, you may still be seen as threatening (Box 5.4).

Recall the discussion in Chapter 4 of the importance of developing cultural competency and Kohli's (2004) eight areas of persons' lives from which cultural differences may arise: Political affiliation, economic class, age, gender, ethnicity, sexual orientation, personal capabilities, and spirituality. The example in Box 5.4 could have emanated from more than one of these; for example, political affiliation and economic class. Patience and a very respectful approach are required to sort through perhaps many layers of distrust before you can plan appropriate interventions.

Regardless of your best efforts to be friendly and helpful, some witnesses are intent on being uncooperative, possibly due to their emotional states, cultural norms, or underlying pathologies. Do not let this scare you. Let them vent. Listen empathetically, and when you get a chance, ask how you can help them deal with the source of their frustration. This usually relieves enough stress to allow the interview to proceed, but not always. If you can no longer bear a harangue, explain that you will reschedule the interview at another time. Be aware of the possibility, however, that the interviewee is using explosive tactics as a calculated means to intimidate you and drive you off. For this reason, among others, seasoned advocates seldom retreat unless they feel physically threatened. They just sit, listen, and wait for openings (Box 5.5).

Questioning Older Witnesses

Once the client is comfortable and indicates a readiness to proceed, start the actual inquiry with open-ended questions. You must be patient, as you will undoubtedly have to endure some slow-paced interviews. Because many older persons think or speak more slowly and laboriously, your mind may be tempted to drift. You must fight this temptation because if you don't, you will lose control of the interview. Good listening skills are critical; very old persons are often less attentive, more forgetful, and less sure about facts than younger adults (Aiken, as cited in Vander Zanden, Crandell, & Crandell, 2003). They are also more likely to voice irrelevant thoughts, stumble, or express inconsistencies (Hasher & Zacks, as cited in Cavanaugh & Blanchard-Fields, 2003). This is not to say that

BOX 5.5

Tips on Building Trust in Interviews

1. Make people comfortable with you and the surroundings.
2. Present yourself as pleasant and conversational (this is not an interrogation!).
3. Find the fine line between conveying sincere care and concern, and condescension.
4. Remember that you are interviewing respected elders in society.
5. Do not treat adults as children.
6. Do not raise your voice unless there is an invitation from the older person to do so; do not assume an older person is hard of hearing. Shouting at older persons who have no hearing impairment may be interpreted as hostility—not conducive to good interviews.
7. Do not offer false hope or things you cannot deliver.
8. Talk about confidentiality sooner rather than later.
9. Ask permission to take notes or record or use other technology.
10. Candidly tell elders your role and goals.
11. If you see signs of apprehension, inquire about the source and correct it.
12. Exercise maximum cultural sensitivity (do your homework before you go).
13. Reassure clients of confidentiality and that they will not be the brunt of retaliation, but only if it is true—if you can deliver on this.
14. Let people vent (it probably has nothing to do with you). When you have opportunities to interject, ask what they think needs to happen to alleviate the course of their frustration.
15. Be aware that a harangue may be an attempt to intimidate you so you will back off.
16. Remember that seasoned advocates rarely retreat unless they feel physically threatened; they just sit and wait for openings.

what the person is telling you is not applicable to the situation, but it means you have to be especially attentive to what is being conveyed both verbally and nonverbally.

Simply asking the interviewees short, direct questions to get them back on track can often mitigate these problems. These also help push reluctant or hesitant interviewees on and can help you fill in gaps and clarify indistinct themes. On the other hand, too many yes/no questions can reduce the information flow. (For more information, a link to the Seniors and People with Physical Disabilities site is on the companion website.) Another technique is to follow the funnel model of questioning: begin by asking broader questions before moving to details. This aids continuity. Avoid asking leading questions as the results of this interview may make

or break your case. Do not get derailed by trying to confirm your preconceptions by suggesting desirable answers.

Concentrate on extracting hard, relevant facts, especially from meandering testimony. Get into the habit of rephrasing and repeating weighty questions to older witnesses to verify your interpretation of their testimony. Listen carefully to differentiate hard fact from opinions and speculation, but never disagree with witnesses. Instead, ask why they hold such sentiments. The ensuing explanation might reveal important clues about what's really going on. At some point in the investigation, you may forget that you are fact gathering and may be tempted to offer the older complainant advice or on-the-spot therapy. Stop! This is not your purpose, at least not yet. Stay focused on staying on task

BOX 5.6

Tips on Interviewing Older People

1. Convey respect for elders' and their cultural ways.
2. Begin with benign open-ended questions when clients are comfortable and ready.
3. Listen intently and watch carefully for both verbal and nonverbal communication.
4. Never convey impatience in any way: repeat, go slowly, explain, and wait for clients to think and respond.
5. Stay focused and gently bring participants back on topic if need be.
6. At the first indication of clients being tired or anxious, stop for a break or for that day.
7. Sometimes short, direct questions will help clients stay on track.
8. Funneling may help to keep the interview focused: begin with broad questions and gradually funnel down to more specific questions.
9. Avoid leading and double-barreled questions.
10. Do not ask questions that tend to confirm your personal preconceived beliefs.
11. Concentrate on obtaining hard, relevant facts.
12. Rephrase and repeat weighty questions.
13. Listen intently to differentiate between hard facts and opinions.
14. Never disagree with what you are being told, but you can follow up by asking respondents why they hold those views.
15. Do not stray from fact gathering to advise or counsel—STOP! This is not what you need to be doing in the investigation and analytic phase.

and finding the facts. You have to know where you're going before you can give directions. Box 5.6 summarizes these tips on interviewing older people.

Closing the Interview

When you are nearing the close of the interview, ask clients if they would like to add anything else, or whether they know of anyone else who knows anything about the situation. Finally, conclude interviews by asking clients how they would like to see the situation resolved. Explain that you will inform them and the complainant of your findings once the investigation is completed. If the allegations cannot be verified, you must explain why. If this upsets them, ask if there is anything else that they can tell you that might change your analysis or give you a reason to reexamine the facts or collect new data. If you are a legal advocate, explain any review or appeal process that may be available to disappointed complainants (Box 5.7).

Chances are that you will interview more than one person, depending on the situation you are investigating. When all of your interviews are completed, ask yourself the following questions and document the answers in your notes:

1. Who is most affected, and what did they tell me?
2. If different people brought this information to my attention, what did they tell me?
3. What have I learned about the situation?

☾ TASK 3. DRAW FROM ALL AVAILABLE RESOURCES

Having identified who is involved in this situation, chances are you will have a good deal of information. In some situations, this may be enough information for you to intervene. However, in many situations, additional sources of information may be needed. Think about what

BOX 5.7

Tips on Closing Interviews

1. Ask whether your client has anything to add or ask.
2. Ask whether the client knows if anyone else has information that would be helpful.
3. If not known before, ask how the client would like the situation to be resolved.
4. Explain that you will inform the client of the results of your investigation.
5. If the allegations cannot be verified, explain why.
6. If the client becomes upset, ask whether there is anything else the client needs to tell you that could affect your finding.
7. Explain any reviews or appeals that are available to your client.

---

other sources might be available and how they might inform you. For example, is some agency already involved in investigating this case? Can they help you, or can you help them in dealing with what has already been done or discovered, and do you have access to this information? Think of the analysis process as a type of scavenger hunt in which you are looking for any information about the elder's needs in context. This means using personal observations, physical evidence, photographs, and any written observations such as medical records, care plans, and incident reports.

Literature, research, theories, or other information may inform the situation. Certainly there are unusual and unique problems, but there are also problems and issues that others have encountered before. Seek out anything that is known about the problem you are encountering because that will help you gain perspective on how frequently it occurs and how others have dealt with similar situations. Internet access has made it easier to find information using evidence-based practice search techniques. These techniques help you ask specific questions about the situation, intervention, and results (Gibbs, 2003).

Which experts might be available for advice in handling this type of situation? No one is an expert in every area; call on other members of an interdisciplinary team (attorneys, colleagues, and other professionals inside or outside of your organization) for their expertise. Who can open

doors and help you when the going gets tough? Ask yourself the following questions and document the answers in your notes:

1. What additional sources of information would be helpful in analyzing this situation?
2. What literature, theory, research, or other information might inform this situation?
3. Are there other agencies or outside experts who need to be involved?

Table 5.2 illustrates how an interview might be documented.

☾ TASK 4. RECOGNIZE NEGLIGENCE

In the process of collecting data from multiple sources, you must be sensitive to any violations of a law, rule, policy, contract, procedure, protocol, or standard. Therefore, we devote a specific task to analyzing negligence. In fact, it is often useful to analyze abuse and other nonaccidental harms or wrongs from the legal perspective of negligence.

Allen (1997) defined negligence as "the failure to exercise the degree of care a reasonable person would exercise under the same circumstances that result in injury to another" (p. 284). The legal meaning of negligence derives from the Latin phrase *res ipsa loquitor,* which means that "the thing speaks for itself" (p. 285). This implies that people are guilty of negligence *if it can be shown*

TABLE 5.2 Documenting an Interview

Questions, Information, or Criteria	Documentation for Trevor (an 80-year-old man)
1. The complainant (whether the victim or a proxy who is reporting on behalf of an elder) typically provides the nature, setting, scope, severity, and priority of the situation.	*Nature and Setting:* To remain client centered, I asked Trevor about what setting he preferred. He suggested meeting in a local restaurant. His choice of venue told me that he wanted to also set the informal nature of the interview. *Scope and Severity:* The client gradually talked about the problem (a woman in his church group seems unable to keep her hands off of him). He told me the story little by little, checking my verbal and nonverbal cues to see whether it was safe to go on. He saw the situation as quite severe but did not want to change churches. He also said that if his wife were still alive (who died 6 months ago) this either would not have been happening or she would have known how to handle it. *Priority:* Given two current scenarios (in his view and before any interventions are planned), put up with it or change churches, Trevor would put up with it.
2. If the complainant is also the victim/client, you must be sure that the complainant is given the opportunity to either direct or influence the problem-solving process. This is essential to staying client centered.	I asked Trevor about the extent to which he wanted to be engaged in the problem-solving process. He said "fully," so we roughed out a plan that we would (a) brainstorm today and (b) decide from whom/where else we might need information. We would each then try to access those bits of information before our next meeting (date and time determined).
3. If the complaint involves any level of risk to the complainant/victim, the investigator must determine the complainant's mental capacity to make an informed choice of accepting or rejecting your assistance.	Trevor appeared to be fully capable and willing to engage in the process.
4. Who is most affected, and what did they tell me?	It is not clear to me whether Trevor is more affected by his embarrassment than Hope, the lady at church. Trevor is my client, and I will, therefore, hold his interests paramount. However, the situation is benign of the more serious complaints of abuse and neglect, although Trevor's angst and discomfort are intolerable to him and, therefore, important to me.
5. If a different person brought this information to my attention, what did they tell me?	Same person.
6. What have I learned about the situation?	Life and limb are not at risk. The problem is a relationship one, and Trevor wants a solution that causes no hard feelings. He is willing and capable of participating in the problem-solving process.
7. What additional sources of information would be helpful in analyzing this situation?	It would be helpful to know (a) why Hope engages in this behavior and her perception of her behavior (maybe she is just a demonstrative person meaning to console Trevor regarding his wife's death) and (b) to what extent other people at Trevor's church are affected by the situation.
8. What literature, theory, research, or other information might inform this situation?	In addition to systems theory, grief and loss, social exchange, symbolic interaction, and social relational theories might be relevant.
9. Are there other agencies or outside experts who need to be involved?	I might look for therapeutic or self-help groups for Hope.

that they failed to act as required by their role according to a reasonable care standard, or, more simply stated, that they failed to act in a way that any reasonable person would in similar circumstances. This type of negligence, also known as **nonfeasance,** exists, for example, when a nurse fails to give an insulin shot as ordered, resulting in the patient's diabetic shock.

Malfeasance, on the other hand, is any sort of wrongdoing by a person in a position of trust, such as when a case manager falsifies a report to secure services for a relative or a friend. **Misfeasance** exists when someone performs a legal responsibility illicitly such as when an ombudsman accepts a client's medical records from a helpful staff person without the client's knowledge or written permission (as required by law). These three types of negligence constitute civil wrongs (torts) and have, at least theoretically, the potential for legal remedies (damages) if they result in actual harm to someone.

Criminal negligence generally entails the intent to cause harm, and the closely related concept of **gross negligence** implies an utterly reckless lack of diligence in caring for another. An example of criminal negligence would be if a caregiver intentionally deprived an individual of sufficient food, water, personal hygiene care, or prescribed medications and treatment.

In examining negligence, you must assess whether any law, rule, policy, or protocol of any organization that has a fiduciary relationship with the client (such as health care facilities, government agencies, and so forth) has been breached. Harms that result from breaches (or noncompliance) constitute conditions of **per se negligence** (Allen, 1997).

A quite different type of negligence is self-neglect. Self-neglect is neither a civil nor criminal wrong, but it constitutes a sort of nonpunishable breach of duty to self. **Self-neglect** exists when older people ignore their own primary health, welfare, or safety needs. It is associated with impaired mental capacity and is "a particularly thorny area for clinicians because the process is riddled with value judgments" (Fulmer & Gould, 1996, p. 96).

The ethical implications for self-neglect (as well as all other forms of negligence) can be clarified by examining whether the cause of the negligence is passive or active (Douglas, as cited Fulmer & Gould, 1996). **Passive neglect** exists when a caregiver or other responsible party carelessly (but unintentionally) fails to do something that is necessary to the older individual's health, safety, or welfare. This type of neglect is closely related to nonfeasance. **Active neglect** is intentional and can be (but is not necessarily) criminal in nature. It exists when there is a deliberate failure to meet important client needs. This is sometimes called *willful privation* or *intentional harm,* and it includes both intentional and non-accidental conditions that constitute physical, psychological, and other forms of abuse. Active neglect is far less common than passive neglect.

Passive and active neglect are especially important for advocates to understand because they hold strong implications for elder rights. In fact, you cannot analyze self-neglect without addressing a client's rights, mental capacity, and legal competence (Fulmer & Gould, 1996). For example, consider the personal rights issues surrounding the legally competent and mentally capable older person's knowing choice to live in squalor. This is active self-neglect, and an advocate may not legally intervene against this older person's wishes to live in this condition. However, in the story of Madeline (Chapter 4), who was living in what Adult Protective Services workers considered filth and squalor, pressures from the community led to her being removed from her home and sent to an assisted living facility. Technically, Madeline was competent to make her own decisions, but what often happens in such situations is that others decide that someone is incompetent because their living conditions do not meet a socially acceptable standard. Competent and mentally capable older individuals have the right to live as they choose. On the other hand (and there is nearly always another hand), when older persons are mentally impaired and repeatedly forget to turn off the stove, take medications, or maintain good hygiene, and caregivers frequently leave them alone to fend for themselves, a condition of passive neglect exists. Interventions are then required, even if the older person resents them. In both of these cases, we enter the realm of client rights. When doing so, ask yourself these questions, and document the answers in your case notes or journal:

1. Is there any type of negligence in this situation?
2. Have any laws, rules, policies, contracts, procedures, protocols, or standards been violated?
3. Is self-neglect (passive or active) a factor in this situation?

☺ TASK 5. EXAMINE POTENTIAL ISSUES REGARDING RIGHTS AND ETHICS

Effective advocates must always remember that U.S. law protects older persons' rights to make free choices and take risks—at least risks that aren't illegal, wanton, reckless, or that endanger others. Advocates understand that people continue to have rights as they age, but access to and ability to enjoy those rights often diminish as people grow older.

In many elder-care and elder-service settings, specific bills of rights are posted that emphasize clients' needs for special protection in historically troublesome areas. For example, nursing homes are required by law to post the *Nursing Home Residents' Bill of Rights,* and the Older Americans Act has a title called *Elder Rights* that focuses on home and community-based settings. Mental health facilities post similar lists of rights, as does the American Hospital Association for acute care settings. (Links to these elder rights sites are on the companion website.)

These posted rights specially protect against historic problems faced by older individuals who find themselves in certain medically restrictive and highly intrusive environments. In a broader sense, all U.S. citizens retain the right, regardless of age, to conduct themselves within the bounds of the law. Technically, this protection includes the right to act somewhat bizarrely, to live in filth, to degrade themselves, and generally to do stupid things as long as their behavior does not do harm. But an elder-oriented rights conundrum

lies in the gap between *having* and being able to *exercise* these rights.

For example, elderly people have the *right* to register and vote, but if they live alone, are poor, and have no readily available transportation, having the right to vote does not *enable* them to vote. Although absentee ballots are available, it is not easy for older people to figure out how to do things differently, and many hesitate to impose on friends and neighbors to take them to the polls. In this situation, ethicists would classify a person's desire (as an informed preference) to vote as reflecting **decisional autonomy** (Collopy, 1988). Here the term *decisional* implies de facto competence, and *autonomy* is defined as the ability to deliberate about personal goals and to act accordingly (The Belmont Report, 1979). (A link to The Belmont Report is on the companion website.) To respect autonomy is to give weight to the autonomous person's considered opinions and choices while refraining from obstructing their actions unless they are clearly detrimental to others. Conversely, older persons' inability to act on their preferences reflects a deficit in **executional autonomy** (Collopy, 1988). Here, the person has the will, but not the physical means to vote.

Persons who lack decisional autonomy lack the legal right to make risky choices, and consequently, may not refuse help in avoiding these risks, regardless of whether they appear to want to assume the risk. Because they lack decisional autonomy, they are usually unable to actively participate in the advocacy process, other than to be observed in order to have their safe preferences identified and protected. Otherwise, when risk is present, the advocate must protectively act in the client's best interest based on the **principle of beneficence.** This fundamental rule requires the advocate to (a) avoid doing harm, (b) maximize possible benefits while minimizing possible harms (The Belmont Report, 1979), and (c) generally err on the side of health, safety, and life.

Older individuals' rights to live freely, if unwisely, often pit rights-based advocates against beneficent-oriented advocates whose professional training invariably prepares them to protect older individuals from dangerous, abased, or

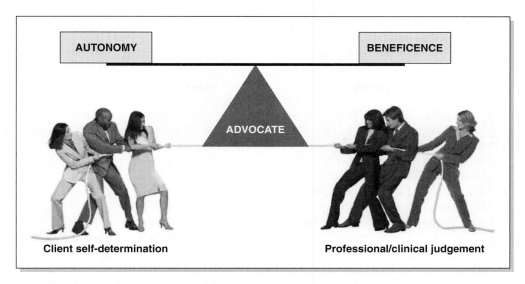

FIGURE 5.2 Conceptual Model of Autonomy Versus Beneficence

squalid conditions. Although these two positions appear to be polar opposites (rights vs. beneficence), and certainly clash often enough, they are really part of a single legally prescribed process that is the only way to analyze and handle elder rights (Nelson, Allen, & Cox, 2005). Advocates must be able to analyze clients' functional competence to determine whether to champion their freedom over their own safety (Fulmer & Gould, 1996) or, conversely, to act protectively or even prohibitively when their clients are mentally impaired and incapable of recognizing the dangers of self-neglect. Unfortunately, the evidence is overwhelming that many well-meaning advocates fall into the pit of paternalism and do things *to* clients instead of *for* them, all in the name of beneficence (Nelson et al., 2005).

The Competing Values of Autonomy and Beneficence

Imagine that you are trying to do the right thing for your 75-year-old uncle whom you know would benefit greatly if only he would go to a rheumatologist, as it is clear to you that he has arthritis. You are a beneficent person: you simply want to do the right thing. However, there are a couple of problems. First, it is not at all clear to your uncle that he has arthritis; in fact, he denies it. Second, you are a professional who knows about autonomy and self-determination, and you are struggling with the competing values of beneficence and autonomy (Figure 5.2).

You stop and think: you have taken your uncle to three doctors a week for the last month, and you cannot fault him for not wanting to go to another one for a condition he doesn't think he has. He does get around, albeit slowly and with considerable pain, and even if you could, you don't want to force him to go to yet another doctor against his will. You opt for his autonomy (which is not to say you don't look for other ways to inform him about treatments for arthritis). From the beneficent perspective, the decision might be to urge him to go to the doctor. Autonomy, on the other hand, considers whether your uncle *wants* to go to the doctor—and he doesn't.

Doing good on behalf of others can also be seen as disempowering elders or being paternalistic. Considerable harm is done in the name of beneficence when it reigns at the expense of autonomy. A great body of gerontological literature suggests that practitioners who act paternalistically tend to view their clients as vulnerable, ignorant (ill informed), and weak (Mitchell & Bournes, 2000). These attitudes are undoubtedly bolstered by professionals' education, which prepares them to use their special knowledge to do what they think is best. Although benefience arises from the desire to help, it is also pushed by the high status professional's (often physicians in particular) failure to carefully elicit and heed client concerns, answer questions, or fully engage in a dialogue about the choice in question (Mueller, Hook, & Fleming, 2004).

Despite the fact that autonomy is safeguarded by the principle of informed consent and is protected by the various codes of residents' rights, defending autonomy often lands rights-based advocates in hot water. It is difficult to derail clinical and professional authorities who cannot accept the older individual's right to make mistakes, live poorly, face danger, refuse help, or die naturally (Agich, 1993). It is equally contentious to challenge caregivers and service personnel who have denied clients' rights for the sake of institutional convenience, the collective rights of others, efficiency, liability protection, or other system-based needs (Nelson, 2000).

Put simply, advocates should not be dominated by the beneficence principle because autonomy is the client's most basic right. Beneficence has its place, but it should never override autonomy when mental impairment is not an issue. Advocates must always put "resident's goals, preferences and ideas" first (Hunt & Burger, 1992, p. 14) and make autonomy the touchstone of their practice, which is the only way to stay client centered.

Precedence Protocol for Autonomy and Beneficence

Staying client centered requires that advocates follow a three-stage precedence protocol designed to safeguard clients' rights while identifying the circumstances in which protective intervention, based on beneficence, is necessary. The protocol's three stages are (a) informed consent, (b) substituted judgment, and (c) beneficence.

The first two stages are designed to protect clients' rights to choice; the third stage, beneficence, is based on the principle of *parens patriae.* This principle means that the state has the right to act as a parent, often through licensed caregivers and government agents, to protect the health, safety, and welfare of vulnerable older individuals, especially those who are mentally impaired.

Stage One: Informed Consent
Protects Autonomy

Informed consent (or informed choice) is often thought of in the context of medical care or medical procedures. **Informed consent** occurs when a person fully understands the essential nature, including the benefits and drawbacks, of a medical procedure, medication, or other process. Complete informed consent includes a discussion of (a) the nature of the decision/procedure, (b) reasonable alternatives to the proposed intervention, (c) the relevant risks, benefits, and uncertainties related to each alternative, (d) assessment of patient understanding, and (e) acceptance of the intervention by the patient (University of Washington, 1998).

Informed consent is not determined by a diagnosis of mental illness or any other medical or mental health condition. Do not make the mistake of thinking that assessing decisional autonomy for informed choice is a "medical question, rather than the application of a legal rule" (Markson, Kern, Annas, & Glantz, 1994, p. 1078). Even clients with mild to moderate mental impairment may be able to make informed choices about end-of-life decisions and other important personal health and welfare problems. Consequently, advocates must examine each individual case involving informed consent on its own merits. Talk with clients to determine their "domain specific" competence regarding a particular situation and choice of options (Kuther, 1999, p. 18). Never arbitrarily dismiss clients' wishes based on some global definition of incompetence, as so many do (Kuther, 1999; Nelson, 2000).

BOX 5.8

The Scalar Principle of Informed Consent

The scalar principle of informed consent means that persons must be competent to assess their risks in making decisions. It is important in elder advocacy because there are times when clients' perspectives, conditions, circumstances, or situations are such that decision making is impaired. Therefore, from what is known you try to predict/ guess the unknown, or what can be expected to happen from then on. You may need to intervene if persons are making choices that will do significant harm to themselves or others. The greater the risk the client wishes to assume, the greater the advocate's need to be sure that the client's decisional capacity is intact (Glannon, 2005).

If clients' informed choices entail risk, advocates must be diligent in determining valid consent. In other words, you must analyze clients' comprehension, logic, and ability to assess the risks and benefits attending their choices. This brings us to the **scalar principle** of determining informed choice, which Glannon (2005) explained in the context of a patient's right to refuse treatment: "The required level of competence to refuse treatment should be on a sliding scale from low to high risk. The greater the level of risk in refusing a treatment the higher the level of competence should be for the patient to make the decision" (pp. 25–26). When patients' decisions to refuse treatment could pose significant risks of harm to self or others, the competence level to advocate for patient autonomy must be high (Box 5.8).

Obviously, the scalar principle also applies to clients who are actively choosing to assume risks. One person wants to walk despite severe balance and muscular coordination problems; another wants to continue to drink herself into nightly oblivion despite a bad liver; someone else wants to smoke despite his emphysema; and another wants to avoid bathing and grooming. All of these things might be reflexively prohibited by well-meaning individuals acting beneficently. Even rights-based advocates would (and should) try to (gently) talk clients out of these chancy choices. But if these dissuasive efforts fail, the dialogues are not wasted because they serve to assure full disclosure by thoroughly airing the risks and consequences of the choices in question. This provides the rights-based advocate with an even stronger mandate to support autonomy or to intervene beneficently.

Stage Two: Substituted Judgment

Informed consent is just the first step in the precedence protocol. Step two is **substituted judgment,** which also supports client choice and autonomy. It comes into play when older individuals are no longer able to make valid decisions because they have become mentally impaired. Substituted judgments include both voluntary and involuntary mechanisms (Page, 1999). Voluntary mechanisms include the durable health care power of attorney in which older people appoint proxy decision makers to act for them should they become decisionally incapable. Advanced directives and living wills are also proxy documents of voluntary substituted judgment. Involuntary mechanisms include court-imposed guardianships and conservatorships.

As an advocate, your stance toward these forms of substituted judgment is straightforward: you must investigate and analyze the nature of any duly executed document of substituted judgment and support your clients' choices unless you conclude that they have subsequently and validly changed their minds and need your help in making this known. You must also respect nonvoluntary mechanisms, but monitor these and analyze their consistency with older individuals' true best interests and valid preferences (Moody, 1992).

Stage Three: Beneficence

The best interest standard constitutes the model's third stage. **Beneficence** is often where providers, caregivers, and advocates begin, even though in all settings and circumstances, without exception, beneficence should really be the last valid recourse. Beneficence should be employed only when the client is decisionally incapable. Once again, the advocate's beneficent stance is simple and straightforward: you must prevent any type of harm to the client. Life, health, and safety are paramount, and you must do what is truly in the client's best interest.

As you can see, focusing on rights and ethics is complicated but absolutely necessary. Once again, ask yourself the following questions and record your answers:

1. In the setting in which this situation occurred (or is occurring), are there specific bills of rights that protect the elder? If so, which ones, and are they posted?
2. Is the elder's decisional autonomy being respected or challenged?
3. Are there limits in the older person's ability to achieve executional autonomy?
4. Are there issues related to autonomy and beneficence?
5. Using the precedence protocol (informed consent, substituted judgment, and beneficence), where does this situation fit?

☾ TASK 6. DEVELOP WORKING HYPOTHESES

When you begin to analyze the situation, try to avoid assuming that you really understand the truth of the matter. Inevitably, advocates begin coming up with hunches about what is going on as they move through the data collection process. **Lay hypothetical theory** predicts that you will begin to make assumptions about how the data fit together and what it means as you are collecting it. These lay hypotheses are educated guesses about what is going on. They are how you begin to make sense of the situation (Kruglanski, Bar-Tal, & Klar, 1993). People do this almost intuitively, and new advocates will be more tentative in their educated guesses than veteran advocates who can draw from a wealth of experience. Virtually everyone, however, formulates plausible explanations about the relationship of cause and effect *during*, and not just *after*, an investigation. In fact, professional investigators are actually trained to develop several feasible working hypotheses to test the "goodness of fit" between the collected data and the encountered problem. Developing more than one hypothesis helps you remain intellectually skeptical and protects you from adopting a pet theory that you might be tempted to make fit your preconceptions.

Analysis Overview: Reconstructing the Data for Verification

In analyzing data, the essential task is to determine whether the complainant's testimony is well connected to (or corroborated by) other testimony, relevant documents, physical evidence, and your own observations. How tight are these connections? Do the data agree with the previously known history of similar events or circumstances? Is your data summary free of any factual or logical error? And most important, do your data allow reasonable observers to infer that a specific cause has resulted in a specific effect (Freeley, 1961)? If your data seem connected, are free of error, and provide reasonable explanations, it is reasonable to assume that the case is *prima facie* valid and is likely to be accepted by decision makers because "it presents good and sufficient reason for adopting a proposition" (p. 167).

Analyzing the Data

Once data are collected, develop a temporal sequence of cause and effect. Drawing from the field of community health, we suggest analyzing causal factors from this three-point framework. The first is the **proximate** or **distinguishing cause** (Freeley, 1961). It comprises the specific, exact, antecedent events that are clearly related to the client's problem (McKenzie & Jurs, 1993). The second, and often more difficult to analyze causal stream, is comprised of **contributing factors.** These typically support the problem's proximate cause. The third, more distantly related factor, measures causation as the client's **relative risk,** which is how the client's risk for the negative outcome in question compares to the general population's risk for the same event (Green & Kreuter, 2005).

Risk to the older individual can include suspected abuse, including any intentional harm, or nonaccidental injury or any condition resulting in pain, humiliation, or financial exploitation. As a general rule, a problem's risk and urgency should be determined by its impact on the client according to the following precedence priority:

1. Life-threatening circumstances
2. Immediate risk of injury or threat of injury
3. Physical pain
4. Severe psychological stress
5. Lesser emotional distress
6. Rights violation
7. Diminished life circumstances
8. Systems access and service difficulties

Returning to Portia

We return to Portia, the older woman introduced earlier in this chapter who was admitted to the hospital with a broken leg. An advocate was pursuing the reasons for her having fallen. Consider how the proximate cause may have been nothing more than a single uncontrollable event that could happen to anybody. Portia simply tripped over her cat, and her injury was a luckless fluke based on a random environmental circumstance—an unforeseen threat that nobody would have reasonably anticipated. As such, you can safely conclude that Portia faced no greater relative risk for tripping over her cat than anyone else. There is no need for advocacy.

Now, consider how the proximate cause and contributing factors of this case may be reassessed based on two other important and all-encompassing causes. **Behavioral causes** entail any human agency, including any individual or collective action or lack of action, either accidental, or based on intent, or based on an actors' attitudes, or any other motive or belief, that contribute to a negative client outcome (Green & Kreuter, 2005). **Environmental causes** include physical or other structural factors such as "things 'around' individuals that may influence their awareness, knowledge, attitudes, skills and behavior" (McKenzie & Smeltzer, 1997, p. 138).

What if your investigation revealed that Portia had tripped over one of her cats due to dizziness and a staggering gate (ataxia) that was brought on by an adverse reaction to a medication that her doctor had just prescribed for insomnia? Now investigation of Portia's broken leg points to controllable conditions caused by human error—circumstances that could have been reasonably anticipated and prevented. The investigation and analysis are now more complex because they move beyond the immediate environmental factors to involve other settings and other players. In this scenario, the proximate cause of Portia's injury still includes the cat as an immediate environmental cause, but it also involves the proximate behavioral effect of her adverse reaction to a medication that lists falling as a possible side effect. Moreover, you discover that Portia had been prescribed a 30 mg dose, which far exceeds the recommended geriatric dosage of 15 mg. Hence Portia faced an unacceptable relative risk for injury. You can also infer that her physician's behavior (the act of prescribing) was, at the very least, an important contributing factor to Portia's injury.

Three other factors should be considered in analyzing whether injuries like Portia's, or any other problem, are accidental. Consider whether the proximate or contributing causes arose from circumstances that were (a) foreseeable (could be anticipated by a reasonable person), (b) preventable (they could be kept from happening), or (c) intentional (done on purpose). In the case of

Portia's ataxia-related fall, her physician clearly should have foreseen the risks of using that particular drug. And since these risks, including falling, could be foreseen, they were, ipso facto, preventable had the physician prescribed an appropriate dosage of some other drug or recommended some nonpharmacological treatment.

Now let us alter Portia's story a bit. This time, the hospital physician becomes concerned by Portia's hesitant and evasive responses and apparent distress over his questions about her injury. He calls in a social worker who gently confronts Portia's anxiety and convinces Portia that she can help (O'Brien, 1996). Meanwhile, the physician discovers signs of older bruises and abrasions. When asked about these injuries, Portia tearfully confesses that her husband, who had been drinking and was angry about his forced retirement, had caused them. She ends by saying, "but I don't think he meant to hurt me." Portia's confession indicates a condition of elder abuse. Recognizing this, the social worker pursues O'Brien's analytical approach to assessing Portia's risk for further harm by asking three questions:

1. How frequently had her husband harmed Portia in the past?
2. What was the severity of the harm?
3. Were the outcomes actually intentional?

The physical evidence and Portia's testimony attest to a probable condition of intentional abuse. The proximate cause of her having been pushed, together with the contributing cause of her husband's alcohol abuse and lost work role, have resulted in profoundly negative behavioral problems that require immediate intervention. In this case, the social worker, who is a mandatory reporter, must refer this situation to Adult Protective Services for further analysis and intervention. Although the definition of abuse varies from state to state, most definitions include elements of physical harm, pain, psychological harm, or unexplained injuries. The issue of whether elder abuse exists can usually be answered by analyzing whether the proximate and contributing causes were foreseeable, preventable, or intentional.

After you have analyzed the data, ask yourself these five questions to generate hypotheses and define the problem (at least for the present time):

1. How do I define the situation at this point? Is it simply a condition, a problem, or a set of problems?
2. What are the proximate causes, contributing factors, and relative risks? Are there behavioral or environmental causes?
3. What are my hypotheses (well-informed hunches) about the direct and indirect causes of the problem?
4. Was the situation foreseeable, preventable, or intentional?
5. Are there gaps in the data that require more digging?

☽ TASK 7. VERIFY THE PROBLEM (OR TEST THE HYPOTHESIS)

In situations that are deemed problematic, need to change, or require some type of intervention, what began as a *condition* will become labeled by the advocate (and perhaps others) as a *problem*. Some problems will be very specific to an individual; others may involve multiple persons. The nature, scope, and severity of a problem can affect individuals, groups, communities, and even larger social systems including a state, a region, or even the nation. Hyman (1982) stressed that you must collect "data that are directly related to the variables of the system being studied" (p. 152), be it the long-term care system, the Adult Protective Services system, the acute care system, the Social Security or Medicare system, or any other system important to the life and well-being of elders. Thus, if the problem is widespread, you could conceivably move from face-to-face interviews to a host of other data collection processes. Focus groups, task forces, even town hall meetings and forums become necessary when the problem is expansive.

But for now think about how to clearly state the problem or hypothesis using the older person's perspective to guide you. If the older adult is not able to participate or communicate, think about what proxies have told you. Think about who, if anyone, could have, or should have prevented or ameliorated the problem. You may even realize that the statement of the problem has changed. The major concern in this part of your analysis is whether the identified needs (or lack thereof) warrant your action as an advocate, and this decision should be based on what the older person needs—not on what you need as an advocate.

If you can verify the problem, identify the decision makers who can change the situation. Target those who have the power and resources to solve the problem. We'll spend more time on this targeting in Chapter 6.

Knowing where to start is often difficult, and the amount of evidence you need will vary due to a range of circumstances. In some cases, the opportunity to investigate and analyze thoroughly will be limited by time, in others the advocate may not have access to people or records. In most cases there won't be any need for extensive, systematic data gathering beyond talking to the older person you are trying to assist. Finally, even in the best investigations, facts can be disputed. However important, facts do not entirely, in and of themselves, make a case. Very often, how the facts are logically packaged and presented is just as important (see Chapter 6). For now, however, use the investigation outline to see what you might do to begin planning for change. Consider these questions:

1. What is the nature, scope, and severity of this problem?
2. From the elder's perspective, what is the problem? Is my statement of the problem different from the elder's, and if so, how and why?
3. Has the statement of the problem changed in the process? How and why?
4. Is the problem verified?

5. Who are the decision makers who have the power to respond to this problem?
6. Where do I start?
7. What do I hope to achieve?

☯ SUMMARY

In this chapter, we focused on seven tasks that advocates perform to investigate and analyze situations. Three rules of evidence were provided: (a) the farther away the investigation is from the time of the incident, the less reliable is the investigation, (b) the farther a person is from witnessing what is (or is not) happening, the less you can rely on the person's information to guide you, and (c) evidence is worthless if it cannot be reliably retrieved once it is collected. The third rule reinforces the importance of keeping good documentation.

We provided information about gathering face-to-face information, interviewing techniques, and ways to reduce tension and build trust. Being sensitive to the issues faced by some older persons and carefully listening are critical factors if voices are to be heard.

Drawing from all available resources includes seeking information from theory, research, literature, experts, agencies, and any other source that may be helpful. The intent is to learn the prevalence of this situation. We also focused on recognizing negligence and its many variations. Negligence leads directly to examining potential issues regarding rights and ethics. The precedence protocol includes informed consent, substituted judgment, and beneficence—concepts every advocate needs to know.

Having gathered data, advocates will have hunches or working hypotheses that emerged in the process. These may evolve and change as more information is gathered. Ask yourself what additional data you need to move forward. Finally, if the problem is verified, its nature, scope, and severity must be determined before you can develop a plan for change. Table 5.3 summarizes the tasks in the investigation and analytic framework.

TABLE 5.3 Investigative and Analytic Framework

Task 1. Consider the Three Rules of Best Evidence

1. What is my role, and how much authority and access to information do I have?
2. How quickly can I act?
3. Am I an eyewitness, or do I need others to tell me about what happened, or didn't?
4. What notes do I need to keep to fully document the situation?
5. Is this a situation similar to others I have encountered or heard my peers discuss?

Task 2. Start by Interviewing the People Involved

1. Who is most affected, and what did they tell me?
2. If a different person brought this information to my attention, what did he or she tell me?
3. What have I learned about the situation?

Task 3. Draw from All Available Resources

1. What additional sources of information would be helpful in analyzing this situation?
2. What literature, theory, research, or other information might inform this situation?
3. Are there other agencies or outside experts who need to be involved?
4. How common (or uncommon) does this situation appear to be?

Task 4. Recognize Negligence

1. Is there any type of negligence in this situation?
2. Have any laws, rules, policies, contracts, procedures, protocols, or standards been violated?
3. Is self-neglect (passive or active) a factor in this situation?

Task 5. Examine Potential Issues Regarding Rights and Ethics

1. In the setting in which this situation occurred (or is occurring), are there specific bills of rights that protect the elder? If so, which ones, and are they posted?
2. Is the elder's decisional autonomy being respected or challenged?
3. Are there limits in the older person's ability to achieve executional autonomy?
4. Are there issues related to autonomy and beneficence?
5. Using the precedence protocol (informed consent, substituted judgment, and beneficence), where does this situation fit?

Task 6. Develop Working Hypotheses

1. How do I define the situation at this point? Is it simply a condition, a problem, or a set of problems?
2. What are the proximate causes, contributing factors, and relative risks? Are there behavioral or environmental causes?
3. What are my hypotheses about the direct and indirect causes of the problem?
4. Was the situation foreseeable, preventable, or intentional?
5. Are there gaps in the data that require more digging?

Task 7. Verify the Problem (or Test the Hypothesis)

1. What is the nature, scope, and severity of this problem?
2. From the elder's perspective, what is the problem? Is my statement of the problem different from the elder's, and if so, how and why?
3. Has the statement of the problem changed in the process? How and why?
4. Is the problem verified?
5. Who are the decision makers who have the power to respond to this problem?
6. Where do I start?
7. What do I hope to achieve?

DISCUSSION QUESTIONS AND EXERCISES

1. Reread Molly's case at the beginning of the chapter and use the investigation and analysis framework to answer the questions. Select a role that you could see yourself playing in this case (there are many), and answer the questions from that person's perspective. Then switch to another role and see how the answers change given the different perspective you are assuming.

2. Using the story of Portia's broken leg as an example, select a likely role that you might play, perhaps as a case manager in the hospital where Portia is admitted. How do the three rules of best evidence apply to her situation? How might the three rules of best evidence be helpful to you as a gerontological practitioner?

3. Why is documentation so important to investigating a situation? What have you learned from reading this chapter that will be helpful to you in documenting your investigation? Why is it important to document what you observe rather than how you feel about or interpret your observations?

4. Interpersonal skills are extremely important in the interviewing process. What are your strengths and challenges in this type of investigative interviewing? What skills do you want to enhance?

5. Where would you go to locate theory, literature, and research that might inform your investigation? Why might that information be important even though it is not specific to the particular situation you are analyzing?

6. Discuss the different types of negligence and see if you can provide examples of what each might look like in your practice. How is negligence dealt with in your state (that is, the legal definitions and procedures)?

7. Locate a bill of rights on the Internet for at least one setting in which older persons are likely to be found. Read over the rights and think about how they might be enforced.

8. Revisit Molly's case in light of the competing values of autonomy and beneficence. How do these values interact in Molly's situation, and what is your analysis in terms of the precedence protocol?

9. What might an initial working hypothesis look like in Portia's case? How might it change if new information is introduced when the physician identifies her injury as having occurred as a result of her husband's actions? Would you want to interview her husband?

10. Think of a situation with which you are familiar. How might the content of this chapter help you in understanding it better? Be specific.

ADDITIONAL READINGS

Beall, S. C. (Ed.). (1996). *Abuse, neglect, and exploitation of older persons: Strategies for assessment and intervention.* Baltimore, MD: Health Professions Press.

Bostick, J. E. (2002). *Relationship of nursing personnel and nursing home care quality.* Ann Arbor, MI: UMI Dissertation Services, ProQuest Information and Learning.

Capezuti, E., Bruch, B. L., & Lawson, W. T. (1997). Reporting elder mistreatment. *Journal of Gerontological Nursing, 23*(7), 24–32.

Dobalian, A. (2001). *Advance directives and resource use in nursing homes.* Ann Arbor, MI: UMI Dissertation Services, ProQuest Information and Learning.

Feezel J., & Hawkins, R. (1997). Myths and stereotypes: Communication breakdowns. In C. W. Carmichael, C. H. Botan, & R. Hawkins (Eds.), *Human communication and the aging process* (pp. 95–110). Prospect Heights, IL: Waveland Press.

Fulmer, T., & Burland, B. (1996). Evaluting the caregiver's intervention in the elder's task performance: Capacity versus actual behavior. *International Journal of Geriatric Psychiatry, 12,* 920–925.

Fulmer, R., Paveza, G., VandeWeerd, C., Fairchild, S., Guadagno, L., Bolton-Bratt, M., & Norman, R. (2005). Dyadic vulnerability and risk profiling for elder neglect. *The Gerontologist, 45*(4), 525–534.

Guadalupe, K. L., & Lum, D. (2005). *Multidimensional contextual practice: Diversity and transcendence.* Belmont, CA: Brooks/Cole.

Henderson, J. E. (2000). *Grounded theory study: Nursing aides learning to care for nursing home residents with dementia.* Ann Arbor, MI: UMI Dissertation Services, ProQuest Information and Learning.

Hiltner, J., & Moore, J. R. (1986, Summer). Training of nursing home administrators: A university-facility experience. *Journal of Long-Term Care Administration*. 14(2), 19–22.

Hubbard, R. S., & Power, B. M. (1993). *The art of classroom inquiry*. Portsmouth, NH: Heineman.

Huber, R., Borders, K., Netting, F. E., & Nelson, H. W. (2001). Data from long-term care ombudsman programs in six states: The implications of collecting resident demographics. *The Gerontologist, 41*(1), 61–68.

Kapp, M. B. (2004). Altering the home care agency/client relationship: Notice requirements. *Care Management Journals, 5*(3), 131–137.

Koff, T. H., Friedsam, H. J., & Shore, H. (1993). *Nursing home administration: A selective annotated bibliography for gerontology instruction*. Washington, DC: Association for Gerontology in Higher Education.

Mikolas-Peters, C. J. (2001). *Nursing home residents' and family caregivers' strategies in financing the costs of long-term care*. Ann Arbor, MI: UMI Dissertation Services, ProQuest Information and Learning.

Moses, D. V. (1979). The nurse's role as advocate for the elderly. In A. M. Reinhardt & M. D. Quinn (Eds.), *Current practice in gerontological nursing* (pp. 221–226). London: The C. V. Mosby Company.

National Center for Long-Term Care Ombudsman Resources. (1992). *Comprehensive curriculum*. Washington DC (Grant number 90-AT-0401). Washington, DC: Administration on Aging, Department of Health and Human Services.

O'Melia, M., & Miley, K. K. (2002). *Readings in contextual social work practice*. Boston: Allyn & Bacon.

Salmon, J. R. (2001). *Contribution of personal control and personal meaning to quality of life in home, assisted living facility, and nursing home settings*. Ann Arbor, MI: UMI Dissertation Services, ProQuest Information and Learning.

Simmons, J. E, (2002). *Transition experiences of community spouses who volunteer in their mates' nursing homes*. Ann Arbor, MI: UMI Dissertation Services, ProQuest Information and Learning.

Singh, D. A. (1997). *Nursing home administrators: Their influence on quality of care*. New York: Garland.

CHAPTER SIX

Planning Interventions

Think before you act and act on facts.   URWICK (1956)

BOX 6.1

The AAA Plan in Region II

It was that time of the year. The Area Agency on Aging (AAA) in Region II prepared to hold public hearings. The regional Council on Aging was meeting in 2 weeks to consider how to proceed, and the hearings themselves were scheduled the next month. The AAA staff had gathered community needs assessment data on numbers of persons served with a small survey of senior center participants and a random telephone survey. The public hearing was designed to gain public comment on community needs that had not been captured in their previous efforts and to reinforce the urgency of the needs they had already identified.

The rural AAA was comprised of five full-time staff people: an area planner (Steve), a coordinator of services (Regina), a case management supervisor (Ramona), and two case managers (Greg and Marilyn). As they talked about how to proceed, Regina was concerned about the number of older persons on the council who had been very angry at the local home health agency last year, which had received the bulk of the AAA's Title III contracts for delivery of in-home services. Last year's hearing had been rather contentious, and several former clients had railed against the politics of the situation, implying that the contracting process had been rigged and that a new faith-based home health

agency had not been able to compete for the limited dollars.

Steve was somewhat defensive when Regina brought this up because he prided himself on very intentionally having selected his proposal review committee based on their fair-mindedness and expertise, not on their political connections. All three of the critical former clients had followed up their comments with biting letters of concern. He wanted to avoid another contentious meeting, and he was anxious to get solid feedback on the planning process and on community needs. The staff decided to face the dilemma head-on and to confide their concerns to the Council on Aging when they met. After all, these folks were older citizens whom they trusted, and they should have a major say in how the hearing was to be conducted.

When the council met, they were more than aware of the controversy over letting contracts to the competing home health agencies. The director of the faith-based agency had personally contacted each of them to discuss his agency's capabilities and their quality mission. The council members had mixed feelings because they were impressed with the sincerity and high moral fiber of the director, yet they did not want to get involved in the contracting process, which

(continued)

BOX 6.1 *(continued)*

was the jurisdiction of the AAA and its reviewers. They did express concern, however, about who would be on the proposal review committee as they were likely to feel a great deal of pressure from community constituents.

At the public hearing the large conference room at the senior center was full. Directors from both home health agencies were present, and both had signed up to speak. The director of the home health agency with the Title III contract provided statistics on the numbers of persons they were currently serving and data on the aggregated characteristics of older persons who were on the waiting list. The waiting list for in-home services had grown since the previous year, and he pleaded with the council to allocate more funds for these services. The director of the faith-based home health agency introduced himself and then turned the podium over to an older woman who was a client of his agency. She slowly moved to the podium, carefully negotiating her walker through the crowd. She began to tell her story—how she was in desperate need after her husband of 55 years had died and her own health had failed, and how the agency staff had literally made all the difference in her life. You could hear a pin drop

in the room as she talked in her quiet, yet convincing, voice.

When the hearing was over, the council met with the AAA staff to debrief. The meeting had not been contentious, and both agencies had been convincing in their statements of needs. Many other speakers had advocated for an increase in in-home service for older persons in local communities. The waiting list was evidence that there were greater needs than they had been able to fund, and the faith-based agency's client had made an emotional appeal for how valuable such services had been. It was clear that there were insufficient funds to cover all the needs identified by either agency and that in-home services needed to be increased. The group agreed that the agencies and individuals from the community had done a very persuasive job of convincing them of unmet needs and advocating for what needed to happen. They began to talk about pooling resources with local municipalities and county boards of supervisors to raise additional funds. They also talked very seriously about how to form a proposal review committee that could fairly consider the requests from multiple agencies, all of which might be worthy of their limited funding dollars.

The Region II Area Agency on Aging planning process is a good example of just how complicated the translation of conditions into problems can be. (A link to the national agency is on the companion website.) The home health agencies in this rural community used two very different tactics to get their problems into the public record. One talked about the long waiting list, putting a face on the characteristics of elders who are not receiving the services they need. The other director brought in a person to tell her story and grab the attention of those present. Both tactics are successful in that the Council on Aging and the AAA staff left the hearing thinking about how to raise additional dollars to allocate for service

delivery. They are convinced that the need is real, that there are problems that need to be addressed, and that they have to plan accordingly because they too have identified a large gap in in-home service provision in their own needs assessment process. Planning is a function that AAAs are responsible for in every region within the United States, making AAAs important resources when unmet needs have been identified.

☾ THE PLANNING PROCESS

In Chapter 5 we examined methods of investigating situations and analyzing data. As situations morph from conditions to problems, it becomes necessary to plan whether and how to intervene. Your plan will only be as good as the needs assessment (Chapter 4) and your situation-based analysis (Chapter 5).

In this chapter, we focus on the planning process and the feasibility issues that must be addressed before action can take place. For example, on an individual level a treatment plan for 24/7 home care for an elderly person will not be feasible unless resources are available to carry it out. This is illustrated very well by the waiting list in our case example. On the macro level, planning a change may not be feasible unless you have sponsors from both parties to amend a state statute or you have secured the funds needed through grants to create or maintain a program. Assessment and planning occur in tandem as you shift back and forth between examining needs and considering resources to meet those needs. Planning is a systematic process to establish justifiably important objectives and the means and resources to achieve them. It is also a fluid, iterative process with enough flexibility for the advocate to shift priorities as new information emerges.

A traditional planning process is typically portrayed as a series of steps, yet it will come as no surprise to you that these steps do not flow in a neat, logical manner even though they may appear at first glance to be linear. The steps are as follows:

1. Investigate, define, analyze, and prioritize problems/needs based on a values-based vision.
2. Assess both the advocate's and the decision maker's strengths and weaknesses (leverage and the situational threats and opportunities).
3. Identify and prioritize goals and objectives.
4. Identify contingency tactics and strategies that are responsive to the goals.
5. Mobilize resources to facilitate change.

Chapter 5 focuses on Step 1, investigating and analyzing the problems. Here we deal with Steps 2, 3, and 4. Chapter 7 focuses on techniques and interpersonal style issues that comprise the action steps of intervention (Step 5) at the individual and group levels (small scale interven-

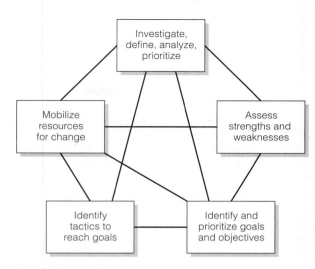

FIGURE 6.1 Nonlinear Steps in Planning

tions), and Chapter 8 focuses on interventions that require large-scale resource mobilization.

Rather than addressing these five steps in a linear manner, think of them as an array of things that you must think about all at once. For example, if you begin by investigating, defining, analyzing, and prioritizing (Step 1), you might wonder how you can do all four of those things before you know the clients' goals and priorities (Step 3). And you may not really want to set goals, perhaps unrealistic ones, before you know what resources are available (Step 5), not to mention various players' strengths and weaknesses (Step 2). Planning requires that you engage in nonlinear thinking as illustrated in Figure 6.1.

The benefits of systematically thinking through a planning process cannot be overestimated. Be sure that you enter each situation sufficiently prepared so that you minimize risks to your clients and reduce uncertainty and ambiguity by building on strengths and reducing the effects of weaknesses (Longest, Rakich, & Darr, 2000). Making quick decisions based on limited information can create even more problems (Donohue & Kolt, 1992). In other words, well-planned confrontations are more successful than unplanned ones.

How much time should you spend planning? Consider this common slogan: There never seems to be enough time to do the job right, but always time to do it over. Planning requires investing time on the front end of the problem as opposed to the back end. Donohue and Kolt (1992) caution advocates against waiting too long to address conflicts lest they grow larger than they might have if the problem had been handled earlier with a little routine maintenance. This chapter provides concrete steps to launch your advocacy efforts, beginning with eight guiding principles. These principles are followed by tasks and conflict resolution strategies.

☾ Guiding Principles of Effective Advocacy Planning

There are many ways to envision the planning process. You might, for example, divide advocacy planning into **long-range planning,** which is the focus of macro systems advocacy, and **short-range planning,** which is more appropriate for individual case or small group advocacy. Planning can be **defensive** and **reactive,** which occurs when advocates respond to environmental circumstances that pose real problems to clients and demand redress (Longest et al., 2000). **Proactive planning** is a preemptive defense strategy designed to protect clients from experiencing harm or to keep small problems from becoming big ones (Longest et al., 2000).

The literature holds multiple plans for planning advocacy. Drawing from a number of sources, we propose eight guiding principles for advocacy planning. *First,* advocacy planning must be client centered. The process must begin and end with the expressed needs, interests, or preferences of the older person. Consequently, the planning process must solicit the elder's input in every reasonable way to clarify wants and needs and to identify outcomes that will satisfy them (Moxley & Hyduk, 2003).

Second, planning processes must be based on sound factual evidence that concretely describes real client needs and their degree of urgency. The needs assessment data discussed in Chapter 5 are important in this part of the planning process.

Third, think before you act and act on facts, not guesses (Urwick, 1956). Gleaning these facts requires "critical observation, cultural sensitivity, and good professional judgment" (Green & Kreuter, 2005, p. 62). The context in which assessment data are gathered and how sensitive these data are to truly understanding clients' needs is critically important.

Fourth, planning should be directed either (a) toward concrete, measurable client specific goals in stable, clearly defined situations, or (b) toward a change in the general direction of target organizations or decision makers in situations that are dynamic, ambiguous, or uncertain (McCaskey, 1974). This principle recognizes that some problems are individually based and others are much bigger, revealing patterns across a number of older persons and indicating the need for a system to change. In situations that involve groups of elders, such as board and care homes in which elders are not receiving appropriate care, the complexity of the situation increases with the number of persons involved. At this point, you must determine whether this is an isolated incident with one person requiring an intervention, or a pattern of incidents that is much greater than one person. Knowing whether you are targeting an individual or group change is critical to the planning process.

Fifth, whenever possible planning should entail face-to-face methods not only between you and the client but also between and among any involved parties, including allied as well as oppositional decision makers. This is not always possible, but when it is feasible, face-to-face interaction may be more effective in persuading others that something needs to occur (or not).

Sixth, embrace a contingency orientation that takes into account the discrete situational variables that commend different approaches to different problems in different circumstances in different settings. Furthermore, you may not have much time to plan because the situation may require immediate action, so you would be wise to have an immediate, or emergency, plan in your brief case (Plan Z—just in case there is no time for Plans A, B, C . . .).

Seventh, advocacy planning is not an amateurish endeavor. Draw upon what is known from all sources, including the literature, practice models, exemplary programs, experts in the field, and

TABLE 6.1 Eight Guiding Principles of Planning Advocacy Interventions

Eight Guiding Principles of Advocacy

1. Advocacy must be client centered and as client directed as possible.
2. Advocacy must be based on sound facts and evidence.
3. Think before you act, and act only on facts.
4. Advocacy must be directed toward measurable goals for individual or systemic changes.
5. Advocacy should be conducted face to face.
6. Advocacy must embrace a contingency perspective (contingent on contextual circumstances).
7. Advocacy is not an amateurish endeavor but must be based on a great deal of knowledge.
8. To be a successful advocate, you must document, document, document.

everything else you can find. This is important not only in the data collection and investigation process but throughout the planning process as new information emerges.

Eighth, formal advocacy on important cases requires that you systematically document every decision and process in the planning process. Include the good decisions and why they were good but also decisions you would make differently next time. Just as in the methodology section of a research article, readers should be able to read your documentation and know what you did and why so that your advocacy experiences can inform advocates who follow in your footsteps. Careful record keeping will also become data in your evaluation of your work.

These eight principles, summarized in Table 6.1, provide the framework for a detailed planning process. We turn now to the six tasks of an ideal planning process.

☺ ADVOCACY TASKS

More specific tasks in the advocacy planning process include: (a) determining whether an advocate is needed, (b) using a situational conflict model, (c) selecting advocacy strategies and tactics, (d) thinking about how to manage conflict, (e) considering the legal implications, and (f) recognizing the power dynamics. Although this ideal process rarely occurs, you can use this template to perform as closely to the ideal as each situation allows.

Task 1. Determine Whether an Advocate Is Needed

After carefully investigating the situation (Chapter 5), you may be able take on the problem without much effort, particularly if the problem is specific to one person. Sometimes, just calling a decision maker's attention to a problem can solve it. In other situations, particularly when the assessment process reveals a good deal of potential conflict, urgency, or risk, or affects more than one person, you may need to spend more time and effort planning how to go about the change process.

As an autonomy-respecting advocate, you will not assume ownership of clients' problems without their consent. Clients should be given every opportunity to determine the need for advocacy, make suggestions, and direct any advocacy efforts. This reflects the assumption that older adults know what they need and want and will act to get it (Moxley & Hyduk, 2003). This includes involvement in selecting options, especially strategies that entail some risk of escalation or retaliation.

Some clients are very articulate and will have no trouble participating in this process. Others have cognitive or communication difficulties that will make it harder for them to become full partners. You must make every reasonable attempt to patiently communicate with clients to determine their needs, wishes, and interests and to assure that they desire help in the first place. After all, older clients have the same rights as anyone to prudently pick or pass on a possible fight

BOX 6.2

Task 1. Determine Whether an Advocate Is Needed

1. Sometimes a problem can be resolved by simply bringing it to the attention of the appropriate decision maker.
2. Even though you are an autonomy-respecting advocate, do not assume ownership of clients' problems without their permission.
3. Some clients will have communication barriers that you must overcome.
4. Obtain clients' informed consent after you have fully explained potential risk or unintended results.
5. Other clients, especially those with cognitive limitations, may need you to advocate for them without their participation.
6. Determine whether the best results could be expected with an internal or external advocate.
7. Beware of clients fearing to be labeled as troublemakers if you advocate for them.

(National Citizens Coalition for Nursing Home Reform [NCCNHR], 1988). (A link to this coalition is on the companion website.)

The older person's informed choice in selecting or accepting an advocate requires that you fully disclose, to the extent possible, the nature of the advocacy situation including any possible risks—this is part of planning. In doing this, you must determine clients' desires for confidentiality, and you may even have to explain to intimidated clients that intervention may not be possible without incidentally divulging their identities (if not their names) by presenting contextual information that may lead decision makers, or other parties, to identify elderly complainants.

You may need to advocate for mentally incapable clients if they are unable to contribute to the planning process except by indicating certain preferences through words, deeds, or affective display (e.g., indications of happiness, fear, displeasure, or agitation). A mentally incapable client may need you to take charge of the whole process.

The need for advocacy is also influenced by the mentally capable client's psychological profile. The client's socioemotional frailty, education, relevant knowledge, culture, and a variety of other factors may influence your plan as well as the tactics you plan to use. Recall the scalar principle of elder advocacy introduced in

Chapter 5—the more risks your client is willing to take on, the more important it is for you, the advocate, to be sure that the client is mentally capable of making such decisions.

The client's setting can also influence the planning and intervention phases of advocacy. For example, clients in specialized care settings are more likely to require external advocates if they lack the stamina to challenge situations by themselves. Furthermore, they may not want to be labeled as troublemakers if they are heavily dependent on the goodwill of their caregivers. Form a hypothetical case in your mind and answer the following questions:

1. Is there is a real need for advocacy?
2. Does this older person need a supportive ally or a full-fledged, take charge of the conflict proxy?
3. Am I the best person to advocate in this situation?
4. Has consent been obtained, and have potential risks been discussed?
5. How is confidentiality being handled? If the older person's name must be revealed to a decision maker, what assurances do I have that this will not result in retaliation?

A summary of the steps for determining whether an advocate is needed is provided in Box 6.2.

Task 2. Use a Situational Conflict Model

In this section we explore (a) the rationale for using a situational conflict model, (b) conflict resolution strategies, including a description of how the model is built on two key concepts (leverage versus urgency or risk), and (c) a return to the AAA Plan in Region II scenario at the beginning of this chapter.

The situational conflict model requires that you assess all facets of the situation to plan the right approach to resolving it. To plan successfully, you must analyze the degree of risk (and its urgency) faced by the older person, including the potential for lost functioning, pain, discomfort, injury, and diminished quality of life. Just as important, however, is to accurately assess your own power, or leverage, to change situations by influencing decision makers who may be cooperative or resistant (which determines conflict tactics and intensity). You must also identify others who may be affected by the proposed changes or who will be responsible and accountable for implementing these changes.

This whole environmental analysis includes the importance of assessing system constraints and the political environment generally, including any ambiguity surrounding a particular situation. In planning, effective advocates must also assess decision makers' potential skills, motives, emotions, and alternatively, their willingness to share power or collaborate. The analysis of unique situations allows you to select the best tactic to solve the presented problem.

To effectively achieve client goals, we present a situational framework of strategies and tactics drawn from the field of conflictology. This model is based on a protocol for micro-level case or client advocacy that focuses on individuals and small groups (Ezell, 2001; Schneider & Lester, 2001; Chapter 7). It is especially useful in situations in which you are initiating action alone, although we also present a tactical conflict model and provide examples that focus on administrative, class, or cause advocacy that targets larger systems for change (Chapter 8).

Rationale for Using a Situational Conflict Model

Using a situational conflict model is important for several reasons (Nelson, Netting, Huber, & Borders, 2001a):

1. To clarify diverse tactical situations that may require equally diverse responses, ranging from cooperation to confrontation
2. To allow advocates to select tactical plans that relay special situational advantages and benefits to elders
3. To clarify the confusion among providers and other elder care professionals about the rights-based advocate's incentives, values, roles, and responsibilities
4. To warn of the danger of inefficiency, suboptimal effects, and potential cooptation in advocates who are too steeped in a conciliation-at-any-cost orientation
5. To increase your awareness of how your own situational leverage (or lack thereof) is crucial to selecting the right plan of action
6. To stress the need for elder conflict surrogates (both within and outside of system boundaries) who are willing to promote elder rights over system imperatives that sometimes unjustly control elders in various settings
7. To link practice and theory via a resident-centered, situation-based conflict guide

These reasons for working from a situational conflict model can help advocates systematically think about the problem resolution process by analyzing situational dynamics that present both barriers to overcome and opportunities for success. With a range of flexible problem-solving and conflict resolution skills, you can use those suited to particular situations involving you, your clients, and the decision makers in a given environment. Each intervention is different, and you will approach each one differently (Deutsch, 1994).

The problems handled by advocates involve people with all their idiosyncrasies, diverse beliefs, values, and roles and may entail solving problems ranging from securing a home delivered meal to forcing medical authorities to honor

Low ▭▭▭▭▭▭▭▭ **LEVERAGE** ▭▭▭▭▭▭▭▭▶ High

FIGURE 6.2 Leverage Continuum

an older patient's desire for a natural death. The advocate's world is full of ambiguity. But no matter how diverse these situations may be, they exhibit certain core dynamics that allow advocates to plan the best intervention by matching encountered situations to a limited range of conflict strategies, which are described in the next section.

Conflict Resolution Strategies

In previous chapters, we introduced the concepts of urgency and risk. We now move to specifics, building on a resident-centered process model to manage long-term care case advocacy (Nelson et al., 2001a). Originally adapted from the Thomas-Kilmann Conflict Mode Instrument (Thomas & Kilmann, 1974), the model is formed along two axes: from low to high leverage and from low to high urgency or risk.

Leverage The advocate's leverage in a given situation is represented on a continuum. **Leverage** can be anything that empowers you in a given circumstance—personal attributes and abilities, including your own status, formal role, credentials, knowledge, support, connections, persuasive ability, legitimate authority, presence, motivation, and courage. Leverage also includes external laws and rules that support your position as an advocate. When these factors leverage or empower you with the decision maker, the resistance to change is minimized (Figure 6.2).

Laws, rules, and regulations that govern various components of the elder-care and human service systems are sources of leverage. Illustrating this point, Nelson and Cox (2003) detailed how nursing home regulations leverage resident advocates by creating an abundance of nonnegotiable circumstances, which establish the way things should be in almost stifling detail. In fact, nursing homes are so heavily regulated that virtually every client problem will involve some violation of law or administrative rule that

may point to the facility's breach of duty to the client. These stringent standards make mediation or extensive problem solving somewhat wasteful because success can be more quickly and efficiently achieved by proving an error to force a concession (Nelson & Cox, 2003). In other words, if you can present a standard and demonstrate that it is not being met (the error), you can, by fiat, force the decision makers to concede that they are in error and must correct it. This leverage, however, can come at a price. Nelson (2000) warned that these conditions invite more intense forms of win-lose conflict, which often spin out of control.

Elder-care advocates in less regulated community-based settings have correspondingly less leverage. Without the power of regulatory standards, they must informally bargain for their clients' interests. Their job is much more complex, far more ambiguous, and altogether more time consuming. It also diminishes the effects of compromise. Interestingly enough, volunteer resident advocates in lightly regulated community long-stay settings served an average of 16 months less than advocates in far more heavily regulated nursing homes. The researchers speculated that this may have been due to the frustration of not having the leverage that accrues when you have comprehensive national standards (Nelson, Netting, Huber, & Borders, 2003).

The importance of a lawful basis for advocacy is important in all elder service settings. Bateman (2000) stressed the inadvisability of performing advocacy without laws, policies, or standards to back you up and emphasized the extreme importance of assessing all legal implications before planning a strategy. He insisted that even simple problems may require legal research to show the other side where it has slipped up. Much advocacy in social and health care is of this type because of the high error rate in decisions on entitlement by welfare bureaucracies. According to Bateman, the department of Social

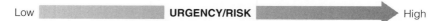

Low ▬▬▬▬▬▬▬ **URGENCY/RISK** ▬▬▬▬▶ High

FIGURE 6.3 Urgency/Risk Continuum

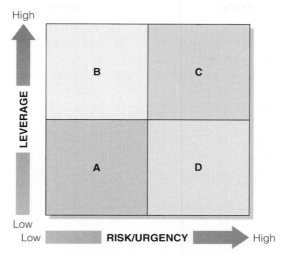

FIGURE 6.4 Situational Conflict Model

Security's own chief adjudication officer has consistently stated that between 5% and 60% of income support decisions are imperfect in some way and that helping professionals are often not well informed about the legalities of their cases.

Urgency or Risk The second axis, urgency or risk, also moves from low to high (Figure 6.3). This continuum assumes that a verified problem exists at some level that requires an intervention based on the advocate's sense of what needs to happen to avoid risk (or more risk) to the older person's quality of care or quality of life. For example, if your client is suffering physical pain or discomfort, or is in imminent risk of danger, the case would be highly urgent. Conditions entailing real psychological pain can also be classified as high urgency, especially if the psychological distress poses other risks.

High-risk or urgent cases require quick plans of sure action, and speed is of the essence. Sometimes the sense of urgency or risk may emanate from what older persons feel about their situations. These two axes merge in the planning framework (Figure 6.4). Examples of problems that fall into the four quadrants of the situational conflict model are discussed next.

Quadrants in the Situational Conflict Model

Quadrant A in Figure 6.4 encompasses situations (clients' problems) that do not pose immediate risks and in which the clients and advocates have very little leverage or power. For example, perhaps your client's (Mark's) local library has a very limited selection of books and CDs, and Mark wants you to lobby the library system to purchase a larger selection. In the grand scheme of things, this is not an urgent matter, and getting the highly bureaucratic library system to make a sizeable purchase will take a great deal more leverage than you have at the moment—thus low risk and low (little) leverage.

Problems in Quadrant B are of relatively low urgency for your client (Mark) but happen to be in an environment in which you have considerable influence or leverage. Perhaps Mark's car is making a strange noise but still runs okay, so he is not in a hurry to spend money on car repairs.

BOX 6.3

Task 2. Use a Situational Conflict Model

1. Assess all facets of each problem to plan the right approach to resolve it.
2. You may advocate for individuals or groups or for classes or causes.
3. Assess your leverage or power against the urgency or risk to client (more regulation provides more leverage or power for advocacy).
4. Learn decision makers' skills, motives, and willingness to share power and collaborate.
5. Understand the political positions of all players.
6. Discuss the rights-based approach with all players.
7. Clarity your own role, values, and responsibilities.
8. You must possess a range of problem-solving skills.
9. Know the legal positions of all parties.
10. Look for an error to force a concession.

You (his advocate) have a friend who is beginning a car repair business and needs customers, so you can refer Mark to that shop right away to get the car fixed before it becomes urgent or risky for Mark to drive. Hence, low urgency and high leverage combine in that particular problem area.

Quadrant C encompasses problems of utmost urgency in which the client is at highest risk, and you (the advocate) have a great deal of leverage. For example, on one occasion the driver of the local van transportation system for people with disabilities did not secure Steve's wheelchair, and it rolled all over the van. Steve had no way to control it, and the loud pleas from Steve and the other two passengers for the driver to stop and secure Steve's wheelchair fell on deaf ears. The runaway wheelchair pinned Steve's arm and broke it. In this case, the law is clear that wheelchairs must be secured before the van moves. Steve's chair was not secured (the error—with two eye witnesses). Given that the laws and standards were clear and clearly not met, the bus company had no option but to concede liability and pay all of Steve's medical expenses as well as a sizable settlement for pain and suffering. This case illustrates high risk and high leverage.

Quadrant D encompasses situations of urgency or high risk to the client in which the advocate has little or no leverage to help—perhaps the most frustrating position for both you and Steve. This situation could emerge if burglars had broken into Steve's home and taken everything on which he relied for his quality of life: TV, CD player, radio, the better pieces of furniture including his bed and lift equipment, all of his medications, and about $750 in cash. The intruders wore hoods and did not speak, so Steve has no way to identify them. The police have very little on which to base an investigation, and there were no witnesses. This situation illustrates high urgency and low leverage.

Back to the AAA Plan in Region II

Return to the case at the beginning of the chapter and think about being the director of the faith-based in-home services program. He is aware that allegations against the other in-home services agency have been made and that there has been contentiousness over who should have received funding last year. He has a choice to make. He can come into the public hearing and blast the other home care agency, or he can reinforce the need for services. In assessing leverage and urgency or risk, he might ask himself these questions:

1. How much leverage do I have in this situation?
2. How urgent is this situation?
3. How much risk to clients is involved if I intervene?

The steps for using the situational conflict model to clarify options are outlined in Box 6.3.

Task 3. Select Advocacy Strategies and Tactics

The conflict model can serve as a planning framework designed to distinguish how different resident risk, need, and urgency levels are balanced against the advocate's leverage to influence the situation. Various combinations of these dimensions determine the selection of the primary strategic approach to solving residents' problems. The interventions advocates plan to improve their chances of causing change include fairly broad general approaches or strategies. A strategy is an overriding direction under which specific actions (tactics) are performed.

Collaboration, for example, can be seen as a win-win strategy for problem solving. It is characterized as a high trust, somewhat time-consuming endeavor, in which the goal is to solve a problem in a way that meets everyone's needs. Specific collaborative tactics include mediation, negotiation, and other forms of bargaining. Techniques are even more refined and are used to support tactics, such as imploring the help of the decision maker by using a distressed, pleading, or forlorn communication style.

Four Broad Situational Conflict Resolution Strategies

The situational conflict resolution model is completed here. In Figure 6.5 four broad strategies have been added to the four quadrants: A: building alliances; B: consultation; C: from persuading to forcing; and D: problem solving. The best strategies employ a manageable number of tactics that preserve good relations in situations of mutual problem solving and interpersonal conflict. We now discuss each of these four conflict resolution strategies.

Building Alliances Building alliances is always your primary strategic choice. However, if there is low urgency or risk and you have little or no leverage, consider not doing anything at all. Deciding *not* to make an issue of this situation is an option. This is avoidance and may be a viable option. Classic conflict theory includes the idea that avoidance is ideal when no problem actually

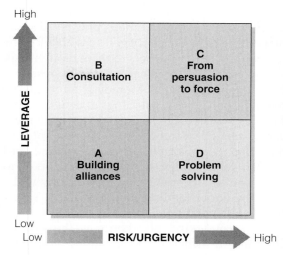

FIGURE 6.5 Situational Conflict Model With Four Main Resolution Strategies

exists, when the problem is so unimportant that it does not warrant the expenditure of time or effort to solve it, or when the risks of conflict escalation make the effort too risky. In the classic conflict model, the need to engage or not engage (avoid) in conflict is determined by whether a verifiable (or expressly desired) client need exists. Avoidance is desirable if the need is nonexistent, dubious, or frivolous. Verifiable needs justify intervention.

Advocates form two fundamental types of alliances. The most effective alliance is often the **internal-external alliance,** which exists when the advocate enlists the direct help of the decision maker to solve clients' problems. Internal-external alliances are more likely in morphostatic systems in which the goal is not to fundamentally change the system structure per se but to repair the normal glitches that occur in any human endeavor. Because both internal and external role holders assume the advocate's mantle in morphostatic systems, and since both generally share the same values regarding the system's worth and integrity, high-intensity conflict is less likely.

An internal-external alliance is ideal in low urgency situations. Forming an alliance is a more complex process than acting unilaterally.

It requires coordination between the external advocate, and perhaps others, and the decision maker. The lack of urgency gives the alliance time to form and for its partners to share thoughts and jointly assess the problem to identify resources and possible solutions. Moreover, an alliance is often the only way to get things done if the advocate has low leverage. This is not to say that alliances cannot be formed to solve urgent problems, but alliances are not always feasible in time sensitive situations, unless the allies have worked together before and can remobilize quickly with a common understanding about each other's roles, beliefs, behaviors, and goals.

A second kind of alliance is the **external coalition** to increase the advocate's leverage to influence decision makers who are not part of the alliance. In this type of alliance, the advocate does not have the power (leverage) to act unilaterally and must form an empowering relationship with another party who has the connections, savvy, or power to influence an otherwise disinterested, distracted, or resistant decision maker.

At the client and administrative levels of advocacy, alliances often form among colleagues within the organization because problems can be solved internally. However, at the community and the highest macro or cause levels, alliances are typically interorganizational given the need to exert the collective power of stakeholders to influence larger systems. A general rule is the larger the system targeted for change, the greater the need for coalition building (Houser, 2002). Advocacy at the community and the highest macro or cause levels often requires alliances to exert the collective power of stakeholders to influence larger systems.

Consultation Like alliances, a consultation strategy is ideal in low urgency situations in which the client is not threatened by imminent harm. Consultation requires working together in an atmosphere of mutual trust and respect (Kintler & Adams, 1997), and this takes time. Consultation is essentially an educational approach intended to gently and naturally lead the decision maker to see the wisdom of changing some circumstance to meet your clients' needs.

Because the client's needs are not urgent, there is no reason for an advocate to push too hard for change—this might stir resentment or build resistance. Consultants need to step back and reflect on how to present and sell the best solution. This may be difficult when the advocate is invested in an issue. Not letting your personal needs and frustrations take over can be difficult when there is a high personal investment in making change.

Consultation is a strategy often associated with conditions of low client risk or urgency and high leverage. As an advocate, you will only be able to consult if your leverage is high enough for you to be accepted as an expert or authority. Successful consultation requires that the decision maker respects and accepts your advice. It doesn't matter whether you see yourself as someone worth listening too, but it does require that the decision maker accept your skills, knowledge, experience, and authority.

From Persuasion to Force The strategic range from **persuading (convincing)** to forcing includes arguing, warning, and literally forcing by fiat or litigation. It is axiomatic that advocates cannot effectively employ such aggressive, competitive, and potentially risky strategies unless their leverage (authority, quantity and quality of evidence, legal mandate) is high. Moreover, these tactics (including win-lose argumentation) invite escalation and even retaliation. They should not be employed unless time is of the essence and the issue is of high importance (risk/urgency) to the client. Under such circumstances, and if the decision maker is resistant, forcing is required because there is not time for lengthy procedural and other forms of bargaining. Other forcing tactics include filing grievances, going over a decision maker's head, bringing in legal experts, hard (win-lose) bargaining, and even large-scale community action or class action lawsuits. Forcing can involve both campaign and contest strategies, which are often described in books on macro level change (Netting, Kettner, & McMurtry, 2004).

Forcing can be highly stressful and should never be implemented unless fully justified and carefully planned. It is rarely a good choice for newly minted advocates, not only because of its high risks but because it requires high leverage, a commodity that neophyte advocates seldom possess. Some advocates, regulators, for example, can punish directly. For most advocates, however, the power to coerce is informal and rests in the implicit ability to cause harm as signaled through a threat or warning. If deftly wielded, this can bring a quick settlement. However, in planning competitive (win-lose) interventions, advocates should consider the effects of the proportionality maxim (Rummel, 1991) and the theory of rational choice. **Proportionality** requires that resistance be met with equal force (in situations where forcing is necessary), and the **rational choice principle** warns that coercive tactics should be employed only if the potential benefits of the goal outweigh the risks to achieve it (Goldman, 1986). If these rules are followed and the advocate has planned to use the right strategy, tactics, and style for the situation, confident and competent forcing can be effective—certainly more so than avoidance, defined by Donohue and Kolt (1992) as doing nothing when something needs to be done.

Our planning framework predicts that more confrontive forms of conflict are required in urgent situations in which the decision maker is uncooperative and the advocate has sufficient leverage to have a reasonable chance of compelling action. Here, the advocate must be clear about the possibility of intensification. This can happen because the client's high risk/urgency forces the advocate to be legitimately more concerned about the client's pressing needs than the decision maker's concerns, goals, and feelings. Even if the advocate advances a case calmly and professionally, decision makers may still misconstrue this relative disregard for their interests as being callous, rude, insulting, unhelpful, or even as a personal attack. If the advocate's communication style is inappropriate, you can be sure that sparks will fly.

Problem Solving This strategy works best when the advocate has low leverage and high urgency. Problem solving involves engaging the appropriate parties and attempting to collaborate with them in solving an important concern that the advocate lacks the essential leverage (including possibly knowledge, skills, legal mandate, or power) to solve alone. When the risk or urgency for the client is high, the advocate must invest time and energy in seeking help by comparing information, thinking with others about possible solutions, and working together in a synergistic effort to make a change. Compromise is often seen as a type of problem-solving strategy in which each party gives up something so that a solution can be agreed upon.

Problem solving may entail milder, collaborative forms of respectful conflict, but does not alienate those persons whose help you need to solve important problems. Compare two people hearing the same complaint. One heard a fuzzy allegation and charged ahead full tilt, hazarding unsupportable assertions and destroying his own credibility. Another, hearing the same complaint, moved ahead cautiously, monitoring potential troubles until the facts warranted a planned intervention. Two advocates, two approaches—one productive, one not (Nelson et al., 2001b).

The following questions provide a guide for the advocate who is trying to determine what approach might work best in a given situation. Consider these questions carefully:

1. In which of the four quadrants do I place myself in this situation (based on my understanding of leverage and urgency/risk)?
2. What strategies will work best?
3. Have these strategies been used before in similar situations I've encountered, and if so, with what success?

Box 6.4 summarizes the tasks in selecting advocacy strategies.

Task 4. Think About How to Manage Conflict Intensity

In planning tactical interventions, successful advocates anticipate the likelihood of conflict and welcome productive, win-win conflict, but they also recognize that some conditions require

BOX 6.4

Task 3. Select Advocacy Strategies and Tactics

1. Determine the quadrant that best fits the present situation.
2. Determine whether that strategy has worked well for you in previous situations.
3. Develop a repertoire of flexible problem-solving skills.
4. The best strategies employ a manageable number of tactics that preserve good relationships.
5. Avoidance is the ideal tactic when no problem actually exists.
6. The larger the system targeted for change, the greater the need for building a coalition.

TACTICS SPECIFIC TO BUILDING ALLIANCES

1. Alliance building should always be your first choice of strategies.
2. Alliances may be the only way to get anything done if you have low leverage (little or no evidence).
3. In morphostatic systems (that do not want to change) the internal and external players both wear the advocate's mantle.
4. Higher level advocacy (class/causes) usually requires alliances.

TACTICS SPECIFIC TO CONSULTATION

1. Work with others in mutual trust.
2. Consultation is an educational approach; gently lead the decision maker to see the wisdom of your plan.

3. It does not matter whether you see yourself as a strong and effective advocate as long as clients and decision makers see you that way.

TACTICS SPECIFIC FOR USING PERSUASION (CONVINCING) TO FORCE

1. Tactics include arguing, warning, and forcing by fiat or litigation, filing grievances, but these invite escalation and retaliation.
2. Forcing can bring quick results, but not without cost.
3. Do not threaten that which you cannot deliver.
4. Remember that actions are met with equal force.
5. Contrary to proportionality, the rational choice principle warns that coercive tactics should be used only if the potential benefits of the goal outweigh the risks.
6. Look for any errors that could, by fiat, force concessions.
7. Going over a decision maker's head could result in a lawsuit against you.
8. Forcing tactics are best left to seasoned advocates.

TACTICS SPECIFIC TO PROBLEM SOLVING

1. Engage appropriate parties to collaborate.
2. Try synergistic tactics.
3. Think through possible compromises.

forcing, which runs some risk for conflict intensification that occasionally spins out of control. Of course, unproductive conflict per se is not limited to forcing. It is just as dysfunctional for an advocate to avoid conflict in the face of pressing client needs or to engage in prolonged mediation over conditions that are really nonnegotiable, such as when an older person's legal rights are thwarted.

For example, a physician may decide to ignore a patient's duly executed advanced directive refusing aggressive treatment. In this circumstance, skirting the issue or trying to negotiate or compromise a friendly solution is dysfunctional. Clearly, the most efficient and effective approach here is to confront the physician with a professionally firm, perhaps even stylistically friendly

BOX 6.5

Task 4. Think About How to Manage Conflict Intensity

1. Analyze how much conflict to expect, anticipated sources and how to handle it.
2. Devise ways to make conflict productive.
3. Know how you will protect the elder from harm if conflict occurs.

4. Be sure you are confident when confronting people in high positions such as physicians.

argument about the nonnegotiability of an advanced directive. Here, there is nothing wrong with fair, firm, and friendly confrontation (about which we will have much more to say later).

Another purpose of advocacy planning is to identify situationally appropriate tactics that minimize the possibilities of unproductive conflict. The model introduced in Figure 6.5 can help you avoid such conflicts by helping you plan and utilize appropriate strategies.

In summary, *forcing* will be required in conditions where the decision maker is uncooperative and the problem is pressing; *avoidance* is best when the decision maker is uncooperative and the problem is not significant (why risk ruffling feathers?). *Collaboration* (problem solving) is both possible and preferable when the problem is pressing but the decision maker is cooperative. *Conciliation*, or relationship building, is desirable when the client's need is low or not urgent but the provider is cooperative. Some friendly fence mending might get some traction for nonurgent issues, and clients stand to gain by friendly (alliance conducive) relationships between advocates and decision makers as long as client needs remain in the forefront.

Regardless of whether resistance is triggered by the advocate's actions or is preexisting based on the decision maker being polarized around issues of needs, goals, personality, and situations, for the advocate to back down in cases of high client urgency constitutes failure. Forceful counteractions may be necessary, but these actions can only be effective if the advocate has high leverage and the decision maker's resistance is low. If

the advocate deems that the client's need is a low priority (hence, low concern), there is no need to intervene. However, if the client's goal is important and the decision maker is cooperative (low resistance), then collaboration is possible and an alliance can be formed to problem solve.

In considering the intensity of the potential conflict in a situation, it may be helpful to ponder these questions:

1. How much conflict do I anticipate?
2. What and who will be the source of conflict? How do I plan to address this confrontation?
3. How can I keep this process from being unproductive? What will I do to make it productive?
4. How will I ensure that the elder is not harmed if potential conflict occurs?

Box 6.5 summarizes the tasks in thinking about how to manage conflict intensity.

Task 5. Consider the Legal Implications

Whether you are dealing with case or cause advocacy, you are always advocating within the context of the legal system. Therefore, it is important to recognize the legal implications of what you are doing. Think about the different standards of evidence used by attorneys in the justice system; many advocacy-borne conflicts end up in court for final settlement (Hocker & Wilmot, 1991). These rules of evidence establish the advocate's persuasive burden, the level of evidence that is required to prove to the court the validity, probable validity, or nonvalidity of case-specific data. For example, in elder abuse cases involving criminal negligence that entail allegations of reckless disregard for the older person's safety, the lawyer-advocate will need to present factual evidence of sufficient quantity and quality to convince a jury **beyond a reasonable doubt** that a crime has been committed. A slightly lower standard of evidence, typically required in guardianship hearings, for example, when the client may face a profoundly devastating loss of rights and prerogatives, requires proof that is clear, cogent, and convincing (Stavis, n.d., para 5).

Most legal proceedings, however, employ a still lower level of proof, requiring only a **preponderance of evidence** showing that the situation is more likely to have occurred (51%) than not (49%). This is the standard for noncriminal negligence, for example, which "constitutes a failure to exercise the degree of care a reasonable person exercises under the same circumstances that results in injury to another" (Allen, 1997, p. 284). This is also the standard of evidence for most tort claims, which, in the context of elder advocacy, include situations where the duty of decision makers (or their agents) to provide a service, or standard of care, is breached, resulting in some harm to clients.

Advocates with lower relative personal or positional power than the decision maker can boost their power by presenting better quality evidence than a more powerful (higher status) advocate might have to present. The higher status advocate is more likely to be listened to because of personal status, expertise, and connection, and these cases will have more traction because of the person presenting them.

Finally, you will need to know the special standards of evidence that apply to each elder-care setting. For example, in many states the duty to report elder abuse or institutional resident abuse requires mandatory reporters (e.g., caregivers, government officials, and social workers) to notify Adult Protective Services based on a very low standard of **reasonable suspicion.** If the mandatory reporter does not reasonably doubt an allegation, physical indication, or even a hearsay claim that abuse has occurred, the advocate

should report the incident. If the advocate has some reason to doubt the received claim, then a preliminary investigation should be undertaken to ascertain whether more evidence might justify a report.

Keeping in mind the potential legal implications of planning for a change, ask yourself these questions:

1. Are there standards of evidence specific to the current setting? If so, do I have and understand them?
2. Can I use a preponderance of evidence to make my case for change or to boost my advocacy role?
3. What is the likelihood that this case will escalate into a formal administrative hearing or judicial process? (Higher risk/urgency cases are often likely to go this route and be subject to higher standards of evidence than those sufficient for negotiation processes of informal advocacy.)
4. Do I need to have someone with legal expertise involved in the planning process?

Box 6.6 summarizes the tasks in considering the legal implications of your actions.

Task 6. Recognize the Power Dynamics

Effective planning requires the ability to exercise power. One way of doing this is to use Rummel's (1991, p. 72) process formula for exerting power:

$$\text{Power} = \text{Interests} \times \text{Capability} \times \text{Will}$$

This equation suggests that your ability to influence (power) equals your *capability* times your *will* or determination to act as an advocate. Your determination will vary by the strength of your commitment to the values involved in the interaction. If you are advocating for a purpose to which you are highly committed, perhaps even with which you psychologically identify, you may be unwavering and your willingness to engage almost inexhaustible.

This formula illustrates the importance of your capability (beyond the desire to help) to influence the decision maker. **Capability** is the

BOX 6.6

Task 5. Consider the Legal Implications

1. Know the standards of evidence for the particular setting you are facing.
2. Present clear, cogent, and convincing evidence.
3. Know the likelihood that your case will escalate into formal administrative hearings.
4. Know when to bring in legal counsel and do so.
5. Know the meanings of legal jargon.

advocate's power base and is comprised of many possible sources. At the most basic level is knowledge. Beyond knowledge, however, advocates have other sources of **personal power,** and some will have the power of position. Etzioni (1961) suggested that high levels of personal power coupled with **position power** (also called legitimate power) accords the advocate control over organizational resources. Consider how advocates who hold high-status roles within their professions or organizations have the clout to get things done. Internal advocates with both position and personal power are especially well poised for effective advocacy.

Effective advocates have keen insight about how their personal power bases can influence others. Thinking about your personal power is essential to planning any intervention. Personal power derives from a range of sources, and one of the most important is **expertise** (French & Raven, as cited in Hersey & Blanchard, 1988). Advocates can empower themselves by developing expertise.

Another critical source of personal power rests on your communication skills, or your ability to persuade (Hocker & Wilmot, 1991). The power of interpersonal linkages has been called **connection power** and involves the ability to get things done (Hersey & Goldsmith, as cited in Hersey & Blanchard, 1988). **Information power** is subtly different from expert power because it implies that the advocate has knowledge of the intricacies of a system's informal processes or "knows the ropes" (Raven & Kruglanski, 1975). **Referent power** refers to the advocate's innate, personality-based likeability, or charisma. Charisma is the ability to convince others to change by virtue of your personality. Probably the least prominent form of power for external advocates is **reward power,** the ability to confer or withhold rewards. Some advocates have position power, or formal authority. For example, AAA directors can fund proposals for advocacy. **Coercive power** is the ability to force someone to change and may be required in situations of extreme situations (French & Raven, as cited in Hersey & Blanchard, 1988).

These types of power are moot without assessing them in the context of the interaction of two or more actors in social relationship (Hocker & Wilmot, 1991). In context, advocates must plan their interventions based on assessments of their own power bases as influenced by the decision maker's power bases. Thus, intervention planning entails assessing your perceived power point by point against the perceived power of the decision makers who can make the needed changes.

Boosting Your Power

As you plan to intervene in any situation, recognize the inherent power dynamics. Aside from working with others, you might also use referent power as you try to build relationships with decision makers (thus building power through interpersonal linkages) before you act

(Pfeffer, 1977). You might ask the decision maker to help you in some way. Or if time permits, you can try to make the decision maker more dependent on you by sharing information or expertise (Hocker & Wilmot, 1991) or helping in some other way (Kolb, 1994). If talking to the decision maker before pursuing the change you need to pursue is not possible, talk to someone who knows your target to learn about the decision maker's values, communication style, tactics, interests, and reactions (Hindle, 1998). In fact, anything you can do to make the decision maker more willing to cooperate, thus increasing your power, is desirable. Other ways to boost your power may be time consuming. Benzinger's nine-step model for acquiring power (cited in Hersey & Blanchard, 1988) can be effective:

1. Know the language and secret codes of the system or organization in which you will conduct advocacy. This boosts your *communication power.*
2. Know the priorities of the target system or organization so you can telegraph your support or empathy for those goals. This will help build your *relational power* of interpersonal linkages by creating common purpose.
3. Learn the power lines, both formal and informal (the grapevine) in the system or organization in which you are advocating. This builds your *information power.*
4. Get to know the decision maker if time permits, this builds your *connection power,* making it extremely unlikely that dysfunctional conflict will ensue because in most conflicts the "attempts to harm another in any way are extremely rare" (Mayer, 1991, p. 8).
5. Hone your formal knowledge about the case at hand. This increases your case specific *expert power.*
6. Take whatever action you can. Initiative increases the perception that you have power, which in turn, increases your actual power (Donohue & Kolt, 1992).

7. Take risks when the situation is urgent, time is of the essence, and you are sure that action is necessary.
8. Don't be shy about applauding your successes. This increases your acceptance by others as an advocate with expertise.
9. Meet the older person's needs, whatever you do, as this is also a clear sign of expert advocacy. It is your reason for being an advocate.

Naturally, you will not be able to do all of these items in a given situation, especially if you are an external advocate, but you may have the time to do one or more of these on short notice in an important situation. Over the long haul, pursue all of these goals in the context of the aging network as these are essential skills for elder advocates. Box 6.7 summarizes the tasks involved in recognizing the power dynamics of the situation.

☻ TARGETS AND LEVELS OF INTERVENTION

Having examined power dynamics, let's move on to determine targets and levels of intervention. If this is a problem involving one older person or a small group, you will engage in case advocacy (Chapter 7). However, if you find that this is a much bigger problem, one that affects a number of people, you may determine that the level of intervention is at the administrative, cause, or systems level. In other words, you may become engaged in macro-level change (Chapter 8).

It is not unusual to begin with individual advocacy to address an urgent need that you cannot put off until you can make a structural change. People's lives often hang in the balance if immediate action isn't taken. Thus you may proceed at the individual level, solve the problem for that one individual, but go forward to join others to advocate for broader scale change. Depending on the evidence you have accumulated and the investigation you have done, you

BOX 6.7

Task 6. Recognize the Power Dynamics

1. Understand this formula and know how and when to use different kinds of power: Power = Interests × Capability × Will.
2. Capability (more than desire) contains all kinds of power and their proper uses.
3. Knowledge is the most basic power, so do your homework.
4. Personal power derives from a variety of sources including your communication skills and ability to persuade.
5. Position (legitimate) power derives primarily from your expertise and official position, or the ability to activate organizational and other resources.
6. Information power accrues when you know a great deal about the problem or issue on the table. Boost it by knowing the communication lines and grapevines.
7. Power includes individuals' referent power, which is innate, or personality or charisma. Referent power increases when you build relationships with decision makers.
8. Power includes your ability to confer rewards such as recognition, jobs, raises, or favors.
9. Coercive power is your ability to force change, but use it very carefully.
10. Knowing the language and codes or the target system will boost your communication power.
11. Know the target systems' priorities so you can build your relational power.
12. Know the power lines of communication and the grapevines.

may be planning a sequential set of interventions. In either case, you must know where to begin. Answering these questions rounds out the planning process:

1. What are the power dynamics in this situation? What types of power do I have (or not)?
2. At what level of intervention is my advocacy effort directed? Whom do I target first?
3. Are there multiple targets? If so, do I need to move from one to the next, or can I target them simultaneously?

☾ SUMMARY

We began this chapter with a case example that focused on a regional planning effort required of all Area Agencies on Aging as they develop their service plans. We then introduced five classic

steps to planning advocacy interventions: (a) defining problems/needs, (b) assessing strengths, weaknesses, threats, and opportunities, (c) prioritizing goals and objectives, (d) selecting strategies and tactics, and (e) taking action. Guiding principles underscored in the literature on advocacy planning include being client centered, using factual evidence, considering context, targeting, using face-to-face methods, embracing contingencies, drawing from what is known, and being systematic.

A planning framework composed of six tasks was then identified: (a) determine if an advocate is needed, (b) use a situational conflict model, (c) select advocacy strategies and tactics, (d) think about how to manage conflict intensity, (e) consider legal implications, and (f) recognize the power dynamics. Table 6.2 outlines this planning framework. We presented the situational conflict model, which combines leverage and urgency, or risk. We

TABLE 6.2 Advocacy Planning Framework

Task 1. Determine Whether an Advocate Is Needed

1. Is there is a real need for advocacy?

2. Does this older person need a supportive ally or a full-fledged, take charge of conflict proxy?

3. Am I the best person to advocate in this situation?

4. Has consent been obtained, and, in the process, have potential risks been disclosed?

5. How is confidentiality being handled? If the older person's name must be revealed to a decision maker, what assurances do I have that this will not result in retaliation?

Task 2. Use a Situational Conflict Model

1. How much leverage do I have in this situation?

2. How urgent is this situation?

3. How much risk to clients is involved if I intervene?

Task 3. Select Advocacy Strategies and Tactics

1. In which of the four quadrants do I place myself in this situation (based on my understanding of leverage and urgency/risk)?

2. What strategies will work best?

3. Have these strategies been used before in similar situations I've encountered, and if so, with what success?

Task 4. Think About How to Manage Conflict Intensity

1. How much conflict do I anticipate?

2. What and who will be the source of conflict? How do I plan to address this confrontation?

3. How can I keep this process from being unproductive? And what will I do to make it productive?

4. How will I ensure that the elder is not harmed if potential conflict occurs?

Task 5. Consider the Legal Implications

1. Are there standards of evidence that are specific to the current setting? If so, do I have and understand them?

2. Can I use a preponderance of evidence to make my case for change or to boost my advocacy role?

3. What is the likelihood that this case will escalate into a formal administrative hearing or judicial process? (Higher risk/urgency cases are often likely to go this route and be subject to higher standards of evidence than those sufficient for negotiation processes of informal advocacy.)

4. Do I need to have someone with legal expertise involved in the planning process?

Task 6. Recognize the Power Dynamics

1. What are the power dynamics in this situation? What types of power do I have (or not)?

2. At what level of intervention is my advocacy effort directed? Who do I target first?

3. Are there multiple targets? If so, do I need to move from one to the next, or can I target them simultaneously?

4. Will I coordinate the advocacy effort myself or hand the plan over to others?

5. What is the time line, and what resources are needed?

6. Do I envision starting at one level of intervention and moving to others (e.g., from individual to community change or from group to policy change)?

describe in detail when to use the four main conflict resolution strategies: building alliances, consultation, a range from persuading to forcing, and problem solving. The chapter ends with a brief section on targets for and levels of advocacy intervention plans.

Chapter 7 focuses on micro-level intervention, and Chapter 8 introduces class or cause advocacy.

DISCUSSION QUESTIONS AND EXERCISES

1. Using the District II Area Agency on Aging public hearing scenario at the beginning of the chapter, describe the strategies and tactics being used by the various players. What types of power are evident?

2. A traditional planning process typically has five steps. How do these five steps relate to the five guiding principles for advocacy planning? Compare and contrast advocacy planning with traditional planning. How are they similar and different? How might traditional planning actually oppress advocates?

3. Think about how you personally deal with conflict. Are there types of strategies that you use more than others or that you prefer to use? How might your preferences affect your role as an advocate?

4. What are the pros and cons of including older persons in the advocacy planning process? What methods might you use to assure maximum participation? Are there times when an advocate might find full participation problematic?

5. Can you think of examples of when you've had high leverage? What contributed to your leverage? Now think of times when you had low leverage. What were the power dynamics in that situation?

6. How would you know whether there is high urgency or high risk? How would you go about determining urgency and risk?

7. Four strategies are presented in the situational conflict model. Tactics typically are the actions that accompany strategies, yet they are not necessarily tied to just one strategy. What tactics might be appropriate under multiple strategies? Can you think of tactics we did not identify in the chapter?

8. Are there standards of evidence in the setting in which you work or in a setting with which you are familiar? What is a standard of evidence, and how might this concept assist you in advocacy planning?

9. What types of power do you hold? What types of power would you like to acquire? How would you go about boosting your power? How might you use power in situations of elder advocacy?

10. Respond to these questions based on the eight guiding principles of advocacy (see Table 6.1):
    - Describe three situations in which it would it be okay for you to deviate from the principle of client centeredness.
    - What if you do not have sound facts and evidence?
    - What if there is no time to think things through before you act? What is your emergency plan?
    - You understand that advocacy should be conducted face to face, but the people you need to interview live elsewhere and the travel distance is prohibitive. What is your plan to overcome this barrier?
    - What does it mean that advocacy must be contingent on contextual circumstances?
    - In what six substantive areas do you need to be knowledgeable to be an effective advocate?
    - What six kinds of information should you document in the investigative and planning phases?

ADDITIONAL READINGS

Bardach, E., & Kagan, R. A. (Eds.). (1982). *Social regulation: Strategies for reform.* San Francisco: Institute for Contemporary Studies.

Friedson, E. (1986). *Professional powers.* Chicago, IL: The University of Chicago Press.

Holder, E. L. (1985). Organizing for change in long-term care facilities. In C. Ewig & J. Griggs (Eds.), *Public concerns community initiatives* (pp. 27–69). New York: United Hospital Fund of New York.

Hunt, S. (2002). *Best practices: Using systems advocacy to improve life for residents.* Washington, DC: National Long-Term Care Ombudsman Resource Center.

Klar, Y., Bar-Tal, D., & Kruglanski, A. W. (1988). Conflict as a cognitive schema: Toward a social cognitive analysis of conflict and conflict termination. In W. Stroebe, A. W. Kruglanski, D. Bar-Tal, & M. Hewstone (Eds.), *The social psychology of intergroup conflict: Theory, research, and applications.* Berlin: Springer-Verlag.

McKenzie, J. F., & Jurs, J. L. (1993). *Planning, implementing, and evaluating health promotion programs.* New York: Macmillan.

Monk, A., Kaye, L. W., & Litwin, H. (1984). *Resolving grievances in the nursing home: A study of the ombudsman program.* New York: Columbia University Press.

Nelson, H. W. (2000). Injustice and conflict in nursing homes: Toward advocacy and exchange. *Journal of Aging Studies, 14*(1), 39–61.

Nelson, H. W. (2003). The causes and consequences of conflict and violence in nursing homes: Working towards a collaborative work culture. *The Health Care Manager, 22*(4), 349–360.

Nelson, H. W., Netting, F. E., Huber, R. & Borders, K. (1999). *The long-term care ombudsman program: An advocacy taxonomy.* Poster presentation to Gerontological Society of America, San Francisco, CA.

Nelson, H. W., Netting, F. E., Huber, R., & Borders, K. (2004). Factors effecting volunteer ombudsman effort and service duration: Comparing active and resigned volunteers. *Journal of Applied Gerontology, 23*, 309–323.

Nelson, W. (1995). *Biennial report, state office of the long-term care ombudsman.* Salem, OR: Office of the State Long-Term Care Program.

Netting, F. E., & O'Connor, M. K. (2003). *Organization practice.* Boston: Allyn & Bacon.

Oberschall, A. (1973). *Social conflict and social movements.* Englewood Cliffs, NJ: Prentice-Hall.

Oregon State Senior and Disabled Services Division. (1997, July 7). *Standards of complaint investigation and report writing: Establishing the burden of proof for corrective action.* Salem OR: Author.

Roloff, E. M., Tutzauer, F. E., & Dailey, W. O. (1989). The role of argumentation in distributive and integrative bargaining contexts: Seeking relative advantage but at what cost? In M. A Rahim (Ed.), *Managing conflict: An interdisciplinary approach.* New York: Praeger.

Ross, H. S., & Mico, P. R. (1980). *Theory and practice in health education.* Palo Alto, CA: Mayfield.

Ross, M. G. (1955). *Community organization.* New York: Harper & Brothers.

Schneider, R. L., & Lester, L. (2001). *Social work advocacy: A new framework for action.* Belmont, CA: Brooks/Cole.

Simmons-Morton, B. G., Greene, W. H., & Gottlieb, N. H. (1995). *Introduction to health education and health promotion* (2nd ed.). Prospect Heights, IL: Waveland Press.

Vander Zanden, J. W. (2003). *Human development* (7th ed.). [Revised by T. L. Crandall & C. H. Crandell]. New York: McGraw-Hill Higher Education.

Wainess, R. (1982). *Role of the ombudsman: Ombudsman technical assistance manual.* Washington DC: Administration on Aging.

Ziegelmueller, G. W., & Kay, J. (1997). *Argumentation: Inquiry and advocacy* (3rd ed). Boston, MA: Allyn & Bacon.

P A R T   THREE

PRACTICING ADVOCACY

Intervening with Individuals

All concessions teach the lesson that more
concessions will be made. GOULD (2000)

BOX 7.1

B E R T H A

Bertha lived in a small brick home in the city. At age 92 she was proud to be able to live alone and to take care of most of her needs. "Being independent is very important to me," she told her friends and neighbors. She had two children who lived across the country from her. They came to visit twice a year, sent notes and cards, and each called Bertha once a week.

During the summer when both her son and daughter were visiting, they became concerned that Bertha seemed unsteady on her feet and more fragile than when they had visited during the holidays. Bertha was honest with them saying, "Your mother is getting old. You've got to realize that. But I'm fine here by myself." Her children wanted someone to check on Bertha once a day, to ease their own minds and to be their eyes and ears when they could not be there. They approached Bertha with their concern.

Bertha agreed that it would be nice to have someone check on her once a day because she knew that if anything happened to her no one would know unless she didn't show up for church or call the one remaining pharmacy in town that still delivered medications. And a list of medications she had! Bertha agreed with her children that they could contact the Friendly

Helpers in town and see if a companionship service could be set up.

Friendly Helpers agreed to send Barb out for an in-home interview to see if there was a good fit with Bertha. Barb arrived right on time, and it was obvious that she and Bertha bonded right away. They had a lot in common. Both liked to knit and crochet, they watched the same soap operas, and they had lived in the same neighborhood all their lives. Bertha's daughter called the supervisor and told her that Barb was perfect for their mother, and a schedule was set up for Barb to come every afternoon from 3:00 to 4:00 o'clock to check on Bertha and see if she needed anything at the store. She would even do some light cleaning during that time as needed.

The children left with a good feeling about Barb and the relationship they could see developing with their mother. Barb and Bertha got along royally, and Bertha began looking forward to their time together as the highlight of her day. Barb would bring her large print books from the library, stop by and get ice cream for her afternoon snack, and even encourage Bertha to take short walks on sunny afternoons. Bertha trusted Barb completely and talked about her when her children called to touch base by phone.

(continued)

BOX 7.1 *(continued)*

One day when Barb arrived Bertha was lying on the living room floor. She was conscious but unable to get up. Barb called 911 and accompanied Bertha to the emergency room. X-rays revealed no broken bones, but the ER physician wanted to admit her just overnight for observation. Barb called the children and reported what had happened, and Friendly Helpers allowed Barb to change her schedule the next day so that she could accompany Bertha home in the ambulance and get her settled. Bertha was very tired and went immediately to bed.

Over the next few days Bertha became increasingly tired and despondent. She told Barb that "it might be my time to go." Barb knew just enough from her training at Friendly Helpers to think there had to be a reason Bertha was suddenly so tired. She knew to start with medications to see if there might be anything going on, and she made a detailed list of the names and dosage amounts of everything Bertha was taking, both prescription and over-the-counter drugs. When Barb showed the pharmacy consultant for Friendly Helpers the list, the pharmacist said that there were several potential problems related to interaction effects that could be causing extreme weakness. One prescription in particular tended to become highly toxic in older adults, which could be at least part of the problem.

Barb told Bertha what she had found out, but she knew that in her role as a companion she did not have (and should not have) access to Bertha's physician. Barb asked permission to call Bertha's daughter and tell her what she had found. Bertha's daughter called the physician that same day, but it was almost impossible to get a call back. She persisted the following morning, calling as soon as she got up. She finally was able to talk with Dr. Raymond's nurse, who said that Bertha needed to come in for a check-up and that they could reevaluate her medications then. It would be a month before they had an appointment time.

Bertha is very tired and there is a distinct possibility that medications may be at least part of the problem. Barb, an aide with Friendly Helpers, has actually gone beyond her role and asked for a pharmacy consult. Given Barb's dependability and the trust that Bertha has in her, Barb has become an advocate for Bertha's welfare. But Barb does not have the power or the leverage to do more than approach Bertha's children, with her permission. It is up to Bertha's daughter to pursue the physician and to seek help. Bertha's condition is getting worse, and waiting a month does not seem like a good idea. Bertha's daughter now has to figure out how to plan for an intervention that will somehow span the geographic distance between them as well as the power differential between her as daughter/advocate and a physician with 1,500 patients, many of whom have very demanding problems.

Bertha does not have the stamina to be her own advocate, and it would be easy for Bertha to fall through the cracks as another invisible old woman with gray hair. These types of situations happen every day in a country with an aging population. Bertha's daughter and Barb are committed to Bertha's welfare, and they will plan an intervention that somehow gets Bertha the attention she needs without waiting a month to see her physician. This is advocacy for an individual, and it is critically important that someone takes Bertha's situation seriously and figures out what to do next.

When investigated, some problems are found to be bigger than originally assumed. These larger advocacy issues that need broader scale attention are addressed in Chapter 8. In this chapter we focus on concerns that affect an individual or a small group and that do not require systemic change (at least initially).

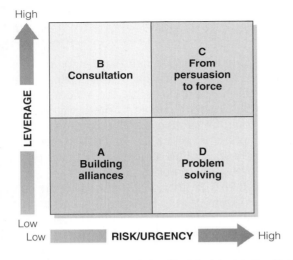

A	Building alliances	Low risk/urgency, no leverage needed
B	Consultation	Low risk/urgency high leverage
C	From persuasion to force	High risk/urgency high leverage
D	Problem solving	High risk/urgency low leverage

Morphogenetic elements create change in otherwise stable systems, and form a core of stability in a changing system, so that events don't spin out of control.

FIGURE 7.1 Situational Conflict Model with Conflict Resolution Strategies

Special attention in both this and the following chapter is devoted to using resources such as volunteers, citizens' advocacy groups, patient advocates, ombudsmen, and a host of other sources that may be needed if the problem escalates. Our intent is to fully inform you about gerontological resources at the local, state, and national levels. More important, we want you to understand the skills that are necessary for effective advocacy.

☾ THE SITUATIONAL CONFLICT RESOLUTION MODEL: STRATEGIES AND TACTICS

Once you, as an advocate, have planfully analyzed a situation, you will have considered the practical skills and strategies necessary to effectively intervene. Four broad strategies were introduced in the situational conflict model: building alliances, consultation, from persuasion to forcing, and problem solving (Chapter 6). Recall that a strategy is an overriding direction under which specific actions (tactics) are performed. This chapter is organized around these four main strategies (Figure 7.1), and we pay close attention to various tactics you might use, depending on the situation. Discussion of each quadrant in the model

(A, B, C, and D) is followed by a summary table listing tactics appropriate for each strategy.

Building Alliances: A Low-Risk Strategy

Alliances are a key strategy used in asymmetrical situations. Locate the point of very low leverage and low risk/urgency for the client in Figure 7.1, and you will see the asymmetry of your position. Alliances are appropriate when your personal leverage is not sufficient to get the job done by yourself and the risk to the client is moderate enough for you to find help. If you feel that you don't have the experience or expertise you need to fully intervene alone or do not yet know the lay of the land, find an ally or two. If the elder's risks are high, this fact alone increases your leverage because emergencies tend to force action.

Alliances work by pooling your intellectual, material, and psychic resources with those of one or more partners, creating a synergy that augments your ability to influence a change (Lamb, 1988). Powerful advocates may also build alliances for many very good reasons, but weaker advocates do not often have as much choice in the matter. The power of the collective is one of the few means available for a less powerful indi-

TABLE 7.1 Quadrant A: Alliance Building Tactics

Low Risk/Urgency for Clients; Advocate Has *Little* Leverage

Nonconflict Tactics		*Conflict Tactics*
Prioritize tasks	Educate/provide information	Write letters
Build your team	Hone surveillance skills	Avoid the conflict
Write care plans	Monitor client problems	Seek conciliation and accommodation
Keep good records	Ask decision maker for help	Create internal-external alliances
Enhance internal alliances		

vidual to influence the otherwise uncontestable power of a decision maker. (Recall that synergy means that the collective is more powerful than the sum of the parts, or everyone acting alone.) The resulting parity makes a fair dialogue possible. As discussed in Chapter 6, your leverage, and hence your general need for an ally, will be greatly influenced by far more than your personality. It also includes your experience, credentials, and cultural competence and your parent organization's setting, structure, credibility, culture, and funding sources.

Nurses (Cavanagh, 1991; Snelgrove & Hughes, 2000), social workers, and government bureaucrats tend to avoid confrontation, as do most new employees in all settings. If you are new to advocacy work, you have not had time to develop a briefcase full of strategies, tactics, and skills for your new role. Consequently, you will logically avoid confrontational advocacy out of fear of getting fired, marginalized, or ostracized—or just out of sheer discomfort of being confrontational in a new setting. But do not feel guilty! You should not feel obliged to assume undue risk. There is no need to abandon your career or hopes of advancement. Building alliances with others is a good option in circumstances in which you do not yet have the personal power to leverage a change.

Nonconflict Preliminaries to Alliance Building

Building alliances entails far more skills and techniques than can be fully addressed here, but we first draw your attention to the nonconflictual aspects of alliance building detailed in Table 7.1. Alliance building entails the threshold surveil-lance skills that are common to all advocates: you must monitor your focal system for any client problems and then prioritize these problems for resolution. If you are an internal advocate, this monitoring is a natural part of doing your job and is accomplished by keeping your eyes and ears open to your clients' needs, whatever they may be. For many providers, care planning and case management are also everyday nonconflictual ways to solve client problems, although they are certainly not immune to conflict, as we shall see.

Using Care Planning as a Tactic

Care planning is a common team-based approach to address client needs. In gerontological settings, interdisciplinary planning is often closely associated (even mandated) for settings such as home care, acute care, hospice care, rehabilitation, nursing home, and subacute care. The care planning process details how treatment teams will work with mentally capable clients and a varying case-specific mix of third party players, including residents' families, close friends, and external consultants. The team's goal is to identify elders' physical, mental, and psychosocial needs and goals, and to decide how, when, and by whom these will be achieved. By doing so, you are taking the first step toward evaluating outcomes (discussed in Chapter 9). **Goals** are end states, or how something will be when the vision is reached. **Measurable objectives** are attached to each goal to detail precisely what is to be done by whom and when to reach the goal. **Process objectives** tell the advocate what has to happen to achieve an outcome. **Outcome objectives** tell the advocate what quality of life change will occur

BOX 7.2

Examples of Goals and Objectives

Goal 1	Outcome Objective
Margaret will have excellent quality care.	Within 2 weeks Margaret will always have water within reach as documented in the medical chart by a staff member 3 times daily.
	Objective 1.1 Within 1 week the Director of Nursing (DoN) will have met with all nurses, orderlies, and aides who work on Margaret's wing, advising them of the importance of Margaret having water within reach at all times.
	Objective 1.2 The following business day the DoN will tell Margaret and any relevant family members that Objective 1.1 has been met.
	Objective 1.3 The DoN will implement a random schedule of when he or one of the nurse supervisors will check to see whether Margaret has water within reach.

Goal 2	Outcome Objective
Margaret will have the opportunity to have a quality spiritual/religious life.	Within 3 months Margaret will indicate that she is very satisfied with the way in which her spiritual/religious life expectations have been enhanced and supported as reported to the facility's social worker.
	Objective 2.1 Within 2 days the social worker will have called Margaret's church and arranged for someone who lives nearby to pick her up each week and take her to church and a visitation program for shut-ins.
	Objective 2.2 Within 2 additional days the social worker will tell Margaret about the arrangements and notify the staff that Margaret needs to be ready for her ride to church on Sundays by 10:30 a.m.
	Objective 2.3 Within 2 months Margaret will have regularly scheduled transportation to attend her church in the community on Sunday mornings and visitors from the church on a regular basis.

for the older person as a result of those processes. Goals may be revised later and need to be fluid and flexible, but you have something concrete to track. If the goal is not attained, you must document that fact and figure out why it was not attained. Teams typically meet on a regular basis to track interventions, review the client's status and goals, and make timely adjustments as needed. See Box 7.2 for some examples of measurable care planning goals and objectives.

Even though care planning is not a conflict strategy or process in and of itself, brainstorming is a critical aspect of team interaction (Tuckman, as cited in Anderson et al., 1999). Team decisions do not always come smoothly or democratically. Disciplinary struggles and forceful tactics are common (Caudron, 2000). Despite the presence of outsiders, the potential for paternalism in provider-dominated teams is so profound that carried to an extreme, one resident activist characterized the process as an "an instrument of terror" (Tulloch, as cited in Kane, 1995, p. 95). The applied advocacy literature stresses the need to involve an informed outside advocate, such as an ombudsman (with the resident's informed permission), to protect the inherently less powerful client's valid preferences and true best interests (Hunt & Burger, 1992). Third parties can either be part of the problem or part of the solution: they might rebalance team power inequities to create a level playing field, or they might fuel dissension.

Teams can face many other challenges based on members' different professional and personal values, role conflict, and miscommunication (Weisbord, 1988). Other problems associated with such teams include ill-defined purposes or processes, power disparities, unrealistic expectations, and closed or asymmetrical dialogues. The biggest challenge is remaining focused on client needs when team members have their own goals and agendas (McLaughlin & Kaluzny, 1983). Steep power asymmetries can be overcome in two ways. High-powered actors can share power to ensure that low-powered players get equal time, or low-power players can form an alliance to rebalance power inequities. The most important thing for you, the advocate, to keep in mind is that care planning teams may have a tendency to plan *without* the older person or a family member present. Ironically, since care planning is about a person's life, you may need to remind yourself and other team members that if at all possible the person whose care plan is being developed needs to be there. It may fall to you to keep the older person's interests, values, and needs always in the forefront of team dialogue.

Alliance Building in Teams

If your occupational status accords you high power on alliance teams and you are truly interested in solving client problems, you will want to encourage mutually respectful team partnering. This will get team members more invested in making the process more open, comfortable, and helpful.

To get people to share and to empower them, you must push the all channel, or go-around, communication process wherein "every team member communicates with every other team member," round robin style if necessary (Jones & George, 2006, p. 582). You must regulate your own comments, and you may even have to suppress the talking time of other high status players. You may also need to advocate for less powerful team members, not just the client, by actively

eliciting their input and giving them information that they might not normally be privy to so that they can contribute fairly. In so doing, no one person or group, including you, can afford to dominate. You must pave the way for mutual respect that will encourage everyone to be more candid about their ideas, values, and agendas (Weisbord, 1988). All of this is essential for building effective alliances (Rader & Crandall, 1995).

These techniques will reduce the frustrations that give rise to negative emotions, but you may also have to regulate affectivity, and not just your own. Set the pace for calm and comforting modes of expression. Team players all have feelings, both good and bad, and emotions will eventually erupt. Most of these explosions will fall within the bounds of team norms and will not be unduly disruptive, but do not be surprised when they occur (Bocialetti, 1988).

Using Case Management as a Tactic

Case management is typically overseen by a designated case manager, but like care planning it requires alliance building. Case managers typically handle 10 to 30 clients, and their roles are similar in scope to care planning. Although there are many types of case managers, in the so-called service and managed care model of case management (Wilson, 1995), the case manager essentially assesses, determines service financial eligibility, implements, and advocates for a client's long-range goals according to a service plan. Case managers accomplish this by coordinating a potentially staggering variety of internal or external health care services, including home health care, rehabilitation, education, psychological testing, housing, and other services that have no single entry point (Wetle, 1995). This makes the case manager's brokering and guidance roles essential, but it also means that case managers are essentially gatekeepers and, hence, decision makers (Pratt, 2004).

You must know who is paying for services. If coordinated by the case manager, services are typically paid for by the case manager's employer, be it Medicaid, Medicare, or some other public or private sector insurer or managed care organization (Pratt, 2004). (Links to Medicare and

Medicaid are on the companion website.) Consequently, case managers' duties to their employers are the key difference between case management and care planning. Pratt goes so far as to argue that case managers' primary responsibility is to assure that the employer's (possibly taxpayers) money is not wasted on unnecessary care. Does this mean that strong case advocacy is impossible? No, at least not as long as the disallowed treatments are truly unnecessary and case managers actively involve clients in decision making and pursue the "least restrictive and most appropriate care"(Wetle, 1995, p. 64). When this happens, case managers are truly enablers who empower clients by connecting them to the best possible public and private supports (Kropf & Hutchinson, 1992). However, the tremendous pressure on case managers to save money can compromise their commitment to advocacy.

Wetle (1995) warned against case managers who too easily accepted system constraints, coerced older clients into the case manager's preferred treatment plans, or were too rigidly focused on safety at the expense of client autonomy. In practice, case managers are sometimes hesitant to fully inform clients of the risk of accepting case management services. For example, the case manager may determine that the client needs to be institutionalized when that is not the client's desire. Clients need to know of this possibility.

For all of these reasons, case managers frequently find themselves targeted by third party advocates who wish to maximize client benefits or to champion those who have been denied services. Moreover, as key decision makers, case managers are clearly far less likely to call in third party advocates as this would be tantamount to falling on their swords (giving up their power). Still, confrontational advocacy clearly happens, especially when case managers become frustrated with specific external providers and alternative services are unavailable.

Alliance Building Conflict Tactics

Once you identify and prioritize client problems, you must decide whether action is necessary. Two conflict tactics commonly associated with advocates who lack leverage and must, therefore, engage in low-intensity advocacy are conflict avoidance and conciliation and accommodation. Of course, allies can certainly engage in more confrontational forms of conflict, which is especially true for macro-level advocates, but in the macro environment one often hears the term *coalition building*, which involves linkages between multiple disparate parties, a subject that we discuss in Chapter 8. At the micro-level of individual advocacy, internal alliance building is a somewhat passive, largely collaborative, and longer range change tactic. However, do not lose sight of the fact that empowered alliances, especially those bolstered by the support of external third parties, can engage in some very pushy confrontation and forcing, a subject that we will discuss as well. But first, we focus on the tactic of avoidance.

Using Avoidance as a Tactic

Avoidance implies ducking overt confrontation to preserve yourself and your good working relationship. Classic avoidance is problem shunning, which would preclude getting help from your colleagues, making it a full-flight mode that is poorly suited to advocacy (Cavanaugh, 1991). Alliance building, on the other hand, is generally (but not exclusively) conflict evasive. It represents an empowering, if relatively passive, form of proactive advocacy that changes situations through learning and communication.

We use the term *avoidance* in two ways: (a) evading confrontation when a client's interest doesn't warrant it (such as wanting a private room when none are available), and (b) in the sense of pursuing valid client needs by means that eschew potentially counterproductive competition. Avoidance is an imminently practical delaying tactic that buys you time to build relationships so that you can effect change through dialogue and power sharing. In this sense, avoidance can be seen as an initial tactical aspect of alliance building that buys time to effect fundamental change. Wilma's situation is a good example of this (Box 7.3).

While not a storm trooper or a guerrilla, Wilma is clearly a fighter. However, unlike Louise, she

BOX 7.3

Wilma, the HMO Case Manager

Wilma is a fledgling case manager in a health maintenance organization (HMO) that has bucked the trend of HMOs leaving the Medicare fold and recently contracted with the federal government to enroll Medicare clients. But things haven't gone well. Wilma discovers that some of her coworkers, especially those with the greatest knowledge and seniority, are filing inaccurate claims and making bad coding choices. At first she assumes that they are ignorant of the Medicare rules. Closer observation, however, leads her to conclude that some of her colleagues are colluding by suppressing the needs of qualifying clients to accelerate their discharge from hospitals and rehabilitation services or to deny them services. She also notices that many clients are specifically being denied services at another rehabilitation center that is partly owned by one of her agency's most threatening and successful competitors. Wilma feels that all of this is fully supported by top management who are strongly pushing cost containment goals. She presumes that her colleagues are complying with this practice, not only to gain managerial favors but to assure job security, as many of them have had the lay-off jitters for the last several months.

Wilma has seen the impact of this denial on several older clients close up, and she is angry. She also sees, however, that tackling this issue head-on would be fruitless. Instead, she chooses to *avoid* manifest conflict, which might jeopardize her fledgling career. But neither can she let the problem go—her conscience won't let her. Wilma perks up her ears and begins to quietly ask around and learn more about this activity. She soon finds others who are equally uncomfortable, including the ill-tempered and self-righteous Louise who is ready to take on the higher ups. But Wilma also sees that Louise is not effective. She is disliked and marginalized by almost everyone because they do not enjoy her angry, moody, and pessimistic attitude (Lieberman, 2000).

Unable to find a powerful internal champion who might take on this issue (Lipsky, Seeber, & Fincher, 2003), Wilma is left with only one good option. She must align herself with the few like-minded, if equally powerless colleagues. With a little luck, they might help her change the situation over time if they can extend their circle, change minds, and exert a little gentle peer pressure. At the very least, Wilma's frustration will have some company. But will she be effective?

---

instinctively understands that building an alliance requires good relationships (Brindle & Mainiero, 2000; Lauffer, 1984). She knows that she must use her referent power (her innate, personality-based likeability as a form of charisma), for getting her colleagues to like her. This is the secret to their opening up to her ideas (Perloff, 1993). She also knows that alliances thrive in stability, and that her virtues of patience, friendliness, and especially her skills of conciliation are crucial to building effective partnerships that will help her clients—to say nothing of her own career. And she knows that her alliance will be energized by the client-centered interest she

must promote, and that the factionalizing blaming that Louise so aggressively dishes out must be avoided at all costs, at least for now—until Wilma has power.

Using Conciliation and Accommodation as Tactics

Conciliation and accommodation are key to building the stable relationships and interactions that might solve Wilma's problem (Donohue & Kolt, 1992). **Conciliation** is the art of pacifying or reconciling others by building trust and reducing differences through communication.

Conciliatory language simultaneously disarms and captivates people. It erodes defensiveness and turns coworkers from potential foes into trusted friends. Conciliatory language minimizes the inevitable disagreements that occur in any group by instilling the idea that it is better to agree to disagree than to confront (Anderson et al., 1999). Conciliation also builds the common ground that is essential for promoting an effective alliance's "goals, norms, and roles" (p. 148).

Wilma recognizes the simple truth that her leverage will increase if her new coworkers find her enjoyable to be around. To this end, she employs conciliatory language whenever possible. She uses supportive statements and offers genuine compliments that signal a positive regard for her colleagues' thoughts, deeds, and emotions (whom she views as potential partners). She freely commiserates with them when they are upset: "I understand your anger," she laments, "it's so unfair!" Such statements show her empathy and solidarity. She also finds it easy to make concession remarks when she is wrong (Hocker & Wilmot, 1991), and she signals that she is willing to change and accept solutions that are acceptable to both parties (Hocker & Wilmot, 1991).

In sum, talking to Wilma is generally rewarding. Her conciliatory language makes her approachable and likeable. Lieberman (2000) holds that likeability and reciprocal affection are key components for building alliances and that colleagues work best with people who are very much like themselves. Further, people need to like you if you want to convince them to do that which is in the best interests of others (Lieberman, 2000).

Louise doesn't understand this, however, and she will probably remain puzzled as to why her courageous and aggressive moral stands not only fail to win friends, or even begrudging admiration, but inevitably make enemies to boot. Louise does not understand the likeability principle. Her inefficacy and frustration will continue until she learns how to compromise, cooperate, and signal respect for others—until she heeds Van Fleet's (1984) reminder to "give before you can get" (p. 189).

Likeability is also the key to building trust, which is a matter of winning your potential partner's confidence (Van Fleet, 1984). This is yet another nuance that is lost to the perennially right and stiffly rigid Louise. Wilma, on the other hand, understands that people will respect her if she helps them, or at least meets them half way. She also sees the link between trust and mutual dependence (Lieberman, 2000), knowing that if she can just make her colleagues depend on her, they will listen to and consider her ideas. Indeed, getting her colleagues to depend on her is the centerpiece of her alliance building plan, which has the following tasks:

1. She must stay upbeat and positive, congratulating her colleagues on deserved successes, reinforcing their desirable behaviors, and showing concern about their well-being at work and at home.
2. She must relentlessly build her expert power—her colleagues must come to respect her knowledge because success also breeds likeability.
3. She will always tell the truth. Deceit is often an unforgivable sin. If you want people to support you and your causes, you must win their confidence by always being honest (Van Fleet, 1984).
4. She will be a good listener and offer advice only when it seems welcome. However, when the opportunity arises, she will attempt to fully air contentious issues, avoiding criticism, to find common ground that can be capitalized upon later.
5. She will identify the group's common values and priorities and emphasize these in all her workaday interactions because she knows that having ideas in common and being liked solidifies teams (Lieberman, 2000).
6. She will avoid confrontation, and especially Louise's blaming style, opting instead for neutrality at least publicly on polarizing issues.
7. She will look for chances to share information that supports her clients' needs and will especially look for safe opportunities to open her high-powered colleagues' minds to her ideas (Brinkman & Kirschner, 2002).

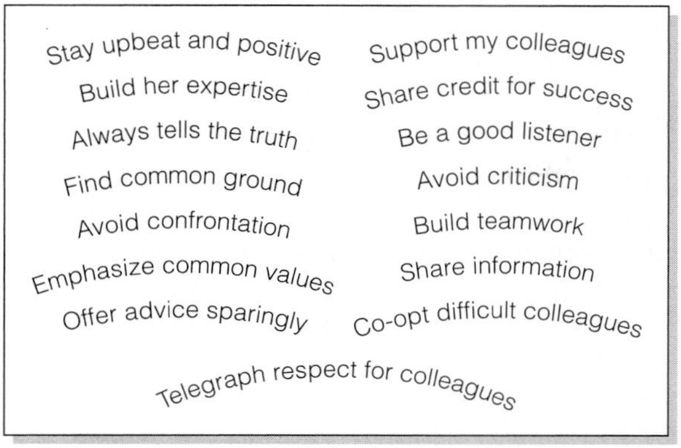

Stay upbeat and positive

Support my colleagues

Build her expertise

Share credit for success

Always tells the truth

Be a good listener

Find common ground

Avoid criticism

Avoid confrontation

Build teamwork

Emphasize common values

Share information

Offer advice sparingly

Co-opt difficult colleagues

Telegraph respect for colleagues

FIGURE 7.2 Wilma's Tactics to Earn the Respect of Her Colleagues

8. She will present her new ideas indirectly, which increases the likelihood that her higher status colleagues will accept them (Brinkman & Kirschner, 2002).
9. Wilma will look for opportunities to invite (or co-opt) particularly troublesome colleagues into being her mentors by praising their work (if it is truly justified), which telegraphs respect and a willingness to learn from others (Brinkman & Kirschner, 2002).

Expanding the Internal Alliance to Promote Change

Despite her awareness that effective advocacy is highly political and often very messy, Wilma succeeds in her pursuit by partnering with a small nucleus of core allies that she consciously expands through conciliatory tactics (Figure 7.2). She carefully primes and nurtures her active allies and builds a peripheral group who might help out, or at least remain neutral, if the alliance ever decides to force its hand.

This approach worked especially well, and Wilma emerged as the dominant voice spearheading the issue. This dominance resulted from her linkage to others who accorded her a leadership role, which massively increased her communication-based leverage. Because Wilma is backed by the collective synergy of her group, she may be able to engage in a meaningful dialogue with management, which could resolve the

problem. In fact, Lauffer (1984) noted that tightly knit groups like Wilma's are more likely to rock the boat because individuals do not feel as vulnerable when advocating from within groups.

Confronting management, however gently, is only one way the alliance might solve the problem. Another way is for the alliance to become a fully participatory self-managing group that develops sufficient internal trust, solidarity, and commitment to cause the learning, or consciousness raising, that builds receptivity to reasonable change throughout the unit's or organization's culture. If the alliance achieves critical mass, unplanned change will occur almost automatically because the alliance's individual constituents will freely abandon the practice out of hand. Peer pressure is likely to make any holdouts feel sufficiently uncomfortable that they will want to adopt the new agency norms to be seen as acting in a morally acceptable way.

Alliances, like any other strategy, are never guaranteed success. The threats of failure are numerous. If Wilma cannot attract key players, competing factions may emerge, leading to conflict, an impasse, or worse. Change may also be resisted if the alliance (a) does not adequately frame the problem, (b) pushes too aggressively, (c) does not link the change to its core client-centered values, (d) fails to make the benefits of the change clear, (e) proposes an impractical scenario, (f) perceives itself as being too weak or otherwise ineffectual, or (g) fears that change may increase workloads or threaten jobs. Under these circumstances, the alliance has three options: abandon the effort (permanent avoidance), give the process more time, or engage an external ally—a third party who will augment the alliance's power or, perhaps, act as a conflict surrogate on behalf of the alliance.

Internal-External Alliances

Third parties play a variety of roles in bringing about change. In this context, they serve as partisan partners whose presence augments the internal ally's power to influence change (Walton, 1987). In some cases the alliance between internal and external advocates is fully declared and out in the open, acknowledged by all parties. This is usually the case when attorneys or regulators are called into play. Of course, an attorney is not a good option for Wilma because she wants to avoid taking legal action against her boss, an expensive way to commit career suicide.

However, Wilma might consider a hidden alliance with an outside party (Hocker & Wilmot, 1991). This is common in long-term care settings, for example, where advocates often engage as hidden allies when called in by internal whistleblowers who need to remain anonymous. Nevertheless, Wilma understands the need for an advocate who has no conflict of interest and who can, as a result, advocate without serious constraints (Nelson et al., 2001a).

Different aging practitioners and involved parties might play this third party advocate role. Wilma, for example, might call in an external social worker from a complementary agency to front her cause. This person's involvement might rebalance power enough for fair bargaining to ensue or may play a consciousness-raising educational role. Many external players shy away from confrontation when resistance hardens. They may back off for fear of ruining a good business relationship that has produced many referrals and other benefits (Nelson et al., 2001b). This, of course, constitutes a serious conflict of interest with the client's needs—a condition that threatens advocacy.

It is not a given, however, that external third parties who are free of any conflicts of interest are always effective. Calling in ombudsmen, lawyers, regulators, and others who are truly independent can be risky. They can heat up fast, precisely because they are not restrained by concerns to either build or keep good relationships with decision makers. Their undivided client loyalty often breeds zealotry, and in a cause such as Wilma's, they may push their own agenda and ideologies (Rubin, as cited in Nelson & Cox, 2003). Their partisanship, if extreme, can unduly bias them against decision makers, inviting harsh, unfair, and otherwise bad judgments (Thompson, as cited in Nelson & Cox, 2003, p. 353). Worse yet, third parties are sometimes duped by their internal allies and are not fully aware of the internal dynamics and challenges that form the situation's context. Overall, building alliances is the safest way to

handle conflict and may be your first choice when it fits your clients' needs and your skills.

Consultation: A Low-Risk Strategy

Similar to developing alliances, consultation (Quadrant B in Figure 7.1) is ideal in low-urgency situations in which an elder is not threatened by imminent harm. Consulting is closely related to the case manager's "advisor" function, and it can represent both nonconflictual and conflictual means of client advocacy. After all, consultants are inherently change agents, and successful consultants have, almost by definition, high leverage due to their proven, recognized, and accepted expert status. Consultants not only have the expertise to effectively advance their cases but, unlike advocates with low leverage, their voices and points may actually be heard. Third parties, or outside consultants, may sometimes be in better positions to advocate effectively. Walton (1987) also advocated for good diagnostic and behavioral skills, coupled with emotional support.

Although we focus here on the classic role of the paid external expert, many third party advocates enter advocacy situations as accepted advisors—some at no charge. In fact, the aging services arena has given rise to all sorts of specialized consultants, such as the commonly encountered geriatric care manager (GCM). Many GCMs are gerontologists, social workers, nurses, or counselors, and they may be members of the National Association of Private Geriatric Care Managers. (A link to this association is on the companion website.) GCMs provide a range of personalized advice to older individuals, their families, and businesses about both long-term and community-based elder services and related subjects. Micro-level case and administrative advocacy elder-service consultants may help with a wide range of problems including, but not limited to, the following:

- Medical treatments and rehabilitation in all fields and specialties
- Psychological interventions
- End of life decisions
- Substance abuse
- Discharge planning

- Family caregiving and support
- Nutrition
- Driving assessment,
- Elder housing outside of and across the continuum of care

Consultants can most certainly influence clients' lives in many powerful ways. They do this by working closely with leaders and practitioners to develop and implement solutions based on assessment, observation, action research, formal studies, and focus groups, and by talking to staff and clients. They promote change through education and training and by recommending improvements in practice, processes, treatments, knowledge, skills, attitudes, and behavior (Table 7.2).

Returning to Wilma's case, we find that even though Wilma's alliance put an end to the HMOs nonfeasance, Louise had still complained to the Medicare fraud unit, resulting in a major investigation that led to some hefty fines and a new management team, which is now headed by Wilma. This team wanted a quick turnaround and contracted with a Medicare consultant to help the case managers do a better job in helping clients navigate through the bewildering array of settings, people, and processes that characterize aging services, and to specifically understand how Medicare requirements apply to these clients. A health care management consultant, Cliff, was also engaged to boost growth, increase productivity, and cut costs by shifting clients from acute care settings to more suitable, but less expensive, subacute care and other geriatric specialty settings.

The Medicare consultant was a gem, but Wilma had a real problem with Cliff. Although she did not fully recognize how common the problem is, Wilma understood that her new supervisory role was being undermined by Cliff, who had excessive power needs, and was trying to overcontrol situations. Byrd (1988) delved into the psychology of consultants like Cliff, concluding that they have lone ranger mentalities that are rooted in their dislike of interdependence and teamwork. Byrd noted that such consultants have authority problems because their needs for independence are fed by anger and defiance instead of clients' needs.

The threats of this messianic mind-set to elder advocacy are twofold. The first problem concerns how controlling consultants such as Cliff are likely to ignore the older person's wishes, acting more like surrogate decision makers than professional advisors (Byrd, 1988). Wilma could certainly analyze the difficulty with Cliff as an interpsychic conflict of interest where an advocate's need for autonomy competes with the client's same need. She also knew that Cliff was violating the resident-centeredness principle that advocates should subordinate their autonomy to mentally capable clients' valid control. Yet this knowledge did not make it much easier. Understanding is one thing, but coping with and continuing to act on the elder's behalf is another in such an oppressive climate.

Another problem relates to the idea of how aggression and anger are contagious. To be sure, most messianic advocates are neither overly aggressive nor overtly hostile, but considerable

TABLE 7.2 Quadrant B: Consultation Tactics

Low Risk/Urgency for Clients; Advocate Has *High* Leverage

Nonconflict Tactics		*Conflict Tactics*
Educate	Build capacity	Conciliate
Collect data	Conduct research and study the issues	Problem solve with leaders
Communicate regularly	Create task forces or subcommittees	and practitioners
Conduct workshops	Develop fact sheets and alternative proposals	Persuade decision makers to
Document for future action	Step back and reflect, monitor the situation	accept your recommenda-
Ask decision maker for help	Recommendations must be resident focused	tions

experience tells us that the two mental states are related. Just think how a highly messianic advocate's zeal to dominate and win (Byrd, 1988) will tend to drive more aggressive forms of conflict and an "us versus them" mentality (Thompson, 1995, p. 840). Advocates with this mind-set tend to believe that what is good for the other party must be bad for them, and vice versa (a win-lose mentality). Partisans who have interests to protect may be especially likely to interpret information provided by the other party as threatening to their interests (p. 840).

If you are the consultant, you must keep an even keel and, as an advocate, you must remain resident centered. To the latter end, it is worth remembering Byrd's (1988) principles for keeping the boss (in this case the client) happy:

1. Despite your expertise, you must communicate with your clients from their understandings, perspectives, and abilities.
2. Engage your older clients and your professional/provider clients in goal setting.
3. Ask your clients for final approval of plans, strategies, and interventions.
4. As you implement solutions, look for opportunities for win-win situations. Work toward outcomes that will minimize risks for your client's bosses or caregivers.

This last point has weighty implications for conflict, the focus of the next section.

From Persuasion to Forcing Strategies

In Chapter 6 we introduced a range of persuading to forcing strategies in situations of high risk/urgency for the client when the advocate has high leverage (Quadrant C in Figure 7.1). Consultants, depending on their skill levels, as well as persons who have clout in their specific systems, may have high leverage. Family members with influential community ties may have high leverage. When you use force tactics, you will reflect a high concern for the client's needs and a low regard for the needs of the opponent. Persuasive tactics include argumentation and some forms of hard negotiation; Forcing commonly involves warnings and threats (Table 7.3). We begin with argumentation.

Argumentation

Argumentation is often seen as a negative characteristic, and argumentative people are considered to be overly aggressive. Much of this discomfort arises from the common misconception that collaborative methods are invariably superior, which is not always the case. Arguments and force can certainly solve (or settle) disputes, and often do.

Many think of an argument as a quarrel. We use the term in the formal tactical sense as a series of propositions, backed by evidence and logic, that lead to a specific claim or conclusion—more of a debate than a quarrel. The calm

TABLE 7.3 Quadrant C: Tactics for a Range of Strategies from Persuasion to Forcing

High Risk/Urgency for Clients; Advocate Has _High_ Leverage

Nonconflict Tactics	_Conflict Tactics_	
Build compelling cases	Argue	Sabotage
Seek legal counsel	Blow whistle	Go over target's head
	File grievances	Coerce when necessary
	Organize a boycott	Community action lawsuit
	Nonviolent protest	Organize letter writing campaigns
	Involve mass media	Refer regulatory issues to regulators
		Warn of dire implications for noncompliance

presentation of your claim, delivered in a direct, fair, professional, nonblaming style (Rogan & Hammer, 1995), is a highly effective way to advance your client's interests. Being able to mount a good argument gives you considerable advantage over your opponents, and good advocates use argument, including language and delivery skills, to convince others of their beliefs (Roloff, Tutzauer & Dailey, 1989; Ziegelmueller & Kay, 1997).

Argumentation is highly suited to circumstances in which the decision maker is oppositional but is still susceptible to reason and, hence, to being influenced. Of course, you should avoid arguing unless you have a case that is backed by sufficient facts to undermine the decision makers' opposition, thus compelling them with your claim. Once you get this agreement, you have convinced the decision maker to share ownership of the problem, which is the key to its effective solution.

Technically, argumentation is a competitive strategy, a win-lose proposition, especially in juridical settings. After all, when you argue, you make the case for your position first, then make accommodations for the opposing position if you can (Donohue & Kolt, 1992). However, not all of your arguments will start intentionally as such. In fact, very often you will approach the decision maker with the simple intent to request and receive help. But if this plea is ignored or rebuffed and the risk to elders is high, the need for action limits the option for time-devouring collaboration. Solid evidence of true risk that is denied or ignored by an oppositional decision maker will pressure you psychologically to see the conflict in simple, high-stakes, win-lose terms (Klar, Bar-Tal, & Kruglanski, 1988). This, in turn, will push you toward a more efficient, direct, and decisive means of gaining compliance; in a word, an argument.

Building a Tight Case

A classic affirmative argument advances a claim for some change beneficial to your client. A good affirmative case is said to be *prima facie*, which means that it is valid "at first glance" (Ziegelmueller & Kay, 1997, p. 29). When you advance

a *prima facie* case, the targeted decision maker must either accept it as presented or articulate a counterargument, which you must not only politely listen to but must also be willing to accept if it is, in turn, *prima facie* valid. This is only fair play. If, however, you do not accept this counterargument, you must continue the dialogue with further rebuttal. This exchange goes on until you either agree to disagree or one of you changes your stance by adopting the position of the other. If your case is truly *prima facie*, the see-saw nature of the case will be diminished. In fact, the more compelling the evidence, the more brief the argument. Consider the scenario in Box 7.4.

If the targeted decision maker perceives that your case is flawed and is not, in fact, *prima facie* like Marty's, the decision maker is likely to make a counterproposal in an attempt to show you that your claim is erroneous, that your evidence or reasoning is flawed, or that your case is somehow overstated. You must listen calmly to this counterargument with an open mind so that you can fairly weigh its merits and either accept or refute it. This back-and-forth repartee constitutes the normal, fair, and expected exchange that is the essence of persuasive argumentation. But, of course, not all the resistance you encounter will be fair or rational. If your target is threatened and fearful, for example, then anger (a secondary emotion that derives from fear) may ensue, or the target may feign anger to throw you off if this tactic that has worked in the past.

In either case, you handle an emotional response by using the techniques of empathetic listening. Listen politely and let your opponents vent. Next, affirm their feelings by verbally reflecting your interpretation of their thoughts. Then, given a window of opportunity, restate your claim or evidence in a calm, leveling way. If the decision maker continues to vent, you may have to repeat this process a number of times like a broken record. In other words, just keep repeating the empathetic listening response cycle until the decision maker's anger is spent, then, seizing the moment, point to your evidence and continue the argument.

BOX 7.4

Bad Air

When Marty dropped by to visit his elderly father, Frank, in his home, he found his dad fretting about the presence of the inspector from the utility company who was downstairs testing for Radon gas. "She said I've got bad air, Marty, bad air, and it costs me plenty to clean it up," said Frank.

"Do you mean she's from the Trustworthy Power Company, Dad?" inquired Marty with some uncertainty.

"Yeah," said Frank.

Marty glanced outside but saw only an older model pick-up truck and no fleet car or utility truck, which seemed odd. He was quite familiar with the ubiquitous Trustworthy orange and green logo-emblazoned fleet vehicles.

"Are you sure she's from Trustworthy?" asked Marty.

"Yes, that's what she said," replied Frank, "and she's downstairs sucking it out now. I guess I could have been in trouble had she not come along,"

Marty went straight to the phone and called Trustworthy to confirm that they were testing for Radon gas. He was not too surprised when he learned that they were not, nor would they.

"Stay here Dad, I'm going to chat with the woman downstairs," said Marty as he headed down the flight of stairs.

Marty approached the "inspector" who smiled in an odd sort of way that didn't seem quite right. "Hi sir, I'm almost done," she chirped, "Mr. Schwartz is getting a good deal today, and I'm just about finished cleaning the air. Let me get this out of your way," she said, averting Marty's intensifying gaze.

"So you work for Trustworthy," Marty blurted.

"Yes," she replied nervously.

"No you don't," Marty countered. "I've called Trustworthy, and they aren't testing for Radon today or any other day. Moreover, Trustworthy told me that their inspectors always wear picture IDs, which you aren't wearing, nor do they use private cars for fieldwork. What's more, that machine you've got there is nothing more than a cheap mist humidifier. I think you'd better come clean. This is a scam, and you're in trouble," Marty stated with conviction.

Faced with this *prima facie* claim, the hapless woman had no counterargument. Her only recourse was an emotional plea: "I just have to feed my kids," she sobbed. "The man who owns the truck told me that we'd be able to get into the homes of older people if we said we're from Trustworthy, but we meant absolutely no harm."

"Tell that to the police," Marty shot back. "How many older people have you scammed like this? I'm sure Dad isn't the first," he said with contempt.

She remained silent, backing toward the door.

Style Issues in Argumentation

Some scholars draw distinctions between argumentation and the style effects of persuasion. For example, Freeley (1961) asserted that argumentation strictly addresses the logical aspect of a claim, whereas "persuasion" relates to an appeal's "ethical and emotional" aspects (p. 7). From our perspective, an argument entails both elements—logic and persuasion. The argument's main thrust is clearly the logical advancement of cause and effect propositions that support your claim, which is, in turn, secondarily, supported by a whole range of style-related persuasive techniques that are interjected into the argument's interactive flow. These include requests (pleas) for help, calm directness, emotional exaggeration, emotional overidentification with clients, and controlled anger.

Requests/Pleas for Help Stylistic techniques include simple requests for help, moral pleas, and other emotional appeals, including ones designed to induce shame, which can trigger compensatory helping from a guilt ridden decision maker (Krebs, 1982). Appeals to self-interest, promises, or rewards or using the psychological techniques of debt (you owe me), liking (helpfulness), and self-feeling ("you'll feel better/worse if you . . .") are all valid tactics or techniques that may help persuade your opponent to act (Perloff, 1993, p. 295). Although helpful, these persuasive techniques are not likely to win the argument by themselves. Persuasion will still ultimately depend on whether you can convince the decision maker that the problem is real and that change is necessary. But these persuasive techniques can subtly make your opponents more susceptible to your logic by giving them additional subjective reasons to listen, cooperate, or conform.

Calm Directness Perhaps the most important style issue relates to directness, which you should project in a calm, assertive way. Even in highly urgent cases, you must keep cool, but you must also signal your resolve by exuding an air of professional intensity. One of the biggest threats to partisan advocates is an aggressive style. Even if you have a compelling case, poor emotional self-governance is typically ineffective. You must understand the bounds of righteous intensity and never become too emotional when making your claim, which imbues your dispute with a dangerous and somewhat desperate quality (Deutsch, 1994).

Emotional Exaggeration Partisan advocates are more prone to emotional arousal for two reasons. First, threat-oriented partisans, especially if they are ideologically motivated by client rights, for example, are more likely to exaggerate potential or perceived interparticipant goal incompatibilities, making them more prone to bias generally (Thompson, 1995). The false impressions that

arise from bias are, in turn, related to hostile attributions.

Emotional Overidentification A second factor pushing partisan advocates toward aggression is that they are more likely to emotionally overidentify with their clients. Client identification has some good points. Most people do not want an unempathetic advocate, and client identification can clearly motivate the commitment to help. In fact, experience shows that fiery advocacy can be useful in certain limited situations— in totally chaotic, dysfunctional, or downright exploitive systems, for example, or where there is nothing left to lose by ratcheting things up.

Controlled Anger Highly expert communicators who read people well and who have much conflict experience know how to read their opponents' leverage, intent, and affect, thus determining when anger might help seal the deal. But for most people, the best rule is to keep calm. We have seen countless cases in which the advocate's hotheadedness rather than the client's problem became the issue. One of our studies, for example, shows that of the 194 grievances filed by external decision makers against one state's volunteer advocates, demeanor (n = 64), including rude, aggressive, demanding, or blaming behavior, accounted for 32% of all complaints, making an aggressive style the number one concern by opponents, ahead of complaints about the advocate's protocol violations, intrusive access behaviors, and confidentiality infractions (Nelson et al., 2003).

Argumentation and Relationship Building

Argumentation can lead to win-win solutions if you can be direct without being aggressive. In fact, arguments can reveal a good deal of common ground, and they often morph into a negotiation exchange. After all, a fair argument can lay bare values, perceptions, and hitherto undiscovered problems. Fair arguments can even improve relationships. Think about your own life. Can you recall an argument that brought you closer to someone? For most people, admittedly, it is probably easier to remember the hurt feelings from bad arguments. Recall disputes in which you and your opponent fundamentally accepted the idea that "partisan advocacy of one's point of view is normal and necessary" and in which winning was really a matter of eliminating perceived goal incompatibilities and agreeing to a fresh start (Klar et al., 1988; Walton, 1991, p. 4). Bad memories of argumentative dysfunction are almost invariably linked to two or more people emotionally violating the cultural rules of fair argumentation—not attributable to the tactical aspects of the argument itself.

Coercion

The conflict law of proportionality (Rummel, 1991) requires that resistance must be met with equal force, and advocates may draw from a range of coercive communication tactics including, most commonly, warnings and threats. Other types of advocates, especially the legal types, will draw from a considerably more confrontational armory, including fines or the threats thereof as well as immersion in formal adversarial administrative processes. This becomes even more intense when elder-law attorneys pull their opponents into the inherently punitive processes of juridical conflict.

Force should always be a last recourse. It should never be employed gratuitously or used in situations that are not urgent, high risk, powerfully important, or that involve clear legal infractions or breaches of fundamental rights. Force has high negatives. It stings feelings and spurs powerful emotions because it inherently disregards the targeted decision maker's interests. But this is exactly why it works! The decision maker must perceive forcing for what it is: a sign of "loss of respect and affiliation, which may signal that a fundamental change has occurred in the nature of the relationship," a change for the worse (Kinney, 1994, p. 186).

Forcing is dangerous; use it only in the following situations. First, because it may destroy a relationship (or a potential relationship), use force only if your *prima facie* case is blindly resisted, especially if this resistance is irrational or duplicitous. Second, use force only when you

determine that the "value of an outcome exceeds the (expected) cost of obtaining it" (Goldman, 1986, p. 181). Third, use force only if you are sure that you can deliver the intended harm and that your conditional promise to do so will be taken seriously. And fourth, enact coercive tactics in calm, nonemotional ways that minimize the chances of incurring emotionally reactive or retaliatory costs.

There are few coercive tactics in the advocate's repertoire, the most common of which is warning. This is where you politely tender a proposition to the decision makers that their failure to comply with your request will escalate the case in some way, by involving a regulator, an attorney, the media, or some other dangerous power elite who will punish or make matters decidedly worse for them. To be effective, the target must rationally conclude that your warning actually poses a looming menace that tarnishes the luster of continued resistance (Hocker & Wilmot, 1991). Here, fear emerges as the stimulus to change, and it is clearly "the most intense persuasion factor," the real key to cowing your opponent (Dawson, 1992, p. 6–7). Now consider the case of Peter who was reviewing his 83-year-old mother's medical bills (Box 7.5).

Peter finally got around to being direct, but he did not bully or browbeat his opponent, which is never a good idea. In fact, effective advocates never completely abandon the rules of likeability; they even sometimes couch their threats in ways that suggest concern for the target's well-being. Here, the advocate is politely, but very indirectly, reminding the decision maker that it will be better to sort things out in a friendly way than to take the chance with an unknown player who has formal punitive powers. As Peter considered what to do next during this episode, he was asking himself questions such as these: Is there time for less dangerous tactics, and if so, what are the risks and benefits to my mother? Do the chances for success outweigh the dangers of failure? Is timely help available? Does the choice not to escalate amount to an unethical abandonment of my mother's cause? Are the consequences of such an abandonment acceptable to my mother?

BOX 7.5

Peter's Mother's Medical Bills

Peter found a serious overcharge in his mother's medical bills, which caused him to dig into his mother's billing statements for the past couple of years. He quickly found more problems, including at least five cases of unmistakable double billing. He familiarized himself with the Medicare regulations and contacted his Medicare HMO to make an appointment with management. He wanted guarantees that this would stop.

Peter's initial claim to the case manager fell on dismissive ears: "These things happen all the time, they're just honest, but sloppy billing errors, you can reduce these problems, and we have, but you can't eliminate them."

Peter verbally described seven incidents he believed were more than mere sloppiness. Again, the manager was dismissive: "We rigorously ascribe to the highest standards, and I can assure you that you don't have what you think you have here." Peter and the manager went back and forth, without any give on either side. In fact, the manager became impatient and emboldened, lecturing Peter about how billing mistakes occur, offering one lame excuse after another, and citing industry norms for acceptable coding error rates. The manager conceded nothing.

Peter tried one last time to be conciliatory. "I'm sorry we couldn't work this out because I really wanted to keep the regulators out of this; they just complicate things, and I'm more of a problem solver. Do you think we've exhausted our options together?" When the manager was not forthcoming, Peter took a deep breath.

"Well, I don't know what you call these," he said as he laid down copies of some 16 erroneous bills, "but I think the Medicare fraud unit or the FBI or the Office of the Inspector General will find these more than a little interesting. Now I might not be a health care administrator, but I'd say that this stuff darn near proves fraud! If you don't make plans to return the misappropriated funds and order an internal audit now, plus give me some evidence that you've done this, I'll take this to the Medicare fraud unit, and we'll see what sorts out."

The manager spent a few minutes looking at the paper trail and blanched. "You're right," he said, "we've got what appears to be a problem here. I didn't mean to be so defensive, but we've had some real personnel issues lately. I'll get on this immediately. I'll order an internal audit. I'm sure we can take care of this, and I'll give you my assurance in writing."

Problem Solving as a Strategy

The last of the four strategies is problem solving (Quadrant D in Figure 7.1). This strategy is used in situations of high urgency or risk in which the advocate has rather low leverage in the system. Many books explain how to achieve goals through conflict management, and we'll cite several as we deal with the problem-solving aspects of collaborative forms of conflict. Problem-solving strategies are often termed fair bargaining, stakeholder conflict, cooperative or win-win conflict, interest-based problem solving, or more broadly, alterna-tive dispute resolution (ADR). We use the term *problem solving* generally as being interchangeable with these various terms.

A problem-solving strategy differs from win-lose or adversarial methods by the mutual commitment of the disputants to preserve or improve their relationship. There is a mutual desire or need to find lasting solutions that satisfy all participants' needs. This approach can fundamentally resolve problems. The desire to dominate, on the other hand, risks competition (win-lose conflict) and concomitant escalations, which may settle a

TABLE 7.4 Quadrant D: Problem-Solving Tactics

High Risk/Urgency for Clients; Advocate Has *Little* Leverage

Nonconflict Tactics	*Conflict Tactics*
Bargain	Mediation
Monitor systems	Seek legal counsel
Compare information	Lobby decision makers
Collaborate with others	Use negotiated consent
Increase consumer awareness	Argue the case/cause and persuade
Monitor agencies and decision makers	Principled negotiation (BATNA)
Seek the oppositions' perspectives and goals	
Establish communication with allies and opposition	

particular dispute for the time being but seldom paves the way for more enduring solutions or productive long-term relationships (Levinger & Rubin, 1994).

It is not possible here to even begin to detail all the how-to tactics and tips pertaining to the classic win-win problem-solving approaches of mediation and principled negotiation. We briefly explore both the benefits and special problems advocates face in using these win-win approaches in elder-service settings where steep power asymmetries between the older client and the surrounding systems abound. We also introduce a special form of mediation designed to empower older clients who face these asymmetrical circumstances and introduce another widely used form of geriatric problem solving called negotiated consent (Moody, 1988; Table 7.4).

The Role of Mediation in Elder Advocacy

Classic win-win mediation tactics are ideal for moderate to high risk situations, especially if these circumstances are complex or ambiguous, or in situations where the outcome isn't in dispute but the means of achieving it are either unclear or in conflict (Nelson et al., 2001a). Mediation attempts to solve a given problem by discovering the problem's underlying causes as well as the disputants' perceptions, true concerns, and needs. In situations in which elders' needs are more urgent or elders are at risk,

mediation is a first line of action before going to a more formal approach.

Mediation requires a mediator who is a "neutral third party with no power over the parties" (National Institute of Dispute Resolution, n.d.). Note the word *neutral.* In fact, neutrality is "the essence of mediators' practice" (Suskind, 1994, p. 323). Theoretically, this impartiality invites the trust of the disputants, which is the key to building common ground (Domenici & Littlejohn, 2001). The mediator can achieve this in part by laying down some rules and by modeling the accommodation and conciliation skills discussed previously. The ultimate goal is to get the disputants to deeply explore all the factors surrounding the problem so they can achieve a mutually acceptable solution.

Despite the stampede to use mediation (or at least the *term* mediation) to solve all sorts of disputes, do not think that mediation will solve all problems, as it will not (Suskind, 1994). In fact, truly client-centered advocates probably use this technique far less than you might suspect for a number of reasons, some obvious, some not. First of all, advocates are not neutral; they are partisan. Second, advocates almost always have some power that the older client may not have. Therefore, a competent advocate will willingly constrain or redirect to advance the client's informed choice. Obviously, when a highly vulnerable client needs your help, the client expects and needs an ally.

Just think of these dynamics: a weak client versus a powerful decision maker, both helped by a neutral advocate. Makes sense, right? Wrong! This potentially sets up the same circumstances that precipitated the client's problem in the first place. It also violates the basic rule of fair mediation: people should not enter mediation processes if they are grossly overpowered because the advantage always stays with the most powerful, no matter how collaborative the process seems.

This does not mean that client-centered advocates should not act as mediators. You can play a classically impartial mediating role in two circumstances. First, if the older client is robust, assertive, and has a need to maintain control but also wants some "process management" (Domenici & Littlejohn, 2001, p. 50), then the appearance of objectivity on the advocate's part is to be expected. The second circumstance justifying impartiality would be a conflict between two older clients who are arguing about preferences or conflicting stipulated rights, such as when two roommates differ about when to turn off the television or radio at night. Because neither is right or wrong, the advocate's goal should be to maximize both clients' interests by facilitating a mutually acceptable arrangement.

Finally, avoid mediating disputes involving a stipulated right or culturally embedded ethical value. After all, why would you try to hash out something that is inherently nonnegotiable? You wouldn't, and shouldn't. You might logically mediate a dispute on how to achieve or comply with one of these stipulated rights, but you would never mediate whether to comply with a right.

In certain heavily regulated elder-service settings, the chances for mediation decline in direct proportion to that setting's regulatory stringency. More rules and regulations mean more nonnegotiables, which means less negotiation. Indeed, the nursing home is one of the most heavily regulated entities in the United States. Almost every aspect of the resident's life is subject to some law or rule, and an exhaustive list of obligations owed by the facility to the resident reduces opportunities for mediation. In fact, when any of these obligations is breached, the facility is, *ipso facto*, duty bound to provide a remedy. In these circumstances, the resident is typically far better served by an advocate who is able to verify the existence of a breach and present this evidence in a claim advanced by persuasive argument, if necessary. This, as we'll see, is a win-lose approach that seldom loses if executed correctly (Nelson & Cox, 2003).

Activist Mediation

Activist mediation is an approach tailor-made for advocacy that borrows many of mediation processes while eschewing the mediator's impartiality (Forester & Stitzel, 1989; Suskind, 1994). In this process, the mediator works to be trusted by both parties, and acceptance is key to success. What is different is that the activist mediator engages in behaviors that empower the client.

Suskind (1994) argued that an activist mediator may "round up representatives" to bring information to the table that will clarify the issue at hand (p. 327). Behind the scenes, activist mediators channel information to disempowered individuals and help them understand complex or difficult issues. Activist mediators also share the implications of any choices the client might face.

At the table, activist mediators make sure that hesitant or reticent older people have enough time to think and get their ideas across. They ask the older person's opponents to use everyday language and avoid jargon. Although activist mediators respect the rights of both parties, they do not hesitate to gently question unfounded assumptions. They are especially attentive to making sure that older disputants understand their rights and how any applicable laws and rules may apply to the situation. They might introduce new ideas and options, and if the older disputants seem to be prematurely giving in or wearing out, activist mediators do not hesitate to call a time out to counsel older individuals in private, to let them regain their strength, or even to reconsider asking for a conflict surrogate.

Still, despite all this power shifting, activist mediators do not become partisans, at least according to advocacy mediation expert Lawrence Suskind (1994): "I am not neutral with regard to the outcome. I'm nonpartisan" (p. 328). He would probably do everything mentioned previously for both parties if the need arose; it's just that more powerful parties need less help. Suskind clearly avoids maximizing the claims of the weaker party over the stronger (which would be a win-lose strategy) because he wants both disputants to own the solution:

> I refuse to adopt the interest of any one side as being more important than the interest of any others. I will not side with any party, including the least powerful. . . . But I'm not neutral with regard to the quality of the outcome. I want an outcome that maximizes mutual gain, that doesn't leave joint gains unclaimed. . . . Maximizing joint gains mean that you haven't left something on the table that would have been better for both sides, even if the parties didn't propose it. (pp. 328–329)

Critics worry that maximizing the interests of both parties does not constitute a pure form of client advocacy. Some advocates, especially those who are legally oriented, have little use for this approach, and we agree that caution in using this approach is certainly advisable. On the other hand, if activist mediation actually achieves optimal outcomes for older individuals and just incidentally produces gains for their opponents, how is this not a viable form of advocacy?

Hard and Soft Negotiation

Negotiation is another win-win process where two individuals who perceive some goal incompatibility try to persuade each other to accept some outcome that is acceptable to both parties. Some forms of negotiation are win-lose. In **hard negotiation,** for example, disputants engage in tough, competitive, no compromise, no concession, win-lose arguments to mislead or overwhelm opponents and gain maximum leverage. Hard negotiation is essentially a bidding war that is highly risky and should be avoided if at all possible. Even if you win a battle, you leave behind a wounded opponent who may be difficult to deal with in the future, or worse, may

want to get even. Even so, hard negotiation has its moments. It can be a viable option under the following circumstances:

1. The risk to the client trumps all other considerations.
2. The issue rests on a moral imperative and is supported by law or rule.
3. The targeted decision maker is not interested in fair bargaining with you or your client.
4. There are no viable alternatives.

Principled, or **soft negotiation** is a win-win process that is without a neutral (or activist) third party facilitator. Soft negotiation is much more widely used by advocates than mediation. It is commonly observed in two basic forms. In the first form an advocate negotiates as a third party on behalf of a client. In the second type the advocate acts as an ally who sits with the client to directly explore each side's perceptions of strengths, weaknesses, opportunities, threats, and goals to find out what can be exchanged to forge a lasting resolution. Exploration of these issues is why soft negotiation is also called *issue negotiation*. The preliminary discussion of issues builds the rapport and trust that are the essential prerequisites to a thorough review of proposed solutions (Donohoe & Kolt, 1992). This is quite different from hard negotiation, which typically begins when one party floats an inflated and unabashedly self-serving proposal that inevitably triggers a counterproposal. In the process, a battle of wits begins, and this process will go back and forth until an impasse is reached or someone capitulates.

Your best alternative to a negotiated agreement (BATNA) determines whether you negotiate in the first place (Gould, 2005). If your BATNA is preferable to what you think you can get by negotiating, then your BATNA is high and your options are good. This allows you to be freer to walk away than the low BATNA players who are more dependent on and more interested in negotiating as the only means to meet their needs. Box 7.6 summarizes some of the basic tenets of finding your BATNA. (A link to BANTA.com is on the companion website.)

BOX 7.6

Best Alternative to a Negotiated Alternative (BATNA)

1. Your power lies in your walk-away alternatives. Make sure that you have real, viable options that do not require an agreement.
2. Do not reveal your walk-away alternatives because your commitment to negotiate appears weakened.
3. Figure out *other* parties' walk-away alternatives. It will help you be creative in developing agreements that benefit both parties.
4. No offer is too high. Any offer is valid provided you can present objective criteria that prove each term of the offer fills to some extent the underlying needs of all parties.
5. Do not react emotionally. When you encounter tactics intended to intimidate, rush, draw out discussions, or otherwise derail the focus from underlying needs and mutual gain, *patiently react to the problem at hand. Draw attention back to substantive interests. Remember: Personal attacks = time to refocus on mutually beneficial outcome.*
6. All needs presented are *not* of equal importance. Focus time on understanding which needs are most likely to influence the outcome.
7. Listen more than you talk. As a listener, you are gathering information that can help you figure out which of the other side's needs must be met for an agreement to be considered acceptable.
8. Listening gives you the advantage. The better your understanding, the more flexibility and creativity you'll have as you create options. Talking gives this advantage to the other side.
9. Know the authority of each person in the room. Make sure you know whether or not you are negotiating with someone empowered to make the final decision. If not, make sure you present options in such a way that they meet the perceived needs of the negotiator and the other members of their organization.
10. Analyze concessions. Look for patterns in the types of concessions made by the other parties, and be attentive to the messages sent by your concessions.
11. Small concessions give the impression that the bottom line is not far off.
12. Large concessions indicate that a lot more can still be conceded before the bottom line is reached.
13. Rapid or large concessions undermine the credibility of the initial offer.
14. All concessions teach the lesson that more concessions will be made.
15. When the other side makes a concession, it is statistically certain that a second concession on the same issue can be secured.
16. Never be bludgeoned into splitting the difference. When an apparent impasse has been reached, splitting the difference is widely regarded as the ultimate fair solution. But the suggestion to split the difference is often used to induce guilt. Guilt is likely to lead to concessions on your part, maybe even concessions that lead to an outcome worse for you than splitting the difference. Splitting the difference rarely results in an outcome that surpasses anyone's expectations, and it does not ensure that the interests of all parties are satisfied.

Source: Fisher & Ury (1983), Gould (2000). Used with permission of Eric Gould at BATNA.com.

To illustrate this technique, consider Martha's situation: she is more willing to compromise or concede points and far less likely to walk away. Martha is representing her client, Katherine, in negotiating the cost agreement with the Shaderton Assisted Living Center. The center uses a point system to determine the costs of any additional support services needed to qualify Katherine for a private apartment. Both Martha and Katherine would do just about anything to get Katherine into Shaderton where assistance with activities of daily living (ADLs) is provided and which has close proximity to Martha's current home and friends. Katherine has been on Shaderton's waiting list for over a year, and there are plenty of people behind her eagerly awaiting their chance to move in.

Martha and Katherine's BATNA is low for a number of reasons. First, the only viable alternatives to Shaderton are a local retirement home without assistance services and a somewhat rundown residential care facility. Consequently, both Martha and Katherine's eagerness to get into Shaderton make them dependent on (and keenly interested in) this negotiation, whereas Shaderton's negotiator couldn't care less due to the facility's long waiting list. Martha and Katherine's lack of options and their weak BATNA robs them of any leverage to negotiate a lower price, whereas the facility negotiator's high BATNA accords her considerable power to propose and impose maximum point rates. If Martha were to attempt to play hardball (which is unlikely given her low BATNA), the facility negotiator would likely walk away to extract the desired fees from another eager customer.

High BATNA makes hard negotiation a more attractive option for the facility, however, which would clearly be a losing approach for the low BATNA duo of Martha and her client. In fact, the only way Martha can get Katherine a room at the Shaderton is to comply with the facility's proposals—submission is the fate of those with low BATNA.

Regardless, in both the hard negotiation of low BATNA and in soft negotiation, the advocate is unquestionably a partisan. After all, Martha's goal is to achieve her client's goal as opposed to the facility's interests, and her presence was needed to level the playing field although she did not have the leverage to prevail.

In soft negotiation, the advocate's pro-client stance, although fully declared, is not at all adversarial in tone, temper, tenor, or technique. Instead, soft negotiation works best when you must find out what your opponents want and give it to them, just as long as what you trade away does not infringe on your client's valid preference or best interest (Hindle, 1998). It also requires "cost-cutting," which is where "each party agrees to help each other avoid the costs associated with helping each other accomplish the goals" (Donohue & Kolt, 1992, p. 128).

Obviously, doing all this effectively requires deft communication. The previously discussed skills of conciliation and likeability are especially important in this regard. Above all, you must avoid personalizing the issue by finger pointing and must keep your discussion focused on the issues as opposed to people and personalities.

Do not forget positive body language, which is integral to communication. Keep your arms open to suggest indecision—you do not want to appear as if your mind is already made up (Hindle, 1998)—and keep your hands away from your head and face. Lean forward (which signals your involvement), maintain good eye contact, and tilt your head slightly to show that you are listening, and above all, smile. This shows your warmth and openness to the others' needs, and an occasional hand-to-chest gesture bespeaks honesty (Hindle, 1998).

How you say something is just as important as *what* you say. Take turns talking, don't monopolize, and do not interrupt! Nod occasionally to show that you are listening, or from time to time inject the nod's verbal equivalent, which is "uh huh," "yes," or "yeah," during your target's pauses to signal your continued attentiveness. Use indirect language when making a request and avoid imperatives. Here are some examples:

Do Say

"Would it be possible to administer the Minnesota Mini Mental to assess Mrs. Anderson's cognitive status?"

"I realize that this will create some difficulty for your staff, but doesn't Mr. Jones have the right to sleep in?"

"How do you think we can improve this assessment process?"

"How does this make you feel and why?"

Don't Say

"You need to administer the Minnesota Mini Mental to assess Mrs. Anderson's cognitive status."

"You must let Mr. Jones sleep in, or you will be breaking the law!"

"You really need to do better assessments."

"You have no right to feel badly. My client is the one who is suffering, and she doesn't have the options that you do."

To give you a flavor of the cooperative talk that supports soft negotiation, we adapted some of Hocker and Wilmot's (1991) soft negotiation communication cues and phrases:

1. "I see that you are really invested in this solution Jim, but although it works well for you, it doesn't work as well for my client. Can we explore some modifications that would better meet my client's needs?" (p. 221)
2. Yes, you're both in a tough situation here, you as well as my client, but I think we can find an agreeable way out. Can't we give it a shot?
3. Please elaborate on why you think this sets a bad precedent.
4. I know how your time constraints are pushing you to offer this compromise, but I think we can find a solution where neither of us has to give a little to get a little.

Isn't it worth trying to meet both of our needs?

5. For this to work fairly for both you and my client, I really need to understand what you want as well as what you need to avoid.
6. I'm ready to do what it takes to find a solution that works for both you and my client; time is not a problem.
7. Tell me more about what you want.
8. What do you see as the circumstances that led to this problem?

Negotiated Consent

Negotiated consent (Moody, 1988) is a collaborative form of political problem solving designed to handle very complex ethical dilemmas that constitute almost no win-win situations in long-term care settings. Although negotiated consent is a more pessimistic process than the ones discussed thus far, it is ideal when "making the best of a bad situation is the most that can reasonably be expected" (Moody, 1992, p. 174).

Negotiated consent represents a significant shift from the previous collaborative conflict models insofar as it seeks to advance client interests apart from the objective and legalistic rules of informed consent and substituted judgment. In fact, Moody goes so far as to imply that in the nursing home the autonomy principle is diluted to "an abstract theory detached from the lives of the individuals" (p. 183). He bases this conclusion on the perspective that the resident's view of reality is too situational, complex, and subjective to be understood outside the transcendent situational meaning that the resident constructs in response to specifically encountered circumstances. It follows, then, that simple legalistic models like autonomy are inadequate to effectively reflect the situational nuances that differ with each resident. Hence, Moody suggested that legalistic models should be abandoned because you "cannot simply appeal to hypothetical rights that patients are supposed to possess, including the right to self-determination and leave the matter there"

(p. 178). Moreover, if the resident's expressed choice is based on a defective interpretation of reality, what is gained by applying a rights-based model? Moody elaborated:

> I argue that the dominant juridical model of informed consent is better replaced by a political model in which the real world of decision making is recognized for what it is: the clash of multiple interested parties with a legitimate stake in the outcome, the presence of competing interpretations, conflicting values, and uncertainty about outcomes. (p. 178)

Moody (1988) believed that this political process is marked by "unrestrained communication" that involves all disputants (p. 67), including the resident's family, facility staff and management, and anyone else who has a stake in the dilemma. It is hoped that this uncurbed communication will lead to a richer, deeper understanding of all involved parties' thoughts and behaviors, thus allowing them, including the resident, to find and accept options that are more beneficial to all participants. Moody's (1992) basic attributes of negotiated consent are as follows:

1. In long-term care conflicts there are "multiple legitimate views" that frequently require compromise (p. 174), which, strictly speaking, is an expedient that does not fully meet any party's needs.
2. The authority for the decision must be shared among all the conflict's stakeholders.
3. Negotiated consent is "not governed by strict deductive rules; it is heuristic in its cognitive style, implying less reliance on codes of ethics and more attention to opportunities for discussion and discovery" (p. 174).
4. Negotiated consent should be applied to situations where optimal outcomes are elusive or impossible.
5. Decisions should be openly justified by reasons that are acceptable to all involved stakeholders.

Another significant difference in negotiated consent is Moody's anecdote to the classic conflict proviso that negotiation should be avoided when the power disparity between disputants is great. He answers this restriction by arguing that the negotiating process should be restructured on a case-by-case basis in ways that promote fair communication (p. 175). This restructuring should follow these principles:

1. The resident or the resident's select surrogate must always be actively involved.
2. The negotiated consent process must assure that all parties are fairly and fully heard.
3. Disempowered parties are fully apprised of their rights and prerogatives.
4. An independent third party should monitor the process to protect the resident's right to withdraw, or not to comply with a negotiated outcome.
5. There should be "publicity about the negotiation process, which is itself subject to negotiation" (p. 175), so that a confidential process is not out of the question.

We believe that if Moody's safeguards are strictly enforced, negotiated consent has a useful niche, exactly as Moody claims—for forlorn cases in profoundly ambiguous circumstances (to which we would add) in facilities with enlightened staff trained in the complex negotiated consent process. We emphasize the need for a vigilant resident-centered advocate, one who not only fully discloses the nature and implications of the negotiated consent process to the resident, but who resists peer pressure to step in and embrace the autonomy model if the resident wants out. With this protection, negotiated consent, like all conflict models, emerges as a situationally appropriate conflict tactic, but it is certainly no cure-all. No tactic is. Hocker and Wilmot (1991) detailed the risks attending negotiation and collaborative processes generally:

1. They overpromote the cooperative tendency to compromise, which is a nonoptimizing approach to problem solving.

2. They bypass confrontational approaches that may be necessary to root out and resolve certain types of problems.
3. They expose good-faith collaborators to the machinations of deceptive players who are actually competitively oriented.
4. They increase the "difficulty of establishing definite aspiration levels and bottom lines because of reliance on qualitative (value-laden) goals" (p. 220).
5. They demand high-level conceptual skills and an outstanding ability to read people, divine their interests and determine, for example, when to time proposals and seek closure.
6. They promote the tendency to negotiate nonnegotiables, such as client rights and other statutory obligations.
7. They tend to engage participants in problem solving for issues that may not warrant the time and effort.

☾ Summary

In this chapter we elaborate on the implementation of four strategies originally identified in Chapter 6: building alliances, consultation, from persuasion to forcing, and problem solving. Considering these tactics in terms of individual or small group change, under each strategy, primary tactics are identified along with multiple techniques used in their implementation. Alliance and consultation strategies are used in situations that are neither urgent nor risky for older persons, whereas persuasion to forcing and problem-solving strategies are more appropriate when the problems are more urgent or risky. As a skilled advocate, your goal is to carefully analyze a situation and match an intervention strategy with the appropriate tactics needed, proceed, and then reassess the situation until a resolution or change occurs.

Building alliances is a key strategy in low-risk, asymmetrical conflict situations. Alliances are necessary when personal power needs support from others. Examples of nonconflictual actions that are used to build alliances are care planning, team building, and case management. Tactics used in alliance building are conflict avoidance and conciliation or accommodation.

Consultation is also a low-risk strategy used in low-urgency situations in which an elder is unlikely to be harmed. Consulting is often used by professionals who have the power of expertise. Consultants work closely with leaders and practitioners to develop and implement solutions based on assessment, observation, action research, formal studies, and focus groups and by talking with staff and clients. Most important is that they do not lose sight of the older person's needs in the process.

Persuasion to forcing as a strategy occurs in high risk/urgency situations and when there is high leverage on the part of the advocate. Argumentation as a tactic in this strategy requires the ability to build a tight case and to use strong persuasion skills. Coercion is a last resort tactic because it will push the power differential and has the potential to alienate the decision maker.

Problem solving occurs when risk/urgency is high but the advocate has less leverage than she or he would like to have. Therefore, tactics include mediation in which a third neutral party may have to be a part of the intervention. Different types of mediation include a classic approach and a method called activist mediation in which the mediator is no longer seen as a neutral party. Both hard and soft negotiation skills are viable tactics in a problem-solving mode. In this process, body language, style, and tone become critically important to successful advocacy. Table 7.5 summarizes the tactics of each strategy.

In Chapter 8 we turn to what happens when more than one person or small group is affected by a problem and how the interpersonal skills discussed in this chapter can be used on a broader scale.

TABLE 7.5 Situational Conflict Resolution Tactics

Quadrant A: Alliance Building Tactics
Low Risk/Urgency for Clients; Advocate Has *Little* Leverage

Nonconflict Tactics		*Conflict Tactics*
Prioritize tasks	Educate/provide information	Write letters
Build your team	Hone surveillance skills	Avoid the conflict
Write care plans	Monitor client problems	Seek conciliation and accommodation
Keep good records	Ask decision maker for help	Create internal-external alliances
Enhance internal alliances		

Quadrant B: Consultation Tactics
Low Risk/Urgency for Clients; Advocate Has *High* Leverage

Nonconflict Tactics		*Conflict Tactics*
Educate	Build capacity	Conciliate
Collect data	Conduct research and study the issues	Problem solve with leaders and practitioners
Communicate regularly	Create task forces or subcommittees	Persuade decision makers to accept your recommendations
Conduct workshops	Develop fact sheets and alternative proposals	
Document for future action	Step back and reflect, monitor the situation	
Ask decision maker for help	Recommendations must be resident focused	

Quadrant C: Tactics for a Range of Persuasion to Forcing
High Risk/Urgency for Clients; Advocate Has *High* Leverage

Nonconflict Tactics	*Conflict Tactics*	
Build compelling cases	Argue	Sabotage
Seek legal counsel	Blow whistle	Go over target's head
	File grievances	Coerce when necessary
	Organize a boycott	Community action lawsuit
	Nonviolent protest	Organize letter writing campaigns
	Involve mass media	Refer regulatory issues to regulators
		Warn of dire implications for noncompliance

Quadrant D: Problem-Solving Tactics
High Risk/Urgency for Clients; Advocate *Little* Leverage

Nonconflict Tactics	*Conflict Tactics*
Bargain	Mediation
Monitor systems	Seek legal counsel
Compare information	Lobby decision makers
Collaborate with others	Use negotiated consent
Increase consumer awareness	Argue the case/cause and persuade
Monitor agencies and decision makers	Principled negotiation (BATNA)
Seek the oppositions perspectives and goals	
Establish communication with allies and opposition	

DISCUSSION QUESTIONS AND EXERCISES

1. In the case at the beginning of this chapter, Bertha's daughter faces a dilemma—how to intervene long distance so that her mother can have professional care in a timely manner. How urgent or at risk do you think Bertha's situation is? How would you define the problem based on the limited information that you have? What would you advise her daughter to do? What strategy (or series of strategies) might the daughter select, and what tactics would be most helpful? What role, if any, might Barb play in this advocacy scenario?

2. Read the following story of Mannie and Lucy and explain what you would do to help them. What strategies and tactics would you use, and why would you use them?

Mannie is a 79-year-old blind man who lives with his 71-year-old wife, Lucy, who is suffering from midstage senile dementia of the Alzheimer's type. Over the last year, Mannie's neighbors, Dave and Mary, have noticed that the couple seem to be deteriorating generally, including grooming and hygiene, and John seems to be losing weight. He also appears to be depressed and was visibly drunk on several occasions. Worse, he began to mutter to both Dave and Mary some philosophical expressions about the peaceful release of death.

Dave and Mary helped out as often as they could, shopping for Mannie on a weekly basis, offering to prepare meals, and so forth. But lately the once affable and garrulous Mannie has grown even more reclusive than Lucy, who had always kept to herself. Alarmed by Mannie's sudden refusal to accept help, Mary called the local aging services agency to ask for help.

The next day a risk assessment social worker visited Mannie and Lucy's apartment. She was appalled by what she found. The apartment was filthy. Woozy from the acrid stench of rotten food, dirty clothes, and human waste, she faced the worst case of self-neglect that she had ever seen. Both Lucy and Mannie had been eating dog food. Mannie was utterly incapable of helping Lucy with her basic activities of daily living. Worse, Lucy suffered multiple bruises from falling, appeared to be dehydrated, and was dangerously thin.

The social worker's report triggered a process whereby Mannie and Lucy were ultimately provided with a court appointed guardian to handle their affairs. Under state law this procedure does not entail a presumption of incompetence but merely a finding that the respondents (Mannie and Lucy) were not reasonably able to provide for their own welfare.

The Guardian placed Mannie in an Adult Foster Care home (up to five residents in a private residential setting) near his former residence. Lucy, however, was moved to a nursing home locked Alzheimer unit across town. Dave and Mary visited Mannie 2 weeks after he was admitted. They were immediately beset by his pleas to be with Lucy.

Mary asked Mannie why he just didn't ask his guardian to find a place where they could be together. "After all," she explained, "my Mom and Dad had shared a room at Crestside Convalescent for years.

Mannie smiled. "Yes," he said. "I need to be with Lucy, she needs me—52 years together and I can't even visit her."

I'll speak to your guardian," offered Mary, but Mannie's smile disappeared. He pursed his lips, dropped his head, and fixed his eyes on the floor.

"No," he muttered, "that wouldn't be a good idea. She might cause trouble, I just don't know, can't you do something?" Mary suggested getting professional help. After promising that nobody would do anything without Mannie's permission, he reluctantly agreed to let Mary try to get some help.

"I just want to be back with Lucy," Mannie reminded his old neighbors as they said goodbye, "but no trouble—just get me back to Lucy."

Several days later Mary met with the local aging services case manager, who referred her to the unit director. When the director heard the guardian's name, warning bells chimed in her brain and a concerned looked crossed her face, but only for a moment. She shook off the expression and turned her attention to Mary. "It shouldn't be hard to find a facility that could accommodate both Mannie and Lucy, she assured Mary, and I don't understand the guardian's decision. Give me a couple of days, and meanwhile I'll need to talk to Mannie.

After Mary left the director recalled a recent run-in with that same guardian. A nursing facility administrator called her office complaining about how one of his resident's guardians had forbidden the resident's friends from shopping for her, which they did once a week. The caseworker knew that guardians needed a general welfare reason to limit a ward's behavior or activities but couldn't figure out what this could be. She soon found out. Court records revealed that the guardian was being reimbursed $45 for each shopping trip, plus expenses. By shopping for Lucy, Mary had been robbing the guardian of her court approved fees.

The caseworker visited Mannie. He was pining to be with Lucy, "to help her." The caseworker assured him that she could make that happen, but Mannie would first have to request assistance from legal aid. "We will have to challenge your guardian in court," she informed him. "And for that we need a lawyer, and we know one who will help you."

Mannie squirmed, "I dunno, isn't there anyway for you just to take me to her? I don't want the guardian to get upset." His fear of the guardian actually trumped his agonizing desire to be with his wife! The caseworker visited him several more times, as did a legal aid attorney. Each time Mannie pleaded to find a way for him to be with Lucy without upsetting the guardian. No amount of reassurance could shake his cold fear.

3. Care planning and case management are described here as alliance building strategies. Whereas care planning may be an internal exercise among clients and staff, case management typically involves collaboration across organizational boundaries. Discuss potential differences in the power dynamics when one builds alliances within organizations and across organizational boundaries. What are the implications for older clients?

4. Case management is often described as a gatekeeping function, but many case managers see themselves as client advocates. If you were hired as a case manager, how might you balance your loyalty to your employer with your concern for your client's welfare? Are there instances in which you can foresee difficult ethical dilemmas in balancing the two? If so, how would you handle them?

5. Avoidance can be used as a tactic when a situation is not urgent and has little risk. It is also a reasonable tactic when you have little leverage. Conciliation and accommodation tactics are also useful in alliance building. Can you think of principles that might assist you in determining when to use avoidance or when to conciliate or accommodate within an alliance building strategy?

6. Consultants have more leverage in systems because they often have the power of expertise and position. Assume you are an external consultant. What would you want to know about the culture of the organization in which you are intervening to fully advocate for an older person? Can family members play the role of external consultants? Why or why not?

7. Persuasion and forcing pertain to situations in which there is high urgency or risk for elders and the advocates have high leverage. Talk about how comfortable or uncomfortable you would be in using this potentially highly conflictual strategy. Under what circumstances might you call in an external advocate to assist you? Under what conditions might it be ethical or unethical to provide information to an external advocate if you feel you cannot force within your own system?

8. Problem solving requires engagement with others to address issues that require attention. How can you assure that older persons are engaged in the problem-solving process? What skills do you consider crucial in working with others when you know that you do not have tremendous leverage?

9. Looking across the strategies and tactics, think about examples in which you might begin with one strategy but need to move to another. How might the framework assist you in knowing how to change your tactics as you move to a different strategy? Provide examples of how this might happen.

Additional Readings

Abramson, J. S. (1993). Orienting social work employees in interdisciplinary settings: Shaping professional and organizational perspectives. *Social Work, 38*(2), 152–157.

Allen, J. E. (2003). *Nursing home administration* (4th ed.). New York: Springer.

Anderson, A. (1996). Nurse-physician interaction and job satisfaction. *Nursing Management, 27*(6), 33–34, 36.

Baumeister, R. F., & Newman, L. S. (1994). Self-regulation of cognitive inference and decision processes. *Personality and Social Psychology Bulletin, 20,* 3–19.

Bell, C. H., & Smith, P. (n.d.). *Coalition facilitator guide.* Ohio State University Fact Sheet. Retrieved February 7, 2005, from http://ohioline.osu.edu/bc-fact/0002.html

Bullough, B. (1978). Stratification. In M. E. Hardy & M. E. Conway (Eds.), *Role theory: Perspectives for health professionals* (pp. 157–176). New York: Appleton-Century-Crofts.

Cherry, R. (1991). Agents of nursing home quality care: Ombudsmen and staff ratios revisited. *The Gerontologist, 31*(3), 302–308.

Cody, M. J., & McLaughlin, M. L. (1985). The situation as a construct in interpersonal communication research. In M. L. Knapp & G. R. Miller (Eds.), *Handbook of interpersonal communication* (pp. 263–312). Beverly Hills: Sage.

Diamond, T. (1992). *Making gray gold*. Chicago: University of Chicago Press.

Eisenhardt, K. M., Kahwajy, J. L., & Bourgeois, L. J. (1997). How management teams can have a good fight. *Harvard Business Review*, 77–85.

Fisher, R., & Brown, S. (1989). *Getting together: Building a relationship that gets to yes*. Boston: Houghton Mifflin.

Freund, T., Kruglanski, A. W., & Shpitzajzen, A. (1985). The freezing and unfreezing of impressional primacy: Effects of the need for structure and the fear of invalidity. *Personality and Social Psychology Bulletin*, 11(4) 479–487.

Gamroth, L., Semradek, J., & Tornquist, E. M. (Eds.). (1995). *Enhancing autonomy in long-term care: Concepts and strategies*. New York: Springer.

Kahana, J. S. (1994). Reevaluating the nursing home ombudsman's role with a view toward expanding the concept of dispute resolution. *Journal of Dispute Resolution*, 2, 218–233.

Kilmann, R. H., & Thomas, K. W. (1975). Interpersonal conflict-handling behavior as reflections of Jungian personality dimensions. *Psychological Reports*, 37, 971–980.

Kraskaupf, J. M., Brown, R. N., Tokarz, K. L., & Bogutz, A. D. (1993). *Elderlaw: Advocacy for the aging* (2nd ed.). St. Paul, MN: West.

Kressel, K., Frontera, E. A., Forlenza, S., Butler, F., & Fish, L. (1994). The settlement-orientation vs. the problem-solving style in custody mediation. *Journal of Social Issues*, 50(1), 67–84.

Kruglanski, A. W., Bar-Tal, D., & Klar, Y. (1988). Conflict as a cognitive schema. In W. Stroebe, A. Kruglanski, D. Bar-Tal, & M. Hewstone (Eds.), *The social psychology of intergroup conflict: Theory and research* (pp. 73–85). New York: Springer.

Kruglanski, A. W., Bar-Tal, D., & Klar, Y. (1993). A social cognitive theory of conflict. In K. S. Larsen (Ed.), *Conflict and social psychology* (pp 34–54). Oslo: Sage.

Litwin, H., Kaye, L. W., & Monk, A. (1984). Conflicting orientations to patient advocacy in long-term care. *The Gerontologist*, 24(3), 275–279.

Litwin, H., & Monk, A. (1984). Volunteer ombudsman burnout in long term care services: Some causes and solutions. *Administration of Social Work*, 8, 99–110.

Lowe, J. I., & Herranen, M. (1978). Conflict in teamwork. *Social Work in Health Care*, 3(3), 323–330.

Lusky, R. A, Friedsam, S. R., & Ingman, S. R. (1994, September). *Provider attitudes towards the nursing home ombudsman program*. Denton, TX: University of North Texas, Center for Studies on Aging.

Mallik, M. (1997). Advocacy in nursing: A review of the literature. *Journal of Advanced Nursing*, 25(1), 130–139.

Martin, B. A. (n.d.). *Mountains into molehills: Managing anger*. Retrieved March 4, 2005, from http://www.brianamartin.co.uk/docs/8.pdf

Martin, G. W. (1998). Ritual action and effect on the role of the nurse as advocate. *Journal of Advanced Nursing*, 27, 189–194.

McDonald, S., & Ahern, K. (2000). The professional consequences of whistleblowing by nurses. *Journal of Professional Nursing*, 16(6), 313–321.

Nelson, H. W. (1995). Long-term care volunteer roles on trial: Ombudsman effectiveness revisited. *Journal of Gerontological Social Work*, 23(3/4), 25–46.

Nelson, H. W., Allen, P., & Cox, D. (2005). Rights-based advocacy in long-term care: Geriatric nursing and long term care ombudsmen. *Clinical Gerontologist*, 28(4), 1–16.

Nelson, H. W., Pratt, C. C, Carpenter, C. E., & Walter, K. L. (1995). Factors affecting long-term care ombudsman organizational commitment and burnout. *Nonprofit and Voluntary Sector Quarterly*, 35(4), 509–514.

Nelson, H. W., & Walter, K. (1996). Sources of volunteer ombudsmen job dissatisfaction and intentions to quit [Unpublished raw data]. Salem. OR: Oregon State Office of the Long-Term Care Ombudsman.

Netting, F. E., Huber, R., & Kautz, J. R. (1995). Volunteer and paid long term care ombudsmen: Differences in complaint resolution. *The Journal of Volunteer Administration*, 13(4), 10–21.

Nicoteria, A. M. (1994). The use of multiple approaches to conflict: A study of consequences. *Human Communication Research*, 20(4), 592–621.

Painter, W. (1999). The battle on B wing: When staff members fight, everyone loses. *Contemporary Long-Term Care*, pp. 22–23.

Pillemer, K., Hegeman, C. R., Albright, B., & Henderson, C. (1998). Building bridges between families and nursing home staff: The partners in caregiving program. *The Gerontologist*, 38, 499–503.

Sellin, S. C. (1995). Out on a limb: A qualitative study of patient advocacy in institutional nursing. *Nursing Ethics*, 2(1), 19–29.

Stafford, F. (1989). If you don't like the care, why don't you take your mother home? Obstacles to family/staff partnerships in the institutional care of the aged. *Journal of Gerontological Social Work, 13*, 1–7.

Sweet, S. J., & Norman, I. J. (1995). The nurse-doctor relationship: A selective literature review. *Journal of Advance Nursing 22*(1), 165.

Trainers Direct. (n.d.). Breakthrough negotiation skills. Retrieved March 12, 2005, from http://www.trainersdirect.com/resources/Orbital/courses/Ngtns/Module1.doc

Vinton, L., & Mazza, N. (1994). Aggressive behavior directed at family members. *The Gerontologist, 34*, 528–533.

Vinton, L., & Mazza, N. (1998). Intervening in family-staff conflicts in nursing homes. *Clinical Gerontologist, 98*, 45–68.

Mobilizing Resources for Macro Interventions

The person-is-political perspective underscores the belief that individuals cannot be viewed separate from the larger society. The actions, and even the inactions, of individuals influence those around them and may have broad implications for others within an organization or community. NETTING, KETTNER, & McMURTRY (2004, p. 11)

 BOX 8.1

SAM and TOM

The gay rights movement has been in the public eye for some time now and will likely be embroiled in heated controversy over the concept of marriage for many years to come. Cheryl, a gerontological social worker, had her own opinions about the conflict, but it had never occurred to her how relevant it would be to her practice . . . until she met Sam and Tom.

Sam began coming to the adult day care center last year. Cheryl knew that his roommate, Tom, brought him in and picked him up in the afternoon. She had exchanged niceties with Tom over the course of the year, and she had become very fond of Sam. He had a number of chronic conditions that impaired his functioning, but with moderate assistance he was able to do a number of things on his own. He participated in the activities she planned at the center, and he was apt to bring her a single flower or a card on special occasions. When Tom called to report that Sam would not be coming to the center that day because he had been hospitalized the night before, Cheryl was genuinely concerned.

That evening Cheryl stopped by the hospital to check on Sam. She stopped by his room,

gently knocked on the door, and was surprised to hear a voice behind her. Turning around she encountered a nurse who said, "Mr. Dyer has company already. You might not want to go in just yet. He's been in there for a very long time with the door closed." Cheryl thought the comment was odd and wondered if the nurse was giving her a meta-message, but Cheryl wasn't sure how to read between the lines. Cheryl paused for a moment, then knocked again.

"Come in," a male voice from inside responded.

When Cheryl walked into the room, she saw Tom sitting close to Sam's bed, an opened book in his hands.

"Oh, hi! How very nice of you to come," Tom said in a very genuine manner. He pointed to the open book and said, "I was just reading to Sam. It helps him fall asleep."

"Well, I don't want to interrupt," Cheryl said. "I just wanted to check on Sam and see how he's doing."

(continued)

BOX 8.1 *(continued)*

Sam looked tired and much smaller tucked under the sheets. An IV bottle and a number of tubes were attached to his body. He smiled weakly, but Cheryl could tell that he was not feeling well. He looked at her for a moment as if he was sizing her up for the first time, trying to determine if he should say something to her.

"Oh, Ms. Cutshaw," he blurted out. "You may be the only person we can trust to tell this to, but I've been telling Tom that we have to seek someone's help." Tom checked to be sure the door was closed, and they began telling her their dilemma, seeking her advice and assistance.

A litany of issues spilled out as they talked. Only relatives or spouses have certain rights and privileges regarding medical matters, and it had become necessary for the men to reveal that their relationship was more than a friendship for Tom to gain full access to Sam. They had literally been "outed" every time they encountered a medical emergency, and they had learned to expect mixed responses. Some professionals were open and inclusive, making sure Tom had all the information he needed and working with them as a couple. Others were obviously very uncomfortable, explaining that only a spouse could do such and such or viewing them as a curiosity, asking questions that did not seem necessary.

In light of the severity of Sam's health conditions and the limited income they had, they wondered if Tom would have to move out of their small home if Sam had to go on Medicaid. Only married couples had the right for one member of the couple to remain in the couple's home for the remainder of his life without harming the partner's access to Medicaid coverage (Cahill & South, 2002). Cheryl was overwhelmed by what Tom and Sam were telling her and by the realization that their relationship was not respected by so many of the policies and procedures she had taken for granted that were in place to protect married couples.

Tom continued, "Gee, we can't even be buried in the same plot because the cemetery in town doesn't allow two unrelated, unmarried people to share the same grave."

Cheryl recognized that she could not take on the federal government or even the local cemetery committee. Calm down, she mentally told herself. They discussed what could be done now, and Cheryl told them about the social worker at the hospital whom she knew personally. She asked for their permission to contact the social worker and set up a meeting for them.

But in the long run Cheryl knew that the multitude of issues raised by Tom and Sam were just the tip of the iceberg for thousands of older same-sex couples who were aging in place, many of whom might not be "out" until their vulnerabilities forced them to share this information with providers. Some providers would do whatever they could to help, and others would be indifferent. Still others would be unaccepting (Hash, 2001), and they would be backed up by policies that discriminate against persons who are not married. Even though Sam and Tom (and others) desperately wanted to marry, they were not allowed to make this commitment in their state.

Advocates often see patterns or themes developing as they go about their work. Obviously, Cheryl had begun to encounter a set of issues that pertained to more than Tom and Sam. Every older person is unique, but there are times when the needs of one person or a group of persons will overlap or when insensitivities, injustices, ageism, and a host of other oppressive acts (or inactions) will seem incredibly familiar. Such acts or conditions seem familiar, of course, precisely because they happen frequently and affect whole groups and even communities of older people. When you encounter such conditions, ask yourself: Is the problem I see here just the tip of an iceberg of similar injustices throughout this system?

You will encounter problems faced by older people that are inherently unfair or unjust through no fault of their own, and the causes are often situational. Sam and Tom, for example, had lost control of being fully informed of one another's health issues because the hospital denied them access to information simply because they were a gay couple—they did not conform to the norm. When you encounter something like this, you may need to advocate at a macro level. Such problems are often caused by the policies of the organizations and communities in which older persons live. To put Band-aids on individuals' problems in such systems may mask the need for organizational, or macro-level, change. Further complicating such situations is the fact that elders may be in very vulnerable positions and be afraid to complain, even though every older person in that organization or group may be experiencing the same injustices. These older individuals can be helped as a class through efforts to change policies, rules, laws, or practices.

☽ WHEN SHOULD YOU WORK ON PROBLEMS AT THE MACRO LEVEL?

This chapter focuses on changing systems, or class level advocacy. Many of the skills, dynamics, and nuances you learned about in Chapter 7 in advocating for individuals also work when your focus is on agencies and other larger systems. Macro advocacy requires the same listening, communicating, negotiating, persuading, and related interpersonal skills that advocates bring to their case or individual level work. But the scope of the intervention greatly expands when you find problems that affect entire groups of people. Here we provide some guidance on how to address those broader scale needs.

We intentionally use the word *guidance* because situations differ, and the strategy you choose must fit the conditions you find. Strategies are dynamic, have overlapping characteristics, and are not mutually exclusive. As soon as you make a move, the situation, and therefore the chosen strategy, changes. This process

is more like a dance than a well-behaved linear list of tasks. In fact, two dances are occurring at the same time: one between your clients' level of urgency/risk and your leverage at the moment, and another between you and your clients together and the decision makers. It is important to reassess as you go to discern the state-of-the-moment of your clients' situations and appropriately adjust your strategies and tactics.

We first explain what it means to conduct large-scale advocacy and provide examples based on five types of systems analogies: mechanistic, organic, morphogenic, factional, and catastrophic systems. We discuss where to begin, how to decide who needs to be involved, and how to determine what approach to take (policy, program, project, personnel, and practice). We then explain how to implement the four main advocacy intervention strategies from the situational conflict model (see Figure 7.1) on a larger scale. We next relate the birth and growth of a grassroots citizen's movement that has had astonishing success as an elder advocacy organization, the Long-Term Care Ombudsman Program. To bridge the micro and macro levels of advocacy, we begin with an example of advocacy needed at both levels at once—the dilemma of some elderly clients at a senior center (Box 8.2).

As an advocate, you might advocate for Chester to be replaced or for the more generous position taken by his elder passengers. In either case, your attention first focuses on Chester and then is elevated to the agency level. To advocate for Chester to be replaced or reprimanded will not prevent similar abuse in the future unless other measures are taken at the agency level. The group of elders first discussed an individual solution—getting Chester fired—but they rather quickly moved to advocate *for* Chester at the second level, that of the agency director. If the director balks or does not have the authority to advance Chester the money to get his car fixed, the group's advocacy effort could move on to a third level, the center's board of directors.

The decision made by the group to take the high road (be generous and gracious and look at the problem from the problem maker's point of view) is worth remembering—not just because it

BOX 8.2

Chester and the Addams Senior Center

The Addams Senior Center van picks up 10 community elders Monday through Friday and brings them to the center for lunch and educational or entertaining programs, then takes them back home. Chester is a 60-year-old man with limited education and skills who was hired to drive the van. He is usually cheerful and eager to help the 10 elderly people, and until last month they responded to him in an equally positive manner.

The director noticed that their attitude toward Chester seemed to have changed in a negative way and investigated. She learned that Chester's car had broken down and that he had a large repair bill to pay before he could get his car back. She did not know that Chester's buddy was urging him to charge each of his passengers $5 for their free rides to and from the senior

center every day. When Chester first mentioned this to his passengers, they wanted to help out and gave him $5 each, but they had no idea he would expect $5 every day from each of them. With urging from his buddy, Chester made this expectation clear.

Some of the elders wanted to go to the director and get Chester fired, but one of the group said no. "Let's see if we can advocate for a better solution so that (a) we are not pressured to tip Chester every day, (b) the director advances Chester the money to get his car fixed, with a reasonable pay-back schedule, (c) he doesn't lose his job, and (d) he learns that such behavior will not be tolerated. He has been good to us for longer than we have had this problem, and it would be hard for him to get another job with this on his employment record."

was a nice thing to do but because it was smart as well. These elders built some goodwill out of a bad situation by advocating for a very specific win-win arrangement. That goodwill may prove to be valuable the next time a problem arises.

☺ What Are Macro Level Interventions?

In the spring of 2004 the American Society on Aging published a special advocacy and aging issue of *Generations*. Various scholars acknowledged that there is a tradition of advocacy in gerontological work. Recognizing that a great deal of advocacy focuses on work with individuals, these articles highlighted broad-scale advocacy. They focused on local organizations and communities working for policy changes at the national level and on national lobbying groups such as the American Association of Retired Persons (AARP). Robyn Stone

(2004) contributed an excellent article to that special issue titled *Where Have All the Advocates Gone?* She recounted her early days in Washington, D.C., during the 1970s, when "a wide range of national organizations advocated for the policies and programs to meet the needs of America's elders. In the Congress, the Senate Aging Committee and the House Select Committee on Aging had dedicated members and a knowledgeable, zealous group of young staffers who worked with the advocates to expand the aging services network and to strengthen health and retirement policies" (p. 59). She went on to say, "Twenty-five years later, just as the United States is about to experience the most significant demographic phenomenon in its history—the aging of the baby boomers— advocacy for aging policies and programs at the national level seems to have lost its compass" (p. 59). She attributed this change to the loss of champions, including legendary figures such as Maggie Kuhn, the founder of the Gray Panthers;

Claude Pepper and Arthur Fleming, who brought their tireless statesmanship to the national arena; and Tish Sommers, a displaced homemaker who literally grew the Older Women's League to national prominence. (Links to all of these organizations are on the companion website.)

Stone also wrote about the "failure of our successes" (p. 60) in which poverty among elders was greatly diminished but the backlash resulted in terms such as "greedy geezers" and to "too many organizations fighting for slices of the pie," "special interests discover[ing] aging," and the "persistence of ageism in U.S. society" (p. 61). The heyday of advocacy to which Stone alluded was a period of seemingly urgent change in a different time and place. Gerontology had yet to become an established curriculum in many colleges and universities, and the popular movement to raise consciousness about aging was high. These were definitely macro-level advocacy efforts, primarily at the national level, before the full extent of devolution had occurred. Stone concluded by saying, "While advocacy is sorely missed at the national level, I believe that the most effective efforts will occur at the local level, where individuals can relate to the importance of creating and sustaining healthy aging communities for all generations" (pp. 63–64).

Today the arenas are somewhat different. With devolution, state houses and local communities are the places in which aging advocacy is likely to occur. At the national level the fight for Social Security seems strangely caught in an *us* versus *them* intergenerational battle that needs to be reframed as simply *us*. We agree that it is at the organizational and community levels that many macro-level interventions will be occurring in the years to come, and general agreement on this point seems to be widespread. Hoefer (2005), for example, is concerned that social work students are not focusing on political processes or developing expertise in advocacy, and others are concerned that students are not being taught the importance of identifying "figurative ground" (Rybacki & Rybacki, 1996) nor developing public argumentation skills (Lens, 2005).

Macro-level interventions occur in complex systems at the organizational and community levels (requiring administrative-level advocacy). When we first discussed complex systems theory in Chapter 2, we introduced five types of systems analogies, which we briefly review here from the perspective of macro advocacy for elders. Box 8.3 provides a quick, oversimplified reminder of how systems work—or do not.

When you look at a system as *mechanistic*, you are using an analogy—that everything should work together like a well-oiled machine. Remember John, the 92-year-old engineer introduced in Chapter 2? Recall John's engineering perspective: that everything should work together in a logical manner. He just could not grasp the idea that if he did everything his physicians told him to do and was totally compliant, he was still going to die. His daughter, as an advocate, realized that he wanted her to push for aggressive treatment even though medical practitioners had essentially given up hope that he would survive. He died, but he died knowing that she was still pushing for the treatment he wanted.

Now consider the possibility that John is not an isolated case. Others believe as he does: that aggressive care should be pursued at all costs—that as long as there is life, there is hope. If you work for a hospice program in which a six months' (or less) to live prognosis is an eligibility criterion and patients and family members agree to comfort or palliative care (but not aggressive treatment), you would not encourage John or his family toward hospice care because John's wishes do not fit your program's goals. If John remains in the hospital, not-so-subtle cost containment pressures may label him as being in denial and staff may encourage him to sign a Do Not Resuscitate (DNR) order. If the hospital either overtly or covertly wants to rush John's discharge, remaining in that hospital is not a good fit for John either.

To advocate for John to continue receiving care even though his prognosis is terminal in any event would require a macro-level intervention because you are seeking policy and practice changes to address the needs of a group of elders who think like John and, therefore, do not conform to the hospital's expectations of a quick discharge. Advocates face myriad dilemmas in their work. Dilemmas are not just hard decisions. They

BOX 8.3

How Systems Work—Or Not

Your public agency is a typical mechanistic and bureaucratic system, one of the most complex organizations on earth. In simplest form, however, it's a magic *black box* between inputs and outputs:

Systems put the hardware and software together in the black box. This is where the interactions occur between all of the components that result in the desired output: elderly clients who have all the services they need.

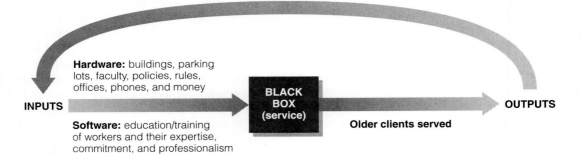

When elderly persons enter your organization, a switch is thrown and your organization starts to hum, focusing all of its resources on the elderly people to create a good output: older clients who are receiving all the services they need. Multiple, very labor-intensive, and expensive inputs are required. These can be thought of as *hardware*, or things you can touch (such as funding, buildings, parking lots, money, phone system, policies, and copiers), and *software*, or things you cannot touch (such as education, training, the expertise of workers, and their commitment to their work, or professionalism).

Your agency (system) is accountable to its *suprasystem*, which both provides the inputs and keeps a close eye on your outputs. If your outputs are not what your suprasystem (elderly people and their families) wants, you will not continue to receive inputs, and your system will die (your agency will be out of business). On the other hand, if the elderly people who exit your system are well served and they (and their families) are satisfied, you will continue to get clients and inputs (resources) and your agency will flourish.

occur when you or your clients must choose between two courses of action that are both either good or not good. In this case, neither setting is just right for John.

A second systems analogy is that systems are *organic*, much like biological organisms: if the parts are kept in harmony, the system will flourish much like plants and flowers do. Certainly, this is a hopeful analogy, but it implies that there

is a cellular connection. Unfortunately, most social and organizational systems are not literally sewn together with interconnective tissue. In fact, sometimes it is hard to know what holds these systems together at all. If you think of a system as being either biological (organic) or mechanistic (machinelike), you may sometimes be disappointed when the system you are dealing with does not meet those expectations. Such systems reinforce the status quo, avoid change if possible, and maintain a sense of equilibrium that looks as much the same as possible over time.

An organic analogy is often used in health care systems because biological ways of understanding things are so prevalent. For example, patient advocates in health care may call themselves the "eyes and ears" of the system. Nurse practitioners and physician assistants have been called "physician extenders" almost as if they literally begin where the physician's physical presence ends. Yet this analogy has its limitations because these eyes and ears and extenders are not one organic whole; they are distinctive and often very different persons. Although they want to coordinate with one another, they may sometimes contradict one another if one person realizes a problem that has not been identified by another. In an organic system, however, there is pressure to perform in a way that does not upset the equilibrium and thus repress conflict.

A third analogy is called *morphogenesis,* or structure changing. Unlike the systems just described, this type of system is recognized as constantly changing, and it is through these changes that new ways of looking at the world emerge. If you have a morphogenic approach to systems, you may expect negative changes but counter them with daily pushes (both gentle and conflictual) that slowly move the system toward your goals.

Morphogenetic systems, in which normal push and pull is experienced as advocates, elders, and decision makers work to make change happen, are described throughout this book. For example, you met Fran, a case manager for an Area Agency on Aging, and her hospitalized client Maria, in Chapter 2. It was Fran who realized that the clash of two organizational cultures meant that she needed to push for change. She was not excessively aggressive but appropriately assertive in prodding the two different sets of players to work together. She was aware that conflict is inevitable but that change can happen if one persists in a collaborative manner. Such changes do not forevermore solve all problems between the two organizations, but they open communication for problems to be identified earlier and for the

system to continue to work for positive changes. These morphogenetic changes often have a positive impact on the lives of elders.

Factional systems are those in which competing interest groups vie for attention and conflict and disorder are high. Things get accomplished, but usually in an aggressive manner, with those who have power dominating those who do not. This can be somewhat disconcerting for people who are not accustomed to conflict or who seek consensus at all costs. In such situations, an outside evaluator can provide much needed perspective. For example, a social worker under contract with a state Department of Health and Social Services (DHSS) was asked to evaluate a waiver program to inform an ongoing funding decision by the Centers for Medicare and Medicaid Services (CMS). The service in question provides limited in-home care to elders, which prevented or delayed their need for skilled (nursing home) care. When it became known that the evaluation was to be conducted by the external social worker, she was approached by representatives from two factions who managed the cases: in-house (DHSS) case managers who managed about 75% of the cases and AAA case managers who managed the other 25%. Representatives from both groups said to the evaluator: "I'm sure you'll find that the cases we handle result in better outcomes." The social worker thanked them and said that she appreciated their commitment to their work. The pressure was not a problem for the evaluator because she had no internal ties to either camp and, therefore, did not have a conflict of interests, one of the clear advantages of external evaluators.

At the beginning of Chapter 6 we presented a case example in which a regional AAA was engaged in a planning process and held public hearings. The two home health providers in conflict used different approaches to present their cases, and private citizens also expressed the needs as they saw them. The home health care agencies were competing for a limited amount of funds, but AAA staff were intent on finding ways to increase the size of the funding pie. This example is typical of a factional system in which there is conflict and various interest groups are competing.

When the parties agree to work toward change (as seemed to be the case in the public hearing), the system becomes more morphogenetic. This is a good example of advocacy directed at an initially factional system in which good, advocacy-oriented workers crafted a solution that held the interests of elders as a priority.

Finally, a *catastrophic* analogy reveals systems in constant flux and great instability. No one is in control, and things are running haywire. If some movement toward a less chaotic system does not occur, advocates will simply burn out (unless they thrive on ambiguity, uncertainty, and high conflict). Catastrophic systems require aggressive social reform, and most practitioners will not engage in this type of change unless they join a broad-scale social movement with radical change in mind. The types of change needed require the organized efforts of powerful people, and even then, it may take a long time to achieve results.

Having briefly reviewed these five theoretical perspectives of systems (mechanistic, organic, morphogenesis, factual, and catastrophic), think about how you and others perceive the system in question. Is the system seen as basically working and needing only minor adjustment for older people to receive a needed benefit? Or is this system riddled with conflict, in which special interest groups vie for their needs to be met? Are elders essentially invisible? Or is it not what one could describe as a system as all? Is it politically volatile? Is it hard to determine where to begin? Do others share your views of this, or do you even know? All of these questions may rush into your mind as you face the challenge of where to start your advocacy intervention.

☺ So Where to Begin?

In Chapter 4 we identified three principal agents who are involved in advocacy efforts: the person in need, the advocate, and decision makers with the power to change things. When you advocate for just one person at a time, you are not likely to be engaged in macro-level intervention. Yet there are multiple ways in which this one person's need may become part of a larger concern or issue. We illustrate with several examples previously introduced and tie these cases to the analogies just reviewed.

Fran and Maria Revisited

Once again we return to the case of Fran and Maria (Chapter 2). Maria was admitted to the Intensive Care Unit (ICU) of a large teaching hospital with a life-threatening illness. Fran, her case manager, was intimidated by the culture of the large hospital system and felt disempowered. She aligned with Maria's physician who had more power within the hospital system. Now let's assume that Fran had a number of older clients who ended up in this large hospital over a period of time. Each time she tried to maintain contact with her clients, her efforts were blocked. These older persons were very ill, had no family members, and were totally isolated from everyone they had known when they entered this large hospital. Fran began to see a pattern. This was the logical place for elders from her community to be admitted when they needed critical care, and it was becoming increasingly evident that Fran would continually be going to this hospital as her clients aged in place. Each time she entered the system, it was as if she had come in for the first time. Each time she had to locate someone who would hear her voice and recognize that she was the sole contact person for these isolated elders.

Fran decided that a systemic link was needed between the AAA and the hospital system. Without some reciprocity between the two organizations, she would continually face this crisis. From her base at the AAA, how might Fran work with local physicians, local elders (while they were well), and the hospital system to assure that the appropriate ground rules, protocols, and agreements were in place so that she would have access to her clients and be able to share information needed for their critical care? This was no longer Fran and Maria as an individual intervention; it became an interorganizational macro intervention, the details of which could make a quality of care (and quality of life) difference to an unknown number of elders. Fran's approach to collaboration between the rural AAA and the city hospital system is similar to a number of interventions in geriatric rural care.

Butler and Webster (2003) provided some possible approaches to collaborating and designing integrated case management models that build on indigenous strengths and capabilities in rural areas.

Fran also recognized that the hospital and the AAA systems had different worldviews. The hospital was highly mechanistic; it needed to maintain strict protocols and standards as its staff dealt with life-threatening interventions. In fact, being mechanistic is critically important when rapid decisions and highly invasive procedures have to occur in sterile environments. On the other hand, the AAA was much less mechanistic in its worldview, often working with multiple constituents within local communities and dealing with the tensions and conflicts that arise in morphogenetic settings. Each worldview was well suited for what that organization needed to do, and Fran recognized that an alliance between the two was a cross-cultural collaboration that would take considerable time and effort. It was worth her effort, however, if older people would benefit in the long run.

Lester, Dorothy, and Mikie

In Chapter 2 we also introduced Lester, an 85-year-old man, and his wife, Dorothy, who were hospitalized the same day. Dorothy had been admitted in the morning, and Lester's admission followed rather quickly when he fell and broke his arm and hip. The apartment manager agreed to oversee Mikie's care (the cat); he was their sole dependent.

Dorothy and Lester had unique personalities and their specific situation was not exactly like any other. Had they not had an advocate (their niece) who could take on the discharge planner, chances are they would not have been discharged to the same nursing facility. The niece was concerned about her relatives and acted as their case advocate, but she had also seen this pattern of hastily made discharge plans repeatedly in her work. The pressure placed on discharge planners was tremendous because each day a patient lingered in the hospital cost the system. Hastily put together discharge plans, often without adequate support at home, varied tremendously, and older

persons were frequently put into perilous situations. Rather than blaming the hospitals or railing at discharge planners, the niece decided to join an advocacy group dedicated to monitoring the fate of older persons discharged prematurely. Their intent was to document patterns in which systems might be held liable for putting older persons in harm's way so that a better process could be implemented. This pattern, repeated throughout the country, required vigilance from advocates who had seen this problem occur over and over again.

Ironically, Mikie (the cat) provided another opportunity for macro-level change. When the niece contacted the apartment manager to let her know how much her aunt and uncle appreciated the manager feeding the cat, the manager indicated that she just could not do this indefinitely. Not only was she allergic to cats, but Mikie was alone in the apartment and was not getting any attention. Lester and Dorothy agreed that they would not be able to care for Mikie even if they returned home and that Mikie needed a new home, but they were adamant that he go to a no-kill shelter.

The niece contacted the local AAA, and a staff person there put her in touch with a regional cat sanctuary. When she called the woman who ran the sanctuary, she was told that they only took in feral and stray cats. The niece persisted, throwing herself on the mercy of this kind-hearted individual. The niece was certain that this was not an isolated problem—that it must be something people dealt with all the time—and she agreed to work with the sanctuary to raise money for animals orphaned when their elder owners either died or were incapacitated. She contacted the local hospice, and they confirmed that they were always trying to place animals as their owners died. Local shelters were reluctant to take in older pets because they were unlikely adoptees. Three hospice workers indicated that they had five cats apiece, having taken in the animals when their older patients died. Working with the regional college of veterinary medicine, the cat sanctuary, and the AAA, the niece formed an alliance for orphaned pets. Word spread and a website for geriatric pets was created and linked to the cat sanctuary. An individual advocacy effort for Lester and Dorothy to have Mikie cared for (easing their minds) became a macro-level intervention designed to facilitate the adoption of older pets orphaned by their elderly owners.

What Do These Examples Have in Common?

Both Fran and the niece in these examples are functioning as external advocates in systems that could be somewhat difficult to navigate in the best of circumstances. The people who staff these systems are not mean-spirited. In fact, they are probably competent and caring professionals. But the very nature of these huge health care systems means that anyone entering this culture will be in a strange place when not in the best physical or mental health. Maria and Lester and Dorothy were already somewhat isolated individuals and were lucky to have one lone advocate pushing for their rights as patients and human beings.

However, Fran had begun to see a pattern as her older clients were whisked away from their rural communities to the large hospital. Each time this happened, she felt she was reinventing the wheel—trying to access decision makers so that she could advocate for the elders she was committed to serving. Similarly, the niece saw a pattern because not only was she personally related to her aunt and uncle, but she worked in the field of aging and knew that older people in cities and communities across the country were entering hospitals every day with discharge planning being imminent. When she had to figure out what to do with Mikie, she recognized another pattern in which older people's beloved companion animals were in jeopardy. She didn't ignore the pattern but began to work interorganizationally to figure out a way to intervene on a broader scale. Essentially that is what advocates do—they see patterns and seize opportunities to work toward broader scale change in systems.

Systems advocacy is more time consuming than case advocacy and requires more resources and energy. Once you determine that a problem's

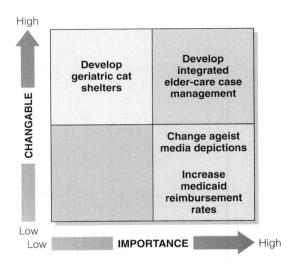

FIGURE 8.1 Importance and Changeability Matrix

scope represents patterns within a system, you next need to determine whether disrupting these patterns is possible and sufficiently important to justify a class-level intervention (Kreuter, Lezin, Kreuter, & Green, 2003). The importance and changeability matrix (Figure 8.1) can help you determine this.

Determining a given problem's importance requires a subjective evaluation. Widespread problems resulting in pain, loss of rights or financial resources, or mental anguish or distress are clearly important on their faces. But other cases, such as a need for geriatric cat shelters, require a more subjective judgment. In such cases, action may be justified due to the problem's prevalence and the fact that something can be done about it without draining important elder-care system resources. You need not worry about the low-importance quadrant of the matrix. If enough people deem the problem important, they will find each other, commiserate, and begin to organize. Next, they will reach out into the community and build coalitions among likeminded stakeholder groups to acquire power, visibility, and clout.

As discussed in Chapter 6, the perception of a problem's importance will not only determine its priority but will also determine the coalition's tactics to cause change. For example, high threat, high urgency macro-problems that fuel anger and anxiety inspire more forceful strategies—grassroots activism, direct legal action, protests, picket lines, and major political power plays.

Advocates who face multiple system problems must rationally choose problems of higher importance, but these must also be realistically changeable. Assessing a system's changeability is crucial because it allows the advocate to decide the "feasibility of making a difference," the time and resources needed to cause the change, and how to "estimate the time it will take to detect a difference" (Kreuter et al., 2003, p. 92).

☾ I See a Pattern That is Important and Changeable: Now What Do I Do?

In Chapter 5 we focused on investigating and analyzing situations, an ongoing process. When patterns are seen and the problem is larger than an individual's concern, it is helpful to return to these tasks, but with the larger context in mind:

1. Consider the rules of best evidence: (a) the farther away you are from the event the less reliable your investigation, (b) the farther away from the event, the less reliable are your informants, and (c) evidence is useless if you cannot retrieve it when you need it.
2. Start by interviewing the persons involved and collect data (collecting evidence).
3. Draw from all available resources.
4. Recognize negligence.
5. Examine potential issues regarding rights and ethics.
6. Develop working hypotheses.
7. Verify the problem.

The difference between focusing on these tasks at the case advocacy level (individuals and small groups) and the cause advocacy level (large systems) is scope. Think in terms of a class of elders who are encountering the same problem and focus on each task with the larger group in mind. This raises the final task: once the problem is verified, just how big does it appear to be? Document the nature, scope, and significance of the problem by drawing from every source you have available.

Next, reconsider the six planning the intervention tasks highlighted in Chapter 6, but focus on the larger context:

1. Determine whether an advocate is needed in this situation.
2. Use a situational conflict model.
3. Select advocacy strategies and tactics.
4. Think about how to manage conflict intensity.
5. Consider legal implications.
6. Recognize the power dynamics.

As you consider each of these tasks, you will realize that macro-level intervention requires the mobilization of resources. Chances are that more than one advocate will be needed in this situation. If this is a big enough problem to affect the lives of many elders and the problem has not been resolved, change may require a great deal of time and effort on the part of multiple parties.

In macro-change situations, resource mobilization takes on added dimensions. To connect multiple advocates or collaborators, advocacy groups must be solicited, joined, or formed. In addition, there will be multiple targets of change, even sequential targets of change.

The selection of strategies may also be sequential, depending on what happens in the process and how long the process becomes. As this process unfolds, conflict intensity will escalate because the depth of resistance will be stronger than anticipated or will be invisible until decision makers are targeted for change. Similarly, legal implications and power dynamics will shift as the push for change gains momentum. When you begin to think about change that affects entire organizational and community systems or change that requires formalized policy alterations, no matter how well you plan you will encounter unexpected reactions and unanticipated residuals.

☾ Decide Who Needs to be Involved

Macro-level interventions require more than one person, and it is important to decide who needs to be involved in the change process. Netting,

Kettner, and McMurtry (2004) introduced a planned change model in which a number of different types of participants are introduced.

First, think about who initiated the need for this macro change. Was it you? Was it you and others? Did someone else call this to your attention? In other words, who started the process of considering that something needs to change? If you are the person, then you are already involved. If someone else called it to your attention, perhaps this person needs to be a co-champion for the cause. In the case of broad-scale change, you may need to join with a whole cadre of advocates to initiate change or to begin the consciousness-raising process.

Second, consider who needs to come together to make a change happen. In the case of Fran and Maria, Fran alone cannot forge a connection between the AAA and a huge hospital system. Are there players in both the AAA and at the hospital who need to connect to make something happen? If so, who are they? And what are their agendas?

Third, who will benefit from this change? Having elder voices in the process is incredibly important; the voices of the very people you are trying to serve can be muted as more people get on the bandwagon to make something happen. Figuring out creative ways to keep those voices heard is often something an advocate must work hard to do.

Fourth, who will support this change process? Established support networks might join forces and throw their weight behind the proposed change. For example, would the American Association for Retired Persons, one of the largest lobbying groups in the country, support the change you want to make? Would groups like the National Council on the Aging, the American Society on Aging, the National Citizens Coalition on Nursing Home Reform, and a host of others be willing to support what you are trying to do? Would the local chapter of the Alzheimer's Association or a branch of the Gray Panthers have a stake in being supportive? Again, depending on your goals, you may find that a number of groups already support this type of action.

Fifth, who has the power to make this change happen? Even with all the support systems available, decision makers who have the power to move change forward must be involved. Sometimes they are the same as some of the players already mentioned, but at other times they are very different. Learn how decisions are made, and by whom, so that you know who actually has decision-making power. This may sound obvious, but if you are an external advocate, you may not have a clue about who has the authority to make a decision. Multiple decision makers may have to be considered because macro changes are rarely directed toward just one person.

Sixth, and closely tied to the previous point, who is being asked to implement the change? In macro-level changes, this may be a very hard question to answer because focus on one person may lead to another and another and another. For example, you may think that the hospital social worker can assist in connecting with the AAA, only to find out that it is the administrator who has to sign a formal agreement. Yet it may not stop there. Once an agreement is signed, it is just an agreement without action until implementation occurs. The discharge planning unit may be tasked to carry out the agreement, yet they may not even know that such an agreement has been signed. In fact, if they are not part of the decision-making process, they may resent the new policy and fail to follow through. Thus multiple players may emerge—first the social worker, then administrators, and then discharge planners.

Finally, who will follow through and monitor the process? Will you be able to oversee it all the way through to its end, or will you need a network of point people, all of whom work together to oversee the process? Planned changes do not just happen, and they certainly do not happen unless there is vigilant oversight. In the beginning of this book we defined advocacy as *being vigilant.* We meant it! Advocacy efforts require focus and energy on an ongoing basis to see changes through—vigilance. In macro-level interventions, these efforts may take months, even years to come to fruition. Succinct reminders of who needs to be involved are listed in Box 8.4.

BOX 8.4

How to Decide Who Needs to Be Involved

1. Who initiated the matter that needs to be changed?
2. Who needs to coalesce to make change happen?
3. Who will benefit from the change?
4. Who will support the change?
5. Who has the power to make it happen?
6. Who is the focus of the advocacy intervention?
7. Who will follow through and monitor the change?

BOX 8.5

Five Approaches to Large-Scale Interventions

Policy: To initiate a new policy or change current policies

Program: Interrelated activities to address a need or set of needs

Project: Short versions of programs such as pilot or demonstration projects

Personnel: Some kind of personnel change needs to happen

Practice: Implement an intervention

○ DETERMINE WHAT APPROACH TO TAKE

Netting et al. (2004) identify five possible approaches to a macro planned change intervention: policy, program, project, personnel, or practice. It is helpful to consider what form the change may need to take, at least in its initial stages, and Box 8.5 provides an introduction to these five approaches. We then briefly examine each type.

Policy Approach

A policy is simply a course of action—a direction set either formally or informally by some authoritative body such as a board of directors, a city council, a county board of supervisors, or a legislature. Policies also may be set by a single person with authority to unilaterally initiate a

policy, such as the head of a state department or someone high in your target organization.

Policy changes can occur at the organizational, community, county, regional, state, federal, or international level. An organizational policy change occurs when a board of directors for a human service agency decides to ration services. Let's say that this rationing was particularly problematic for older persons because it became a justification to accept only clients who had the best chance of success (younger people). Older people were being deemed ineligible far more often than younger people. Convincing the organization that their rationing policy is resulting in age discrimination against older clients becomes the focus of your intervention. The goal is to change the policy.

A community policy is exemplified by a city council that decides to establish a public transit system. Everyone may be thrilled that there is

BOX 8.6

Summary of the Policy Approach

Policy: A course of action or a direction set by some authoritative body such as a board of directors, a city council, a county board of supervisors, or a legislature.

1. Policies can be set unilaterally by a chief executive officer with such authority.
2. Policy changes can occur at all levels of systems: organizational, community, county, regional, state, federal, and international.

3. Policy changes are usually well intentioned but can have deleterious unintended consequences.
4. The intention may have been to document accountability, but older people may be seen as ineligible more often than younger people if better outcomes are anticipated for younger people.
5. Sometimes no policies exist in the areas in which you are concerned (for example, smoking in public places).

finally a way to get around town until persons with disabilities and older persons discover that the vehicles are not fully accessible. Although the disabilities and aging advocates may be pleased that transportation is available, it is incumbent upon them to bring this inaccessibility issue to the attention of the newly established transit authority. City council members may not have had any idea that they would be limiting accessibility when they voted to make public transportation a priority. The breakdown is in implementation of the policy, and advocates would work toward a change that results in vehicular accessibility.

Another current example is city council members who decide to ban smoking in all public places—a policy that would be welcomed by myriad elders with respiratory problems as well as a large part of the population. As expected, opposition comes from hotel, restaurant, and bar owners and managers who are well organized and supported by the tobacco industry, so inroads there must be forged.

Similarly, mandated bodies at the state and national levels enact policies. Sometimes it is not that an existing policy needs to be amended but that no policy exists. For example, advocates

may want to ensure that caregivers receive special dispensation for the time they spend caring for older relatives. State legislators are willing to support this cause, but no bills were introduced in last year's session to provide a tax break for caregivers. Advocates bring this to the attention of legislators so that a bill can be prepared to support caregiving activities and compensate caregivers.

If a policy approach is needed, advocates must clearly identify the targets of their efforts. Advocates need to know when to target an existing policy that needs to change or be reversed, and when to address a gap in which there is no policy. The main points of the policy approach are summarized in Box 8.6.

Program Approach

A program is a set of interrelated activities that occur over an extended period to address a need or set of needs. A program is sometimes the result of a policy change. A policy is enacted and everyone feels good about it, but the question remains: How will it be implemented? What will happen? Policies are only a beginning—nothing really happens until older people's needs are addressed through programming.

BOX 8.7

Summary of the Program Approach

Program: A set of interrelated activities that occur over an extended period to address a need or set of needs—sometimes the result of policy changes.

1. A policy to create a program is useless until the program is actually implemented.
2. Like policies, programs can occur at all levels.
3. Programs may be federally mandated but implemented at the state level, such as the Medicaid program and the Long-Term Care Ombudsman Program.
4. A program change that affects elders in local senior centers may need to be changed at the state or federal level.
5. Program evaluation is an important and valid reason to conduct research: (a) to what extent is this program doing what it is supposed to be doing, and (b) what are the outcomes for its clients?

Programs, like policies, may occur at various levels. A community-based organization may design a program for elders unique to that community's needs. However, programs may be designed at the national and state levels as well. For example, Medicare is a federally mandated health care program for older people. What Medicare covers and doesn't cover may become a bone of contention. Advocates focus on needed program changes such as the addition of prescription drug coverage or certain health care procedures.

Program evaluation is an important and valid reason to conduct research. Existing programs may come under fire because they are not doing what they need to do. Other programs may be developed to address a void in the health and human service delivery system. Regardless of whether the advocate is pushing for a programmatic change or seeking to establish a new program, macro changes occur in response to the needs of groups of people, not just those of an individual.

Moxley and Hyduk (2003) elaborated on the logic of what they call "personal advocacy" for program management in community-based settings. Based on the assumption that elders know what they need but may need support from a personal advocate to achieve desired outcomes, this empowerment approach can be incorporated into existing human service programs. "It assists [elders] to sort out specific stressors without pointing to personal deficits or incompetence, and without labeling the elder diagnostically" (p. 10). This approach could become part of a local provider network, replacing existing deficit-based models with a strengths-based perspective. Although the actual impact would be individual, a major change in programmatic philosophy would require a macro-level intervention. Box 8.7 summarizes the main points of the program approach.

Project Approach

By definition, projects are short versions of programs. They are typically called projects because they are easier to sell to decision makers who may not be willing to buy into full-fledged programs but are willing to try new ideas. Sometimes projects are called *pilot* or *demonstration projects* to test the waters with new possibilities.

Projects can occur at any level, but typically they are thought of as being on a smaller scale than programs and may be localized in a city or region. A project may be tied to a specific agency that is going to try its hand at addressing a need in a different or innovative way. Advocates may

BOX 8.8

Summary of the Project Approach

Projects: Short versions of programs, typically called projects because they are easier to sell to decision makers who may not be willing to buy into a full-fledged program but are willing to try a new idea; sometimes called pilot or demonstration projects.

1. Projects occur at all levels and are smaller; a program may have several ongoing projects.
2. Advocates can push for new projects to test new ideas or interventions.

3. Employees who see special needs may more easily obtain permission to launch a new project than a new program.
4. Creating a project can be a very politically astute way to pilot a new program.
5. Projects are usually time limited, whereas programs are generally intended to be permanent.

---

push for projects to try something new that may address an identified need.

For example, a local homeless shelter wants to address the needs of a number of older men and women who are sleeping on the streets at night in the area. The shelter is only open to families, but they agree to open their doors to single men and women over the age of 60. They work with the local aging network to refer these older people to the case management program and to locate housing. The focus on families has all but eliminated the possibility that these older persons would receive services. By piloting a senior project, the shelter identifies a greater need: word gets out that they are open to singles over a certain age and people literally come out of the woodwork. Once this happens, aging advocates begin to push for the possibility of a specialized shelter tied to the local senior center so that a plethora of services will be easily accessible, including a nutritious meals program for drop-ins. Box 8.8 provides a summary of the project approach.

Personnel Approach

Sometimes a person or persons need to change for the problem to be resolved. We are not suggesting that advocates try to cause people to lose their jobs or move on, but there are times when it is obvious to the advocate that a personnel change has to happen. For example, it came to the attention of the director of a foster grandparent program that the van driver she had hired was going to be a problem staff person. The van driver was delightful to talk with, always seemed enthusiastic about picking up the grandparents at their respective sites, but seemed to drive a little too fast. Grandparents liked her and often said she was a lot like their granddaughter, but occasionally one would comment, "Susan can really make time on the road!"

The director of the program had talked with Susan a number of times about her driving habits, and she vowed that she was keeping within the speed limit. One day the high school principal was watching her leave the school grounds after having picked up several grandparents, and she wheeled off the grounds, leaving a cloud of dust. The principal reported this to the agency, and Susan was fired. However, she soon reappeared as the driver for the local senior nutrition program. What had begun as an individual van driver being fired raised a question about the safety of passengers in another program. The director debated over whether to talk with the senior nutrition director and decided to do so when they had an opportune encounter.

BOX 8.9

Summary of the Personnel Approach

Personnel: The staff or volunteers who are involved in a problem.

1. The personnel change could be to hire, dismiss, or reassign workers, or even volunteers.
2. Care needs to be taken that the person doesn't simply go to a different agency and resume the same behavior.

3. If caseloads are too large, it is appropriate to advocate for additional staff.
4. If an agency is in severe financial jeopardy, advocacy may be directed toward eliminating a position, possibly the lesser of two bad outcomes.

Now this personnel change had evolved into a macro intervention beyond the walls of one agency and across organizational boundaries. This was good work, right? The director intervened when a problem employee moved from one agency to another, but does the director's action entail an ethical dilemma? Is it permissible to discuss a personnel issue of a former employee with the director of another program in the area? In doing so, has the director made the agency a prime target for litigation? If so, was this still the *right* thing to do? Such questions should never be very far from your thinking before such decisions are made.

Advocating for additional personnel could have been appropriate if Susan had so many stops on her van route that she always felt pressured to drive fast to complete her assigned pickups or, in the nutrition program, to deliver meals within set lunch hours. Caseloads are often too high for high-quality work. This is especially true in Adult Protective Services in many cities and states. Regardless of whether internal or external advocacy is planned for hiring more employees, advocates must do their homework by documenting caseloads and determining whether they are higher than designated or best practice standards would allow. The consequences to clients when caseloads are too high should be clearly described.

The other side of this dilemma is when, for example, a hospice census is down and a social worker must be laid off. If the workers put their heads together, they may generate creative solutions to reduce personnel costs without laying off workers such as having everyone cut back to 4 days a week, job sharing, and shorter shifts. The inviolate criterion must always be that clients' needs are met. There are ample opportunities for advocacy to occur within personnel decisions. Box 8.9 provides a summary of the personnel approach.

Practice Approach

A practice involves the specific activities that occur in providing an intervention. Practice changes may be as simple as deciding what assessment tool to use or as complicated as which type of therapeutic mental health intervention is needed with dually diagnosed clients. A practice change occurs when individual practitioners decide to change the way in which they provide treatment or try a new client intervention. A macro practice change occurs when an entire unit or service provider shifts how they practice to meet multiple clients' needs.

A local nursing home was proud of its family council and was viewed by the state association of homes for the aged as exemplary in implementing the family council concept. Nursing homes are encouraged to have family councils composed of persons who have relatives in their facilities, and there is great unevenness across facilities in the structure and functioning of these groups.

BOX 8.10

Summary of the Practice Approach

Practice: The specific activities that occur in providing interventions.

1. A macro practice change occurs when an entire unit or service needs to shift how they practice.
2. The need for a practice change may arise from clients' needs, from new documentation and accountability standards, or in response to environmental events.
3. Environmental and historical events may cause changes in practice at all levels.
4. Investigation may uncover practices that do not conform to established policies and need to be aligned with them.

A visiting social worker inquired about the home's council and was told by the administrator that they met once a month and that he personally attended each event. It was important to him to hear what families had to say, and he always tried to respond appropriately, making small changes as requested. When he could not attend for any reason, he asked another staff member to attend and take notes so that he would not miss anything.

The visiting social worker was aware that the purpose of a family council was to be an *autonomous* body that met independently of administrative oversight. The intent was for families to talk candidly and identify any problems faced by their older relatives. Having any staff person in the room was a sure way to reduce the opportunity for honest conversation and allowed the administrator to guide the dialogue in certain directions. If this home was viewed as exemplary in the state, she wondered just how prevalent this model of family councils was across facilities. It looked like an organizational intervention might be in order here, but it might be much broader than that—perhaps homes across the state needed to be educated as to the nature of family councils. A change in how family councils are structured would be an example of a practice change. This administrator in this facility, however, may be very different from the norm. For example, the residents' friends and family members may have invited the administrator to attend so that their concerns are heard first-hand.

Myriad individual practice sessions as well as agency protocols across the country surely changed on September 12, 2001—the day following the 9/11 terrorist attacks on the World Trade Center in New York and the Pentagon in Washington, D.C. This and other events in the lives of colleagues enter into and affect how agencies and businesses function—or fail to function. Box 8.10 summarizes the practice approach.

Now that you (a) know what it means to implement macro-level interventions, (b) have insight on five types of systems, (c) have an idea of where to begin, (d) know how to decide who needs to be involved, and (e) understand how to determine what approach to take (policy, program, project, personnel, and practice), we return to the four main strategies in the situational conflict model (see Figure 7.1). Think about how you will use these strategies in large-scale advocacy.

☾ CONFLICT STRATEGIES AND TACTICS AT THE MACRO SYSTEM LEVEL

Houser (2002) stated that the most salient difference between case advocacy and cause or systems advocacy is that the latter is much more time consuming. "Quick fixes" are more common in case advocacy, but rarely exist at the systems level (Hunt, 2002, p. 10). It is much more difficult to change large systems and communities than to change the mind of a single decision maker about an individual situation. Therefore, systems advocacy entails "fundamental modification of a broader sort of change than that which affects only one person" (Houser, 2002, p. 7). Systems advocates must take a longer range view, and their work will entail long-range strategies and intensive campaigns that may take months, years, or even decades to implement (Houser, 2002).

At the administrative and systems levels, the meaning of a highly urgent case is very different than at the individual case level of advocacy. Aside from a truly catastrophic event or a national disaster, highly urgent macro-level issues do not usually involve a group of clients in immediate jeopardy. Rather, like systems advocacy itself, the impending harm is long term and progressive in its effects.

Otherwise, all the factors of individual advocacy, including strategies, tactics, conflict, power, and leverage, have similar bearing on planning for effective macro-systemic interventions. Consider, for example, how "exchanges occur between organizations as well as between people" (Lauffer, 1984, p. 130). Organizations can form alliances and work toward common goals, or they can oppose each other, both informally and in the justice system. They can even try to eliminate each other through blatantly destructive forms of conflict. The political power dynamics of systems-level advocacy shares the essential features of power discussed earlier. After all, organizations control resources, have status (which is closely tied to the personal power bases of their members), seek influence, and enjoy different degrees of legitimacy, expertise, and intellectual capital.

The implications for systems-level advocacy planning are obvious. Systemic advocacy is more "labor intensive and time consuming" (Houser, 2002, p. 7) and will almost invariably involve the principle of "community integration" (Ross, 1955, p. 50), entailing building alliances and coalitions between individuals and groups who coalesce around shared values. This shared vision propels

members to take action to meet some perceived need. Moreover, systems advocacy is closely linked to case advocacy insofar as case advocacy "provides the basis for changing systems" (Hunt, 2002, p. 5) because social problems are the aggregated problems of individuals. When these problems reach critical mass, the collective issue is picked up by the cultural radar and becomes the target of reformers.

At the class or cause level of advocacy, culturally competent advocates contact local cultural group leaders (spiritual, political, and cultural) and ask a few questions to be sure that they do not sabotage their own advocacy work by not being well informed of the cultural aspects of their clients and their problems. Even if advocates must use interpreters, they must have some knowledge of the context in which their clients live (see Chapter 4). Because this is so important to an advocate's self-awareness, we repeat these questions here. Ask yourself as well as your clients or involved associates these questions:

1. How do your culture's values, beliefs, and goals relate to the current problem?
2. What would be an acceptable solution to this apparent problem?
3. What are your values and beliefs regarding this situation?
4. In what manner might you help others achieve their desired solutions?
5. Who else in the community might support your efforts to obtain a solution?

The extensive and ongoing planning involved in systems advocacy is very time consuming, but is absolutely "vital [for] long-term efficiency and effective program organization and management. The neglect of ongoing serious planning shows itself in the long run through loss of supporters, unmet objectives, failed projects, and disorganization" (Holder, 1985, p. 39). Systems advocacy planning maps out "a wide range of activities" (Houser, 2002, p. 8) that have to be closely prioritized, coordinated, and sequenced. Marshaling significant resources, including marketing and fund-raising campaigns, forming task forces, and using the media effectively, cannot be approached haphazardly. Tactics like these are long remembered and may result in the targeted leaders waiting for opportunities to retaliate if they feel they have been inappropriately or unfairly targeted. Therefore, carefully weigh the risks and advantages before implementing measures that may come back to haunt you in the future.

Finally, advocates must carefully select an overall strategy to facilitate change. This strategy may shift as new information evolves in a cause-oriented change, and it requires tremendous vigilance and flexibility. Once again, we use the conflict model introduced in earlier chapters, pulling the strategic threads into and through this chapter as a familiar framework (see Figure 7.1). The four advocacy strategies are building alliances, consultation, from persuasion to forcing, and problem solving. These strategies call for different types of tactics at the macro level.

Building Alliances

Building alliances is important in individual case advocacy, but it is absolutely critical in macro-level change. Alliance building and collaboration are similar concepts, but there are some important differences. Alliance building entails building a coalition of likeminded advocates and their supporters to cause change through a variety of strategies (such as education, culture change, and other forms of problem solving). On the other hand, in the language of conflict collaboration implies a respectful approach to resolving issues between two opposing parties. Numerous resources are available for those who want to fully explore this strategy, including Albrecht and Brewer (1990), Bailey and Koney (1995, 1996), Bailey, Koney, and Jones (1997), Gray and Wood (1991), Mizrahi and Rosenthal (1993), and Roberts-DeGenarro (1997).

Alliance-building strategies are particularly effective when there is low urgency/risk to elders and the advocate has little leverage. In a way, alliances are built to gain leverage, to raise the level of pressure by literally using the power of numbers. No matter how much risk and urgency is present, an alliance-building strategy may be used as a first step to gain support even in situations in which high risk is evident.

Planners might, for example, choose a **consensus organizing** tactic to improve organizations or systems that are seen as fundamentally healthy. Consensus organizing works in open systems where people share similar goals and accept the proposed change as beneficial. A consensus model that is widely used by health promotion advocates is PATCH (**Pl**Anned **T**actic to **C**ommunity **H**ealth; McKenzie & Jurs, 1993). Through the actions of citizen health advocates who organize to promote health within their own communities, this grassroots tactic focuses on forming alliances with governmental and other health providers who provide technical resources that promote change.

Consultation (Campaigning)

Consultation may sound like an individual case strategy, but it can also be a macro intervention strategy. Used in this way, it is typically called a **campaign strategy.** "Campaign is used when the target must be convinced of the importance of the change, but when communication is still possible between the two systems" (Netting et al., 2004, p. 345). Tactics typically used in this method are education, persuasion, and mass media appeal. The intent is to use the leverage that advocates have to get the word out and to leverage others who are willing to listen to and join the cause.

Another consultation tactic widely used by health planners is the **social planning model.** Here planners promote system change by raising citizen and provider awareness of social problems and their basic causes. The so-called normative reeducation of these stakeholder groups will succeed if the planners undertake a thorough technical needs analysis, a complex social and environmental analysis, and plan to motivate behavior change by designing interventions based on sound theoretical models (Chin & Genne, cited in Ross & Mico, 1980). Social planners might also employ the "power educative tactic," which uses moral reasoning to enlighten both the harmed and those who perpetrate harm about the need for behavioral change. Confrontation and legal and political action to promote system improvements through regulatory change are also used (Green & Kreuter, 1999), moving it toward a persuading strategy. Other technical aspects of the social planning model involve careful assessment of cost-effective resources and ongoing monitoring of program effectiveness (Ross & Mico, 1980).

From Persuasion to Forcing (Contesting)

When you have strong leverage and the risk/ urgency for your elder clients is also high, strategies ranging from persuasion to forcing are appropriate. This is an aggressive push to make change happen and is often called **contesting** in the literature. Contesting implies conflict and becomes a necessity when decision makers or targets are either not open to change or are adamantly against it. This is a useful strategy when push has come to shove. Pushed to the extreme, this strategy can spark the motivation and stamina that fires entire social movements. People are typically angry enough to be motivated to advocate for the cause in the most aggressive and persistent social activist manner.

Social action planners eschew planned educational and behavioral interventions in favor of a more highly charged power/conflict orientation (Ross & Mico, 1980), which is seen as a legitimate means to redistribute "resources, power, and decision making" in unjust or oppressive systems. Here, you act as a reformer who serves as an "activist, agitator, negotiator, and a partisan" (Simmons-Morton, Greene, & Gottlieb, 1995, pp. 364–365).

A more coercive tactic would be to plan for the nonviolent disruption of systems that are seen as primarily serving the interests of privileged groups. To be effective, this tactic requires mobilizing large numbers of disenfranchised people to collectively pursue social justice by peacefully interrupting the normal operation of systems that favor the power elite and that previously have been accepted by the masses. For example, changes were implemented when women and minorities were no longer willing to tolerate not being allowed to vote. Passive resistance works by forcing the elite to share their power by establishing "new understandings between ruler and ruled" (Ross & Mico, 1980, p. 177).

Finally, radical advocates might adopt the methods of violent disruption, a "form of planned social change that has been used throughout history" (Ross & Mico, 1980, p. 178) although to our knowledge it has never been used in the context of elder-care advocacy. At the macro political cause level of advocacy, forcing is more likely to occur in factional systems where advocacy groups see the need for significant change and in catastrophic systems that people are trying to radically change or destroy.

Cause-level forcing, can, in extreme cases, actually threaten social stability, especially if the goal of the mobilized advocates is to destabilize a major social institution (or society itself). Sociology's legitimization theory predicts that the threat of this turbulence, if sufficiently intense, can spur government to act. This typically results in an attempt to cool things down by channeling the conflict into more orderly avenues of judicial or governmental regulatory processes designed to settle conflict in reliably predictable and theoretically equitable ways. When this happens, a forcing strategy may become a problem-solving strategy.

Problem Solving

At the macro level problem solving is an appropriate strategy when leverage is not yet great enough that compromises have to be made but change is critically important because need is high and risk is great. Here both advocates and targeted decision makers respect each other's legitimacy and recognize the need for system change but differ on how reform should occur, primarily due to worries about how their own interests might be disrupted. Intergroup problem solving is more likely to occur when the power between the two negotiating groups is not out of balance. When each side has roughly equal ability to help or harm the other, there is typically a mutual attempt to avoid the latter.

Problem solving at the macro level is different from problem solving (or collaborative conflict) at the individual level. As Blake and Mouton (1984) pointed out, when two people engage in collaborative forms of conflict, they are much freer to change their minds "on the basis of new evidence and to give or withhold cooperation in keeping with personal desire" (p. 6). But members of groups and coalitions are much more locked into a form of groupthink, and group members cannot operate as freely as can individuals acting independently (Blake & Mouton, 1984). A major result of this within-group interdependence and aggregated thought is that intergroup conflict lasts a lot longer, and the larger the groups involved, the harder it is to change minds and achieve true win-win resolutions.

☾ AN EXAMPLE: THE LONG-TERM CARE OMBUDSMAN PROGRAM

The following story illustrates the interaction of different strategies and the use of different tactics to effect macro-level change in the nursing home reform movement of the 1970s and the emergence of the Long-Term Care Ombudsman Program.

A grassroots citizens' movement was spurred in the 1970s by media exposés of multiple nursing home scandals. Large numbers of energized citizens became intent on changing an industry that was seen as exploitive, dangerous, and clearly unwilling to change itself (Nelson, 2000). In accordance with mobilization theory, this movement was motivated by hostility toward nursing home owners and their political allies who were seen as "responsible for grievances, hardship and suffering" (Oberschall, 1973, p. 119). This level of anger was an excellent mobilizer, but in the beginning individual groups did not have a great deal of leverage. It was incumbent upon them to build alliances among interested persons at the local level to get the attention they needed.

What began as an alliance building strategy among disparate and fragmented nursing home reform groups at the local level mushroomed into a national movement to effect change in the nursing home industry. The alliance-building strategy essentially had shifted to a forcing mode in which the power of mobilized constituents (in sheer numbers and degree of outrage) tipped leverage into an aggressive stance. To cool this level of concern, powerful decision makers were pushed to act, and they used a problem-solving strategy to contain the energy of the growing movement. President Nixon and Congress channeled angst over poor nursing home care into the regulatory processes. Policies were changed, and government imposed new standards for inspection and enforcement. Finally, they developed the ombudsman program.

The Long-Term Care Ombudsman Program (LTCOP) was kicked off in a five-state demonstration project. Note that what started as a *policy* approach to change had shifted to a *project* approach designed to demonstrate how the policy could be implemented in local areas.

Following the successful demonstration of the ombudsman concept, grants were provided to most states in 1975 to develop ombudsman programs, and by 1978 each state was *required* to establish and operate a statewide long-term care ombudsman program. The program's original purpose was to respond to complaints from residents, families, staff, and others involved in nursing home facilities in the United States. Subsequently, the purpose expanded to include monitoring of board and care, assisted living, and even home care programs in some states. What had morphed from a *policy* to a *project* approach had become a *program* approach.

However, the ombudsman-as-partisan advocate did not arise full-blown overnight. It was the result of multiparty policy planning headed by a Department of Health, Education and Welfare task force, which involved representatives of different nursing home stakeholder groups in a classic problem-solving mode. The planning process was not easy because of the divergent views about the need for and extent of the change desired. Planners carefully considered which conflict model would best serve resident interests. Aging activists, those who had been mobilized in the first place, preferred a forceful resident-centered advocacy model. Government task force representatives worried that this partisan orientation would be unacceptable to providers, so they favored a more neutral and collaborative model. Nursing home leaders, whose power was threatened by the change, understandably rejected an advocacy model as illegitimate and argued for a noninvestigative, nonadvocacy, friendly visitor model (Monk, Kaye, & Litwin, 1984). Of course, disagreement arose over which strategy to use in implementing the reform.

In 1972 the Department of Health, Education and Welfare planners who identified serious needs on behalf of institutionalized elders recommended that ombudsmen effect "fundamental changes within the nursing home industry" (Wainess, 1982, p. 1–3). This partisan shove was fortified in 1981 when the program was folded into the advocacy portion of the Older Americans Act (Wainess, 1982). By the late 1980s advocates superseded most conciliation models and dominated the most successful programs (Nelson, 1995).

Although ombudsmen emerged as resident advocates, their powers were intended to be informal. Unlike regulators, they had no ability to force or compel but had to change minds through the power of persuasion. Their leverage, therefore, was somewhat low. To succeed, ombudsmen either had to ask for help, collaborate with the willing, or present evidence-based arguments to compel change. They could not threaten punitive action and were not in positions to use force unless they aligned with decision makers who had the power to force. At the individual advocacy level, the most intensely coercive tactic was to warn the decision maker of an impending referral to a regulatory agency for failure to comply with the ombudsman's request if that request dealt with a breach of some legal code.

In 1982 the program's mandate required ombudsmen to investigate complaints in long-term care facilities, but data were not systematically collected to document what paid and volunteer ombudsmen did in their daily work. All the

Administration on Aging had to report to decision makers at the national level were aggregate numbers of complaints. There was no national database for analyzing what really happened in long-term care settings around the country, who investigated the complaints, who complained, or how complaints were resolved. Because the complaint reporting system was pivotal to what ombudsmen do, its lack of viability was viewed with concern (Netting, Paton, & Huber, 1992). Each state was required by law to develop a systematic reporting system, but this requirement was not closely monitored. Some states had computerized systems, and others had very limited reporting methods.

A push by a number of advocates to improve the reporting system began in the early 1990s. Their intent was to raise consciousness about how tragic it would be to have an advocacy program that was unaccountable and therefore could not use the data they collected to leverage for change in the nursing home industry (Huber et al., 2001). Over a period of years the development of a standardized reporting system was institutionalized, and comparable data are now collected within and across states—data that document the kinds of problems that occur in the nation's long-term care facilities and how problems are resolved.

Today the Long-Term Care Ombudsman Program remains an important source of resident-centered advocacy in long-term care. Although hostilities have cooled mightily, ombudsmen still face considerable opposition from long-term care facilities. Furthermore, some radical nursing home groups worry that the program has become a bureaucratized fixture that tends to support the status quo rather than pursue the widespread changes they see as essential to improving long-term care.

Debriefing

As you read, we hope you discovered just how interactive were the strategies and tactics used in development of the Long-Term Care Ombudsman Program, as well as how the different approaches to change were carried out. Beginning with an alliance building strategy, a number of concerned citizens coalesced into a nursing home reform movement. This movement began with alliance building, moved to consultation (educating the public and others), and into a forcing/persuasion strategy. Once the agenda of nursing home reform was established, a problem-solving strategy ensued, led by decision makers as high as the President of the United States and the Congress. This policy approach worked in facilitating legislation to mandate greater enforcement of nursing home oversight.

However, a policy approach inevitably must result in implementation or efforts are hollow. A demonstration project approach was used to test the Long-Term Care Ombudsman Program model in five local communities. As a result of these successful pilot projects, a full-blown program approach was used to develop a nationwide program mandated by the Older Americans Act.

Having a program might have ended the process as everyone settled into making the program happen, but controversy arose over the practice approaches being taken within the program. Would the ombudsmen simply be friendly visitors, which would certainly make the nursing home industry comfortable, or would they be forceful advocates who challenged questionable practices and worked toward change? Advocates pushed again for the practice approach to be one of advocacy.

Subsequently, another practice approach controversy arose in which the data collection process was questioned. An advocacy program designed to make change needs documentation; this information can be used to effect additional change as needs are discovered. Without an adequate information system, the program was essentially disempowered in getting the word out. Conversely, with data all kinds of possibilities could occur. By questioning the efficacy of the information system, advocates pushed again for change at the national level.

The Long-Term Care Ombudsman Program illustrates how various strategies, tactics, and approaches interact over time. What began as a grassroots effort eventually spread to affect the entire nation. Macro-level intervention requires commitment and dedication, and a constellation of relationships typically is needed to make it work. Ongoing advocacy is necessary as changes are implemented.

☯ SUMMARY

We began this chapter with a discussion of what it means to implement macro-level interventions and how individual advocacy can move into the macro arena when a client's problems affect all of the elders in a particular group. We also discussed the impact of devolution on advocacy—that more successful advocacy efforts are expected to occur at the local level for aging baby boomers as less responsibility is assumed at the national level, abdicating it to local groups and communities.

We revisited the five analogies of systems—mechanistic, organic, morphogenic, factual, and catastrophic—originally introduced in Chapter 2. We revisited the story of Fran advocating for Maria in the hospital environment and the tragedy of Lester and Dorothy being shuffled off to two different long-term care facilities—and how the advocate committed herself to finding a good home for their cat Mikie. We explored what these three scenarios had in common and provided guidance for where to begin your advocacy work.

We explained how the importance and changeability matrix can help you sort out and weigh those two concepts when considering different conflict resolution strategies. We discussed how to decide who needs to be involved in a planned intervention and what approach would be best (policy, program, project, personnel, or practice), noting that sometimes you may start with one approach and then switch to another as needed. Table 8.1 summarizes these five advocacy approaches.

We then returned to the situational conflict model and applied the four main strategies to large-scale interventions. We closed the chapter by describing the birth and growth of an extraordinarily effective macro advocacy program, the Long-Term Care Ombudsman Program.

TABLE 8.1 Summary of the Five Approaches to Large-Scale Interventions

Policy Approach

1. Policies can be set unilaterally by a chief executive officer with such authority.
2. Policy changes can occur at all levels of systems: organizational, community, county, regional, state, federal, and international.
3. Policy changes are usually well intentioned but can have deleterious unintended consequences.
4. The intention may have been to document accountability, but older people may be seen as ineligible more often than younger people if better outcomes are anticipated for younger people.
5. Sometimes no policies exist in the areas in which you are concerned (for example, smoking in public places).

Program Approach

1. A policy to create a program is useless until the program is actually implemented.
2. Like policies, programs can also occur at all levels.
3. Programs may be federally mandated but implemented at the state level, such as the Medicaid program and the Long-Term Care Ombudsman Program.
4. A program that affects elders in local senior centers may need to be changed at the state or federal level.
5. Program evaluation is an important and valid reason to conduct research: (a) to what extent is this program doing what it is supposed to be doing, and (b) what are the outcomes for its clients?

Project Approach

1. Projects occur at all levels and are smaller; a program may have several ongoing projects.
2. Advocates can push for new projects to test new ideas or interventions.
3. Employees who see special needs may more easily obtain permission to launch a new project than a new program.
4. Creating a project can be a very politically astute way to pilot a new program.
5. Projects are usually time limited, whereas programs are generally intended to be permanent.

Personnel Approach

1. The personnel change could be to hire, dismiss, or reassign workers, or even volunteers.
2. Care needs to be taken so that the person doesn't simply go to a different agency and resume the same behavior.
3. If caseloads are too large, it is appropriate to advocate for additional staff.
4. If an agency is in severe financial jeopardy, advocacy may be directed toward eliminating a position, possibly the lesser of two bad outcomes.

Practice Approach

1. A macro practice change occurs when an entire unit or service needs to shift how they practice.
2. The need for a practice change may arise from clients' needs, from new documentation and accountability standards, or in response to environmental events.
3. Environmental and historical events may cause changes in practice at all levels.
4. Investigation may uncover practices that do not conform to established policies and need to be aligned with them.

DISCUSSION QUESTIONS AND EXERCISES

1. Can you identify a series of related events that became a pattern requiring a macro-level intervention? What recent news stories reveal an individual problem that has become a concern of the larger public? Can you identify one person whose individual case became the basis for a social change, even a social movement?

2. Why do you think Stone asks the question, "Where have all the advocates gone?" Do you agree or disagree with her concerns? Why or why not?

3. What age-related associations are you familiar with (or belong to) that are engaged in advocacy work? How would you use them if you identified something needing attention? Can you give an example?

4. Explain how the five systems analogies relate (or not) to the systems in which you find yourself. Discuss how different people might have different perspectives on the same system. For example, can you think of a system you believe is highly mechanistic but that others might see as being more factional? How might these analogies be helpful to you in your practice?

5. Think of something in the aging delivery system you would like to see changed. Who would it be important to include in the process, and why would you include them? Whom might you co-opt to become part of the effort in the hope of neutralizing their opposition?

6. Five approaches to change are provided in this chapter. With which approaches are you most familiar? What news events in the last month have reported on changes that use one or more of these approaches? Can you identify a group or organization that is currently using one or more of these approaches to change something in the aging service delivery system in your local community?

7. Are there gerontological causes that you would like to pursue if you had the time? If so, what are they, and what might you do to join groups that are pursuing those causes? In what strategies would you feel comfortable participating, and which ones might you tend to use less? Why?

8. What did you learn from the Long-Term Care Ombudsman example at the end of the chapter?

9. Read the following story about Fred. Put yourself in the role of the occupational therapist or the social worker (your choice). What would you do?

Fred is a 50-year-old African American man who was admitted to a long-term rehabilitation facility after falling in his home and lying on the floor for 2 days. He has two large open wounds on his shoulder and back and numerous abrasions. Fred had fallen because he had been drinking excessively, and upon admittance to the rehabilitation center he was still suffering the effects of alcohol withdrawal. In a family conference with his daughter, you learn that Fred's wife died last year. Since then, Fred has been drinking very heavily. A psychiatric evaluation indicates that Fred is clinically depressed.

Fred was put on a rigorous regimen of five appointments each week for 6 weeks with speech, physical, and occupational therapists, for a total of 3 hours per day, or 15 hours each week. He was told that he must complete this program before he could go home. After 6 weeks, Fred appeared to be making little to no progress. He was still depressed, and his wounds were taking a long time to heal. Fred was able to make his needs known in therapy but typically stated that he was feeling too tired to stay a full hour with each professional. The physical and speech therapists stated that Fred had reached a plateau and was not making any progress, and they discharged him from their services.

The occupational therapist (OT) continued to see Fred for another 3 weeks, and he began to make some progress. His wounds began to heal, but the depression lingered. The OT brought in a social worker to help with the depression. Two weeks later, he stated that he was feeling better and demonstrated a spark of motivation toward his goals. At this point the OT asked the physical therapist to rescreen Fred in order to pick him up again. The physical therapist did so and sent a request to the insurance company to resume physical therapy, stating that with one more month of social work and occupational therapy he would be ready for placement in a group home or assisted living facility.

At this point, the insurance company representative called and stated that he had read the notes and did not believe Fred was making enough progress and that he would have to be discharged to a nursing home because he was not independent enough to return home. Fred stated that he did not want to go to a nursing home but that he would be willing to go to an assisted living facility. The occupational therapist reported that to the insurance company and noted that with another month of therapy this would be achievable. Both the social worker and the OT personally called the insurance company representative and explained the situation.

The representative stated that he was unclear on the meaning of the assistance levels in the charts and did not see any progress being made. The OT then had to explain the differences between each level of treatment and each piece of progress that Fred had made so far. She restated that one more month of social work and physical and occupational therapy would further the progress, and Fred could then be discharged to a less restrictive (ergo less expensive) environment.

The insurance company representative decided that he would allow occupational therapy to continue but that he would have to be updated on Fred's progress every 2 days to determine whether treatment would be allowed to continue. No social work or physical or speech therapy was to be allowed. The OT continued to see the patient, reporting to the insurance company every 2 days.

Both the social worker and the OT noted a dramatic increase in that insurance company's denials of treatment over the 2 months they worked with Fred, even when another month's treatment would result in clients being discharged to less expensive settings. In other words, if the insurance company would approve eight more sessions (four with the OT and four with the social worker), they would be paying about $1,000/month for Fred's long-term care in an assisted living facility rather than $3,000/month for nursing home care. This made no sense even from a financial perspective, not to mention their client's health and well-being. They began to wonder what was going on and learned two things: (a) this particular representative of the insurance company was hired 2 weeks before they began to notice the excessive (and illogical) denials, and (b) the representative's wife is half-owner of a local nursing home. Suddenly they realized that this was not just about Fred—it's a larger problem.

ADDITIONAL READINGS

Baldridge, D. (2004, Spring). Double jeopardy: Advocating for Indian elders: The principles are the same, but the task is harder from Indian Country. *Generations, 28*(1), 75–78.

Bateman, N. (2000). *Advocacy skills for health and social care professionals.* Philadelphia, PA: Jessica Kingsley.

Binstock, R. H. (2004, Spring). Advocacy in an era of neoconservatism: Responses of national aging organizations: Current policy proposals amount to dismantling the old-age welfare state. Who cares? *Generations, 28*(1), 55–58.

Blancato, R. B. (2004, Spring). Advocacy and aging policy: The prognosis: The best advocacy often comes when people and programs are threatened. *Generations, 28*(1), 65–69.

Brindle, M., & Mainiero, L. A. (2000). *Managing power in lateral networking.* Westport CN: Quorum Books.

Brotman, S., Ryan, B., & Cormier, R. (2003). The health and social service needs of gay and lesbian elders and their families in Canada. *The Gerontologist, 43*(2), 192–202.

Browdie, R. (2004, Spring). Introduction: The tradition of advocacy remains an essential underpinning of our mission. *Generations, 28*(1), 5–7.

Callahan, Jr., J. J. (2004, Spring). Advocacy in an aging society: The varied roles of attorneys: Thinking like a lawyer. *Generations, 28*(1), 36–40.

Cohen, E. S. (2004, Spring). Advocacy and advocates: Definitions and ethical dimensions: From jawboning to community organizing to lobbying to legal proceedings. *Generations, 28*(1), 9–16.

Deutsch, M. (1994). Constructive conflict resolution: Principles, training and research. *Journal of Social Issues, 50,* 13–32.

Dodd, S., & Jansson, B. (2004). Expanding the boundaries of ethics education: Preparing social workers for ethical advocacy in an organizational setting. *Journal of Social Work Education, 40*(3), 455–465.

Donohue, W. A., & Kolt, R. (1992). *Managing interpersonal conflict.* Newbury Park, CN: Sage.

Ezell, M. (2000). *Advocacy in human services.* Belmont, CA: Brooks/Cole.

Freeman, I. C. (2000). Uneasy allies: Nursing home regulators and consumer advocates. *Journal of Aging and Social Policy, 11*(2/3), 127–135.

Freeman, I. C. (2004, Spring). Advocacy in aging policy: Working the bills on Capitol Hills: How to do it in the real world. *Generations, 28*(1), 41–48.

Goldman, A. I. (1986). Toward a theory of social power. In S. Lukde (Ed.), *Power.* New York: New York University Press.

Hornbostel, R. (2004, Spring). The power of local advocacy: Funding for senior services in Ohio: Can one person change a state law? *Generations, 28*(1), 79–82.

Hudson, R. B. (2004, Spring). Advocacy and policy success in aging: What role has advocacy played in the expansion of aging policy? *Generations, 28*(1), 17–23.

Kane, R. A. (2004, Spring). The circumscribed sometimes-advocacy of the case manager and the care provider: Where does advocacy and gatekeeping begin? *Generations, 28*(1), 70–74.

Kapp, M. B. (2004, Spring). Introduction: The tradition of advocacy remains an essential underpinning of our mission. *Generations, 28*(1), 31–35.

Kelly, M. A. (2004, Spring). Developing an advocacy coalition with varied interests and agendas: A Pennsylvanian experience: Elders, families, caregivers, and businesses. *Generations, 28*(1), 83–85.

Mayer, R. J. (1991). *Conflict management: The courage to confront.* Columbus, OH: Battelle Press.

McConnell, S. (2004, Spring). Advocacy in organizations: The elements of success: The power to bring about change. *Generations, 28*(1), 25–30.

McNutt, J.G. (2002, February 15). New horizons in social work advocacy. *Electronic Journal of Social Work, 1*(1).

Roloff, E. M., Tutzauer, F. E., & Dailey, W. O. (1989). The role of argumentation in distributive and integrative bargaining contexts: Seeking relative advantage but at what cost? In M. A Rahim (Ed.), *Managing conflict: An interdisciplinary approach.* New York: Praeger.

Rother, J. (2004, Spring). Why haven't we been more successful advocates for elders? AARP's policy chief on the need for flexibility. *Generations, 28*(1), 5–7.

Rummel, R. J. (1991). *The conflict helix.* London: Transaction.

Schneider, R. L., & Lester, L. (2001). *Social work advocacy.* Belmont, CA: Brooks/Cole.

Ziegelmueller, G. W., & Kay, J. (1997). *Argumentation: Inquiry and advocacy* (3rd ed). Boston, MA: Allyn & Bacon.

CHAPTER NINE

Evaluating Advocacy Outcomes

A commitment to effectiveness requires that we collect new kinds of data—data that will inform us about client conditions at entry into and exit from services so that we can learn more about our ability to have an impact on their problems. KETTNER, MORONEY, & MARTIN (1990, p. 6)

BOX 9.1

CINDY

Cindy and Nancy both had been advocating and lobbying for elderly clients and their causes for 15 years. Although they lived in different parts of the country, they had met at professional meetings and always looked forward to seeing one another face to face. They communicated via e-mail several times a week, sharing strategies and advice.

Both women recently had applied for a high-level position at the Administration on Aging to direct a massive nationwide education and media campaign targeted toward the plague of neglect of our nation's elderly people. Both were contacted by the Administration on Aging and told they were finalists for the position based on their advocacy work on behalf of elderly people. Interviews for the position were scheduled during the conference. Nancy's interview was scheduled for a breakfast meeting on Tuesday morning, and Cindy's was scheduled for dinner that evening. Neither woman knew that the other had applied for this position, and they arranged to have lunch together on Tuesday in the hotel coffee shop.

Nancy was so excited about the possibility of securing the position that she just couldn't keep it to herself any longer and began to tell Cindy all about the position. Cindy said, "Wow, Nancy,

how did the interview go? And I should tell you that I also have applied for that position and meet with the search committee this evening."

Nancy was only slightly daunted by the news that Cindy was competing with her for the position, and they continued to talk about the position and all of the ideas and strategies they both had in mind. They even talked about their individual strengths: Nancy had more direct experience with neglect cases in the community, and Cindy had worked more with institutional neglect. Neither was desperate for the position, as each had a strong advocacy practice of her own, and they even fantasized about job sharing the position—what fun it would be to work together on such an important and monumental job! Although they both wanted the position, Nancy said that if she didn't get it she hoped Cindy would, and Cindy felt the same way. When they parted, Nancy made Cindy promise to call her after her dinner interview that evening, no matter how late it was.

When Cindy met with the search committee at dinner that evening, she felt like she already knew the committee members based on what

(continued)

BOX 9.1 *(continued)*

Nancy had told her about them. They questioned Cindy extensively about her experience, and when Cindy told them about her strategies and approaches, a member of the committee always asked something like, "And what was your success rate with that strategy?" Cindy always responded with a percentage and a graph showing the trend or magnitude of success. Furthermore, Cindy defined "success" when she first began describing a different tactic or intervention.

Cindy was very impressed with the committee members, one of whom was the Secretary of Aging for the current administration, the person to whom she would report. She was even comfortable enough to tell them that she and Nancy were friends and that they had frankly shared support for one another in securing the position at lunch, and had even speculated about some arrangement whereby they could share the position. The committee members exchanged eye contact, and Cindy could tell that some important communication had just taken place. Then the secretary said, "Cindy, the job is yours. We had 95% decided that before we met you, due in no small part to your evaluation and statistical acumen; it was yours to lose and you didn't. There will be times that you must report numbers to Congress and to me quickly, and you have those skills. We need you in this position! Can you begin next week?"

When Cindy called Nancy to report in that evening, she was a little chagrined. How would she tell Nancy that she got the job right on the spot? They were good friends, and Nancy was very excited for her. When Cindy told her friend what the search committee members had said, Nancy responded by saying, "You are so much better equipped than I am for the job. You always focus on the importance of evaluation, and I get so passionate that sometimes I forget that there must be a way to measure effectiveness. This is a lesson that you have taught me, and I need to remember it."

By now we hope you are getting the idea that we strongly believe in taking action that works for the benefit of elders. When you take action, you need be thinking about how to evaluate your efforts and present what you have learned to others. In the case of Cindy and Nancy, this made the difference in Cindy's interview and consideration for a high-level position in the national aging network.

We conclude this book by providing some ideas on how to evaluate the outcomes of your advocacy work. Information really is power and is powerful, and it can increase your influence. Both Nancy and Cindy had relevant experience and education, and no doubt several other valuable attributes as well. The main difference between the two was that Cindy had had the foresight to know the value of collecting and displaying data and had established protocols at the beginning of her professional life to collect and analyze data as a routine part of her work. It paid off for Cindy, and we trust this story illustrates why you need empirical data to evaluate the outcomes of your advocacy work.

In this chapter we examine goals and objectives, asking you to assess your objectives using this mantra: *Who* is going to do *What* by *When?* This is followed by a brief overview of single subject designs and a sample codebook to spark your thinking about what should be included in your advocacy outcomes database. Next we revisit the dilemma faced by Sam and Tom (Chapter 8) and pose goals and measurable objectives for their case. The chapter closes with the now familiar summary, a framework for developing and implementing a plan for evaluating your advocacy work, discussion questions and exercises, and additional readings.

We will not attempt to cover the intricacies of intervention research skills and methods or program evaluation, neither quantitative nor qualitative. Many excellent research books cover this material in depth, and several are listed in the Additional Readings section. Our goal is to guide you toward the simplest way to set up an ongoing evaluation database so that you, too, could have answered the questions posed to Cindy and Nancy in their job interviews. Some of you may have considerable research and statistical expertise; others may appreciate our intent to keep it simple. In fact, simplifying difficult tasks is a laudable goal in many arenas.

☾ GOALS AND MEASURABLE OBJECTIVES

We discussed using care planning as an alliance-building tactic in Chapter 7, and used the story of Margaret to illustrate that by writing goals and measurable objectives you have taken the first step toward evaluating outcomes. Let's revisit Margaret's first goal: *Margaret will have excellent quality care.* Remember that goals are general statements about the way things should be when a plan or intervention is successful. They are end states— *excellent quality of care.* The goal is accompanied by outcome objectives that are more specific and answer the question "Who will do what by when?"

Goal 1
Margaret will have excellent quality of care.

Outcome Objective
Within 2 weeks Margaret will always have water within reach as documented in the medical chart by a staff member 3 times daily.

Objective 1.1 Within 1 week the Director of Nursing (DoN) will have met with all nurses, orderlies, and aides who work on Margaret's wing, advising them of the importance of Margaret having water within reach at all times.

Objective 1.2 The following business day the DoN will tell Margaret and any relevant family members that Objective 1.1 has been met.

Objective 1.3 The DoN will implement a random schedule of when he or one of the nurse supervisors will check to see whether Margaret has water within reach.

The easiest way to check to see that objectives are measurable is to test them with our mantra: Who is going to do what by when? By creating measurable, time-limited, specific objectives you have, ipso facto, posed a research question. For example, the above goal is followed by an Outcome Objective: Within 2 weeks Margaret will always have water within reach as documented in the medical chart by a staff member 3 times daily. Now dissect this objective by our mantra, *Who* (staff member) *is going to do what* (see that Margaret has water within her reach 3 times a day and document it in her chart) *by when* (within 2 weeks from the current date on the chart). Notice that this objective is also a verbatim alternative hypothesis (ponder this last phrase for a few moments), so turning it into a research question is primarily accomplished by rearranging the words: Within 2 weeks from this date, will staff members have documented, 3 times every day, that Margaret has water within her reach?

Some of the canons and rules of research are helpful here. *First,* there is a huge assumption that Margaret having water within her reach is a valid component of receiving quality care, which is fine. No problem there, but we point it out to remind you to recognize and acknowledge the assumptions that underlie your goals and objectives. Of course, having water within reach is but one small, albeit critical, indicator of the overall quality of care Margaret receives (assuming there are no physician's orders prohibiting Margaret from having water).

Second, another assumption is that if it's documented, it happened. When staff noted in the chart that Margaret had water within reach, are you sure they really checked? And if water was not in reach, did the staff person physically take water to her room and put it within her reach? This somewhat paranoid way of thinking (like a purist researcher) could go on to measure what "within reach" meant in inches, but that would depend on how Margaret was positioned in a bed or chair, or how far she could move her arm, and so forth, which can get rather silly. At some point, elements of trust are allowed, and falsifying charts is a serious offense that few health care staff would commit. (It is unlikely that it would be worth losing their job just to avoid getting water for Margaret.)

Third, this is a triple-barreled question—it really asks three questions: *Did Margaret have water? Was it within her reach?* and *Was it charted?* These are not good research questions, however: to be able to answer them, we would have to ask "when?" They would work well if they pertained to one point in time, such as when her daughter was there on Tuesday at 3:00. Even then, the answers would only yield nominal data (yes/no), which severely limits the analyses that can be conducted. So we need to operationalize the question, stating exactly how to get answers. To do this, we add the following question:

1. Between (*2-week date*) and (*a later date when data are being collected*), how many times did staff chart (document) that Margaret had water within her reach?

Note that you continue with your assumption that if it was charted it occurred. The answer to this question will be an integer (for example, 90 times, which is ratio data, the highest level), allowing you great flexibility in analyses. You would simply divide that number by the number of days between the two dates and you have an *average* of how many times a day Margaret reportedly had water within reach. But is the *average* adequate information? No. So you ask for more detail:

2. On how many days was the event (water-within-reach) charted 3 times?
3. On how many days was the event charted twice?
4. On how many days was the event charted only once?
5. On how many days was there no evidence in the chart that Margaret had water within her reach?

This could continue to include the shifts (day, evening, night) and even the workers, so you could learn whether, for example, there was only one staff person on one shift who was charting the water-within-reach event, but she was doing so 3 times every time she went to work.

Now look at the first stated objective under the outcome objective: Within 1 week the Director of Nursing (DoN) will have met with all nurses, orderlies, and aides who work on Margaret's wing, advising them of the importance of Margaret having water within reach at all times. This objective is more easily answerable, although checking on whether the DoN met with all of those staff members presents a challenge, but we will not belabor that here. Making objectives measurable is not a simple task but one that must be thoroughly thought out—all the way through each communication, action, or task.

In the next section we suggest a simple database that you could maintain in the Statistical Package for the Social Sciences (SPSS), or even Microsoft Access or Excel. The data Cindy had in her hands were also used to write grants for new initiatives in her agency and community and to mount expensive advocacy efforts pro bono when her clients could not afford, for example, travel expenses to lobby legislators. It is difficult to imagine that you could overestimate the importance having such a database.

☾ SINGLE SUBJECT DESIGN

Single subject design (SSD) research was borne of practitioners' frustration with researchers not understanding the difficulties inherent in conducting classic experimental research designs, when in their clinical practices they saw clients only singly or in very small groups. There is no generalizability with SSDs—you cannot generalize results to any group or individuals other than those in your study as you can with a scientifically drawn random sample. However, if you collect the same *kinds* of data across all of your advocacy cases, you have the power of data from aggregated single subject designs, which allows you to at least speculate a little (Benbenishty, 1989; Bloom, Fischer, & Orme, 1999; Blythe & Rogers, 1993). The methodology suggested here is classified as a single subject design because the cases have virtually nothing in common except being your clients and being tracked in your database. Estimating the percentage of goal reached is a concept that does not change, for example, from one problem to another, one individual to another, or from one agency, city, or state to another. In fact, the concept does not even change if you compare percentage of goal reached for an individual client, or a class action targeting your county or state. Once again, synergy works for you in that aggregate knowledge (percentage of goals reached) carries more weight than the results from a single advocacy case. In other words, the whole is greater than the sum of its parts.

Margaret's case for water within reach was a case example at the micro level in which the advocate was working on behalf of one person, which is one reason the SSD is appropriate for advocacy work. However, a case (or a line in a database, the unit of analysis) can be an individual, a group, an organization, an agency, a city or town, a state or nation—whatever constitutes an advocacy case. Table 9.1 shows some possible variables (pieces of information) in codebook format for an advocacy database.

Notice that the first four variables (pieces of information that vary from one person, or case, to the next) are not used for statistical analysis, but can be used for mailing labels and so forth, depending on the software you use. Column 1 is simply a number for the first, second, and so on variables in your database. Column 2 is the *variable name*, which is restricted to eight characters in some databases but not in others. Column 3 is the *variable label* for (very!) short descriptions of the variable—as you can see, just two or three words will do the trick. Column 4, *type of data*, tells you whether numbers, letters (alpha, or sometimes called string variables, for entering a string of letters), or dates will be entered and thereby constitute the data. Some codebooks include another column for level of data that each variable will yield: nominal, ordinal, ratio, or dates. Column 5 is the *length* variable, which refers to how many spaces you want allocated to enter data for each variable. You can see that we allow up to 15 letters and spaces for names, and up to 100 for (very!) short descriptions of the problem. Here are some examples: *The client was tricked into moving* (Jeanine in Chapter 1), *advocate in trouble due to faulty assessment* (Clara's dementia assessment in Chapter 4), *Out of control daughter* (Molly's out of control daughter Zoe in Chapter 5), or *gay civil rights issue* (Sam and Tom's dilemma in Chapter 8).

The far right-hand column contains coded information for nominal data variables, and herein lies a critical factor in establishing this kind of database: *the values and value labels must be the same for parallel variables.* Notice that we have used exactly the same coded strategies in variables 13 through 15 in Table 9.1. If you add to or change the list in one of the parallel variables, you must match it by changing the other two in exactly the same way (or your analyses will be *much* more difficult). You may even want to change the list to begin with, perhaps separating persuasion and forcing, thereby increasing your strategies to five. The same holds true for the tactics variables (16 through 18 in Table 9.1). If you change one, change them all.

Notice that the goal variables are also parallel, with three variables for each of two goals (7, 8, and 9 for Goal 1; 10, 11, and 12 for Goal 2). Look at variable 7, *Goal1* (for a short statement of the first goal), and *G1Pct* (the percentage of the goal reached), which can be determined by you or the client. You can make your assessment periodic (adding more variables: these three goals for the first assessment, second assessment, and so on) or simply enter the results when the case is closed. The last variable for Goal 1, *Goal%1Da*, is the date of that assessment. The same three parallel variables are provided for the second goal (variables 10 through 12).

This is a simple example of information that can serve you well as you begin your advocacy work—you can modify the database according

TABLE 9.1 Sample Codebook for Advocacy Evaluation Database

	Variable Name	**Variable Label**	**Type of Data**	**Length**	**Values to Enter**
1	NameLast	Client's last name	Alpha	15	
2	NameFrst	Client's first name	Alpha	15	
3	NameMid	Client's middle name or initial	Alpha	15	
4	Title	Client's title	Numeric	1	1 = Dr. 2 = Mrs. 3 = Miss 4 = Ms 5 = Mr. 6 = Senator (etc.)
5	Referred	Client referred by (person or agency name)	Numeric	1	1 = Former client 2 = AAA 3 = AARP 4 = APS (etc.)
6	DateRef	Date of referral	Date	10	
7	Problem	Summary of problem	Alpha	100	
8	Goal1	First goal	Alpha	100	
9	G1Pct	Percentage of Goal 1 achieved	Numeric	5*	
10	G1Date	Date of Goal 1 percentage achieved	Date	10	
11	Goal2	Second goal	Alpha	100	
12	G2Pct	Percentage of Goal 2 achieved	Numeric	5*	
13	G2Date	Date of Goal 2 percentage achieved	Date	10	
14	PrimStrt	Primary strategy used	Numeric	1	1 = Alliance Building 2 = Consultation 3 = Persuasion to Force 4 = Problem Solving
15	Strat 2	Secondary strategy	Numeric	1	1 = Alliance Building 2 = Consultation 3 = Persuasion to Force 4 = Problem Solving
16	Strat 3	Third strategy used	Numeric	1	1 = Alliance Building 2 = Consultation 3 = Persuasion to Force 4 = Problem Solving
17	Tactic 1	Primary tactic used	Numeric	1	1 = Present & ask 2 = Argue 3 = Warn 4 = Threaten 5 = Legal counsel 6 = Coerce 7 = Error to force concession 8 = Use the media (etc.)

18	Tactic 2	Secondary tactic used	Numeric	1	1 = Present and ask
					2 = Argue
					3 = Warn
					4 = Threaten
					5 = Legal counsel
					6 = Coerce
					7 = Error to force concession
					8 = Use the media (etc.)
19	Tactic 3	Third tactic used	Numeric	1	1 = Present and ask
					2 = Argue
					3 = Warn
					4 = Threaten
					5 = Legal counsel
					6 = Coerce
					7 = Error to force concession
					8 = Use the media (etc.)
20	MicroMac	At what level was advocacy attempted?	Nominal	1	1 = Micro
					2 = Macro
					3 = Both
21	Continuum	On a continuum from 1 to 10, where would you place this case?	Ordinal	** 5/2	1 = Micro
					10 = Macro

*The length of the variable will total five spaces, two of which come after a decimal; for example, 85.75.

**This will accommodate an average during analysis of, for example, 9.75 or 10.00. The 5/2 signifies that the length of the variable will be 5 spaces, 2 of which come after the decimal.

to your needs as you gain experience. You may be surprised, however, at how many research questions can be asked and answered with such a simple database; here are some examples (with cursory suggestions for analytic procedures):

1. From where do I get most of my referrals? (Run frequency of 5 *Client referred by*)
2. What are the main problems? (Run frequency of 7 *Summary of Problem*)
3. What is the relationship between referral source and the main problems? (Run a chi square of 5 *Referred by* 7 *Problem*, although you might want to first recode the main problems into fewer categories.)
4. What is the average percentage of goals achieved? (Run frequencies of 9 G1Pct and 12 G2Pct, asking for the means)
5. What is the relationship between the average percentage of goals reached and strategies used? (One-way Analysis of Variance [ANOVA] of 9 G1Pct by 14 PrimStr; and 12 G2Pct by 15 Strat2)

6. What is the relationship between average percentage of Goal 1 being reached and primary tactics used? (Again, run a one-way ANOVA of 9 G1Pct and 17 Tactic1)

Many other questions could be posed, and perhaps these examples will spark your imagination for both additional variables and questions.

☉ SAM AND TOM REVISITED

Now let's turn to some goals and objectives that could be posed in working on the macro level with Sam and Tom's (Chapter 8) dilemma. Recall that Sam's health was deteriorating, Sam and Tom had limited income, and they both feared that if Sam had to go on Medicaid Tom would have to move out of their home. Here are potential goals and measurable objectives for this macro advocacy work. Remember to read critically, thinking of the mantra, *Who* is going to do *what* by *when?*

Goal 1

Same-sex couples will have the same rights and access to government subsidized health care benefits as those extended to heterosexual couples.

Outcome Objective

Sam and Tom will be able to remain in the same household if Sam's health conditions require him to go on Medicaid coverage.

Objective 1.1 Cheryl will have met with the local gay advocacy group within 2 weeks of hearing Tom's concern regarding his ability to remain in the home if Sam becomes a Medicaid client.

Objective 1.2 Within 1 week Cheryl will have raised this issue within her professional network and asked them to assess the number of similar situations with their age 65 and older clients, and report back to her within 1 week.

Objective 1.3 Within 2 weeks Cheryl will have collected the data from the professional network to use in support of Objective 1.4.

Objective 1.4 Within 3 weeks Cheryl will have written a letter to the local legislature advocating for an amendment to Medicaid laws that applies the same rules and policies to same-sex couples that apply to heterosexual relationships.

Cheryl is employed full time by a nursing home and has clearly advocated for Sam and Tom on several occasions. In this instance we know *who* is doing the advocating and *what* the advocacy actions are. We also know *when*. Cheryl will be raising the issue with her colleagues in the coming week and meeting with the gay advocacy group within 2 weeks of first hearing about Sam and Tom's dilemma. During the fall session of the legislature, Cheryl learned that her letter had prompted a debate on this issue to be scheduled for the next session.

☾ The Importance of Both Numerical and Word Data

In developing a codebook, words are usually translated into numbers so that data can be quantitatively analyzed. For example, if marital status is a variable, being widowed might be coded as "1" and being married might be coded as "2." It is very important to know how to code the words we use. For example, in doing the background work for developing a policy proposal, Cheryl will probably want to have statistics on how many older gay men are in the state and aggregated information on their characteristics in order to make her case.

Just as powerful as numbers in advocating for change, however, is recording word data so that you have the voices of elders at your fingertips. For example, in interviewing other older gay couples, a student at the university may have transcripts of the issues they face. Without disclosing who said what, words from those transcripts can be used to enrich Cheryl's arguments when she advocates for state-level change. She may go before a legislative committee, present the statistical background on why things need to change, then read the statement, "If only I could change who I am, but this is who I am. I would not have chosen all this heartache if this wasn't who I am—a gay person." Such statements allow Cheryl to use the voices of real people as data to get points across. Testimonials, combined with numbers, are ways to sway public opinion, get information to persons who don't quite understand the plight of elders, and to combine the best of numeric and word data in your advocacy efforts. But both have to be captured to fully evaluate the intervention.

TABLE 9.2 Advocacy Outcomes Framework

Task 1. Determine a model for evaluating advocacy outcomes.

1. Choose or develop an evaluation model that fits well with your work and personality.
2. Give considerable thought to the *kinds* of outcomes you want or need to document.
3. How will your outcomes be used? To market your services? To advocate before the legislature or other bodies?
4. Check on clearance from any applicable institutional review boards, human studies committees, or research integrity reviews.

Task 2. Establish goals and objectives.

1. Can your client be involved in developing the goals and objectives?
2. Is there sufficient time within the situation to reach proposed goals? Are the goals realistic in both time and scope?
3. Is there potential for unintended harm to innocent parties if the goals are reached? If so, how can the goals be revised to prevent this?
4. Have you considered the client's social, economic, and cultural contexts?

Task 3. Collect data and enter it into your database.

1. Make a list of questions you would like to be able to answer from your database.
2. Create a codebook so you can be sure that you have operationalized every variable.
3. Know exactly what kind of data your questions and codebook will yield:
   - Nominal (race, gender, problem)
   - Ordinal (Likert type scales or the extent to which your client is satisfied with something: 1 = Not at all, 2 = Somewhat satisfied, 3 = Completely satisfied)
   - Ratio (anything counted, such as the number of times, days between two dates, or percentages of goals attained)

Task 4. Disseminate your data to appropriate sources.

1. Who needs your findings? Who benefits from them?
2. Who could be hurt by your findings?
3. What ethical and moral issues must you consider before you publicly disseminate your results?
4. What have you learned from this project that will make you a better advocate?

☾ SUMMARY

We began this chapter with Cindy and Nancy, two women who are friends competing for the same position. Cindy, who answered the search committee's questions with hard data, won the position.

We then provided a simple way to begin collecting data on advocacy outcomes. We suggested single subject designs as an appropriate methodology and discussed the value of aggregated data from all of a worker's (or agency's) advocacy cases, even though the individuals have little or nothing in common. If the right kinds of data are collected in the right ways, comparisons can be made between the outcomes and other factors, such as strategies and tactics used, main problems, and percentages of goals reached. Table 9.2 outlines the advocacy outcomes framework.

We then discussed how to write goals and measurable objectives, and included an example of a codebook that could be used to initiate a working database. We posed six questions that could be answered with the data from the example variables. We then proposed a goal and five objectives for the macro level advocacy example of Sam and Tom not having the same civil rights as heterosexual couples.

We ended with a reminder that it is important to collect both numerical and word data. The best way to evaluate effective interventions is to have multiple ways of knowing that something has happened. Capturing the statistics as well as the voices of real people is a dynamite combination.

DISCUSSION QUESTIONS AND EXERCISES

1. Why do you think Nancy did not pick up on the several questions put to her about how she evaluated the outcomes of her advocacy work?
2. What kinds of data would be helpful for you to track for your own advocacy work with elders?
3. Define the place or words in the objectives for Sam and Tom in which the *Who, What,* and *When* questions are satisfied.
4. Write goals and measurable objectives for the opening stories in Chapter 1 (*Jeanine kidnapped?*), Chapter 3 (*Patrice*), Chapter 5 (*Molly, or rather Zoe*), and Chapter 6 (*the AAA home health allocations*).
5. Pose two additional questions that can be answered from the codebook, including the statistical procedures that would yield the answers and why.
6. Consider how you might capture both numerical and word data in your practice. What would be important to capture? How might your methods differ, and how could numerical and word data be used in tandem to evaluate what you have done?

ADDITIONAL READINGS

Briar, S. (1968). The casework predicament. *Social Work, 13,* 5–11.

Briar, S. (1973). The age of accountability [Editorial]. *Social Work, 18,* 114.

Briar, S., & Blythe, B. (1985). Agency support for evaluating the outcomes of social work service. *Administration of Social Work, 9*(2), 25–36.

Kirk, S. A., & Fischer, J. (1976). Do social workers understand research? *Journal of Education for Social Work, 12,* 63–70.

Penka, C., & Kirk, S. (1991). Practitioner involvement in clinical evaluation. *Social Work, 36,* 513–518.

Reid, W. (1993). Fitting the single-system design to family treatment. *Journal of Social Service Research, 18*(1/2), 83–99.

Rubin, A., & Babbie, E. (1997). *Research methods for social work.* Belmont, CA: Brooks/Cole.

Wood, K. (1978). Casework effectiveness: A new look at the research. *Social Work, 23,* 437–458.

Tabachnick, G. G. & Fidell, L. S. (2001). *Using multivariate statistics* (4th ed). Boston: Allyn & Bacon.

GLOSSARY

active neglect Intentional neglect that is often criminal in nature; a deliberate failure to meet an individual's needs.

activities of daily living (ADLs) Eating, bathing, dressing, transferring, and caring for your own personal hygiene.

acute episode An event (often medical) that threatens an individual's life or safety, then stabilizes.

aging in place Growing older in the same environment such as living in your own home over a long period of time as opposed to changing settings or locations.

alleged perpetrator The alleged source of the problem identified by the initial complainant or through victim interviews.

allying Being in a friendly association; uniting or connecting with others in a helpful relationship.

array of services The collection of services for an identified population such as Meals on Wheels, Adult Day Care, congregate living and meal services for aging persons.

attorneys-in-fact Health proxy advocates (not lawyers) with legally binding powers to make decisions on behalf of older individuals on the basis of personal trust by executing a durable health care power of attorney.

autonomy Often used in conjunction with self-determination, the right to seek one's own personal goals.

avoidance Ducking overt confrontation to preserve yourself and your good working relationship.

axiomatic Self-evident; without proof or argument.

behavioral cause Any human agency, including any individual or collective action or lack of action, either accidental, or based on intent, or based on an actor's attitudes, or any other motive or belief, that contributes to a negative client outcome.

beneficence or best interest standard Often used in conjunction with paternalism, the desire on the advocate's part to prevent any type of harm to the client who may not be able to self-determine. Life, health, and safety are paramount, and the advocate attempts to do what is truly in the client's best interest.

beyond a reasonable doubt Evidence requires proof that is clear, cogent, and convincing, the standard typically required in guardianship hearings, for example, where the client may face a profoundly devastating loss of rights and prerogatives.

campaign strategy A change strategy used when communication is open between the target and the advocate but when a great deal of effort has to be made to convince the target or a series of targets that change needs to occur.

capability The advocate's power base, which is comprised of many possible sources.

care planning A nearly universal term to describe what is to be done for clients.

case advocacy Situations in which an identified, individual case (whether a person or a larger unit) is the subject of change efforts.

case manager A person, either paid or voluntary, who helps an older person secure services; case management typically involves assessment, care planning, resource mobilization, monitoring, and reassessment processes.

catastrophic analogy Describes a social system in constant flux, in which everything is random or in motion and there is extreme conflict.

causal factors A three-point framework: (a) the *proximate* or *distinguishing cause* comprises the specific, exact, antecedent event, which is clearly related to the client's problem; (b) the often more difficult to analyze causal stream comprised of *contributing factors,* which typically support the problem's proximate cause; and (c) more distantly related factors that measure causation as the client's relative risk, which is how the client's risk for the negative outcome in question compares to the general population's risk for the same event.

class (or cause) advocacy Advocates target larger systems and champion the needs or rights of groups of people, groups of organizations, and even multiple communities with the same problems or in similar situations.

coercive power The ability to force someone to change, which may be required in situations of extreme urgency.

collective (the) A group of people advocating for the same person or cause, which has more power than one individual acting alone.

collective self-advocacy Individuals join with others in cooperative efforts (often under the leadership of paid coordinating staff) to promote shared interests.

community-based Services provided throughout communities in people's homes, not in congregate living institutions.

complex systems theory Most systems are composed of other systems nested within one another, particularly social systems.

conciliation The art of pacifying or reconciling others by building trust and reducing differences through communication.

conferenced All involved disciplines coming together with clients and even family members when appropriate to discuss treatment options and decisions.

congregate living institutions Nursing homes or smaller board and care facilities where a group of older adults live.

connection power The ability to get things done because of your contacts.

consensus organizing Advocates focus on forming alliances with governmental and other health care providers who provide technical resources that promote change.

construct A creation of systematically arranged ideas or terms.

continuum of care An ideal, seamless service delivery system or consortium in which the same professionals work with clients from the first time they enter a system so that clients are not always encountering new people who do not know their names or histories.

contributing factors Events that support the problem's proximate cause.

criminal negligence Generally entails the intent to cause harm.

cultural competence The ability to work successfully with people from various cultural backgrounds, including race, culture, gender, sexual orientation, physical or mental abilities, age, and national origin (Kohli, 2003).

cultural environment The values, norms, symbols, and traditions that may or may not be familiar to the older person in a particular setting.

de facto In reality or fact, actually.

decisional autonomy In reference to the rights of elderly people, *decisional* implies de facto competence, and *autonomy* is defined as the ability to deliberate about personal goals and to act accordingly.

deep structures General racial and ethnic population characteristics and cultural factors that may influence specific behaviors.

defensive or reactive planning Advocates responding to environmental circumstances that pose real problems to clients and demand redress.

devolution Delegating or transferring authority to a lower level of government to do something that has previously been done at a higher level. For example, since the 1990s there has been a push to have state governments assume responsibilities previously assumed by federal authorities.

dialectic The art or practice of arriving at the truth by the exchange of logical arguments: stating a thesis, developing a contradictory antithesis, and combining and resolving them into a coherent synthesis.

dilemmas Situations in which individuals must choose between two courses of action that are both equally good or bad, or between two good choices or two bad choices.

discharge planner A person, usually employed by a hospital or other agency, whose job is to coordinate with other workers to arrange the client's discharge from the agency as soon as possible.

distinguishing (proximate) cause The specific, exact, antecedent events that are clearly related to the client's problem.

dually diagnosed clients Individuals who have both a physical and a mental health diagnosis, usually an addiction to drugs or alcohol, or those who have two physical or mental health diagnoses.

elder advocacy Vigilant efforts by, with, or on behalf of older persons to influence decision makers in structures of imbalanced power and to promote justice in providing for, assisting with, or allowing needs to be met.

environmental causes Physical or other structural factors that may influence elder persons' awareness, knowledge, attitudes, skills, and behavior.

error to force a concession Presenting a standard and demonstrating that it is not being met (the error), thereby forcing the decision makers to concede the error and correct it.

executional autonomy Older persons' ability to act on their preferences and control their own fate.

executional power The ability to execute documents on your own behalf.

extended family Family members who live outside of the client's household.

external coalition Forming an empowering relationship with another party who has the connections, savvy, or power to influence an otherwise disinterested, distracted, or resistant decision maker.

factional analogy Systems are viewed as special interest groups, all with their own agendas, divided into factions and bent on conflict.

faith-based Organizations sponsored by religious groups, such as Catholic Charities, Jewish Community Centers, Presbyterian, Catholic and Baptist hospitals, and Muslim community centers or health clinics.

fiduciary Held in trust or confidence.

figurative ground The center for elder advocacy, which rests with the founders of the movement, such as Elma Holder, founder of the National Citizens Coalition for Nursing Home Reform, or Maggie Kuhn of the Gray Panthers.

first rule of best evidence Stipulates that the farther away the investigation is from the time of the incident, the less reliable the investigation.

formal decision makers Persons who have the power and authority to promote, influence, control, or maintain group, professional, or organizational norms that sometimes (even in highly functional prosocial systems) block the legitimate interests of less powerful people.

geriatric assessment tools Assessment instruments, tools, or surveys that measure various domains of importance to the quality of life of elders.

goal An end state, or how something will be when the vision is reached.

gross negligence An utterly reckless lack of diligence in caring for another person. An extremely careless action; recklessness, disregard for cautionary behavior.

groupthink Decision making by a group, especially in a manner that discourages creativity or individual responsibility; members may feel coerced into going along with the group or may become lulled into thinking in a specific way.

guardian *ad litem* Individuals (court visitors) who advocate for the rights and best interests of older persons in guardianship proceedings.

guardians A subcategory of involuntary surrogate advocates judicially imposed upon older persons who have been legally deemed mentally incapable (de facto incompetent) or are otherwise unable to provide for their own care.

hard negotiation Disputants engage in tough, competitive, no compromise, no concession, win-lose arguments to mislead or overwhelm opponents and gain maximum leverage.

informal decision makers Individuals who do not hold roles of authority within established organizations or groups whose power derives from their role in relation to older persons, a relationship in which they have the ability to influence the quality of care and the quality of life of that person.

information power Derives from advocate's knowledge of the intricacies of a system's informal processes.

informed consent Fully understanding the essential nature, including the benefits and drawbacks, of a medical procedure, medication, or other process.

institutionalized Living in a long-term care facility.

instrumental activities of daily living (IADLs) Daily activities that are less personal (intimate) than ADLs, such as shopping, writing checks, planning activities, driving a car, and using the phone.

interaction theories Power, social exchange, and conflict theories that convey the pervasive tension and the inevitable conflicts that occur between people in the aging service arena where scarce resources, lean staffing, and burgeoning service needs can create many frustrations.

internal-external alliance The advocate enlists the direct help of the decision maker to solve clients' problems.

intrarole Multiple roles that are inherent in a profession such as nurse or social worker, some of which are incompatible with one another.

ipso facto By the fact itself; by that very fact.

lay advocates Individuals who are not paid to be advocates.

lay hypothetical theory Predicts that you will begin to make assumptions about how the data fit together and what it means as you are collecting it.

leverage Anything that empowers you in a given circumstance—personal attributes and abilities, including your own status, formal role, credentials, knowledge, support, connections, persuasive ability, legitimate authority, presence, motivation, and courage.

long-range planning The focus of macro systems advocacy in which large-scale changes are sought.

malfeasance Any sort of wrongdoing by a person in a position of trust.

measurable objectives Attached to each goal, objectives detail precisely what is to be done by whom and when to reach the goal.

misfeasance A civil wrong (tort), when someone wrongfully exercises lawful authority.

morph To transform something into something else, such as changing a morphostatic organization into a morphogenic form.

morphogenic Structure changing; generative.

morphostatic Maintaining the status quo, remaining static or set.

negligence Failing to exercise the care that any reasonable person would in similar circumstances.

nonfeasance Failing to do what ought to be done to perform an act that is a legal requirement or responsibility.

old-old Ages 75 to 85.

oldest-of-the-old Over age 85.

ombudsman Someone who investigates complaints and mediates fair settlements between aggrieved parties of an institution or organization. (The Older Americans Act retained this gendered form, "ombudsman," as it originated in Sweden.)

operationalize Defining concepts for purposes of quantitative measurement.

organizational culture Shared basic assumptions taught to new members that reinforce internal integration (Schein, 1992).

organizational culture theory Examines the self-maintaining attitudes, values, habits, rituals, and goals that comprise a given agency's procedural, social, and psychological belief system.

outcome objective Describes the quality of life change that will occur for the older person when the process objectives are met.

outpatient An individual who goes to a hospital or clinic for a medical procedure and returns home the same day.

parens patriae A function of a state acting as legal guardian.

passive neglect Carelessly (but unintentionally) failing to do something that is necessary to an individual's health, safety, or welfare.

paternalism Often associated with beneficence, paternalism (or maternalism) occurs when a person does something for, or makes assumptions about, another person as if knowing what is best for the other person.

paternalistic Treating or governing people in a fatherly manner, thereby limiting their rights and responsibilities.

per se negligence Harm resulting from breaches or noncompliance of fiduciary responsibilities.

personal power Individuals' ability to persuade others due to their expertise and communication skills.

persuading (convincing) Includes arguing, warning, and forcing by fiat or litigation.

physical environment The material things in the elder's environment, everything from stairs to toileting facilities.

pioneer network A network of people dedicated to supporting elders and those who work with them. They are elders, family members, administrators, nurses, certified nursing assistants, resident assistants, physicians, social workers, educators, researchers, ombudsmen, advocates, regulators, and architects, all working to create a better culture in all settings where elders live, with the intention of building loving, elder-directed communities.

planning advocacy interventions A systematic process to establish justifiably important objectives and the means and resources to achieve them, allowing enough flexibility for the advocate to change and shift priorities as new information emerges.

plenary guardians Guardians/conservators who assume the ward's full rights (*sui juris*).

policy A course of action—a direction set either formally or informally by some authoritative body such as a board of directors, a city council, a county board of supervisors, or a legislature.

position power Also called legitimate power, the power of advocates who have control over organizational resources.

preponderance of evidence Lower level of proof showing that the situation is more likely to have occurred (51%) than not (49%).

prima facie True, authentic, or adequate at first sight.

principle of beneficence When risk is present, the advocate protectively acts in the client's best interest.

proactive planning A preemptive defense strategy designed to protect clients from experiencing harm or to keep small problems from becoming big ones.

process objectives Detailed descriptions of what has to happen to achieve an outcome.

program A set of interrelated activities that occur over an extended period and are intended to address a need or set of needs.

project Short versions of programs, typically called projects because they are easier to sell to decision makers who may not be willing to buy into a full-fledged program but would be willing to try a new idea.

proportionality Resistance must be met with equal force in situations where forcing is necessary.

protocol A code of conduct; a proceeding.

prototype An original that later serves as a standard.

provider Institution or person providing care, usually refers to nursing homes or people working in them.

provider advocate Any elder-service worker who sees something not working for an older person and speaks out or takes action.

proximate or distinguishing cause The specific, exact, antecedent events that are clearly related to the client's problem.

proxy Authorization to act on another's behalf.

psychogeriatrician A physician who specializes in the psychological needs of elders.

psychological environment How the person is affected by the setting, such as how interactions between people or the memories attached to this setting are perceived.

public guardian A form of involuntary surrogate legal advocate appointed in some jurisdictions to protect the legal and financial rights of individuals who are unable to manage their own affairs, usually due to mental incapacity.

quality of care The extent to which personal care and treatment are of high quality and administered in a caring and culturally sensitive manner.

quality of life Elders' perceptions of their current levels of well-being, including but not limited to the quality of the care they are receiving.

rational choice principle Coercive tactics should be employed only if the potential benefits of the goal outweigh the risks to achieve it.

reasonable suspicion Standard for reporting when the mandatory reporter does not reasonably doubt an allegation, physical indication, or even a hearsay claim that abuse has occurred.

referent power Advocates' innate, personality-based likeability as a form of charisma.

relative risk How the client's risk for the negative outcome in question compares to the general population's risk for the same event.

resorption To dissolve and assimilate such things as bone tissue.

reward power The ability to confer or withhold rewards.

scalar principle Persons must be competent to assess their risks in making decisions: the greater the level of risk in refusing a treatment the higher the level of competence should be for the client to make the decision.

second rule of best evidence Stipulates that the farther a person is from witnessing what is (or is not) happening, the less you can rely on that person's information to guide you.

self-advocate An individual who feels certain wants and needs and is motivated and able to strive for them.

self-neglect People ignoring their own primary health, welfare, or safety needs.

short-range planning Individual case or small group advocacy focused on achieving changes for particular individuals.

single subject design (SSD) Results from individual cases that cannot be generalized to any group or other individuals, as is done with a scientifically drawn random sample, but you can speculate a little if you collect the same *kinds* of data across all of your advocacy cases.

situational conflict model A model for assessing all facets of the situation to plan the right approach to resolving it.

social action planners Reformers who serve as activist partisans, eschewing planned educational and behavioral interventions in favor of more highly charged power/conflict strategies.

social environment Interactions among people in that setting and the degree of privacy or crowdedness.

social planning model Planners promote system change by raising citizen and provider awareness of social problems and their basic causes.

soft negotiation A win-win process in which the advocate negotiates as a third party on behalf of a client or acts as an ally who sits with the client to directly explore each side's perceptions of strengths, weaknesses, opportunities, threats, and goals to find out what can be exchanged to forge a lasting resolution.

strategy An overriding direction under which specific actions (tactics) are performed.

subacute care An intermediate type of medical institution between a nursing home and a hospital. It provides more intense, but shorter duration care than a nursing home but is lower tech, longer stay, and less expensive than a hospital. Home health care is also part of this continuum.

substituted judgment When older individuals are no longer able to make valid decisions because they have become mentally impaired, others may support client choice and autonomy.

sui juris Capable of managing one's own affairs; having full legal capacity to act on one's own behalf: not subject to the authority of another.

suprasystem The systems that surround an identified or target system, sometimes called the "task environment." For example, agencies to which discharge planners refer clients comprise a hospital's suprasystem.

surface structures The materials that integrate the obvious cultural characteristics of your advocacy population.

surrogates People who are willing to engage in a wide range of persuasive efforts, both mild and strong, that are intended to aid or empower vulnerable others, either on their behalf or under their direction.

synergy, synergistic The interaction of two or more agents or forces so that their combined effect is greater than the sum of their individual effects.

system A group of interrelated or interdependent elements that form a complex whole.

systems theory A belief that the whole is greater than the sum of its parts.

tactics Activities and techniques performed to carry out strategies.

theory A set of interrelated principles that guide action or facilitate comprehension or judgment.

theories of interaction Theories of interaction, including power, social exchange, and conflict theories, convey the pervasive tension and the inevitable conflicts that occur between people in the aging service arena.

third party citizen advocate An individual distinguished by altruistic involvement on behalf of dissimilar others.

third rule of best evidence Warns that evidence is worthless if it cannot be reliably retrieved once it is collected.

Title III A clause of the Older Americans Act that establishes the basic services either contracted out or provided by Area Agencies on Aging.

tort Injury or wrongful doing in which a civil suit may be brought.

waiver program Programs approved for the expansion of eligibility for those who would otherwise not be eligible for the Medicaid program.

writ large Signified, expressed, or embodied in a greater or more prominent magnitude or degree.

wrongdoing Any sort of wrongdoing by a person in a position of trust, also called *malfeasance.*

young-old Ages 65 to 74.

REFERENCES

Administration on Aging. (2001). *A guidebook for providers of services to older Americans and their families.* Washington, DC: Author.

Agich, G. J. (1993). *Autonomy in long-term care.* New York: Oxford University Press.

Agress, C. R. (1985). The nursing home long-term care committee of the United Hospital Fund of New York: A visiting program. In C. Ewig, J. Criggs, C. R. Agress, & S. J. Rogers (Eds.), *Public concerns community initiatives: The successful management of nursing home consumer information programs* (133–144). Proceedings of a 1984 Conference of The United Hospital Fund of New York.

Albrecht, L., & Brewer, R. M. (Eds.). (1990). *Bridges of power: Women's multicultural alliances.* Philadelphia: New Society.

Allen, J. E. (1997). *Nursing home administration.* New York: Springer.

Alspach, G. (1998). Patient advocacy—have we ascended to new heights or fallen to new depths. *Critical Care Nursing, 18*(4), 17–19.

Anderson, R. E., Carter, I., & Lowe, G. R. (1999). *Human behavior in the social environment* (5th ed.). New York: Aldine De Gruyter.

Bailey, D., & Koney, K. M. (1995). Community-based consortia: One model for creation and development. *Journal of Community Practice, 2*(1), 21–41.

Bailey, D., & Koney, K. M. (1996). Interorganizational community-based collaboratives: A strategic response to shape the social work agenda. *Social Work, 41*(6), 602–611.

Bailey, D., Koney, K. M., & Jones, R. L. (1997). *Creating and maintaining strategic alliances: From affiliations to consolidations.* Course taught at the Kellogg School of Management, Northwestern University, Chicago.

Bateman, N. (2000). *Advocacy skills for health and social care professionals.* Philadelphia: Jessica Kingsley.

Beaver, M. L. (1983). *Human service practice with the elderly.* Englewood Cliffs, NJ: Prentice-Hall.

Belmont Report (The). (1979). *Ethical principles and guidelines for the protection of human subjects of research.* Retrieved September 28, 2004, from http://ohsr.od.nih.gov/guidelines/belmont.html

Benbenishty, R. (1989). Combining the single-system and group approach to evaluate treatment effectiveness on the agency level. *Journal of Social Service Research, 12*(3/4), 31–47.

Binstock, R. H., & Day, C. L. (1996). Aging and politics. In R. H. Binstock & L. K. George (Eds.), *Handbook of aging and the social sciences.* San Diego, CA: Academic Press.

Bird, A. W. (1994). Enhancing patient well-being: Advocacy or negotiation? *Journal of Medical Ethics, 20*(3), 152–157.

Bisno, H. (1988). *Managing conflict.* Newbury Park, CA: Sage.

Blake, R. R., & Mouton, J. S. (1984). *Solving costly organizational conflicts.* San Francisco, CA: Jossey-Bass.

Blau, P. (1964). *Exchange and power in social life.* New York: Wiley & Sons.

Bloom, M., Fischer, J., & Orme, J. G. (1999). *Evaluating practice: Guidelines for the accountable professional* (2nd ed). Boston: Allyn & Bacon.

Blythe, B., & Rodgers, A. (1993). Evaluating our practice: Past, present, and future trends. *Journal of Social Service Research, 18*(1/2), 101–119.

Bocialetti, G. (1988). Teams and the management of emotions. In W. B. Reddy & K. Jamison (Eds.), *Team building* (pp. 62–71). Alexandria, VA: National Institute of Applied Behavioral Science.

Botan, M. (1988). Communication and aging in organizational contexts. In Carl W. Carmichael, Carl H. Botan, & Robert Hawkins (Eds.), *Human communication and the aging process* (pp. 141–154). Prospect Heights, IL: Waveland Press.

Brindle, M., & Mainiero, L. A. (2000). *Managing power through lateral networking.* Westport, CN: Quorum Books.

Brinkman, R., & Kirschner, R. (2002). *Dealing with people you can't stand.* New York: McGraw-Hill.

Burns, T., & Stalker, G. M. (1961). *The management of innovation.* London: Tavistock.

Butler, S. S., & Webster, N. M. (2003). Advocacy techniques with older adults in rural environments. *Journal of Gerontological Social Work, 41*(1/2), 59–74.

Byrd, R. E. (1988). How to stay in charge—even with a consultant. In W. B. Reddy & K. Jamison (Eds.), *Team building* (pp. 150–160). Alexandria, VA: National Institute of Applied Behavioral Science.

Cahill, S., & South, K. (2002). Policy issues affecting lesbian, gay, bisexual, and transgender people in retirement. *Generations, 26*(2), 49–54.

Campbell, P. R. (1996). *Population projections for states by age, sex, race, and Hispanic origin: 1995 to 2025.* Retrieved August 5, 2005, from http://www.census.gov/population/www/projections/ppl47.html

Caudron, S. (2000). Keeping team conflict alive: Conflict can be a good thing. Here's what you can do to make the most of this creative force. *Public Management, 82*(2), 5–9.

Cavanagh, S. J. (1991). The conflict management style of staff nurses and nursing managers. *Journal of Advanced Nursing, 16*, 1254–1260.

Cavanaugh, J. C., & Blanchard-Fields, F. (2003). *Adult development and aging* (4th ed.). Belmont, CA: Wadsworth Thomson.

Charters, M. A. (1993). The patient representative role and sources of power. *Hospital and Health Services Administration: Quarterly Journal of the American College of Hospital Administrators, 38*(4), 429–442.

Clegg, S. R., Hardy, C., & Nord, W. R. (1996). *Handbook of organization studies.* London: Sage.

Cohen, E. S. (2004, Spring). Advocacy and advocates: Definitions and ethical dimensions. *Generations, 28*(1), 9–16.

Cohen, P. (1994). Aging matters: Advocates for independence. *Nursing Times, 90*(9), 66.

Coleman, N. (1985). Confronting the legal issues in nursing home consumer information programs. In Carol Ewig & John Griggs (Eds.), *Public concerns, community initiatives* (pp. 98–138). New York: United Hospital Fund of New York.

Collins, R. (1994). *Four sociological traditions.* New York: Oxford University Press.

Collopy, B. J. (1988). Autonomy in long term care: Some crucial distinctions. *The Gerontologist, 28*, 10–17.

Copp, L. A. (1993). Response to 'Patient advocacy—an important part of the daily work of the expert nurse.' *Scholarly Inquiry for Nursing Practice, 7*(2), 137–140.

Cross, T. (1988). Cultural competence continuum. *Focal Point Bulletin.* Retrieved August 28, 2002, from http://www.nysccc.org/T-Rarts/CultComp.Cont.html

Cutler, L. (2000). Assessment of physical environments of older adults. In R. L. Kane & R. A. Kane (Eds.), *Assessing older persons: Measures, meaning, and practical applications* (pp. 360–379). New York: Oxford University Press.

Dawson, R. (1992). *Secrets of power persuasion.* Englewood Cliffs, NJ: Prentice Hall.

Deutsch, M. (1994). Constructive conflict resolution: Principles, training and research. *Journal of Social Issues, 50*(1) 13–32.

Diwan, S., Shugarman, L. R., & Fries, B. E. (2004). Problem identification and care plan responses in a home and community-based service program. *The Journal of Applied Gerontology, 23*(3), 193–211.

Domenici, K., & Littlejohn, S. W. (2001). *Mediation: Empowerment in conflict management.* Prospect Heights, IL: Waveland Press.

Donohue, W. A., & Kolt, R. (1992). *Managing interpersonal conflict.* Newbury Park, CA: Sage.

Dychtwald, K. (1999). *Aging power: How the 21st century will be ruled by the new old.* New York: Jeremy P. Tarcher/Putnam.

Etzioni, A. (1961). *Complex organizations.* New York: Holt, Rinehart & Winston.

Ezell, M. (2001). *Advocacy in the human services.* Belmont, CA: Brooks/Cole.

Fisher, R., & Ury, W. L. (1983). *Getting to yes: Negotiating agreement without giving in.* New York: Penguin Books.

Forester, J., & Stitzel, D. (1989). Beyond neutrality: The possibilities of activist mediation in public sector conflicts. *Negotiation Journal, 5*(3), 251–259.

Freeley, A. J. (1961). *Argumentation and debate: Rational decision making.* Belmont, CA: Wadsworth.

Freidland, R. B., & Summer, L. (1999). *Demography is not destiny.* Washington, DC: National Academy of an Aging Society: A Policy Institute of the Gerontological Society of America.

Freire, P. (1970). *Pedagogy of the oppressed.* New York: Continuum International.

Fulmer, T. T., & Gould, E. S. (1996). Assessing neglect. In L. A. Baumhover & S. C. Beall (Eds.), *Abuse, neglect, and exploitation of older persons: Strategies for assessment and intervention* (pp. 89–99). Baltimore, MD: Health Professions Press.

Gibbs, L. E. (2003). *Evidence-based practice for the helping professions.* Pacific Grove, CA: Brooks/Cole.

Gibelman, M., & Kraft, S. (1996). Advocacy as a core agency program: Planning considerations for voluntary human service agencies. *Administration in Social Work, 20*(4), 43–59.

Giordano, J. A., & Rich, T. A. (2001). *The gerontologist as an administrator.* Westport, CT: Auburn House.

Glannon, W. (2005). *Biomedical ethics.* New York: Oxford University Press.

Goldman, A. I. (1986). Toward a theory of social power. In S. I. Ludke (Ed.), *Power* (pp. 156–202). New York: University Press.

Gould, E. (2005). *Powerful tips: A quick reference guide.* Retrieved August 15, 2005, from http://www.batna.com/tips_v4.html

Gray, B., & Wood, D. J. (1991). Collaborative alliances: Moving from practice to theory. *Journal of Applied Behavioral Science, 27*(1), 3–22.

Green, L. W., & Kreuter, M. W. (1999). *Health program planning: An educational and ecological approach* (3rd ed.). Mountain View, CA: Mayfield.

Green, L. W., & Kreuter, M. W. (2005). *Health program planning* (4th ed.). Boston, MA: McGraw-Hill.

Hardina, D. (2002). *Analytical skills for community organization practice.* New York: Columbia University Press.

Hash, K. (2001). Preliminary study of caregiving and post-caregiving experiences of older gay men and lesbians. *Journal of Gay & Lesbian Social Services, 13*(4), 87–94.

Helman, C. G. (2001). *Culture, health and illness.* London: Arnold.

Hersey, P., & Blanchard, K. H. (1988). *Management of organizational behavior.* Englewood Cliffs, NJ: Prentice-Hall.

Hindle, T. (1998). *Negotiation skills.* New York: DK Publishing.

Hocker J. L., & Wilmot, W. W. (1991). *Interpersonal conflict* (3rd ed.). Dubuque, IA: William C. Brown.

Hoefer, R. (2005). Altering state policy: Interest group effectiveness among state-level advocacy groups. *Social Work, 50*(3), 219–227.

Holder, E. L. (1985). Organizing for change in long-term care facilities. In C. Ewing & J. Griggs (Eds.), *Public concerns community initiatives* (pp. 27–69). New York: United Hospital Fund of New York.

Hooyman, N. R., & Kiyak, H. A. (1999). *Social gerontology: A multidisciplinary perspective* (5th ed). Boston, MA: Allyn & Bacon.

Houser, E. (2002, January 31–February 2). Systems advocacy in the long-term care ombudsman program. In *The Long-Term Care Ombudsman Program: Rethinking and retooling for the future* (app. V). Midland, MI: National Association of State Long-Term Care Ombudsman Programs.

Huber, R., Borders, K., Netting, F. E., & Kautz, J. R. (2000). Interpreting the meaning of ombudsman data across states: The critical analyst-practitioner link. *The Journal of Applied Gerontology, 19*(1), 3–22.

Huber, R., Borders, K., Netting, F. E., & Nelson, H. W. (2001). Data from long-term care ombudsman programs in six states: The implications of collecting resident demographics. *The Gerontologist, 41*(1), 61–68.

Hudson, C. G. (2000). At the edge of chaos: A new paradigm for social work? *Journal of Social Work Education, 36*(2), 215–230.

Hunt, S. (2002). *Ombudsman best practices: Using systems advocacy to improve life for residents.* Washington, DC: National Long-Term Care Ombudsman Resource Center.

Hunt, S., & Burger, S. (1992). *Using resident assessment and care planning as advocacy tools: A guide for ombudsmen and other advocates.* Washington, DC: National Citizen's Coalition for Nursing Home Reform.

Hyman, H. H. (1982). *Health planning: A systematic approach* (2nd ed). Rockville, MD: Aspen.

Jones, G. R., & George, J. M. (2006). *Contemporary management* (4th ed.). New York: Irwin/McGraw-Hill.

Kane, R. A. (1995). Decision making, care plans, and life plans in long-term care: Can case managers take account of client values and preferences? In L. B. McCullough & N. L. Wilson (Eds.), *Long-term care decisions* (pp. 87–109). Baltimore, MD: Johns Hopkins University Press.

Kane, R. A. (2003). Definition, measurement, and correlates of quality of life in nursing homes: Toward a reasonable practice, research, and policy agenda. *The Gerontologist, 43*(Special Issue II), 28–36.

Kane, R. L. (2000). Choosing and using an assessment tool. In R. L. Kane & R. A. Kane (Eds.), *Assessing older persons: Measures, meaning, and practical applications* (pp 1–13). New York: Oxford University Press.

Kane, R. L., & Kane, R. A. (Eds.). (1981). *Assessing the elderly: A practical guide to measurement.* Lexington, MA: Lexington Books.

Kane, R. L., & Kane, R. A. (Eds.). (2000). *Assessing older persons: Measures, meaning, and practical applications.* New York: Oxford University Press.

Kettner, P. M., Moroney, R., & Martin, L. L. (1990). *Designing and managing programs: An effectiveness-based approach.* Newbury Park, CA: Sage.

Kinney, T. A. (1994). An inductively derived typology of verbal aggression and its association to distress. *Human Communications Research, 21*(2), 183–222.

Kintler, D., & Adams, B. (1997, October). *Streetwise independent consulting: Your comprehensive guide to building your own consulting business.* Holbrook, MA: Adams Streetwise Consulting.

Klar, Y., Bar-Tal, D., & Kruglanski, A. W. (1988). Conflict as a cognitive schema: Toward a social cognitive analysis of conflict and conflict termination. In A. W. Stroebe, A. W. Kruglanski, D. Bar-Tal, & M. Hewstone (Eds.), *The social psychology of intergroup conflict: Theory, research and applications* (pp. 73–85). New York: Springer-Verlag.

Kohli, H. K. (2003). *Building an assessment model to measure cultural competence in graduating social work students.* Unpublished doctoral dissertation, Kent School of Social Work, University of Louisville, Kentucky.

Kolb, D. B (1994). *When talk works: Profiles in mediators.* San Francisco: Jossey-Bass.

Krauskopf, J. M., Brown, R. N., Tokarz, K. L., & Bogutz, A. (1993). *Elderlaw: Advocacy for the aging* (2nd ed., vol. 1). St. Paul, MN: West.

Krebs, D. (1982). Prosocial behavior, equity, and justice. In J. Greenberg & R. L. Cohen (Eds.), *Equity and justice in social behavior* (pp. 261–308). New York: Academic Press.

Kreuter, M. S., Lezin, N. A., Kreuter, M. W., & Green, L. W. (2003). *Community health promotion ideas that work* (2nd ed.). Boston, MA: Jones and Bartlett.

Kropf, N. P., & Hutchinson, E. D. (1992). Effective practice with elderly clients. In R. L. Schneider & N. P. Kropf (Eds.), *Gerontological social work: Knowledge, service settings, and special populations* (pp. 3–24). Chicago: Nelson-Hall.

Kruglanski, A. W., Bar-Tal, D., & Klar, Y. (1993). A social cognitive theory of conflict. In K. S. Larsen (Ed.), *Conflict and social psychology* (pp. 34–54). Oslo: Sage.

Kuther, T. L. (1999). Competency to provide informed consent in older adulthood. *Gerontology and Geriatrics Education, 20*(1), 15–30.

Lamb, J. A. (1988). Social work and the changing health care picture. *Arête, 13*(1), 16–22.

Lang, L. (n.d.). House sends governor mental health reform legislation to protect mentally ill in nursing homes [Online]. *Lang News.* Retrieved January 27, 2005, from http://www.reploulang.com/News/News/News1/news1.html#top

Larson, E. B., & Shadlen, M. (1999). Diagnostic tests. In W. R. Hazzard, J. P. Blass, W. H. Ettinger Jr., J. B. Halter, & J. G. Ouslander (Eds.), *Principle of geriatric medicine and gerontology* (pp. 275–286). New York: McGraw-Hill.

Lauffer, A. (1984). *Understanding your social agency* (2nd ed.). Newbury Park, CA: Sage.

Lee, P. R., & Estes, C. L. (1994). *The nation's health.* Boston: Jones & Bartlett.

Lens, V. (2005). Advocacy and argumentation in the public arena: A guide for social workers. *Social Work, 50*(3), 231–238.

Levinger, G., & Rubin, J. Z. (1994). To a more general theory of conflict. *Negotiation Journal, 10*(3), 201–216.

Lieberman, D. J. (2000). *Get anyone to do anything.* New York: St. Martins, Griffin.

Lipsky, D. B., Seeber, R. L., & Fincher, R. D. (2003). *Emerging systems for managing workplace conflict.* San Francisco: Jossey-Bass.

Little Brothers Friends of the Elderly (The). (2005). *Special Services.* Retrieved August 4, 2005, from http://www.littlebrothers.org/html3/usa/e/activity.shtml

Litwin, H. (1982). Change agents and gatekeepers: A study of collaborative and contest strategy orientations to a nursing home ombudsman program. *Dissertation Abstracts International, 1707.*

Loewenberg, F., & Dolgoff, R. (1988). *Ethical decisions for social work practice.* Itasca, IL: F. E. Peacock.

Longest, B. B., Rakich, J. S., & Darr, K. (2000). *Managing health services organizations and systems* (4th ed.). Baltimore, MD: Health Professions Press.

Luthans, F. (1981). *Organizational behavior* (3rd ed). New York: McGraw-Hill.

Mallik, M. (1997). Advocacy in nursing—a review of the literature. *Journal of Advanced Nursing, 25*(1), 130–138.

Markson, L. J., Kern, D. C., Annas, G. J., & Glantz, L. H. (1994). Physician assessment of patient competence. *JAGS, 42,* 1074–1080.

Martin, J., & Frost, P. (1996). The organizational culture war games: A struggle for intellectual dominance. In S. R. Clegg, C. Hardy, & W. R. Nord (Eds.), *Handbook of organizational studies* (pp. 599–621). London: Sage.

Martin, P. Y., & O'Connor. G. G. (1989). *The social environment: Open systems applications.* New York: Longman.

Mayer, R. J. (1991). *Conflict management: The courage to confront.* Columbus, OH: Battelle Press.

McCann, T. (2003). Holocaust survivors with Alzheimer's can relive old horrors. *Chicago Tribune.* Retrieved July 12, 2004, from http://

www.sanluisobispo.com/mld/sanluisobispo/news/nation/5101690.htm?template=cont

McCaskey, M. B. (1974). A contingency approach to planning: Planning with goals and planning without goals. *Academy of Management Journal, 7*(2), 281–291.

McKenzie, J. F., & Jurs, J. L. (1993). *Planning, implementing, and evaluating health promotion programs.* New York: Macmillan.

McKenzie, J. F., & Smeltzer, J. L. (1997). *Planning, implementing, and evaluating, health promotion programs.* Boston: Allyn & Bacon.

McLaughlin, C. P., & Kaluzny, A. D. (1983). *Continuous quality improvement in health care.* Gaithersburg, MD: Aspen.

McPherson, B. D. (1983). *Aging as a social process.* Toronto, Canada: Butterworths.

Mitchell, G. J., & Bournes, D. A. (2000). Nurse as patient advocate? In search of straight thinking. *Nursing Science Quarterly, 13*(3), 204–209.

Mizrahi, T., & Rosenthal, B. (1993). Managing dynamic tensions in social change coalitions. In T. Mizrahi & J. Morrison (Eds.), *Community organization and social administration: Advances, trends, and emerging principles* (pp. 11–40). New York: Haworth Press.

Monk, A., Kaye, L.W., & Litwin, H. (1984). *Resolving grievances in the nursing home: A study of the ombudsman program.* New York: Columbia University Press.

Moody, H. R. (1988). From informed consent to negotiated consent. *The Gerontologist, 28 ,* 64–70.

Moody, H. R. (1992). *Ethics in an aging society.* Baltimore, MD: Johns Hopkins University Press.

Mor, V., Berg, K. Angelelli, J., Gifford, D., Morris, J., & Moore, T. (2003). The quality of quality measurement in U.S. nursing homes. *The Gerontologist, 43*(Special Issue II), 37–46.

Moxley, D. P., & Hyduk, C. A. (2003). The logic of personal advocacy with older adults and its implications for program management in community-based gerontology. *Administration in Social Work, 27*(4), 5–23.

Mueller, P. S., Hook, C., & Fleming, K. C. (2004). Ethical issues in geriatrics: A guide for clinicians. In *Symposium on Geriatrics* (pp. 554–562). Rochester MN: Mayo Foundation for Medical Education and Research.

National Citizens Coalition for Nursing Home Reform. (1988). *The rights of nursing home residents.* Washington, DC: Health Care Financing Administration (contract No. 87-0392, HSQB-87-0013).

National Council on the Aging. (n.d). *About us.* Retrieved August 9, 2004, from http://www.ncoa.org/content.cfm?sectionID=58

National Institute of Dispute Resolution. (n.d.). Conceptions of mediation. In *Performance-based assessment: A methodology* (chap. 3). Retrieved March 9, 2005, from http://www.convenor.com/madison/concept.htm

Nelson, H. W. (1995). Long-term care volunteer roles on trial: Ombudsman effectiveness revisited. *Journal of Gerontological Social Work, 23*(3/4), 25–46.

Nelson, H. W. (2000). Injustice and conflict in nursing homes: Toward advocacy and exchange. *Journal of Aging Studies, 14*(1), 39–61.

Nelson, H. W., Allen, P., & Cox, D. (2005). Rights based advocacy in long-term care: Geriatric nursing and long term-care ombudsmen. *Clinical Gerontologist, 28*(4), 1–16.

Nelson, H. W., & Cox, D. (2003). The causes and consequences of conflict and violence in nursing homes: Working towards a collaborative work culture. *The Health Care Manager, 22*(4), 349–360.

Nelson, H. W., Hooker, K., Dehart, K. N., Edwards, J. A., & Lanning, K. (2004). Factors important to success in the volunteer long-term care ombudsman role. *The Gerontologist, 44*(1), 116–120.

Nelson, H. W., Netting, F. E., Huber, R., & Borders, K. (2001a). The social workers-ombudsman partnership: Using a resident-centered model of situational conflict tactics. *Journal of Gerontological Social Work, 35*(3), 65–82.

Nelson, H. W., Netting, F. E., Huber, R., & Borders, K. (2001b). Training residents' rights case advocates in effective situational conflict skills. *Gerontology & Geriatrics Education, 22*(2), 29–46.

Nelson, H. W., Netting, F. E., Huber, R., & Borders, K. (2003). Managing external grievances against volunteer advocates. *The Journal of Volunteer Administration, 21*(4), 10–16.

Nelson, H. W., Pratt, C., Carpenter, C. E., & Walter, K. L. (1995). Factors affecting volunteer long-term care ombudsman organizational commitment and burnout. *Nonprofit and Voluntary Sector Quarterly, 35*(4), 509–514.

Netting, F. E. (1998). Interdisciplinary practice and the geriatric care manager. *Geriatric Case Management Journal, 8*(1), 20–24.

Netting, F. E., Kettner, P. M., & McMurtry, S. L. (2004). *Social work macro practice* (3rd ed). Boston: Pearson Education.

Netting, F. E., Paton, R. N. & Huber, R. (1992). The long-term care ombudsman program: What does the complaint reporting system tell us? *The Gerontologist, 32*(6), 843–848.

Nursing home compare. (2002). Medicare: The official U.S. government site for people with Medicare website. Retrieved July 2002, from http://www.medicare.gov/NHCompare/home.asp

O'Boyle, R. (1999). *Family councils help nursing homes maintain quality care.* Retrieved August 10, 2004, from http://www.ec-online.net/Knowledge/Articles/familycouncil.html

O'Brien, J. G. (1996). Screening: A primary care clinician's perspective. In L. A. Baumhover & S. C. Beall (Eds.), *Abuse, neglect, and exploitation of older persons: Strategies for assessment and intervention* (pp. 51–64). Baltimore, MD: Health Professions Press.

O'Donnell, M. P. (2002). *Health promotion in the workplace* (3rd ed.). Albany, NY: Delmar.

Oberschall, A. (1973). *Social conflict and social movements.* Englewood Cliffs, NJ: Prentice-Hall.

Oregon Senior and Disabled Services Division. (1992). *Standards of complaint investigation and report writing: Establishing the burden of proof for corrective action.* Salem, OR: Oregon Department of Human Services.

Page, J. B. (1999, September 5). Informed consent and substituted judgment: A synopsis. *Stanford Medical Review, 1*(1), 1–5.

Pannick, D. (1992). *Advocates.* New York: Oxford University Press.

Parsons, T. (1960). *Structure and process in modern societies.* Glencoe, IL: Free Press.

Perloff, R. M. (1993). *The dynamics of persuasion.* Hillsdale, NJ: Lawrence Erlbaum.

Pfeffer, J. (1977). Power and resource allocation in organizations. In B. M. Staw & G. R. Salanicik (Eds.), *New directions in organizational behavior* (pp. 255–260). Chicago, IL: St. Clair Press.

Pratt, J. R. (2004). *Long-term care: Managing across the continuum.* Boston: Jones & Bartlett.

Rader, J. (Ed.). (1992). *Reclaiming the magic of caring: Strategies for understanding behaviors and reducing psychoactive mediations.* Mt. Angel, OR: Benedictine Institute for Long Term Care.

Rader, J. (1995a). Assessing the external environment. In J. Rader & E. M. Tronquist (Eds.), *Individualized dementia care* (pp. 47–82). New York: Springer.

Rader, J. (1995b). Use of skillful, creative psychosocial interventions. In J. Rader & E. M. Tronquist (Eds.), *Individualized dementia care* (pp. 191–195). New York: Springer.

Rader, J., & Crandall, L. (1995). Identifying the underlying cause of the resident's behavior. In J. Rader & E. M. Tronquist (Eds.), *Individualized dementia care* (pp. 83–94). New York: Springer.

Raven, B. H., & Kruglanski, W. (1975). Conflict and power. In P. G. Swingle (Ed.), *The structure of conflict* (pp. 177–219). New York: Academic Press.

Reisch, M. (1986). From cause to case and back again: The re-emergence of advocacy in social work. *Urban and Social Change Review, 19,* 20–24.

Roberts-DeGannaro, M. (1997). Conceptual framework of coalitions in an organizational context. *Journal of Community Practice, 4*(1), 91–107.

Rogan, R. G., & Hammer, M. R. (1995). Assessing message affect in crisis negotiations: An exploratory study. *Human Communication Research, 21*(4), 553–574.

Roloff, E. M., Tutzauer, F. E., & Dailey, W. O. (1989). The role of argumentation in distributive and integrative bargaining contexts: In M. A. Rahim (Ed.), *Seeking relative advantage but at what cost? Managing conflict: An interdisciplinary approach.* New York: Praeger.

Ross, H. S., & Mico, P. R. (1980). *Theory and practice in health education.* Palo Alto, CA: Mayfield.

Ross, M. G. (1955). *Community organization.* New York: Harper & Brothers.

Rubin, J. S. (1994). Models of conflict management. *Journal of Social Issues, 30,* 34–45.

Rummel, R. J. (1991). *The conflict helix.* London: Transaction.

Ryan, E. B., Hamilton, J. M., & See, S. K. (1994). Patronizing the old: How do younger and older adults respond to baby talk in the nursing home. *International Journal of Aging and Human Development, 39*(1), 21–32.

Rybacki, K. C., & Rybacki, D. J. (1996). *Advocacy and opposition: An introduction to argumentation* (3rd ed). Boston: Allyn & Bacon.

Schein, E. H. (1992). *Organizational culture and leadership* (2nd ed.). San Francisco: Jossey-Bass.

Schneider, R. L., & Lester, L. (2001). *Social work advocacy: A new framework for action.* Belmont, CA: Brooks/Cole.

Shafritz, J. M., & Ott, J. S. (2001). Classics of organization theory (5th ed.). Fort Worth, TX: Harcourt.

Simmons-Morton, B. G., Greene, W. H., & Gottlieb, N. H. (1995). *Introduction to health education and health promotion* (2nd ed.). Prospect Heights, IL: Waveland Press.

Singh, D. A., & Schwab, R. C. (1998). Retention of administrators in nursing homes: What can management do? *The Gerontologist, 38,* 362–369.

Snelgrove S., & Hughes, D. (2000). Interprofessional relations between doctors and nurses: Perspectives from South Wales. *Journal of Advanced Nursing, 31*(3), 661–667.

Sosin, M., & Caulum, S. (1983). Advocacy: A conceptualization for social work practice. *Social Work, 28*(1), 12–17.

Stavis, P. F. (n.d.). *Standards of evidence in child abuse investigations.* Retrieved October 30, 2004, from http://www.cqc.state.ny.us/counsels_corner/cc33.htm

Stein, H. (1994, January). Change, loss and organizational culture: Anthropological consultant as facilitator of grief work. *NAPA Bulletin, 14*(1), 66–80.

Stone, R. (2004). Where have all the advocates gone? *Generations, 28*(1), 59–64.

Sullivan, M. S.-J., & Rader, J. (1995). Assessing the resident's needs. In J. Rader & E. M. Tornquist (Eds.), *Individualized dementia care* (pp. 29–46). New York: Springer.

Sullivan, W. M. (2000). Medicine under threat: Professionalism and professional identity. *Canadian Medical Association Journal, 162,* 673–675.

Suskind, L. (1994). Activist mediation and public disputes. In D. M. Kolb & Associates (Eds.), *When talk works: Profiles of mediators* (pp. 309–337). San Francisco: Jossey-Bass.

Syme, S. L., & Berkman, L. F. (1997). Social class, susceptibility, and sickness. In P. Conroad (Ed.), *The sociology of health & illness: Critical perspectives* (5th ed., pp. 29–34). New York: St. Martin's Press.

Tennstedt, F. L. (2002). "I've Fallen and . . ." *Generations, 26*(4), 5–6.

Thomas, K. W., & Kilmann, R. H. (1974). *Thomas-Kilmann conflict mode instrument.* Woods Road, NY: Xicom.

Thompson, D. (1993). Generations, justice and the future of collective action. In P. Laslett & J. Fishkin (Eds.), *Philosophy, politics, and society. Vol. VI: Relations between age group and generations.* New Haven, CT: Yale University Press.

Thompson, L. (1995). "They saw a negotiation": Partisanship and involvement. *Journal of Personality and Social Psychology, 68*(5), 839–853.

Tulloch, G. J. (1975). *A home is not a home: Life within a nursing home.* New York: Seabury Press.

Turnham, H. (n.d.). Federal Nursing Home Reform Act from the Omnibus Budget Reconciliation Act of 1987 (or simply OBRA '87 Summary). Retrieved July 13, 2004, from http://www.ltcombudsman.org/uploads/OBRA87summary.pdf

University of Washington. (1998). *Informed consent.* Retrieved September 28, 2004, from http://eduserv.hscer.washington.edu/bioethics/topics/consent.html

Urwick, L. F. (1956). The manager's span of control. *Harvard Business Review,* 39–47.

Van Fleet, J. K. (1984). *Lifetime conversation guide.* Englewood Cliffs, NJ: Prentice-Hall.

Van Kleuned, A., & Wilner, M. A. (2000). Who will care for mother tomorrow? *Journal of Aging & Social Policy, 2*(2/3), 1–11.

Vander Zanden, J. W., Crandell, T. L., & Crandell, C. H. (2003). *Human development* (7th ed.). Boston: McGraw-Hill.

Wainess, R. (1982). Role of the ombudsman. In *Ombudsman technical assistance manual.* Washington DC: Administration on Aging.

Walton, D. N. (1991). Bias, critical doubt, and fallacies. *Argumentation and Advocacy, 28,* 1–22.

Walton, R. E. (1987). *Conflict: Interpersonal dialogue and third party roles* (2nd ed). Reading, MA: Addison-Wesley.

Ward, R. A. (1979). *The aging experience.* New York: Lippincott.

Warren, K., Franklin, C., & Streeter, C. L. (1998). New directions in systems theory: Chaos and complexity. *Social Work, 43*(4), 357–370.

Weisbord, M. R. (1988). Team work: Building productive relationships. In W. B. Reddy & K. Jamison, K. (Eds.), *Team building* (pp. 35–44). Alexandria, VA: National Institute of Applied Behavioral Science.

Wetle, T. (1995). Ethical issues and value conflicts facing case managers of frail elderly living at home. In L. B. McCullough & N. L. Wilson (Eds.), *Long term care decisions* (pp. 63–86). Baltimore, MD: Johns Hopkins University Press.

Wilson, N. L. (1995). Long-term care in the United States: An overview of the current system. In L. B. McCullough & N. L. Wilson (Eds.), *Long term care decisions* (pp. 35–59). Baltimore, MD: Johns Hopkins University Press.

Windsor, R. S., Baranowski, T., Clark, N., & Cutter, G. (1994). *Evaluation of health promotion, health education, and disease prevention program* (2nd ed.). Mountain View, CA: Mayfield Press.

Ziegelmueller, G. W., & Kay, J. (1997). *Argumentation: Inquiry and advocacy* (3rd ed). Boston: Allyn & Bacon.

Zimny, G. H., & Grossberg, G. T. (1998). *Guardianship of the elderly: Psychiatric and judicial aspects.* New York: Springer.

N A M E   I N D E X